Weimar's Long Shadow

Weimar casts a long shadow over postwar political thought. The Weimar Republic is used to understand contemporary threats to democracy and to critique or defend modernity. It has generated a series of political lessons that are invoked whenever democracies are challenged. This book questions the historical validity of many of these lessons and their applicability to contemporary political orders. It shows how Weimar lessons are often influenced by partial and superficial readings of events, often intended to advance particular political projects. The chapters give detailed accounts of how so-called Weimar lessons have influenced, if not shaped, political debates in Germany, elsewhere in Europe, and in the United States.

Richard Ned Lebow is Professor of International Political Theory, Emeritus at King's College London; Honorary Fellow of Pembroke College at the University of Cambridge; and James O. Freedman Presidential Professor, Emeritus at Dartmouth College. He is a Fellow of the British Academy.

Ludvig Norman is Associate Professor of Political Science at Stockholm University and Senior Fellow at the Institute of European Studies at the University of California, Berkeley.

Weimar's Long Shadow

Edited by

Richard Ned Lebow
King's College London

Ludvig Norman
Stockholm University

CAMBRIDGE
UNIVERSITY PRESS

CAMBRIDGE
UNIVERSITY PRESS

Shaftesbury Road, Cambridge CB2 8EA, United Kingdom

One Liberty Plaza, 20th Floor, New York, NY 10006, USA

477 Williamstown Road, Port Melbourne, VIC 3207, Australia

314–321, 3rd Floor, Plot 3, Splendor Forum, Jasola District Centre,
New Delhi – 110025, India

103 Penang Road, #05-06/07, Visioncrest Commercial, Singapore 238467

Cambridge University Press is part of Cambridge University Press & Assessment,
a department of the University of Cambridge.

We share the University's mission to contribute to society through the pursuit of
education, learning and research at the highest international levels of excellence.

www.cambridge.org
Information on this title: www.cambridge.org/9781009484343

DOI: 10.1017/9781009484329

First published 2024

A catalogue record for this publication is available from the British Library

Library of Congress Cataloging-in-Publication Data
Names: Lebow, Richard Ned, editor, author. | Norman, Ludvig, 1976- editor, author.
Title: Weimar's long shadow / edited by Richard Ned Lebow, King's College
   London, Ludvig Norman, University of Stockholm.
Description: Cambridge ; New York : Cambridge University Press, 2024. |
   Includes bibliographical references and index.
Identifiers: LCCN 2023057238 (print) | LCCN 2023057239 (ebook) |
   ISBN 9781009484343 (hardback) | ISBN 9781009484305 (paperback) |
   ISBN 9781009484329 (ebook)
Subjects: LCSH: Germany–Politics and government–1918-1933. | Germany–
   Politics and government–1918-1933–Historiography. | Germany–History–1918-
   1933. | Germany–History–1918-1933–Historiography. | Sozialdemokratische
   Partei Deutschlands. | Democracy. | Failed states–Historiography.
Classification: LCC DD240 .W3937 2024 (print) | LCC DD240 (ebook) |
   DDC 943.085–dc23/eng/20240131
LC record available at https://lccn.loc.gov/2023057238
LC ebook record available at https://lccn.loc.gov/2023057239

ISBN 978-1-009-48434-3 Hardback
ISBN 978-1-009-48430-5 Paperback

Contents

Contributors

AMEL AHMED specializes in democratic studies, with a special interest in elections, voting systems, legislative politics, party development, and voting rights. She examines these issues from historical and comparative perspectives, and her work combines a regional focus on Europe and the US. She is author of *Democracy and the Politics of Electoral System Choice* (Cambridge, 2013), which won the Best Book Award from the European Politics and Society section of the American Political Science Association. She has a special interest in research methods and has written about mixed-method research designs, the position of historical analysis within the social sciences, and comparative areas studies. Her work has appeared in various journals, including *Comparative Political Studies, Perspectives on Politics, Democratization, Studies in Comparative International Development,* and *Journal of Politics.*

PETER BREINER is an associate professor of political science at the University at Albany, State University of New York. He is the author of *Max Weber and Democratic Politics* (Cornell University Press, 1996) and of numerous articles on Weber, Mannheim, and German political theory, along with articles on Machiavelli, Rousseau, and Tocqueville. He is working on a book entitled *Political Equality,* in which he argues that the tension between liberal rights and Schumpeterian democracy leads to a constant and unending struggle over political equality, much like Polanyi's recurrent movement and countermovement between the market and democracy.

PETER C. CALDWELL is Samuel G. McCann Professor of History at Rice University. He is a Humboldt Fellow and has received grants from the DAAD, the Humboldt Foundation, and the Center for German and European Studies at Georgetown University. His scholarly work has focused on the meanings of democracy and constitutionalism in Germany's first republic, conservatism and state theory, legal theory and the welfare state, and the economics and law of planning under state socialism. His books include *Popular Sovereignty and the Crisis of German Constitutional Law* (Duke University Press, 1997), *Dictatorship, State Planning, and Social Theory in the German Democratic Republic* (Cambridge, 2003), and *Democracy, Capitalism, and the Welfare State* (Oxford University Press, 2019). Currently, he is looking at the rhetoric of democracy in contemporary Mexican politics.

RICHARD NED LEBOW is Professor Emeritus of International Political Theory in the War Studies department of King's College London; Honorary Fellow of Pembroke College, University of Cambridge; and James O. Freedman Presidential Professor Emeritus at Dartmouth College. He is a Fellow of the British Academy and a member of the Atheneum. His most recent books are *The Quest for Knowledge in International Relations* (Cambridge, 2022), *Justice and International Order* (Oxford University Press, 2022; co-authored with Feng Zhang), and *The Robustness and Fragility of Political Orders* (Cambridge, 2022; co-edited with Ludvig Norman). He has also recently published a novel and book of short stories.

JAN-WERNER MÜLLER is Roger Williams Straus Professor of Social Sciences and Professor of Politics at Princeton University. He works mainly in democratic theory and the history of modern political thought, but also has research interests in the relationship between architecture and politics, as well as the normative implications of the current structural transformations of the public sphere. Publications include *Constitutional Patriotism* (Princeton University Press, 2007), *Contesting Democracy* (Yale University Press, 2011), *What Is Populism?* (University of Pennsylvania Press, 2016), which has been translated into more than twenty languages, *Furcht und Freiheit* (Suhrkamp, 2019), which won the Bavarian Book Prize, and *Democracy Rules* (FSG, Penguin, and Suhrkamp, 2021).

LUDVIG NORMAN is Associate Professor of Political Science, Stockholm University, and Senior Fellow at the Institute of European Studies at the University of California, Berkeley. His research focuses on European politics and the EU, democratic theory, and social science methodology. His most recent books are *Dilemmas of European Democracy* (Edinburgh University Press, 2023; co-edited with Niklas

Bremberg) and *Robustness and Fragility of Political Orders* (Cambridge, 2022; co-edited with Richard Ned Lebow). He previously authored the book *The Mechanisms of Institutional Conflict in the European Union* (Routledge, 2016). His articles have appeared in *Democratization, Constellations, Political Studies, European Journal of International Relations, European Journal of Social Theory, Journal of Common Market Studies, Journal of European Public Policy*, and *Cooperation and Conflict.*

WILLIAM E. SCHEUERMAN is James H. Rudy Professor of Political Science and International Studies at Indiana University Bloomington. His primary research and teaching interests are in modern political thought, German political thought, democratic theory, legal theory, and international political theory. His most recent books are *The Cambridge Companion to Civil Disobedience* (Cambridge, 2021), *The End of Law* (Rowman & Littlefield, 2020, 2nd edition), and *Civil Disobedience* (Polity Press, 2018). He is also the author of *Between the Norm and the Exception* (MIT Press, 1994), which won two prestigious awards, as well as *Carl Schmitt* (Rowman & Littlefield, 1999), *Liberal Democracy and the Social Acceleration of Time* (Johns Hopkins University Press, 2004), *Frankfurt School Perspectives on Globalization, Democracy, and the Law* (Routledge, 2008), *Hans J. Morgenthau* (Polity, 2009), and *The Realist Case for Global Reform* (Polity, 2011). He has edited *The Rule of Law Under Siege* (University of California Press, 1996), *From Liberal Democracy to Fascism* (Humanities Press, 2000; with Peter Caldwell), and *High-Speed Society* (Penn State University Press, 2009; with Hartmut Rosa). He has published in many professional journals, including *Constellations, History of Political Thought, International Theory, Journal of Political Philosophy, Politics & Society, Review of International Studies*, and *Social Research.*

JILL SUZANNE SMITH is an associate professor of German at Bowdoin College in Maine. She is the author of the book *Berlin Coquette* (Cornell University Press, 2013). Her research and teaching focus on gender and sexuality, Jewish studies, and the city of Berlin from the Wilhelmine era to the present. She is currently working on a book-length study on the representations of Weimar Berlin in contemporary German and American popular culture. Her previous publications have appeared in *Modern Jewish Studies, The German Quarterly, Feminist German Studies*, and *The Germanic Review.*

DOUGLAS WEBBER is an Emeritus Professor of Political Science at the international business school INSEAD (Fontainebleau, France, Singapore, and Abu Dhabi). Prior to joining INSEAD, he worked at the universities of Essex, Strathclyde (Glasgow) and Sussex in the UK and at the Max Planck Institute for the Study of Societies (Cologne) in Germany. He has been a guest professor at the University of California, Berkeley, a visiting fellow at Monash University (Melbourne) and at the Australian National University (Canberra), and a Jean Monnet Fellow and Robert Schuman Fellow at the European University Institute (Florence). He has published extensively on issues of German politics and foreign policy, Franco-German relations, EU politics, and European and Asian regional political integration. His last book was *European Disintegration? The Politics of Crisis in the European Union* (Red Globe Press/ Macmillan, 2019).

Note on Bauhaus Font and the Cover Design

The Bauhaus school sought to modernize, unify, and standardize design into an idealistic form that would combine function with aesthetics. One aspect of their many proposed reforms was a series of related Bauhaus typefaces. They were intended to replace Gothic with more readable and aesthetically pleasing fonts. Many of these fonts are still in use and may represent the most universal and enduring feature of the Weimar era. We use a more colorful Bauhaus font, intended for posters, book covers, and other designs. The editors thank Jayden Lawrence for conceiving the cover, choosing the font, and preparing several mock-ups.

1   Why Weimar?

Richard Ned Lebow and Ludvig Norman

The Weimar Republic lasted a mere fifteen years – from the end of the First World War to Hitler's dictatorship in 1933. It nevertheless became *the* paradigmatic historical event shaping political thinking about fragility and robustness in the postwar West. While seemingly falling out of public debate after the end of the Cold War, Weimar is now back with a vengeance. It is routinely invoked in scholarly writings, op-eds, and political commentary to make sense of the rise of far-right populism, acute political polarization, the erosion of liberal democratic institutions, economic crises and their consequences, and ruptures in the "liberal world order."[1] The assumption motivating many of those who invoke the Weimar analogy is that the Western democracies, like those in the 1930s, are at risk – even at the brink – of possible collapse. One of the principal reasons for writing this book is to challenge this analysis. Our authors demonstrate that the supposed lessons of Weimar are highly questionable, but they have been mobilized to support a broad range of political and cultural projects.

Our book explores the origins and evolution of the "Weimar lesson" – really, Weimar lessons. We ask when and how they arose, who invoked them, under what circumstances, and for what purposes, and how they played out in particular contexts. Weimar and its lessons offer a cautionary tale, resembling a Rorschach test that is likely to tell us more about the people mobilizing it and the political culture in which they function than about the former German republic. Our volume also explores analogies based on Weimar lessons. The two are closely related. Lessons generate analogies but the process also works in reverse. To advance political projects, people have made comparisons between Weimar and their democratic orders to warn others against policies they opposed or to mobilize support for those they favor. As we will see, they invented lessons to support their analogies.[2]

We ask a set of interconnected questions about Weimar lessons and analogies. We are interested in why some so-called lessons are learned but not others. How much are they influenced by superficial versus

1

deeper readings of events? To what degree are lessons the products of political agendas? What aspects of the Weimar experience have generated lessons? The political lessons are the most prominent, but there are also cultural lessons. To what extent are they related? Finally, we are interested in the life history of lessons. Which Weimar lessons have endured, and why? Have they remained the same over time or have they evolved in content or taken on a different valence?

Weimar analogies, our contributors demonstrate, have proven flexible. They adapt to circumstances and are applied in political cultures quite different from the one in which they emerged. They are also prominent in the sense of being benchmarks or flashpoints of political and cultural dialogue. When mobilized, they are invariably contested, making them expressions of opposing political views and providing circumstances in which they assume meaning. Our contributors show that Weimar has come to play a cautionary tale for both the conservative right and political actors on the left. Weimar lessons are mobilized because people think they will influence the thinking of others. Their use raises deeper questions about their conceptual utility. Do they frame contemporary issues in useful ways? Or do they impose frames of reference that are inappropriate, misleading, and unhelpful? To what extent, therefore, can Weimar serve as a guide for understanding politics at the present juncture?

There is impressive scholarship on the Weimar era. We ask if it supports or contradicts the lessons people have drawn. If it does not, does it suggest more accurate and useful alternatives? Are there political and cultural lessons that can be drawn from Weimar that are germane today, or should these alleged lessons be retired gracefully? And what do Weimar lessons tell us about the relationship between history and political learning – or what passes for political learning? What incentives are there to learn particular lessons and not others?

We are not the first to acknowledge the influence of Weimar. Several recent works focus on how the Republic's demise has shaped postwar political thought.[3] However, we may be the first to evaluate these works critically by placing Weimar lessons in a comparative perspective and to use them to reflect on historical analogies and historical learning more generally.[4] Given the increased presence of Weimar analogies in contemporary Western societies, these are urgent tasks.

Historical Analogies

Historical analogies often shape how political actors understand their political present and what needs to be done to avoid repeating past catastrophes. Attempts to escape the past may nevertheless increase its hold over the present to the degree that political actors are guided by its supposed lessons. Margaret Macmillan observes: "Even when people think they are striking out in new directions their models often come from the past."[5] Assimilation of lessons provides guidance but also blinds people to alternatives. Good policymaking requires knowledge of history and its possible lessons, but also recognition of the limitations of such lessons and the way in which different contexts might render them ineffective or counterproductive. It further demands openness to change and to new ways of identifying and thinking about problems. These are nearly impossible conditions to meet in practice, which may help explain why policymakers so often err. For leaders facing fraught and risky challenges shrouded in uncertainty, facile historical analogies offer cognitive guidance and emotional support.[6] Policymakers cannot make sense of the world in the absence of historical analogies and lessons, but policy suffers when they become prisoners of these analogies and lessons.

The political consequences of the mobilization of historical analogies are unpredictable. It can sometimes generate lessons that help produce beneficial outcomes, as it seems to have done in the Cuban missile crisis. In *The Guns of August*, published shortly before the crisis, Barbara Tuchman argued – incorrectly, we now know – that European political leaders took the risks that led to war because they had no appreciation of its likely length and cost and because they were unaware of their countries' military plans.[7] President John F. Kennedy was very taken by Tuchman's book and is said to have kept it in mind during the crisis, and it was arguably one of the reasons he was cautious and shied away from military action.[8]

In the aftermath of the 1991 Gulf War, Vietnam was one of the historical analogies invoked by President George H. W. Bush and his advisers.[9] They were keen to avoid a long war and to retain public support.[10] Vietnam served, in this case, as a cautionary example. However, like many historical events, the Vietnam War spawned multiple and contradictory lessons.[11] Some historians and political scientists concluded that the US was defeated because it framed the problem incorrectly in terms of containment of the Soviet Union and China.[12] Others contend that American leaders failed to understand the local political and cultural situation in Vietnam and tried inappropriately to win a political conflict by military means.[13] Still others maintain that the US suffered from hubris, was unreasonably confident in its military capability, and was arrogantly dismissive of the Vietnamese.[14] These interpretations of the Vietnam War have continued to provide a lens for understanding the US's campaigns in Iraq and Afghanistan in the first decades of the twenty-first century.[15] Some observers have argued that the Vietnam analogy even served as a self-fulfilling prophecy, not least for the Biden administration, culminating in the rapid and chaotic exit by the US from Afghanistan in 2021.[16]

There is also a revisionist narrative that draw different lessons from Vietnam. It relies on the notion that the war was winnable and identifies internal scapegoats for the failed victory. It, too, takes several forms. Some argue that the right military strategy would have been victorious, and others that political interference kept the military from pursuing such a strategy.[17] The claim is widely voiced that the US lost the war in Vietnam because people at home did not support the troops, due in large part to the peace movement and protesters. This version of the *Dolchstoss* (stab in the back) thesis makes the case that if only the US had persevered and been less restrained in its use of force it could have won. Some revisionists also deny or downplay the civilian casualties for which the US was responsible.[18] From these perspectives, the Vietnam analogy is thus not only used to defend particular policies but also feeds into different conceptions of civic duties and patriotism.

The Vietnam case leads us to posit two ways in which historical analogies or lessons become part of political life. Analogies form part of the shared understandings of particular societies. People deploy them to make sense of their world and to identify and respond to its challenges. They also use them strategically as political tools to bolster and legitimize particular policies and identities and to delegitimize others. The creation and application of historical lessons capture the reflexive, creative, and intentional aspects of political action as well as the habitual and unreflective. An accurate and nuanced understanding of how historical lessons become influential in particular societies and at specific junctures requires that we pay attention to both these dimensions.

Sense-making has to do with the stories that politicians, academics, and people in general tell themselves about themselves and others. Historical narratives underpin foundational myths that serve as rallying points around which national and political identities are built. Significant past events are transformed into cautionary or triumphalist stories that provide meaning to political action and serve as guides for pushing society in a particular direction or for organizing its institutions in specific ways.[19] For scholars, such historical events or eras become focal points that serve as illustrative examples; they help direct the scholarly gaze in particular directions and provide the scaffolding for new theoretical understandings that are generalized and applied to contemporary circumstances. The French Revolution became such an undeniable

reference point for nineteenth-century European political thought; pro-
gressives and conservatives made it "an object of worship or of horror."[20]
Vietnam serves this function in the US – and, we argue, Weimar plays the
same role more generally for Western democracies. A marker of the
extent to which such reference points are embedded in a particular
society is that the intrinsic importance of such historical episodes is rarely
questioned. People disagree about the lessons that one should draw from
them, but the significance of the event as a source of lessons is firmly
ensconced in shared understandings of social and political life.

How does this happen? The premodern notion that history can be
uncritically mined for exemplars and serve as a reservoir for lessons in
line with the idea *Historia Magistra Vitae* (history as life's teacher) should
by now have loosened its grip on our political consciousness.[21] However,
frequent turns to history for lessons by policymakers and analysts indi-
cate a continuing tendency to think in this way.[22] Drawing lessons from
history may be a powerful, if not inescapable, cognitive predilection.
Current events and problems are almost always framed in terms of
collective understandings of past significant episodes and events.

High-profile policy decisions frequently make use of historical analogies to impart significance and weight to problems at hand and to their
responses. Scholars of international relations have documented how the
so-called lesson of Munich has been used to justify and highlight foreign
policy decisions at various junctures in the postwar era.[23] Neville
Chamberlain's appeasement and assurances to the British people that
war with Hitler's Germany had been averted "in our time" obviously
turned out to be erroneous. But, as often happens with lessons and
analogies, "Munich" was divorced from its historical context and its
power enhanced by transforming it into a freestanding principle of foreign policy.[24] It has encouraged and justified confrontational and mili-
taristic foreign policies in widely varying circumstances. This includes
the disastrous French campaigns in Vietnam and then in Algeria in the
1950s, British prime minister Anthony Eden's response to Nasser's
seizure of the Suez Canal, US intervention in Vietnam, and Margaret
Thatcher's response to Argentina's 1982 occupation of the Falkland
Islands.[25] Munich was also used to justify deterrence and Cold War
military buildups against the Soviet Union. Deterrence was repeatedly
reconfirmed tautologically and was falsely given credit for the end of the
Cold War.[26]

We should not assume a priori that historical lessons and analogies to
buttress contemporary political decisions are problematic. If based on
sensitive historical interpretations, treated with caution, and reformu-
lated in response to new evidence, historical analogies can help crystallize

core problems facing particular societies. They can also serve as effective communicative tools that provide perspective on contemporary challenges.[27] Scholarly evaluation and periodic reformulation of lessons have the potential to improve the choice of historical analogies mobilized in political discourses and the way in which they are used. Toward this end, we think it useful to focus equally on the collective understandings about history and its lessons that emerge in a society and how such analogies are used to formulate policies, justify them, and rally support.

The cognitive and instrumental perspectives on historical analogies and lessons capture different features of social and political reality. They overlap in the sense that lessons that have been taken to heart are easier to mobilize for instrumental purposes and will be more successful if they are shared and make sense to the target audience. Some scholars have attempted to determine if historical analogies shape the outlooks of politicians or are mobilized by them to justify and gain support for or against particular policy decisions.[28] This is a useful question to ask, but we should also focus on the ways in which these two uses of historical analogies are analytically and substantively related, and how they reinforce one another in practice.

Historical analogies and lessons are bundled together. Analogies are made between some past event and a present situation and the lessons learned from that event applied to the present one.[29] People can question the analogy between the past and present situations, the validity of that lesson, or its applicability to a particular situation. Our contributors make it apparent that Weimar has been mobilized in a range of different settings and for a variety of different ends. The most extensively used historical analogies are usually ones that have become deeply embedded in a political culture. Munich and Weimar qualify in this regard. The lessons of both are open to challenge, but, given how entrenched they are, it is usually more politically effective to challenge their application. Because they are so frequently invoked, they generate many cases in which their applicability or the lessons themselves can be evaluated. We are interested in knowing the extent to which scholars, the media, and policymakers think retrospectively about the application of these lessons.

The Paradigmatic Lesson

For political scientists and the media, the Weimar Republic and its downfall have become something of a just-so story. They have been a recurring reference point to make sense of threats to democracy and the possibility of political, economic, and societal breakdown.[30] Weimar has been mobilized to understand the limits and fragility of political orders; it supplies a concrete instance of a possible outcome which, if we are not careful, might come to pass in other polities. The interpretation of Weimar, as the exemplar of societal and political breakdown, is intimately bound up with what followed it. The moniker "the Weimar Republic" became widely spread only posthumously, after it had been eclipsed by the Nazi regime.[31] As political analogies go, however, Weimar may be unparalleled in its richness and scope of application. In recent years, Weimar has most frequently been used to understand the growing support for far-right movements and parties in Europe and more recently in the US. It assumes and encourages a homology between today's politics and the social, economic, and political dynamics that produced fascism in the 1930s. Donald Trump and those who voted for him have been described as fascists.[32] Trump's claim that the 2020 presidential election was stolen from him has been compared to the "stab in the back" myth, and his supporters' occupation of the capitol to Hitler's 1924 failed Beer Hall Putsch.[33] Weimar has also been weaponized by the far right. Their propagandists blame the Republic's collapse on homosexuality and other forms of perceived degeneracy and warn that the same outcome is likely in America.[34]

Early accounts of the re-emergence of the radical right in Europe built explicitly on interpretations of the rise of the Nazis in Weimar.[35] A common starting point of these analogies is a comparison of modernization and its effects in Weimar with contemporary globalization and the groups these processes marginalize and anger. Longstanding and well-institutionalized sociopolitical cleavages and coalitions became obsolete, creating a situation in which the center did not or seems not to hold. Much of the burgeoning literature on antidemocratic movements and political parties consists of variations on this theme.[36] The association of socioeconomic hardship and status decline on the one hand, and the rise of the radical right on the other, has also been contested; scholars have advanced other, mostly non-Weimar, explanations.[37] Similarly, the many efforts to analyze Trump's rise to power in the light of the Weimar analogy have been criticized for their lack of historical accuracy and progressive potential. It is accordingly a propitious moment to explore the Weimar analogy and its lessons as they are being widely used and widely criticized in the US, Europe, and elsewhere.

By far the most important Weimar analogies are associated with the fragility of democracies and what can be done to defend them and make them more robust. Scholars and pundits have drawn different lessons from Weimar. Some have emphasized the need for a substantive democracy that successfully addresses the material and other needs of citizens.[38] Social democrats have long regarded the comprehensive welfare state as the *sine qua non* and guarantor of a well-functioning democracy, inoculating societies from extremist politics. Social equality enables broad popular participation in politics in a positive way and fosters support for democratic institutions.[39] Conservatives have drawn the opposite lesson. Convinced that a mobilized population constitutes a threat to political order, they argue for a minimalist democracy primarily focused on safeguarding procedures for the non-violent change.[40] Beginning with Karl Loewenstein, constitutional scholars have focused on those aspects of the Weimar Constitution that made it inherently vulnerable to abuse. Loewenstein described Hitler's appointment to *Reichskanzler* (imperial chancellor) and the subsequent destruction of democracy as in no little part facilitated by "the generous and lenient Weimar republic," speaking then about how the constitution allowed for the dismantling of democracy through legal means.[41]

Recent discussions on democratic self-defense also take their cues from the fall of Weimar democracy. They rework the ideas of Loewenstein in a contemporary context.[42] Critics have questioned to what extent the notion of a democracy that abolishes itself is an accurate one; they have instead argued that it is an idea that ultimately helps legitimize a diminished and constrained form of democracy based on distrust of the electorate and their ability to withstand the emotional allure of charismatic leaders.[43] Others have highlighted fundamental differences between today's far-right populists and the extremist supporters of totalitarian ideologies in the interwar years.[44]

The Weimar analogy has not been limited to understanding political phenomena with a direct lineage to European fascism. It is often invoked in settings where this parallel is less obvious or absent. A prominent example is the student protests and social and political upheavals of the late 1960s and early 1970s in the US. They were seen by some as analogous to the turmoil of the Weimar era.[45] Others – with some justice, in our view – dismissed this comparison as superficial and indicative of a fear of democracy.[46]

From the point of view of the student movements, "fascism" was a pejorative used freely against a wide range of ideological opponents. For others, it came with more specific connotations, based in more palpable experiences of authoritarianism and war. This was especially evident in the German and Italian nationalist movements, both of which sought to reckon with the legacy of actual fascism in their countries.[47] The Weimar analogy is so flexible because there are multiple readings of its collapse, each with a different villain. For many German refugees, what put an end to Weimar was the mobilization of the masses by extremists on the right and the left. For socialists, then and now, it was the alliance of industry and the fascist right. For postwar constitutionalists, it was the special powers provision of the Weimar Constitution.[48] Others have singled out the failure of intellectuals to commit to the Republic; political division on the left; Weimar's troubled version of semi-presidentialism; bad leadership by Hindenburg and his chancellors; and the supine response of the socialists and Prussian police to Hitler's efforts to consolidate power.[49] Each of these interpretations of Weimar offers different lessons and serves to underpin conflicting social and political diagnoses of present-day problems. They include the dangers of polarization, the erosion of established institutions, the recklessness of the emotional masses, and authoritarian or psychopathological leaders. Weimar is mobilized to challenge the status quo but also to defend it.

The Weimar analogy has also been employed to assess the viability of new political orders, their instability or stability. In this sense, Weimar came to represent something of a shadow figure to the triumphalist liberal narratives of the end of the Cold War. For some, post-Soviet Russia provides a striking analogy with the tumultuous and instable Weimar Republic.[50] In a similar way, it has been applied to post-occupation Iraq as part of the counternarrative to American triumphalism and the claim by US occupiers that liberal democracy was expanding its reach and on the march throughout the world.[51] Weimar also has a foothold in the economics literature, where it is associated with hyperinflation in the scholarly and popular imagination.[52] Images of wheelbarrows of cash used to purchase a loaf of bread, or of *Reichsmarks* set aflame to light the wood stove, became emblematic of the dangers of irresponsible financial policies and their potential for precipitating more general social and political collapse. In many countries, and above all in Germany, the experience of hyperinflation and its putative lessons were exploited in the postwar era to remove financial policy from the sphere of democratic decision-making and to sacrifice all other economic goals to that of avoiding inflation. This lesson has finally lost some of its luster among economists, prompting a Nobel prize laureate to proclaim that the first person to bring up Weimar hyperinflation in a debate is considered to have lost.[53]

Weimar is also invoked to identify the tensions and limits of modern society more generally. Some thinkers, writing during and after the war, framed the collapse of Weimar as part of a larger struggle between modernity and rationality versus premodern, myth, and emotion. Liberal thinkers such as Hans Kelsen and Karl Popper elaborated these themes, as did Ernst Cassirer.[54] Influenced by Nietzsche, Cassirer argued that, despite all the efforts to supplant myth with reason, modern societies are built on the volcanic soil of mythical thinking and risk eruptions in times of uncertainty and crisis.[55] In this connection it is useful to define what we mean by myth. We follow Cyril Buffet and Beatrice Heuser in attributing two qualities to historical myths. "Myth" is a "shorthand" for an historical interpretation that is invoked frequently to justify certain kinds of policies. It is also in many instances an untrue, or largely untrue, representation of the past.[56] Weimar "myths" are mobilized at two levels. They are used to sell policies – mostly conservative ones – that are intended to preserve democracy, but which, as we have seen, in practice make societies less democratic. They are also used to evaluate modernity and its consequences, and again, for the most part, to attack them as dehumanizing, demoralizing, and corrupting. Not surprisingly, the two myths intersect as the conservative versions are mutually supporting. This is most evident with the so-called Claremonster conservatives (see Chapter 3), who explicitly draw on Leo Strauss's condemnation of modernity to justify their support for Donald Trump and authoritarian rule.

Weimar is contested every time it is deployed, no matter by whom and for what purpose. This is particularly apparent in the famous *Historikerstreit* in Germany in which opposing interpretations of Weimar emerged. These readings offered sharply contrasting takes on the Weimar Republic and the rise of the Nazis. The *Historikerstreit* generated a more general debate on the nature of the lessons that might be learned from the Weimar and Nazi eras and how both should be understood in relation to German history.[57]

Weimar and its downfall provide lessons about the West more generally and about modernity. While specific lessons drawn from the Weimar era are always contested, its continuing allure as an illustration of collapse and societal breakdown seems undiminished. Whenever it is invoked, it is a response to perceived crisis, and its embeddedness also helps us to determine when we confront a crisis. For some, it alerts us to being at the edge of chaos, and, for critics, imagining a crisis when none may exist. Either way, it has significant policy consequences.[58]

Structure of the Book

Douglas Webber's chapter (Chapter 2) explores why the reputedly strongest labor movement party in Europe, the German Social Democratic Party (SPD), failed to stave off the collapse of the Weimar Republic. Webber distinguishes between structural and contingent variables, and between those that were internal and external to the labor movement, that explain this inaction. The preponderantly antidemocratic orientation of the German middle and aristocratic classes, the continuity of bureaucratic, military, and legal elites from authoritarian pre–World War I Germany, the Weimar Constitution, and the division of the labor movement between the SPD and the German Communist Party meant that, in defending the new republic, the SPD faced an uphill struggle from the outset. It was also hindered in its efforts by the cautious stance adopted by the free trade unions, which had grown increasingly independent of the party and constrained its capacity to organize mass strikes as a political weapon, as well as by its own ideological orientation – its orthodox Marxism fostered passivity in the face of growing threats to the Republic and dissuaded it from adopting new economic policy ideas that might have won it broader support among German working-class and other voters.

Webber argues that, from 1930 onward, the Great Depression – the mass unemployment, the poverty and social distress, and the class and party-political polarization that it provoked – tipped the balance of power decisively against the Social Democrats, as their former bourgeois allies turned to the right, the Communist Party intensified its attacks on the SPD, and the labor market situation destroyed the trade unions' capacity and willingness to strike for political or any other ends. The SPD's decision not to take any direct protest action against the "Prussian Coup" that ousted the SPD-led government in Prussia in July 1932 – which contrasted with the successful opposition against the "Kapp Putsch" that aimed to overthrow the Republic in 1920 – reflected and acknowledged how weak its political position had become. The party leaders could have called on its paramilitary organization, the *Reichsbanner*, to oppose the coup – and later Hitler's accession to power. The *Reichsbanner*, however, would have had no chance of winning a physical confrontation – in effect, a civil war – against the German police and army, which would have been supported by the Nazis' and the right's own paramilitary forces. The party leadership's decision to oppose the coup and Hitler's rise to power by strictly political and legal means was unheroic, but it was understandable in as far as it was based on a realistic assessment of the balance of political forces in Germany in 1932–3.

According to Webber, the SPD parliamentary party's vote in March 1933 against the Enabling Law that Hitler used to install the Nazi dictatorship allowed the party to save its honor in a way that no other German party to its left or right could. Still today, scarcely any Social Democratic reference to the collapse of Weimar democracy fails to refer to the courageous speech made in this last parliamentary session by the parliamentary party's chairman, Otto Wels, which thus has a legitim-izing function for the SPD. The main lesson that SPD leaders drew from

Weimar's failure after World War II was about the importance of avoiding any deflationary economic policies and repetition of the Great Depression and the mass unemployment and poverty, as well as the political radicalization and democratic breakdown that it engendered. However, although the collapse of the Weimar Republic and the SPD's unsuccessful efforts to avert it remain very present in the Social Democrats' collective memory and are regularly recalled and commemorated, it did not take long after the war for contemporary issues to displace the "lessons of Weimar" as the SPD's principal preoccupation in day-to-day political action. The SPD made two key decisions in the late 1950s – to accept the "Western integration" of the Federal Republic and to transform itself from an avowedly working-class party into a catch-all "people's party" (*Volkspartei*) – that arguably contributed significantly to the consolidation of democracy in West Germany. But these decisions were not made in the shadow of Weimar, but rather in response to the pressures of party-political competition at the time, to the growing gap in support between the SPD and Chancellor Konrad Adenauer's Christian Democrats.

In Webber's view, there is little if any reason to fear a renewed democratic breakdown in contemporary Germany. However, the process of executive *aggrandizement* – the expansion and abuse of their powers by political chief executives – that undermined the Weimar Republic can be seen at work in many recent or contemporary cases of democratic breakdown. The principal lesson of Weimar may be how important it is to combat such trends as early as possible, before the process has gained too much momentum – in German, "*Wehret den Anfänge!*"

Peter C. Caldwell's contribution to this volume (Chapter 3) examines the role of the Weimar analogy in West Germany after 1945. For the actors who helped found and shape the Federal Republic of Germany, Weimar was both a concrete event in German history and an example of how democracies fail from which the new Germany had to learn: What were the conditions that destroyed Weimar democracy? And, by analogy, what conditions should the new German polity avoid? The problem was that there never was just one "Weimar analogy." Two general causes came to dominate West German debates about the threats to democracy in Germany's future. One stressed the role democracy itself played in its own destruction: The threat lay in political parties, unlimited rights, and a weak state. The other emphasized the way actors both on the far left and on the right had actively undermined and eventually destroyed Weimar democracy: The threat lay with those who rejected democracy. Caldwell reconstructs the discussion about the practical lessons from Weimar's end from the initial public discussions directly after the war, to the conferences creating the Basic Law, to the first major historical debates on the end of Weimar in the 1950s, in order to show how eventually a clear distinction developed between these two different views of the end of Weimar – and, indeed, of the nature of democracy. Caldwell does not dismiss analogy as a method because of the way it creates contradictory explanations. His point is rather that analogy can serve as a tool for making sense of complex, indeed nonreplicable, historical events, in a way that opens up discussion about an uncertain future.

In Chapter 4, Peter Breiner examines how Otto Kirchheimer constructed his account of the struggle of the Social Democratic Party of Germany to redirect the Weimar Constitution into a model of socialist democracy and how the outcome of this failed struggle contained in Weimar provided him with an exemplary lesson – what he calls a "paradigmatic example" – on how the logic of liberal democracy could spawn a shift of authority to administration and the courts and eventually to dictatorship.

At the core of this account is Kirchheimer's insistence that constitutions must be understood in terms of the sociology of power within which they must operate, rather than there being an exclusive focus on a priori legal structure and reform. With this account in mind, Breiner examines how American political science turned Kirchheimer's powerful left criticism of the logics of liberal democracy based on the Weimar example into support for that political form by redefining the Weimar example itself into a dangerous warning of what can happen if we do not accept a liberal pluralist regime. This move left the force of Kirchheimer's criticism and the complex meaning of the Weimar example blunted, though still relevant. Focusing on Kirchheimer's continuous preoccupation with sustaining a left political opposition against its neutralization by the liberal parliamentary state, we see a continuity between his Weimar work and his influential postwar political science, even though this work was often reinterpreted in a way that was at odds with its meaning. Breiner concludes that Kirchheimer's original argument, forged in the crucible of the Weimar Republic, on the need to preserve a left political opposition in the face of its neutralization by the liberal parliamentary state continues to have the critical force that American political science has so attenuated.

Ludvig Norman, in Chapter 5, analyzes Swedish social democratic thinking in the 1930s and the form that Weimar lessons took there. Focusing on the writings of Alva and Gunnar Myrdal, both enormously influential intellectual figures for social democracy during this period, it traces how the reevaluation of democratic politics, informed by its collapse that occurred elsewhere, shaped Swedish social democracy. Norman shows that prevalent lessons pertaining to democracy – and, in particular, the discrediting of democracy as mass politics – were largely absent in social democratic thinking in Sweden. Rather, the rise of totalitarianism in Germany was seen as the result of an intellectually damaged society where science and rationality had been abandoned.

From Norman's analysis of social democratic thought in Sweden emerges a more general point regarding analogical reasoning and lesson-drawing in politics. The Swedish self-image as an avant-garde in rational social reform provided a degree of blindness that reduced the scope for critical self-reflection. In the writing of the Myrdals, we encounter a view of Swedish society as an exemplar, a model for a different path into modernity from the one that dominated in Europe at the time and which was playing out as the demise of democracy and the rise of totalitarian regimes.

Its unique position in Europe during the 1930s and 1940s allowed social democracy to play out unbounded in its self-perceived rationality in what could be achieved through state intervention, allowing for both highly progressive reforms and more troubling and intrusive aspects of social programs. This is exemplified in particular by the Myrdals' strong advocacy for programs designed to ensure a healthy population stock. This, the Myrdals argued, would be achieved by, among other things, the use of forced sterilization of individuals deemed "asocial" and of "lesser quality." In spite of the clear parallels with prevalent ideas of eugenics, which were also central to the ideational underpinnings of the Nazis, the Myrdals were adamant about how the population programs they suggested represented a wholly democratic set of policies, in stark contrast to the undemocratic ones found elsewhere – in Germany in particular. The failure or unwillingness to see these parallels, Norman argues, can be partly explained by how lesson-drawing and the use of analogies may shield actors from self-reflection.

Amel Ahmed (Chapter 6) engages recent works that have sought to harness the lessons of Weimar to offer guidance to ailing democracies around the globe. Utilizing a Weberian evaluation of ideal types, she examines the model of democracy and democratic defense employed by these accounts. She argues that what they offer as a general model of democracy defense reflects a very particular understanding that emerged during the Cold War. It was not so much about democracy preservation as it was intended to serve particular foreign policy goals. It was designed to defend domestic actors aligned with the West and diminish the influence of those aligned with the East. It came to be closely associated with the idea of *political democracy*, a particular postwar creation related to but distinct from both liberal and elite democracy. It might be described as an approach to democracy that theorized tactics for the preservation of democracy.

This Cold War model of democracy is today an atavism, but it still dominates much thinking about democracy preservation. It is embedded in recent works on the lessons of Weimar. The model's lack of reflexivity and analytical problems distort the history of Weimar, rendering dubious any analogies based on it to present-day politics. Its analytical flaws become political pitfalls, as the works that draw on it misconstrue the terrain of the political fight and miss opportunities to appeal to those who support democracy but seek more radical changes. Accounting for the historical particularity of this vision reveals important insights into the problem faced by contemporary democracies. It may also help to open up space for theorizing democracy in a way that would better serve its defense.

Recent scholarship regularly interprets the rise of Donald Trump and other authoritarian populists with recourse to the Weimar Republic and its tragic fate. Often penned by liberal democrats hoping to ward off growing authoritarian threats, it tends to identify parallels between the political conditions that enabled Trump and those that destroyed Germany's first democratic experiment. William E. Scheuerman's chapter (Chapter 7) brings to our attention the use of Weimar "lessons" by right-wing intellectuals in support of Trump. This tendency has been especially striking among those Trump partisans who trace their intellectual genealogy to the influential German Jewish émigré political philosopher Leo Strauss (1899–1973). Even though Trump garnered little enthusiasm among the ranks of America's mostly liberal intelligentsia, Straussian lawyers and political scientists based at the right-wing Claremont Institute (and at California's Claremont McKenna College) constituted an exception to the generally anti-Trumpian mood. Strauss's self-described "west coast" – or "Claremonster" – disciples quickly remade the Institute's main publications, *Claremont Review of Books* and *The American Mind*, into pro-Trump ideological vehicles. They served in prominent official and semi-official posts for President Trump, and worked both publicly and behind the scenes to subvert the November 2020 presidential election results.

For Scheuerman, contemporary Straussians' politically charged, methodologically limited, and distorted view of the Weimar Republic played a pivotal role in justifying their irresponsible political choices. Their redeployment of Weimar, he suggests, highlights the many ways in which its legacy can serve both antidemocratic and authoritarian ends. The Claremonsters' recourse to Weimar has its origins in Strauss's own critical, yet far more nuanced, view of Weimar's relevance for postwar liberal democracy. Traumatized by the Republic's destruction and the Nazi regime that succeeded it, Strauss became postwar America's most influential conservative political theorist. Nonetheless, the story of how Strauss's ideas morphed into the pro-Trump partisanship of the Claremonsters remains messy. To explore it, Scheuerman examines how US-based Straussians have come to favor open-ended notions of executive power, a trend he believes eventually culminated in their disastrous interpretation of Donald Trump as a redemptive political figure tasked with returning a decadent republic to its original, morally superior bases.

By exploring recent Straussian views of executive power, Scheuerman offers an explanation for why many "west coast," but not most "east coast," Straussians were susceptible to Trump's appeal. He concludes by briefly revisiting the controversial matter of Strauss's intellectual and political relationship to Carl Schmitt. Eager to ward off a repeat of Weimar's fate, Scheuerman argues, some Straussians are embracing a brand of authoritarian presidentialism with striking parallels to Schmitt's political ideas during Weimar Germany's final years. Although there are real differences from Strauss's original Weimar-inflected theoretical narrative, elements of contemporary Straussian political analysis stem from theoretical lacunae that already plagued Strauss. Specifically, Strauss's soft spot for ideational or *geistegeschichtliche* (spiritual and/or intellectual-historical) analysis forced him to marginalize systematic historical, political, and social analysis. According to Scheuerman, precisely that flawed methodological orientation, with even more disastrous political consequences, has invited contemporary Straussians to join the Trumpist bandwagon.

The very definition of political learning is one of the key questions posed by this volume, and, in Chapter 8, Jill Suzanne Smith ponders what counts for political learning when it comes to the realm of popular visual culture. In her close analysis of the hit streaming series *Babylon Berlin*, which takes place in the German capital in the late 1920s and early 1930s, Smith explores the tension between political lessons about Weimar that the series' creators articulate in the media and the representation of those lessons in the series itself. Does the series inspire viewers to a robust defense of democracy, even when Weimar's democratic center is barely depicted in the series? Does the series' portrayal of Weimar-era "New Woman" praise the era's emancipatory potential, or does it often reenact the withholding of socioeconomic and sexual freedoms from those very women? Is sexuality seen as an indicator of democratic freedom, or is it associated instead with Weimar's descent into Nazism? The combination of so-called deviant sexuality, hedonistic club culture, and fascism is most potent in Bob Fosse's 1972 film adaptation of the hit musical *Cabaret*, a clear point of inspiration for *Babylon Berlin*.

Acknowledging the sway that *Cabaret* holds over the makers of the contemporary series, Smith points to the fact that Fosse's film is just one of many cultural citations that make up this kaleidoscopic work. In hopes of getting closer to some of the lessons the showrunners may have drawn from the Weimar era itself, Smith looks to novels from the time, most prominently Irmgard Keun's 1932 novel *The Artificial Silk Girl*, using the depiction of the New Woman and politics in those novels as lenses for a closer examination of *Babylon Berlin*'s own political and social dynamics. Because the club acts as a key space for political, social, and sexual negotiations across cultural depictions of Berlin, from the Weimar-era novels of Keun and others, through films and music of the 1970s and 1980s, to today's streaming television, Smith interprets three separate club scenes from the television series in order to explore how these cultural genres and time periods work both with and against one another, giving viewers a contradictory, multidimensional view of Weimar and its subsequent revivals. When it comes to pop-cultural representations of Weimar Berlin, Smith notes, sense-making easily becomes myth-making, unless we subject the myth of sexual hedonism and decadence that is so obvious on the surface of *Babylon Berlin* to intense scrutiny. When we do, we discover other multiple, conflicting narrative strands that may aid in our cultural understanding of Weimar.

Jan-Werner Müller (Chapter 9) discusses Weimar as a theme in contemporary understandings of the threats against democracy that feed into discussions on "militant democracy" and specifically on the role of the concept of "fascism" in this context. References to "Weimar" and "fascism" have played an increasingly important role in trying to make sense of the present, and also to mobilize various constituencies. Related to the diagnosis of contemporary political movements as fascist or neo-fascist, the question discussed in Müller's chapter is whether some of the lessons drawn in the postwar period from the failures of Weimar – especially the ones that inspired the creation of the legal toolkit generally known as "militant democracy" – should be central to attempts to defend democracy today.

Müller's chapter engages both issues and argues that it is, first, ultimately problematic to designate today's forms of "autocratization" as involving anything plausibly called fascism. A key aspect that is missing, Müller argues, for large parts of the contemporary far right, are political programs that revolve around the glorification of violence. In this sense,

it seems, today's far-right populist movements have also taken lessons –
but, in their case, perhaps, from the fall of fascism. As Müller discusses,
these political actors are highly proficient in navigating what counts as
publicly acceptable forms of speech in democratic societies. Second, and
in spite of the fact that the actors associated with contemporary threats to
democracy generally fall within the realm of what is permissible, Müller
argues that the toolkit of militant democracy remains valuable in many
ways. However, he cautions that the instruments included in this framework are less well suited to dealing with today's challenges to democracy
than is often assumed.

In a final chapter (Chapter 10), Lebow and Norman tie together
insights from the volume's contributions and discuss how Weimar as a
paradigmatic historical lesson has served as a focal point for competing
visions about modernity and politics, democracy in particular. Weimar as
a cultural and a political symbol is also discussed, and Lebow and
Norman highlight the sense of drama and tragedy that analogies to
Weimar rely on, helping to explain its continued grip on our political
imaginations. The chapter finally offers some generalizations regarding
historical lessons. Historical lessons and their associated analogies may
be an inescapable part of making sense of contemporary politics, but they
sometime take on a deterministic tinge that hems in political thought.
When employed with care, however, they can be a tool for thinking
creatively about current political predicaments, used to highlight the
things we care about in politics and as starting points for
political analysis.

Notes

1 Ben Mercer, "Trump, Fascism, and Historians in the Post-Truth Era" in Marius
   Gudonis and Benjamin Jones, eds., *History in a Post-Truth World* (London:
   Routledge, 2020); Gavriel Rosenfeld, "An American Führer: Nazi Analogies and
   the Struggle to Explain Donald Trump," *Central European History* 52, no. 4 (2019),
   pp. 554–87. The notion of "Weimar America" is an oft-employed image in relation
   to the Trump administration, and seemingly is as often criticized for its inaccuracy.
   See, for instance, Roger Cohen, "Trump's Weimar America," *New York Times*,
   14 December 2015, www.nytimes.com/2015/12/15/opinion/weimar-america.html;
   Niall Ferguson, "'Weimar America'? The Trump Show Is No Cabaret,"
   Bloomberg, 6 September 2020, www.bloomberg.com/opinion/articles/2020-09-06/
   trump-s-america-is-no-weimar-republic (both accessed 10 November 2020).
2 See chapter 2 in Richard Ned Lebow and Feng Zhang, *History, Lessons,
   Analogies: Learning from Wars and Pandemics*, under review, Oxford
   University Press, on the complex relationship between lessons and analogies.
3 Daniel Bessner, *Democracy in Exile: Hans Speier and the Rise of the Defense
   Intellectual* (Ithaca, NY: Cornell University Press, 2018); Udi Greenberg, *The*

Weimar Century: German Émigrés and the Ideological Foundation of the Cold War (Princeton: Princeton University Press, 2015).

4 In the field of international relations, numerous studies have addressed the use of historical analogies, studying in particular how the Munich and Vietnam analogies have been employed in a variety of settings to bolster foreign policy decisions. See Lebow and Zhang, *History, Lessons, Analogies*; Yuen Foong Khong, *Analogies at War: Korea, Munich, Dien Bien Phu, and the Vietnam Decisions of 1965* (Princeton: Princeton University Press, 1992); Scott MacDonald, *Rolling the Iron Dice: Historical Analogies and Decisions to Use Military Force in Regional Contingencies* (Westport, CT: Greenwood, 2000); David Chuter "Munich, or the Blood of Others" in Cyril Buffet and Beatrice Heuser, eds., *Haunted by History: Myths of International Relations* (Oxford: Berghahn Books, 1998), pp. 65–79; Mikkel Vedby Rasmussen, "The History of a Lesson: Versailles, Munich and the Social Construction of the Past," *Review of International Studies* 29 no. 4 (2003), pp. 499–519; Margaret Macmillan, *Dangerous Games: The Uses and Abuses of History* (New York: Modern Library 2009); Hal W. Brands and Jeremi Suri, eds., *The Power of the Past: History and Statecraft* (Washington, DC: Brookings, 2016). For a discussion on other historical analogies employed in US foreign policy, see Jan Ångström, "Mapping the Competing Historical Analogies of the War on Terrorism: The Bush Presidency," *International Relations* 25, no. 2 (2011), pp. 224–42.

5 Macmillan, *Dangerous Games*, p. 8.

6 Richard Ned Lebow, *Between War and Peace: The Nature of International Crisis* (Baltimore: Johns Hopkins University Press, 1981), chapters 5–6; Khong, *Analogies at War*, p. 252.

7 Barbara Tuchman, *The Guns of August* (New York: Random House, 1962).

8 Jordan Michael Smith, "Did a Mistake Save the World?," *Boston Globe*, 21 October 2012, www.bostonglobe.com/ideas/2012/10/20/cuban-missile-crisis-did-mistake-save-world/hYf8nEauKjnul3fmFCg3PM/story.html (accessed 2 December 2020).

9 For a description of how American political and military officials employed the "lessons" of Munich and Vietnam, although neither was really applicable, see Hal W. Brands, "Neither Munich nor Vietnam: The Gulf War of 1991" in Brands and Suri, *Power of the Past*, pp. 73–98.

10 Ibid.

11 Mark Atwood Lawrence, "Policymaking and the Uses of the Vietnam War" in Brands and Suri, *Power of the Past*, pp. 49–72.

12 Arthur M. Schlesinger, Jr., *Bitter Heritage: Vietnam and American Democracy, 1941–1966* (New York: Houghton-Mifflin, 1966);George C. Herring, *America's Longest War: The United States and Vietnam, 1950–1975*, 4th ed. (New York: McGraw-Hill, 2001).

13 Frances Fitzgerald, *Fire in the Lake: The Vietnamese and the Americans in Vietnam* (Boston, MA: Little, Brown, 1972); George McT. Kahin, *Intervention: How America Became Involved in Vietnam* (New York: Knopf, 1986); Eric M. Bergerud, *The Dynamics of Defeat: The Vietnam War in Hua Nghia Province* (Boulder, CO: Westview, 1996); Jeffrey Race, *War Comes to Long An: Revolutionary Conflict in a Vietnamese Province* (Berkeley: University

of California Press, 1972); James Trullinger, *Village at War: An Account of Conflict in Vietnam* (Stanford: Stanford University Press, 1993).

14 Loren Baritz, *Backfire: The Myths That Made Us Fight. The Illusions That Helped Us Lose, The Legacy That Haunts Us Today* (New York: Ballantine, 1986); James William Gibson, *The Perfect War: Technowar in Vietnam* (New York: Atlantic Monthly Press, 1986); Mark Philip Bradley, *Imagining Vietnam and America: The Making of Postcolonial Vietnam, 1919–1950* (Chapel Hill: University of North Carolina Press, 1950).

15 Andrew Gawthorpe, "Afghanistan and the Real Vietnam Analogy," *The Diplomat*, 18 August 2021, https://thediplomat.com/2021/08/afghanistan-and-the-real-vietnam-analogy/ (accessed 22 September 2022).

16 Paul D. Miller, "How a Misguided Vietnam Analogy Sealed the Afghanistan Disaster," *The New Atlanticist*, 5 October 2021, www.atlanticcouncil.org/blogs/new-atlanticist/how-a-misguided-vietnam-analogy-sealed-the-afghanistan-disaster/; Marvin Ott, "Afghanistan: Echoes of Vietnam?," Wilson Center [blog], 13 July 2021, www.wilsoncenter.org/blog-post/afghanistan-echoes-vietnam (both accessed 22 September 2022).

17 Harry G. Summers, *On Strategy: A Critical Analysis of the Vietnam War* (Novato, CA: Presidio, 1982); Bruce Palmer, Jr., *The 25-Year War: America's Military Role in Vietnam* (Lexington: University of Kentucky Press, 1984); Philip R. Davidson, *Vietnam at War: The History, 1946–1875* (Novato, CA: Presidio, 1988); Andrew F. Krepinovich, *The Army and Vietnam* (Baltimore: Johns Hopkins University Press, 1988); Mark Moyar, *Triumph Forsaken: The Vietnam War, 1954–1965* (New York: Cambridge University Press, 2006); Michael Lind, *Vietnam: The Necessary War* (New York: Free Press, 1999).

18 Gunter Lewy, *America in Vietnam* (New York: Oxford, 1979); Norman Podhoretz, *Why We Were in Vietnam* (New York: Simon & Schuster, 1982); Lind, *Vietnam*; Moyar, *Triumph Forsaken*. See Andrew Wiest and Michael Doidge, eds., *Triumph Revisited: Historians Battle for the Vietnam War* (London: Routledge, 2010), for a review and critique of revisionist claims.

19 Chiara Bottici and Benoit Challand, *Imagining Europe: Myth, Memory, Identity* (Cambridge: Cambridge University Press, 2013).

20 François Furet, *Interpreting the French Revolution* (Cambridge: Cambridge University Press, 1981), p. 6; William Doyle, "The Revolution and Its Historians" in *The Oxford History of the French Revolution*, 3rd ed. (Oxford: Oxford University Press, 2018), pp. 440–58.

21 Reinhart Koselleck, *Futures Past: On the Semantics of Historical Time* (New York: Columbia University Press, 2004), chapter 2.

22 Javier Fernández-Sebastián argues that, even though nineteenth-century Western culture began to perceive the past as a qualitatively different place, it also ushered in a golden age of the use of historical parallelisms in discussions about all aspects of social and political life. Javier Fernández-Sebastián, "Waving the Historian's Wand: Temporal Comparisons and Analogies in the Writing of History," *Time & Society* 30, no. 4 (2021), pp. 517–35.

23 Jeffrey Record, *The Specter of Munich: Reconsidering the Lessons of Appeasing Hitler* (Washington, DC: Potomac Books, 2006); Brands, "Neither Munich

nor Vietnam." While this volume focuses on Weimar, Munich is widely regarded as the paradigmatic equivalent for international relations.

24 Chuter, "Munich, or the Blood of Others."

25 Ibid.; Richard Ned Lebow, "Miscalculation in the South Atlantic: British and Argentine Intelligence Failures in the Falkland Crisis," *Journal of Strategic Studies* 6 (1983), pp. 1–29; Rasmussen, "The History of a Lesson."

26 Richard Ned Lebow and Janice Gross Stein, *We All Lost the Cold War* (Princeton: Princeton University Press, 1994); Ellen Schrecker, ed., *Cold War Triumphalism: The Misuse of History After the Fall of Communism* (New York: New Press, 2006).

27 For a discussion on how to differentiate more or less useful applications of historical analogies in political debate, see Markus Kornprobst, "Comparing Apples and Oranges? Leading and Misleading Uses of Historical Analogies," *Millennium* 36, no. 1 (2007), pp. 29–49.

28 Khong, *Analogies at War.*

29 See chapter 2 in Lebow and Zhang, *History, Lessons, Analogies* for further exploration of this connection.

30 Graf Rüdinger, "Either-Or: The Narrative of 'Crisis' in Weimar Germany and Historiography," *Central European History* 43, no. 4 (2010), pp. 592–615. Rüdinger argues that Weimar as an image of crisis has been the most prevalent one; some have also argued against this understanding, pointing to how it serves as an overly constrained and partial view of Weimar society. Peter E. Gordon and John P. McCormick also depart from the singular focus on Weimar as a site of crisis, characterized by a unified *Zeitgeist*, and instead study Weimar thought as constituted by a variety of intellectual traditions and impulses. Peter E. Gordon and John P. McCormick, *Weimar Thought: A Contested Legacy* (Princeton: Princeton University Press, 2013).

31 Colin Storer *Britain and the Weimar Republic: The History of a Cultural Relationship* (London: Bloomsbury, 2010), p. 4.

32 Jan-Werner Müller's contribution to this volume looks more closely at the use of the fascist epithet.

33 Cohen, "Trump's Weimar America"; Robert Gerwarth, "Weimar's Lessons for Biden's America," *Foreign Policy*, 6 February 2021, https://foreignpolicy .com/2021/02/06/weimars-lessons-for-bidens-america/ (both accessed 7 July 2021).

34 Jill Suzanne Smith's contribution to our volume focuses on the cultural significance of Weimar in relation to these themes. See also Eric D. Weitz, *Weimar Germany: Promise and Tragedy*, 2nd ed. (Princeton: Princeton University Press, 2009), p. xiii; Joel Kotkin, "Is American About to Suffer Its Weimar Moment?," *Daily Beast*, 31 December 2009, www.thedailybeast .com/is-america-about-to-suffer-its-weimar-moment (accessed 7 July 2021).

35 Hans-Georg Betz, *Radical Right-Wing Populism in Western Europe* (Basingstoke: Macmillan, 1994), p. 27.

36 Pippa Norris and Ronald Inglehart, *Cultural Backlash: Trump, Brexit, and Authoritarian Populism* (Cambridge: Cambridge University Press, 2018); Noam Gidron and Peter A. Hall, "The Politics of Social Status: Economic and Cultural Roots of the Populist Right," *British Journal of Sociology* 68, no.

S1 (2017), pp. 57–84; Daphne Halikiopoulou and Tim Vlandas, "Risks, Costs and Labour Markets: Explaining Cross-National Patterns of Far-Right Party Success in European Parliament Elections," *Journal of Common Market Studies* 54, no. 3 (2016), pp. 636–55.

37 Cas Mudde, "The Myth of Weimar Europe," *Open Democracy*, 20 August 2013, www.opendemocracy.net/en/can-europe-make-it/myth-of-weimar-europe/ (accessed 28 October 2020).

38 Alf Ross, *Why Democracy?* (Cambridge, MA: Harvard University Press, 1952). For discussions of the welfare state and law in Weimar, see Peter C. Caldwell and William E. Scheuerman, *From Liberal Democracy to Fascism: Legal and Political Thought in the Weimar Republic* (Boston, MA: Humanities Press, 2000). For a comprehensive engagement with the cultural dynamics of socialists and communists in Weimar, see Sabine Hake, *The Proletarian Dream: Socialism, Culture, and Emotion in Germany, 1863–1963* (Boston, MA: De Gruyter, 2017).

39 Hermann Heller, "Political Democracy and Social Homogeneity" in Arthur J. Jacobsen and Bernhard Schlink, eds., *Weimar: A Jurisprudence of Crisis* (Berkeley: University of California Press 2000 [1928]), pp. 256–65; Sheri Berman, *The Social Democratic Moment: Ideas and Politics in the Making of Interwar Europe* (Cambridge, MA: Harvard University Press, 1998).

40 Karl Popper, *The Open Society and Its Enemies* (Princeton: Princeton University Press, 1945).

41 Karl Loewenstein, "Autocracy Versus Democracy in Contemporary Europe," *American Political Science Review* 29, no. 4 (1935), pp. 571–93. There is a comprehensive and more contemporary literature on legal and political thought in Weimar and its influence on postwar thought, in particular in the field of constitutional law. See, for instance, David Dyzenhaus *Legality and Legitimacy: Carl Schmitt, Hans Kelsen, and Hermann Heller in Weimar* (Oxford: Oxford University Press, 1997); Jan-Werner Müller, *A Dangerous Mind: Carl Schmitt in Post-War European Thought* (New Haven: Yale University Press, 2003); Cindy Skach, *Borrowing Constitutional Designs: Constitutional Law in Weimar Germany and the Fifth Republic* (Princeton: Princeton University Press, 2005); William E. Scheuerman, *The End of Law: Carl Schmitt in the Twenty-First Century* (Boulder, CO: Rowman & Littlefield, 2020).

42 Alexander Kirchner, *A Theory of Militant Democracy: The Ethics of Combatting Political Extremism* (New Haven: Yale University Press, 2014); Anthoula Malkopoulou and Alexander Kirchner, eds., *Militant Democracy and Its Critics: Populism, Parties, Extremism* (Edinburgh: Edinburgh University Press, 2019); Jan-Werner Müller, "Protecting Popular Self-Government from the People? New Normative Perspectives on 'Militant Democracy,'" *Annual Review of Political Science* 19 (2016), pp. 249–65.

43 Anthoula Malkopoulou and Ludvig Norman "Three Models of Democratic Self-Defence: Militant Democracy and Its Alternatives," *Political Studies* 66, no. 2 (2018), pp. 442–58.

44 Cristóbal Rovira Kaltwasser "Populism and Militant Democracy" in Malkopoulou and Kirchner, Militant Democracy and Its Critics, pp. 92–111.

45 Daniel Bessner, "The Ghosts of Weimar: The Weimar Analogy in American Thought," *Social Research* 84, no. 4 (2017), pp. 831–55; Bruno Bettelheim, "The Anatomy of Academic Dissent," *Change in Higher Education* 1, no. 3 (1969), pp. 18–26.

46 Theodore Draper, "The Spectre of Weimar," *Social Research* 39, no. 2 (1972), pp. 322–40; Hans Morgenthau, "Remarks on the Validity of Historical Analogy," *Social Research* 39, no. 2 (1972), pp. 360–4.

47 Ben Mercer, "Spectres of Fascism: The Rhetoric of Historical Analogy in 1968," *Journal of Modern History* 88, no. 1 (2016), pp. 96–129.

48 Loewenstein, "Autocracy Versus Democracy in Contemporary Europe."

49 Hans Rosenberg, *A History of the German Republic* (London: Methuen, 1936); Erich Eyck, *A History of the Weimar Republic*, 2 vols. (Oxford: Oxford University Press, 1962); Andreas Dorpalen, *Hindenburg and the Weimar Republic* (Princeton: Princeton University Press, 1964); Richard F. Hamilton, *Who Voted for Hitler?* (Princeton: Princeton University Press, 1982); Henry Ashby Turner, *German Big Business and the Rise of Hitler* (New York: Oxford University Press, 1985); Martin Broszat, *Hitler and the Collapse of Weimar Germany* (New York: St. Martin's Press, 1987); Anthony James Nicholls, *Weimar and the Rise of Hitler* (New York: St. Martin's Press, 2000); Skach, *Borrowing Constitutional Designs*; Anthony McElligott, ed., *Weimar Germany* (Oxford: Oxford University Press, 2009); Frank Bajohr, Werner Johe, and Uwe Lohalm, *Zivilisation und Barbarei: Die widersprüchliche Potentiale der Moderne* (Hamburg: Hamburger Beiträge zur Sozial- und Zeitgeschichte, 1991); Shelley Baranowski, *The Sanctity of Rural Life: Nobility, Protestantism, and Nazism in Weimar Prussia* (Oxford: Oxford University Press, 1995); Donna Harsch, *German Social Democracy and the Rise of Nazism* (Durham, NC: Duke University Press, 2011); Paul Gerhard, *Gegen Hitler und für die Republik: Die Auseinandersetzung der deutschen Sozialdemokratie mit der NSDAP in der Weimarer Republik* (Dusseldorf: Droste Verlag, 1989); Heinrich August Winkler and Peter Fritsche, "Did Weimar Fail?," *Journal of Modern History* 68, no. 3 (1996), pp. 629–56.

50 Rogers Brubaker, *Nationalism Reframed: Nationhood and the National Question in the New Europe* (Cambridge: Cambridge University Press, 1996); Stephen E. Hanson and Jeffrey S. Kopstein, "The Weimar/Russia Comparison," *Post-Soviet Affairs* 13 no. 3 (1997), pp. 252–83.

51 David Runciman, *The Politics of Good Intentions: History, Fear and Hypocrisy in the New World Order* (Princeton: Princeton University Press, 2006), p. 117.

52 Adam Fergusson, *When Money Dies: The Nightmare of the Weimar Hyperinflation* (London: Old Street Publishing, 2010). It should be noted that this work is not necessarily representative of the comprehensive literature on the financial crisis in Weimar. It is interesting to note, however, for the sake of the discussions here that the work was first published in 1975 and received limited attention until it was republished in 2010 in the midst of the Great Recession.

53 Paul Krugman "Partying Like It's 1923: Or, The Weimar Temptation," *New York Times*, 27 December 2010, http://krugman.blogs.nytimes.com/2010/12/27/partying-like-its-1923-or-the-weimar-temptation/ (accessed 10 November 2020).

54 Popper, *The Open Society and Its Enemies*; Ernst Cassirer, *The Myth of the State* (New Haven: Yale University Press, 1974 [1946]); Hans Kelsen, "God and the State" in Ota Weinberger, ed., *Hans Kelsen: Essays in Legal and Moral Philosophy* (Boston, MA: Springer, 1973), pp. 61–82.
55 Cassirer, *The Myth of the State*, p. 280.
56 Cyril Buffet and Beatrice Heuser, "Introduction" in Buffet and Heuser, *Haunted by History*, pp. vii–x.
57 Richard J. Evans, "The New Nationalism, and the Old History: Perspectives on the West German Historikerstreit," *Journal of Modern History* 59, no. 4 (1987), pp. 761–97; Matthew P. Fitzpatrick, "The Pre-History of the Holocaust? The Sonderweg and Historikerstreit Debates and the Abject Colonial Past," *Central European History* 41, no. 3 (2008), pp. 477–503.
58 See Richard Ned Lebow and Ludvig Norman, eds., *The Robustness and Fragility of Political Regimes* (Cambridge: Cambridge University Press, 2023) for a discussion of these consequences.

2 An Unheroic but Understandable Failure
German Social Democrats and the Collapse of the Weimar Republic

Douglas Webber

On 30 January 1933, President Paul von Hindenburg appointed Adolf Hitler as German chancellor. In his diary, Julius Leber, a member of parliament in the SPD (Sozialdemokratische Partei Deutschlands – German Social Democratic Party), noted, "The dangers are enormous. But the resoluteness of the German working class is unshakable. We are determined to take up the fight."[1] Four days later, the leaders of the SPD and the free trade unions met to decide what they should do in response to Hitler's appointment. Union leaders cautioned that enthusiasm or support for a general strike among factory workers was "not very strong."[2] The Social Democratic intellectual and former finance minister Rudolf Hilferding, whom the Gestapo would later murder, warned that a general strike would rapidly culminate in a civil war. The union chairman Theodor Leipart recommended that the party and unions should wait until the constitution had clearly been broken before taking any action.[3] Instead of trying to initiate strike action against Hitler's appointment, the SPD focused instead on mobilizing support in the elections that Hitler had announced for 5 March. Before these elections could take place, Hitler's government took the fire in the German parliament, the Reichstag, on 27 February as a pretext to ban the German Communist Party, curtail the freedom of political expression, and arrest numerous political opponents – from the Communist and other parties. The elections themselves produced a majority for the Nazis and their allies. On 23 March, with the support of the Catholic Center Party, they secured the two-thirds majority they needed to adopt the "Enabling Law" (*Ermächtigungsgesetz*) that buried the Weimar Republic.

Only the SPD voted against the Enabling Law. The party chairman, Otto Wels, made a courageous and defiant speech opposing National Socialism and emphasizing the party's commitment to the Weimar Constitution. Wels's stance arguably saved the honor of German social democracy. As a well-known German comedian later remarked, Wels's speech and the party's rejection of the Enabling Law made the SPD, after the Third Reich and World War II, the only major political party in the

Federal Republic that did not have to change its name. Some leading Social Democrats, such as the former Prussian interior minister Carl Severing, subsequently withdrew from political activity and acquiesced in the National Socialist dictatorship. Some fled abroad to set up a party organization and oppose Hitler from exile. Some, including the party's first post–World War II leader, Kurt Schumacher, stayed in Germany, went underground, and tried to organize resistance from within, but they were quickly arrested and interned in the Nazis' first concentration camps.[4] Overall, save for campaigning and participating in elections and parliamentary work, the German Social Democrats did little in the end to stave off the collapse of the Weimar Republic.

The objectives of this chapter are as follows: first, to analyze why the SPD failed to stop the collapse of the democratic republic and whether it could have averted this outcome; second, to discuss the lessons that German Social Democrats drew from their failure and the collapse of Weimar; and third, in the concluding section, to assess to what extent the history of Weimar democracy and its collapse is relevant for the analysis of the threat or reality of the erosion or breakdown of democracy in the contemporary world.

The Collapse of the Weimar Republic: Determinants of the SPD's Failure

The collapse of the Weimar Republic has given rise to a voluminous literature. The catalogue of the German National Library, for example, contains more than 7,200 titles relating to the topic.[5] It is safe to say that no other single case of democratic breakdown has attracted more attention among social scientists, commentators, and political practitioners. This may be explained by the fact that, as it led directly to the Third Reich, the Second World War, and the Holocaust, the collapse of the Weimar Republic was the most consequential of all democratic breakdowns. Given the power and role of Germany in Europe and international relations in the late nineteenth century and the first half of the twentieth century, any political regime change was likely to have important consequences and repercussions. However, the collapse of Weimar was all the more notable and attracted all the more attention due to the fact that it involved the defeat of what had long been – or at least had widely been seen to be – the strongest of all the European labor movements, one that, especially in ideological and programmatic terms, had exercised a strong influence on labor movements in other European countries. How could the German Social Democrats have failed so completely to resist the rise and conquest of power by Hitler and the

Nazi movement? To what extent was the SPD's failure inevitable? Or, to what extent, in retrospect and at various key turning points, could it have decided differently and, in so doing, prevented the collapse of Weimar and changed the course of German, European, and world history?

In analyzing this question, I distinguish between four sets of independent variables on two different dimensions. On the first dimension, I distinguish between "external" and "internal" variables, according to whether these factors are located "within" the SPD or outside it. On the second, I distinguish between "structural" variables, on the one hand, and "contingent" variables, on the other, according to whether these factors were intrinsic, entrenched, quasi-permanent traits of the political environment of Weimar and the SPD between 1918 and 1933 or whether, in contrast, they were more temporary, transient, or ephemeral.

Structural Determinants

Several factors made it difficult for democratic politics to sink solid roots in Germany after the First World War and for the SPD thus to stabilize the Weimar Republic. Following the collapse of the monarchy in November 1918, it was the SPD that, in the chaos of the immediate postwar period, engineered the transition to democracy and provided the new republic's main bulwark. At the outset, to its political right, it had two allies: the Center Party (Zentrumspartei), which organized German Catholics, especially in the Rhineland; and the DDP (Deutsche Demokratische Partei – German Democratic Party), a left-liberal party that appealed to more progressive groups among the German middle class. How quickly popular support for the so-called Weimar Coalition of these parties shrank is shown by the fact that already in June 1920 they lost the big majority of seats that they had won in the first post–World War I elections in early 1919. The rapid waning of support for the "Weimar Coalition" parties illustrated the relatively weak or shallow commitment to democracy of the German middle class as well as of the aristocratic landowning class. This is the first external structural variable that constrained the SPD's capacity to consolidate democracy in Germany. In contrast to the UK and France, Germany did not witness the development of a strong liberal bourgeoisie in the nineteenth and early twentieth centuries.[6] Rather, it became an "industrial feudal society," in which the landowning aristocracy transformed the bourgeoisie rather than the other way around.[7] An alliance of these two classes sustained a semi-authoritarian monarchy that finally collapsed only under acute external pressure, under the weight of Germany's war defeat, in 1918. Given this inherited pattern of class alliances, the task of consolidating German democracy fell more heavily on the SPD than it did on social democratic or labor parties in other otherwise comparable countries. To paraphrase – or rather, to revise – Barrington Moore Jr.: "No [liberal] bourgeois, no [stable] democracy."

Second, the magnitude of the task of consolidating German democracy that the SPD faced was increased enormously by the fact that the political left was divided in its attitude to parliamentary democracy. The party had already split over the issue of Germany's war aims in 1917, with left-wing critics of the party leadership's stance founding the USPD (Unabhängige Sozialdemokratische Partei Deutschlands – Independent German Social Democratic Party), from which the most radical faction split off in December 1918 to form the Spartacist League. Led by Karl Liebknecht and Rosa Luxemburg and inspired by the Russian revolution, the Spartacists aimed to create a state based on workers' and soldiers' councils. Liebknecht and Luxemburg were murdered when the Spartacists launched a futile uprising to overthrow the new SPD-led government in late 1918 and early 1919. The fact that the government deployed not only the army but also the volunteer conservative militias, the *Freikorps*, to crush the Spartacist uprising served only to deepen the gulf between competing political movements on the German left. In 1920, most delegates at the USPD's congress voted to join the Third International, thus opting to align and eventually subordinate themselves to the Soviet Communist Party – and transforming the Communist Party in Germany from "an impotent sect ... to a great mass party."[8] Henceforth, the SPD had to fight a two-front political struggle – against a growing antidemocratic party to its left and, heading into the 1930s, numerous political parties that were either increasingly cool or overtly hostile toward a democratic state to its right. In theory, the SPD might conceivably have been able to avert this debilitating irreconcilable split on the German left by making concessions to the USPD and Spartacists. However, if the party had adopted a more radical stance to try to forge a more united left, this would inevitably have come at a cost in terms of its commitment to parliamentary democracy and the life of the Weimar Republic may have been even shorter than it already was. In fact, though, the goal of preventing Germany from following the "Russian path" was a major motive for the SPD leaders' efforts to establish a strong government in the wake of the collapse of the monarchy.[9] There never seemed to be any genuine prospect of their abandoning their goal of creating and maintaining a parliamentary democratic state on the altar of the unity of the left. In any case, following the second postwar elections in 1920, in which the SPD lost a lot of support and the USPD made substantial gains, the latter rejected an offer from the SPD to "defend the republic against all attacks from the right" and to maintain the gains made in the social field, such as the eight-hour day.[10]

The third external structural factor that may have contributed to the SPD's ultimate failure to save the Weimar Republic relates to the absence of any transformation within German bureaucratic, legal, and military elites. An important consequence of the division and violent conflict between the Social Democrat and Communist left was that it made the SPD-led government in the immediate postwar period reliant on the state apparatus and power structures inherited from the imperial period to suppress the Spartacists' and subsequent uprisings.[11] Historians disagree, however, on the extent to which the undoubted continuity of bureaucratic, legal, and military elites weakened or undermined the new republic and/or on the extent to which the SPD failed to exploit windows of opportunity to reform the state more comprehensively. In one view, "fear of chaos and of economic breakdown, genuine commitment to the paramountcy of parliamentary democracy and probably a lack of perception of the potential scope for peaceful radical change contained in the Workers' Council movement caused the leadership of the majority socialists and the social democratic government to reject any experiments in this direction."[12] It was in this period, when the "situation was fluid," that, according to Hilferding, the SPD made "the most serious political mistakes."[13] In a different view, in contrast, if the SPD leadership had followed a more radical course immediately after the war, this would have jeopardized the supply of basic goods and services and security and might have further exacerbated already high levels of political violence and instability – and, by implication, might have brought about a more rapid collapse of the new republic.[14] Insofar as the state bureaucracy submitted to the political control of successive Weimar governments, it does not seem to have played an influential role in the collapse of Weimar.[15] This was not the case, however, for the German army, on which the first Social Democratic president of the Republic called to put down the Spartacists' uprising, but whose leaders played a central role in the machinations that helped to undermine the Republic in the early 1930s.

The fourth external structural variable that shaped the SPD's capacity to defend the Weimar Republic was its constitution. In the National Assembly elected in January 1919, the SPD naturally exercised a strong influence on the provisions of the new constitution, which a leading Social Democrat described at the time as founding the "most democratic democracy."[16] By the early 1930s, however, the party was no longer in a sufficiently strong political position to contest or change those provisions – relating to the proportional representation electoral system, the powers of the president, and the scope for popular referenda – that facilitated first the shift from parliamentary to authoritarian government and then the accession to power of Hitler. The referendum provision provided a platform for Hitler to mobilize nationalist opposition to the Versailles Treaty and reparations as well as support for himself and the Nazis; the electoral system facilitated the fragmentation of the party system and militated against the formation of stable governments; the president's extensive powers, as exercised by Hindenburg, enabled the appointment of a chancellor, Hitler, who resolved to put an end to parliamentary democracy and the Republic.

The SPD's capacity to shore up the Weimar Republic was also affected by *internal* structural factors that, in effect at least, limited the range of options from which party leaders could choose. Of these, the most significant related to the relationship between the party and the (free) trade union movement. Founded originally by the party, the trade unions started to grow rapidly after the repeal of the anti-socialist laws in 1890. By the early twentieth century, reversing the previous situation, there were far more trade union than party members and the unions were increasingly asserting their independence from the party.[17] This trend was particularly visible in the debate within the labor movement over the use for political ends of the mass strike – about which the unions, which had increasingly developed a stake in the existing order, were decidedly unenthusiastic, in contrast to the party's radicals. At the SPD's 1906 Mannheim congress, the unions had won this conflict and "passed from a position of independence of the party to one of effective control over it."[18] The consequence of the shift in the balance of power between the party and unions was that the SPD no longer wielded the most potent weapon that could be deployed in a fundamental clash with its opponents over the nature of the political order. The party's role was henceforth to be limited to agitating and organizing.[19]

The other internal factor that conditioned the SPD's action in the Weimar Republic concerned its ideological orientation. One aspect of this was the notion, as illustrated in and by the (orthodox Marxist) thinking of the party's longtime chief ideologue Karl Kautsky, that the socialist revolution would come about inexorably, of its own accord, through the progress of history, irrespective of the volition of the party.[20] This is indeed akin to what happened in November 1918, when the monarchy collapsed and, to the annoyance of the party chairman Friedrich Ebert, the SPD politician Philip Scheidemann proclaimed the foundation of a republic to head off the proclamation of a socialist republic based on the workers' and soldiers' councils by Liebknecht later the same day. This worldview fostered an attitude of passivity and a policy of *attentisme* (wait and see). Imprisoned as it was in this collective mindset, the SPD leadership was typically inclined to wait and see at key turning points – while other political actors seized the initiative. The other aspect of the party's ideological orientation that affected its capacity to defend democracy, again related to its Marxist heritage, was its self-conception as a party of the working class, which arguably limited its appeal to members of other social classes and its capacity to find among them pro-democratic political allies.[21] In contrast to Scandinavian social democratic parties, which found partners in the independent peasantry and succeeded in defending democracy in the 1930s, the SPD antagonized this group in Germany through its efforts to organize and mobilize the support of agricultural workers.[22] It was only in the Federal Republic, well after the Second World War, with the adoption of a new program in 1959, that the SPD finally shed its identity as a working-class party for that of a "catch-all" or "people's party" (*Volkspartei*).

All in all, the Weimar Republic possessed only a "very narrow democratic potential."[23] As its main champion, the SPD was thus always going to have to wage an uphill struggle to defend it. It would nonetheless be mistaken to think that this was a lost cause to begin with and that the first German democracy was bound to fail. After all, at its outset the Republic survived several years of extreme economic, social, and political turmoil and sporadic civil war. At arguably the most precarious moment, the so-called Kapp Putsch in 1920, the SPD ministers in the government resisted a violent attempt to overthrow the Republic by right-wing extremists and the trade unions launched a general strike that was followed by most civil servants and quickly defeated the coup. According to one historian, the situation in Germany at the peak of hyperinflation in 1923 was "more dangerous" than that in the early 1930s, yet there was no democratic breakdown then.[24] In the analysis of another historian, having seen off "some serious challenges," the Republic, by the end of 1923, seemed "politically more stabilized than ever."[25] At this point, "the failure of democracy would have seemed far less probable than its consolidation ... The future of the Weimar Republic was wide open."[26] Why, in 1933, did the SPD fail to save the democratic system that it had managed to shore up between ten and fifteen years earlier?

Contingent Determinants

When Germany went to the polls in May 1928, the SPD emerged as the biggest party, with 28.7 percent of the vote; this was almost three percentage points more than four years previously, and provided the chancellor in a new coalition government comprising the other parties of the Weimar Coalition plus the business-friendly DVP (Deutsche Volkspartei – German People's Party). Little if anything suggested at this point that within five years the Weimar Republic would be dead. The single most important contingent determinant of its collapse – the Great Depression – began to unfold after the New York stock market crash in October–November 1929. By 1932, compared with 1929, the German economy had contracted by more than 50 percent, unemployment had risen from 8.5 percent to almost 30 percent, and collective social welfare provision had been slashed: Fewer and fewer unemployed persons were entitled to unemployment benefits and the value of the benefits themselves were cut by almost half.[27]

The impact of the Great Depression on the Weimar Republic "cannot be overestimated." Without it, "the political system would not have entered a prolonged crisis, nor would a large segment of the population have been mobilized by the Nazi movement" – which had won no more than 2.6 percent of the vote in the 1928 elections.[28] But if the Depression was indeed a necessary condition for the collapse of Weimar, it was by no means a sufficient one. If, in some countries, the extreme right prospered and democratic political systems crumbled, in others democracy survived the 1930s and parties of the democratic left were strengthened. In the US, the Depression helped to bring about the election of the Democratic president Franklin Roosevelt and the New Deal. In Scandinavia and New Zealand, it led to the election of labor or social democratic parties. Across the most advanced industrial countries, the political fallout of the Depression thus diverged widely.

In Weimar Germany, one of the first consequences of the Depression and the economic crisis was more intense distributional conflict and class and party-political polarization. This trend manifested itself in more turbulent labor relations between employers and trade unions, and, within the political system and in the government, in heightened tensions over issues of government finance between the SPD and especially the DVP. In March 1930, the latter led to the collapse of the coalition over how to bridge the growing hole in the unemployment insurance fund budget and to the resignation of the Social Democratic chancellor Hermann Müller.[29] Although a vote by the SPD parliamentary party to oppose a compromise package on this issue was the proximate cause of the coalition's collapse, the driving force behind it was the DVP, which insisted that the fund's budget be balanced mainly by cuts in the unemployment benefit.[30] If the SPD had accepted the compromise, the DVP would have soon brought down the government in any case – and the concessions made by the SPD would have been to no avail, while damaging its credibility among its supporters.[31] As the crisis intensified, the DVP and the Center Party, alongside the more conservative DNVP (Deutschnationale Volkspartei – German National People's Party), moved to the right and were increasingly inclined to manage the crisis by sidelining parliament and by governing by emergency decree.[32] They took their cue from German business organizations, which pushed for a reduction in the collective bargaining rights of trade unions, for lower wages and welfare provision, for a deflationary economic policy, and also for a government less dependent on political parties and parliament.[33]

The other contingent factor that sapped the SPD's capacity to defend Weimar was precisely the shift in the locus of political decision-making away from parliament; this began with the fall of the coalition government in 1930, gathered momentum while the Center Party politician Heinrich Brüning was chancellor over the following two years, and reached its erstwhile climax under the short-lived chancellorships of Franz von Papen and the army general Kurt von Schleicher in 1932–3. The other side of this trend was the growing empowerment of a "very small and politically irresponsible group of people" in the entourage (*kamarilla*) surrounding the aging president and former army commander Hindenburg.[34] Sensitive notably to the interests of the East Elbian landowning aristocratic circles from which Hindenburg originated, this group was closely involved in the key decisions made by the president, including those to replace Brüning with von Papen and to appoint Hitler as chancellor.[35] With Brüning and his two successors governing after March 1930 by presidential decree, the only means that the SPD possessed to try to influence government policy was to oppose or threaten to oppose them in confidence votes in the parliament. After the SPD had helped to bring down the first Brüning government in parliament, however, the subsequent election produced a big increase in support for the parties of the extreme left and right: the Communists and the Nazis. Faced with the prospect that fresh elections – if they had to be held – would strengthen the Nazis, the SPD resolved to "tolerate" Brüning's administration, despite its lack of influence over its political direction. In so doing, it of course made itself co-responsible – and paid the political cost – for the disastrous consequences of Brüning's deflationary economic policies.

Mass unemployment and social distress, intensifying class and political polarization, the rightward shift of the traditional center and right-wing parties, and the SPD's growing exclusion in a system of government based increasingly on presidential decree – combined, these factors would have made it very difficult for the SPD to shore up the Weimar Republic in the early 1930s. This task was rendered even more daunting, however, by the ongoing – indeed deepening – conflict on the left between the SPD and the KPD (Kommunistische Partei Deutschlands – German Communist Party). In the mid-1920s, under Stalin, the Soviet Communist Party, which gradually asserted its control over the KPD, developed and followed a thesis of "social fascism," an "extraordinary political aberration" according to which social democracy was the chief obstacle to the achievement of (Soviet) socialism and hence the Communist parties' principal political foe.[36] In 1931, the KPD joined the Nazis in supporting a popular referendum to dissolve the parliament in Prussia, which was still governed by an SPD-led "Weimar Coalition," as discussed above.[37] Relations between the two parties were also embittered by a series of clashes, such as when, in 1932, the Prussian government suppressed a KPD-staged May Day demonstration – during which the Berlin police killed several participants – and when the KPD co-organized a strike of Berlin transport workers with the Nazis. Even after the July 1932 elections, in which the Nazi vote surged from 18 to 37 percent, the KPD hardened its stance against the SPD and the free trade unions, proclaiming that there was "absolutely no difference" between the SPD and the Nazis.[38]

The KPD's tactics might have had a lesser impact – and been less destructive – if the party had remained as marginal a political force as it had been at the outset of the Weimar Republic. However, like the Nazis, albeit to a much more limited extent, it had also profited from the process of political polarization and radicalization fueled by the Depression. By the elections of November 1932, it had become a serious competitor of the SPD for the support of German workers; the KPD gained almost 17 percent of the vote, fewer than three percentage points less than the SPD. Only three months later, the Communists were to become the first victims of the Nazi regime. The KPD called for a general strike when Hitler was appointed chancellor,[39] but this appeal found no visible echo among German workers, very few of whom belonged to Communist trade unions . The SPD chairman Wels conceded that, in the factories, there was a lot of talk about the need to form a united front with the KPD. However, the party and free trade union leaders were opposed to cooperating with the Communists, on the grounds that the latter's goal was to erect a Soviet state in Germany and hence was irreconcilable with the aims of the SPD.[40]

This, then, was the situation in Weimar Germany in the run-up to Hitler's appointment as chancellor. First, the *political* balance of power was shifting away from the SPD. Its vote had declined at all three elections staged between 1930 and 1932. It was bereft of political allies and coalition partners, to both its left and its right. The process of "executive aggrandizement" deprived it of any leverage it might otherwise have possessed thanks to the (diminishing) size of its bloc in the German parliament. Second, and simultaneously, the *economic* balance of power was also changing to the detriment of the SPD and organized labor. Mass unemployment gravely weakened the capacity of the SPD's allies in the free trade union movement to strike, whether for political or other ends. A reserve army of workers stood ready to occupy strikers' jobs if necessary. In any case, as the unions had long since established their independence from the SPD, this was an issue on which not the party but rather the unions had the last word. Third, and finally, the "*military*" balance of power was also strongly skewed against the SPD. Reflecting the growing political polarization in Weimar, numerous political parties had established paramilitary organizations. In 1924, the SPD had launched the *Reichsbanner* as a "republican defence league."[41] The *Reichsbanner* was larger than its rival organizations, including the Nazis' SA (*Sturmabteilung* – Storm Division) and the nationalist and anti-republican *Stahlhelm*, which comprised mainly World War I veterans. Unlike these, however, the *Reichsbanner* did not engage in serious military training until 1932.[42] If, because of a general strike or other direct action initiated by the unions or the SPD, a civil war or equivalent physical confrontation were to break out, the odds – in the conditions of the early 1930s – that the SPD and the labor movement would come out on top were, to say the least, very limited – above all as their political opponents controlled the organs of state repression: the police and the army.

Failing without a Fight

Out of government at the national level in Germany from April 1930 onward, the SPD was confronted during the next almost three years with a series of immensely consequential political choices: whether, for example, to bring down or to tolerate the Brüning government, how to position itself vis-à-vis Brüning's two successors, with what kind of crisis policy or program to contest elections, and how to react to Hindenburg's appointment of Hitler as chancellor.

In retrospect, the most fateful decision that the SPD made related to the "Prussian Coup" of 20 July in which the freshly appointed German chancellor von Papen dismissed the SPD-led administration in Prussia and put it under the control of the central government. This was the "decisive turning-point" in Weimar's slide from democracy to Nazi dictatorship.[43] Its significance was grasped immediately by the Nazi propagandist Joseph Goebbels, who noted triumphantly in his diary that day: "The reds [the Social Democrats] have missed their big moment. It will never recur."[44]

Prussia was by far the biggest state in the Weimar Republic, comprising roughly five-eighths of Germany's territory and population. From 1920 onward it was governed by the Weimar Coalition of the SPD, Center Party, and DDP, headed almost continuously by the Social Democrat Otto Braun. To keep this government in office – and to keep the Nazis out of power in both Prussia and Germany – was one major motive for the SPD's decision to tolerate Brüning's government in the Reichstag after the September 1930 elections.[45] In Prussian state elections in April 1932, the parties of the Weimar Coalition suffered severe losses and lost their parliamentary majority, while support for both the Nazis and the Communists surged. As the parties of the two extremes could not agree on a successor to Braun, despite controlling a majority of seats in the new parliament, the incumbent government remained in office. Amid rising levels of political violence, and using as a pretext a bloody clash between Nazis and Communists in Altona (Hamburg) that resulted in nineteen deaths, the new German chancellor, von Papen, exploited emergency provisions relating to law and order in the Weimar Constitution to dismiss Braun's administration and put Prussia under the direct control of the central government.[46]

A quasi-official Social Democratic account of the Prussian Coup argues that, among the rank-and-file members of the party, the unions, and the *Reichsbanner*, there was a "considerable preparedness to fight" against the coup.[47] This analysis seems to have been shared by at least some top officials in the Berlin police force, which was an important potential actor in the conflict. The commander of the Berlin police believed that there would have been time to mobilize the 16,000-strong, well-armed force against the coup and that the police would have defeated the only army battalion stationed in Berlin in a direct confrontation.[48] In his view, however, President Hindenburg, wanting to avoid a clash between the police and the army, would not have declared a state of siege in this scenario. If the Prussian government had cut the lines of communication to his office, as it could have done, and had it sent a representative to see him, the coup could have been stopped bloodlessly. It was "known" that the *Reichsbanner* and the workers in the factories were all ready to act in response to an appeal from Prussian interior minister Severing.[49] His superior, the police president, was more pessimistic about the capacity of his force to stand up to the army, as the latter could have deployed "many thousands of soldiers" in Berlin in "no more than one or two hours."[50] Nonetheless, he too pleaded with Severing that the coup was illegal and that the Prussian government could not simply capitulate to von Papen.

In the absence of Braun, who was on sick leave in this period, Interior Minister Severing's stance was decisive for the SPD's reaction and the outcome of the coup. In contrast to his staff, Severing was apparently not convinced that the coup was illegal and argued that the government could "not allow any blood to be shed" opposing it.[51] The coup had not come as a surprise. It was an open secret that, as demanded by the right-wing parties, von Papen would try to overthrow the Prussian government: Only the date and the way in which it would be carried out were still uncertain.[52] The Berlin police president had tried – unsuccessfully – to persuade Severing to make plans to preempt such an eventuality. In line with the stance taken by Severing, the SPD's national leadership refrained from opposing the coup by any kind of force or strike action. They reacted instead in two main ways. First, as a campaign for national elections on 31 July was in full swing, they urged Germans to express their opposition to the coup at the ballot box by voting for the SPD. This – in the light of the Prussian election result just a few months previously – "completely unfounded" hope failed to materialize, as the SPD vote slumped from 24.5 percent in 1930 to 21.5 percent – while support for the Nazis more than doubled, from 18 to 37 percent.[53] Second, pursuing its path of strict legality, the SPD leadership appealed to the Prussian Supreme Court to reverse the coup and reinstall the Prussian government. However, this tactic also failed. Several months after von Papen had created the "facts on the ground," the court basically ratified his takeover of power in Prussia. Ultimately, the SPD forfeited control of its last political bastion in Germany without putting up a meaningful fight.

Did the SPD's retreat from a direct confrontation in Prussia with von Papen and the central government reflect an accurate analysis of the balance of power in Germany in mid-1932? Nowadays, most historians believe that it did. Thus, "even in the unlikely event that the Prussian police would have followed orders from Severing, the sides in a civil war would have been massively uneven. Resistance most likely would have failed."[54] A semi-official Social Democratic analysis concludes similarly that, pitched against the German army, the SA, and the *Stahlhelm*, the SPD and its allies would hardly have been able to win a civil war.[55] Winkler argues that there were "compelling grounds" for the SPD's self-restraint.[56] Given the party's heavy defeat in the Prussian elections, mass unemployment, the "uniquely deep split" between the KPD and SPD in the working class, and the lack of military and psychological readiness to engage in armed opposition, the democratic left would have lost any civil war at the "most fearful" cost in terms of the number of victims. For Bracher, too, given that no preparations to resist it had been made beforehand, the "concrete relations of power on 20 July" made it extremely unlikely that the coup could have been successfully opposed. He nonetheless regretted the absence of any even "limited action of opposition" that could have averted the "psychological-moral collapse" of the pro-democratic forces in Weimar and had a moderating effect on the new wielders of political power.[57] In the same vein, Harsch wonders whether some kind of "heroic action" would have provided "an inspiration to resist the horror to come and, even in failure, might have changed the course of history."[58]

It is indeed conceivable that, if the SPD had undertaken even an entirely symbolic or token act of practical resistance against the Prussian Coup or later against the takeover of power by Hitler, it would have emerged from the ruins of the Weimar Republic and the Third Reich with a stronger sense of pride and self-respect than that which it gleaned from Wels's courageous parliamentary speech in March 1933. In the absence of any such act, its failure to defend German democracy more offensively was distinctly unheroic. But given the very high probability that any more vigorous opposition would have been crushed by force, the course of action chosen by the party leadership was understandable. It is notable that, during the interwar period in Europe, democracy also failed and right-wing or fascist dictatorships also came to power in several countries – for example, Italy, Austria, and Spain – in which the political left did not submit as meekly to their defeat as the SPD in Germany.[59] To this extent, Hilferding is probably right that, even if the SPD had decided and acted differently in the dying years of the Weimar Republic, this would not have altered the outcome.[60]

More difficult, important, but ultimately impossible to answer than whether the SPD could have successfully resisted the breakdown of Weimar by extra-parliamentary action are questions about whether, in the early 1930s, the SPD could have averted its continuous electoral decline and retained greater political influence by proposing an economic policy that offered the growing number of increasingly impoverished Germans the prospect of a brighter material future, and why it did not do so. With the WTB (Woytinsky, Tarnow, and Baade) plan that was the brainchild of the trade union economist Wladimir Woytinsky, the free trade unions came up with a "proto-Keynesian strategy" to stimulate the German economy by deficit spending.[61] The WTB plan was strongly opposed, however, by the former finance minister and the party's chief economic theoretician, Hilferding, who argued that the only solution to the economic crisis was to accept the "logic of capitalism" and wait for the business cycle to run its course.[62] Even after the election of July 1932 – which was disastrous for the SPD – and even though Hilferding lamented the fact that "we can't say anything concrete to the

people about how and with what means we would end the crisis," the
party continued to reject Woytinsky's proposals.[63]

The Lessons of Weimar: Social Democratic Accounts

Prominent post-Second World War German Social Democrats cited a
variety of divergent reasons for the collapse of the Weimar Republic and
the SPD's failure to prevent it. For some, such as Schumacher and Willy
Brandt, their first chancellor after 1945, who, then still a teenager, left the
SPD to join a more radical left-wing party in the early 1930s, the party
could and should have opposed the Nazis' accession to power much
more vigorously.[64] In his memoirs, Brandt castigated the SPD leadership
for its lack of courage and for not having exploited the preparedness of
the party's rank-and-file supporters to strike and fight to save the
Republic.[65]   Wilhelm Hoegner, an early postwar prime minister of
Bavaria, emphasized the negative impact of the party's ideological orientation – specifically its expectation, rooted in the thought of its most
influential thinker, Karl Kautsky, that the socialist revolution would
come about more or less by itself and that the party would have to be
no more than its midwife.[66] While the SPD waited, other, more volun-
taristic political forces, such as the Nazis, acted. It is unclear, however,
whether these Social Democrats genuinely thought that the SPD could
have *successfully* resisted the Nazis and saved Weimar democracy.

For other leading Social Democrats, implicitly or explicitly, it had
simply been beyond the SPD's capacity to avert this outcome. Thus,
for Hans-Jochen Vogel, for example, at different times a federal minister,
mayor of Berlin, chairman of the parliamentary party, and chancellor
candidate, the Weimar Republic collapsed primarily because antidemocratic values dominated among the German right, among the traditional
elites – military, bureaucratic, clerical, scientific, business, and landowning – and among the German middle classes. There were simply
too few defenders of democracy – they were in the minority.[67]

Almost all notable Social Democrats – from the period in which the
Basic Law was being negotiated in the late 1940s to the present day –
assign a key part in Weimar's collapse to the "social question," to the
radicalizing, politically destabilizing impact in Germany of the mass
unemployment and poverty that accompanied the Great Depression.[68]
The thinking of the former Social Democratic chancellor Helmut
Schmidt (1974–82) best typifies this strand of analysis. As German
finance minister, he warned already in the early 1970s of the prospective
destabilizing consequences of significant unemployment. Every German,
he argued, "should know what that would mean: Half a million people

unemployed[!], fear for one's livelihood, radicalism. Things cannot be allowed to come to that."[69] As chancellor, Schmidt would regularly refer to the political dangers of pursuing a deflationary economic policy of the kind followed between 1930 and 1932 by the government of the then German chancellor Heinrich Brüning – an analysis he also applied later, during the Eurozone crisis, to the European Union.[70] For Schmidt and other leading Social Democrats of his generation, a strong welfare state, labor codetermination, and good and close relations between business, labor, and the government were key ingredients of the Federal Republic's relative (democratic) political stability – ingredients that distinguished it from the failed Weimar Republic. In 1982, during the final weeks of his chancellorship, before the Social–Liberal coalition of the SPD and the FDP (Freie Demokratische Partei – Free Democratic Party) collapsed, Schmidt also referred to the SPD's withdrawal from the government in the conflict over unemployment insurance in 1930 to caution his party against giving up its position in government too carelessly. But Schmidt's motive for this observation was tactical – he wanted to assure that the FDP would carry the blame for the government's collapse in public opinion. He was well aware of the "inaccuracy of the historical parallel."[71]

Unsurprisingly, given his personal experience, the collapse of Weimar left a deep imprint on Schumacher, who was to lead the party in West Germany from 1945 to 1952. Although he professed to "distrust historical parallels" and maintained that socioeconomic and political conditions in the immediate post–World War II period were "completely different from those in the past," Schumacher referred increasingly to "analogous past situations" after the foundation of the Federal Republic and feared that the new republic would be undermined by a resurgence of economic crisis and hostility to democracy among conservative political movements and the German capitalist class, now supported "from abroad."[72] This analysis of the situation, combined with the SPD's failure to prevent the Nazis' conquest of power in Weimar, certainly seemed to shape the course that Schumacher set for the post-1945 SPD. As a "militant Socialist," he rejected any compromises or coalitions with other political parties, such as those that the Weimar SPD had made with the Center Party and left- and right-wing liberal parties.[73] Aiming thus to forestall any resurgence of aggressive nationalist sentiment, he was also a fierce champion of what he deemed to be German national interests vis-à-vis the Allied powers, as manifested in the priority he attached to promoting German reunification over the Western integration of the Federal Republic.[74] Schumacher's strategy, however, proved to be a failure on almost all fronts. It took three consecutive and increasingly decisive electoral defeats by Konrad Adenauer and his Christian

Democrats for the SPD to jettison Schumacher's strategy and heritage and shed its identity as a party of the industrial working class for that of a modern "people's party" with the adoption in 1959 of its Bad Godesberg program. This document – historic for the SPD – made several references to the threat posed by Soviet Communism but not a single explicit one to the collapse of the Weimar Republic or any lessons that the SPD should learn from this catastrophe.[75] By this time, at the latest, the experience of Weimar seems to have become strictly "history," devoid of any significant contemporary relevance.[76]

Conclusions: How Relevant Is Weimar Today?

Since the early 2000s, and not for the first time since the Second World War, the world has witnessed a significant, albeit hitherto limited, process of democratic recession.[77] It no longer seems as self-evident as it seemed at the end of the Cold War that the future belongs to liberal democracy. Are there, in this troubling context, almost a century later, any or many lessons that can be learned from the experience of democratic breakdown in the Weimar Republic?

If the comparison is drawn with the countries in the North Atlantic region – notably, with contemporary Germany – it is the divergences from Weimar Germany that stand out more than the parallels.[78] The evolution of capitalism has transformed the social structures of these countries. The peasantry has virtually disappeared, the industrial working class is much smaller, and the service sector-based urban middle class is vastly bigger than in interwar Germany. In socioeconomic terms, the center is much broader now than it was in the interwar period. There is no longer a plausible threat of Communism of the kind that contributed to right-wing radicalization between the wars. In general, levels of social, political, and ideological polarization are (much) lower, as illustrated in the German case by the capacity of the Social and Christian Democratic and liberal and Green parties to coalesce with each other in order to form stable governments at the state or federal level.

As we have witnessed in the global financial and Covid-19 crises, state capacities to intervene in the economy and to contain potentially highly destabilizing crises are also much stronger today than in the 1920s and 1930s. Collective social welfare provision, which dampens the anxieties that such crises can provoke, is much more comprehensive. More citizens of the North Atlantic countries adhere to liberal democratic values than in Weimar Germany, even if this adhesion is far from universal and its depth uncertain. Especially in Europe, many states are now also integrated into regional or other international organizations that help to anchor liberal democracy – although it remains unproven whether, in the final analysis, they can prevent complete democratic breakdowns among their members, and although the constraints that they place on members may prejudice democratic accountability.[79]

Another striking difference between Weimar and contemporary Germany and interwar and contemporary Western Europe relates to levels of political violence and the "paramilitarization" of society and politics. There are scarcely any parallels today to the scale of political violence that marked Weimar Germany in its final years and especially earlier, when such violence cost the lives of several thousand people.[80] And there are no parallels to the formation during the Republic of mass paramilitary organizations – Nazi, national-conservative, Social Democratic, and Communist. Such organizations – the SA, *Stahlhelm*, and *Reichsbanner*, for example – were leading protagonists in this violence; by the early 1930s, they had as many or more than three million members, and their existence and activities pointed to Weimar being in a state of incipient civil war.

In this latter respect, however, the contemporary US appears increasingly to be diverging from the democratic states of Western Europe. Since the 1990s, the US has witnessed a sharp growth in arms sales and the number of (especially white supremacist) militias.[81] Over the same period, relative to population, no other North Atlantic democracy has deployed so many soldiers in so many military conflicts for so long as the US. Among the members of these militias and among the persons arrested for the assault on the Capitol on 6 January 2021 was a disproportionately high number of military veterans.[82] This suggests that, analogous to Weimar, albeit still on a much smaller scale, the propensity to engage in political violence and paramilitarization tendencies in the US have been fostered by a similar process of the "brutalization of soldiers through war," which has occasionally been blamed for political violence and the paramilitarization process in Germany after 1918.[83] However plausible the argument is that the US is already a good way down the road to civil war if not democratic breakdown, it remains an exceptional rather than a representative case in comparison with other North Atlantic democracies.[84]

The experience of Weimar warns us nonetheless to guard against complacency concerning the durability or longevity of democracy. True, post–World War I Germany provided stony soil for democracy from the outset. But as late as 1928–9, democracy did not seem to be in mortal danger. Once the Depression began to unfold in Germany, though, democracy rapidly began to break down. Support for new, radical parties, such as the Nazis and, to a lesser extent, the

Communists, surged – as has occurred in numerous North Atlantic countries this century. Even if levels of unemployment and material distress are not comparable with those in Germany in the early 1930s, growing and pervasive feelings of economic, social, and cultural insecurity or unfairness and globalization- or immigration-related fears of a loss of social status may nonetheless fuel political radicalization. In response to these trends, especially as "ethnic entrepreneurs" seek to exploit them for political gain, existing political parties' attitudes and support for democracy may change and erode, as appears increasingly and above all to be the case for the US Republican Party.[85]

Above all, perhaps, Weimar furnishes a very instructive case of *from where* and *from whom* threats to democracy typically emanate. Its collapse, in short, was an inside job, executed by the political representatives of traditional elites who had become increasingly hostile toward democracy and sought to engage Hitler and the Nazis to provide them with the mass political base they lacked themselves and that they needed to crush the labor movement and the left.[86] Weimar is thus a shining early example of the most common route by which democratic breakdowns occur today, namely by executive aggrandizement, by the abuse and expansion of power by political chief executives.[87] For Weimar democracy did not break down suddenly, from one day to the next, on 30 January 1933, when Hindenburg named Hitler as chancellor. Rather, its collapse stretched over a period of three years in which the scope for parliamentary control of the government was curtailed step by step. A bit like the bankruptcy of the character Bill in Ernest Hemingway's novel *The Sun Also Rises*, Weimar democracy first collapsed gradually, then (fairly) suddenly.

In as far as in Weimar Germany the collapse of democracy was a process rather than a single one-off event, the principal lesson that may be derived from analyzing this issue is the importance of combating threats to democracy as soon and as quickly as they materialize – as in the German phrase "*Wehret den Anfängen!*" (loosely translated: "Combat them from the start!").[88] This implies at least the timely mobilization of pro-democratic political forces in a common front to defend democracy and the timely deployment of the agencies of law enforcement to the same end. Precisely because the breakdown of democracy today, as it was in Weimar, is usually a process, something that occurs "piecemeal, in baby steps," the task in the real world of identifying the first signs of democratic breakdown and mobilizing to avert it in good time may, however, be extremely challenging.[89] This is a task that champions of liberal democracy nonetheless cannot allow themselves to shirk.

Notes

1 Josef Becker and Ruth Becker, eds., *Hitlers Machtergreifung: Dokumente vom Machtantritt Hitlers 30. Januar 1933 bis zur Besiegelung des Einparteienstaates 14. Juli 1933* (Munich: Deutscher Taschenbuch, 1983), p. 31.
2 Ibid., pp. 50–1.
3 Ibid., p. 50.
4 Donna Harsch, *German Social Democracy and the Rise of Nazism* (Chapel Hill and London: University of North Carolina Press, 1993), pp. 234–8.
5 Ursula Büttner, "Ausgeforscht? Die Weimarer Republik als Gegenstand historischer Forschung," *Aus Politik und Zeitgeschichte* 68 (2018), pp. 18–26.
6 Ralf Dahrendorf, *Society and Democracy in Germany* (New York: W. W. Norton, 1979); Friedrich Engels, *Revolution and Counter-Revolution* (London: George Allen and Unwin, 1891); Barrington Moore, Jr., *Social Origins of Dictatorship and Democracy: Lord and Peasant in the Making of the Modern World* (Boston, MA: Beacon Press, 1966); Karl-Dietrich Bracher, *Die Auflösung der Weimarer Republik: Eine Studie zum Problem des Machtverfalls in der Demokratie* (Dusseldorf: Droste, 1984).
7 Dahrendorf, *Society and Democracy in Germany*, p. 60.
8 Carl E. Schorske, *German Social Democracy, 1905–1917* (New York: Russell and Russell, 1970), p. 328.
9 W. L. Guttsman, *The German Social Democratic Party, 1875–1933* (London: George Allen and Unwin, 1981), pp. 308–9.
10 Ibid., p. 313.
11 Robert Gerwarth, *November 1918: The German Revolution* (Oxford: Oxford University Press, 2020), pp. 173–83.
12 Guttsman, *The German Social Democratic Party*, p. 332.
13 Ibid.
14 Büttner, "Ausgeforscht?," p. 20; Andreas Wirsching, "Die paradoxe Revolution 1918/19," *Aus Politik und Zeitgeschichte* 50–1 (2008), pp. 6–12.
15 Hagen Schulze, *Weimar: Deutschland, 1917–1933* (Berlin: Severin und Siedler, 1982).
16 Eduard David, quoted in Franka Maubach, "Weimar (nicht) vom Ende her denken," *Aus Politik und Zeitgeschichte* 68 (2018), pp. 4–9.
17 Schorske, *German Social Democracy*, pp. 8–16.
18 Ibid., p. 52.
19 Ibid., pp. 114–15.
20 Guttsman, *The German Social Democratic Party*, p. 311; Susanne Miller and Heinrich Pothoff, *Kleine Geschichte der SPD: Darstellung und Dokumentation 1848–1983* (Bonn: Neue Gesellschaft, 1983), p. 71; Schorske, *German Social Democracy*, pp. 112–15; Fernando Claudin, "Democracy and Dictatorship in Lenin and Kautsky," *New Left Review* 106 (1977), pp. 59–76.
21 Thomas Meyer, Susanne Miller, and Joachim Rohlfes, eds., *Lern- und Arbeitsbuch deutscher Arbeiterbewegung: Darstellung, Chroniken, Dokumente. Band 2* (Bonn: Neue Gesellschaft, 1984), pp. 516–17.
22 Gregory Luebbert, "Social Foundations of Political Order in Interwar Europe," *World Politics* 39, no. 4 (1998), pp. 449–78.

23 M. Rainer Lepsius, "From Fragmented Party Democracy to Government by Emergency Decree and National Socialist Takeover: Germany" in Juan J. Linz and Alfred Stepan, eds., *The Breakdown of Democratic Regimes* (Baltimore and London: Johns Hopkins University Press, 1978), pp. 34–79.

24 Büttner, "Ausgeforscht?," p. 26.

25 Gerwarth, *November 1918*, p. 217.

26 Ibid., p. 221.

27 Wolfgang Michalka and Gottfried Niedhart, eds., *Die ungeliebte Republik: Dokumente zur Innen- und Aussenpolitik Weimars 1918–1933* (Munich: Deutscher Taschenbuch, 1980), pp. 408, 412; Wilhelm Adamy and Johannes Steffen, "Arbeitsmarktpolitik in der Depression: Sanierungsstrategien in der Arbeitslosenversicherung," *Mitteilungen aus der Berufs- und Arbeitsmarktforschung* 15, no. 3 (1982), pp. 276–91.

28 Lepsius, "From Fragmented Party Democracy to Government by Emergency Decree and National Socialist Takeover," p. 50.

29 Ludwig Preller, *Sozialpolitik in der Weimarer Republik* (Dusseldorf: Athenäum/ Droste, 1978), pp. 418–29.

30 Martin Vogt, "Die Stellung der Koalitionsparteien zur Finanzpolitik, 1928–1930" in Hans Mommsen, Dietmar Petzina, and Bernd Weisbrod, eds., *Industrielles System und Politische Entwicklung in der Weimarer Republik. Band 1* (Dusseldorf: Athenäum/Droste, 1977), pp. 439–62; Harsch, *German Social Democracy and the Rise of Nazism*, p. 51; Bracher, *Die Auflösung der Weimarer Republik*, pp. 262–71.

31 Vogt, "Die Stellung der Koalitionsparteien zur Finanzpolitik."

32 Lepsius, "From Fragmented Party Democracy to Government by Emergency Decree and National Socialist Takeover," pp. 45–6; Guttsman, *The German Social Democratic Party*, p. 320; Harsch, *German Social Democracy and the Rise of Nazism*, p. 144; Meyer, Miller, and Rohlfes, *Lern- und Arbeitsbuch deutscher Arbeiterbewegung*, p. 581.

33 Michalka and Niedhart, *Die ungeliebte Republik*, pp. 285–6, 300–4; Michael Schneider, *Unternehmer und Demokratie: Die freien Gewerkschaften in der unternehmerischen Ideologie der Jahre 1918 bis 1933* (Bonn: Neue Gesellschaft, 1975); Lepsius, "From Fragmented Party Democracy to Government by Emergency Decree and National Socialist Takeover," pp. 56–8.

34 Lepsius, "From Fragmented Party Democracy to Government by Emergency Decree and National Socialist Takeover," p. 49.

35 Bracher, *Die Auflösung der Weimarer Republik*, pp. 449–54, 616–17; Meyer, Miller, and Rohlfes, *Lern- und Arbeitsbuch deutscher Arbeiterbewegung*, p. 586.

36 Theodor Draper, "The Ghost of Social-Fascism," *Commentary* (February 1969), pp. xx; KPD chairman Ernst Thälmann in a speech to the German Communist Party congress, in Meyer, Miller, and Rohlfes, *Lern- und Arbeitsbuch deutscher Arbeiterbewegung*, p. 610.

37 Harsch, *German Social Democracy and the Rise of Nazism*, pp. 129–31.

38 Ibid., p. 216.

39 Becker and Becker, *Hitlers Machtergreifung*, pp. 32–3.

40 From the protocol of a joint meeting of the SPD executive board and representatives of the free trade unions, 5 February 1933, as published in Becker and Becker, *Hitlers Machtergreifung*, pp. 49–51.

41 Harsch, *German Social Democracy and the Rise of Nazism*, p. 20.
42 Ibid., p. 21.
43 Bracher, *Die Auflösung der Weimarer Republik*, p. 510.
44 Meyer, Miller, and Rohlfes, *Lern- und Arbeitsbuch deutscher Arbeiterbewegung*, p. 588.
45 Harsch, *German Social Democracy and the Rise of Nazism*, p. 134l; Meyer, Miller, and Rohlfes, *Lern- und Arbeitsbuch deutscher Arbeiterbewegung*, p. 585.
46 Heinrich August Winkler, *Der lange Weg nach Westen. Band I: Deutsche Geschichte vom Ende des Alten Reiches bis zum Untergang der Weimarer Republik* (Munich: C. H. Beck, 2000), p. 513.
47 Meyer, Miller, and Rohlfes, *Lern- und Arbeitsbuch deutscher Arbeiterbewegung*, p. 588.
48 Magnus Heimannsberg, from a memo reprinted in Bracher, *Die Auflösung der Weimarer Republik*, p. 641.
49 Heimannsberg, as quoted in Bracher, *Die Auflösung der Weimarer Republik*, pp. 641–2.
50 Albert Grzesinksi, memo reprinted in Martin Broszat, *Die Machtergreifung: Der Aufstieg der NSDAP und die Zerstörung der Weimarer Republik* (Munich: Deutscher Taschenbuch, 1984), p. 196.
51 Grzesinksi, as reprinted in Broszat, *Die Machtergreifung*, p. 195.
52 Grzesinksi, in Broszat, *Die Machtergreifung*, p. 192; Bracher, *Die Auflösung der Weimarer Republik*, p. 521.
53 Bracher, *Die Auflösung der Weimarer Republik*, p. 519.
54 Harsch, *German Social Democracy and the Rise of Nazism*, p. 199.
55 Meyer, Miller, and Rohlfes, *Lern- und Arbeitsbuch deutscher Arbeiterbewegung*, p. 588.
56 Winkler, *Der lange Weg nach Westen*, p. 514.
57 Bracher, *Die Auflösung der Weimarer Republik*, p. 523.
58 Harsch, *German Social Democracy and the Rise of Nazism*, p. 200.
59 Paolo Farneti, "Social Conflict, Parliamentary Fragmentation, Institutional Shift, and the Rise of Fascism: Italy" in Linz and Stepan, *The* Breakdown of Democratic Regimes, pp. 3–33; Juan J. Linz, "From Great Hopes to Civil War: The Breakdown of Democracy in Spain" in Linz and Stepan, *The Breakdown of Democratic Regimes*, pp. 142–218; Walter B. Simon, "Democracy in the Shadow of Imposed Sovereignty: The First Republic of Austria" in Linz and Stepan, *The Breakdown of Democratic Regimes*, pp. 80–121.
60 Harsch, *German Social Democracy and the Rise of Nazism*, p. 239.
61 Sheri Berman, *The Primacy of Politics: Social Democracy and the Making of Europe's Twentieth Century* (Cambridge: Cambridge University Press, 2006), pp. 110–15; Harsch, *German Social Democracy and the Rise of Nazism*, pp. 155–268.
62 Harsch, *German Social Democracy and the Rise of Nazism*, pp. 112–13.
63 Ibid., p. 113; Robert A. Gates, "German Socialism and the Crisis of 1929–1933," *Central European History* 7, no. 4 (1974), pp. 332–59.
64 Lewis Edinger, *Kurt Schumacher: A Study in Personality and Political Behavior* (Stanford: Stanford University Press, 1965); Willy Brandt, *Erinnerungen* (Frankfurt and Berlin: Ullstein, 1995).

65 Brandt, *Erinnerungen*, pp. 93–6.
66 Kurt Klotzbach, *Der Weg zur Staatspartei: Programmatik, praktische Politik und Organisation der deutschen Sozialdemokratie 1945 bis 1965* (Berlin and Bonn: Dietz, 1982), pp. 30–1.
67 Hans-Jochen Vogel, "Die Zerstörung der Demokratie in Deutschland vor 75 Jahren: Ansprache in der Gedenkstunde des Deutschen Bundestages am 10. April 2008," *Bulletin der Bundesregierung* 30, no. 2 (2008).
68 Jörn Leonhard, "Die Weimarer Republik als Metapher und geschichts-politisches Argument," *Aus Politik und Zeitgeschichte* 68, nos. 18–20 (2018), pp. 11–20.
69 CDU (Christliche-Demokratische Union), *Arbeitslosigkeit, Inflation und Rezession: Argumente, Dokumente, Materialien*, no. 5336, April 1975, p. 3.
70 Helmut Schmidt, "Speech to the SPD party congress," *Protokoll des Ordentlichen Bundesparteitages der SPD*, Berlin, 4–6 December 2011, pp. 14–27.
71 Klaus Bölling, *Die letzten 30 Tage des Kanzlers Helmut Schmidt: Ein Tagebuch* (Hamburg: Rowohlt/Der Spiegel, 1982), pp. 14–15.
72 Edinger, *Kurt Schumacher*, pp. 77–84.
73 Klotzbach, *Der Weg zur Staatspartei*, p. 45; Edinger, *Kurt Schumacher*, pp. 89, 120.
74 Edinger, *Kurt Schumacher*, pp. 91–3, 152–3, 171–3, 227–8.
75 Klotzbach, *Der Weg zur Staatspartei*, pp. 417–21, 449–54; Dieter Dowe and Kurt Klotzbach, *Programmatische Dokumente der deutschen Sozialdemokratie* (Berlin and Bonn: Dietz, 1984), pp. 361–84.
76 Klotzbach, *Der Weg zur Staatspartei*, p. 55.
77 Vanessa Boese, "Demokratie in Gefahr?," *Aus Politik und Zeitgeschichte* 71 nos. 26–7 (2021), pp. 24–31; Larry Diamond, *Ill Winds: Saving Democracy from Russian Rage, Chinese Ambition, and American Complacency* (New York: Penguin, 2019); Steven Levitsky and Daniel Ziblatt, *How Democracies Die* (New York: Crown, 2018); David Runciman, *How Democracy Ends* (London: Profile Books, 2019).
78 Elke Seefried, "Die Krise der Weimarer Demokratie – Analogien zur Gegenwart?," *Aus Politik und Zeitgeschichte* 66, nos. 40–2 (2016), pp. 18–23; Alain Salles, "Eloge de la démocratie allemande," *Le Monde*, 22 October 2021.
79 Wolfgang Streeck, *Gekaufte Zeit: Die vertagte Krise des demokratischen Kapitalismus* (Berlin: Suhrkamp, 2013).
80 Büttner, "Ausgeforscht?"; Seefried, "Die Krise der Weimarer Demokatie."
81 Edward Luce, "Forever at War," *Financial Times*, 11–12 September 2021; Barbara F. Walter, *How Civil Wars Start – and How to Stop Them* (New York: Crown, 2022), p. 157.
82 Walter, *How Civil Wars Start*, p. 207; Luce, "Forever at War"; Kathleen Belew, "On assiste à une lame de fond massive du militantisme white power" [interview], *Le Monde*, 9–10 January 2022.
83 Büttner, "Ausgeforscht?"
84 Walter, *How Civil Wars Start*.
85 On the concept of "ethnic entrepreneurs," see Walter, *How Civil Wars Start*, pp. 44, 95.

86 Von Papen, as quoted in Michalka and Niedhart, *Die ungeliebte Republik*, p. 362; Levitsky and Ziblatt, *How Democracies Die*, p. 17.

87 M. Steven Fisch and Jason Wittenberg, "Failed Democratization" in Christian Haerpfer, Patrick Bernhagen, Ronald F. Inglehart, and Christian Welzel, eds., *Democratization* (Oxford: Oxford University Press, 2009), pp. 249–64; Ethan Kapstein and Nathan Converse, *The Fate of Young Democracies* (Cambridge: Cambridge University Press, 2008); Levitsky and Ziblatt, *How Democracies Die*, pp. 3–4, 6; Diamond, *Ill Winds*, p. 55.

88 Vogel, "Die Zerstörung der Demokratie in Deutschland vor 75 Jahren."

89 Levitsky and Ziblatt, *How Democracies Die*, pp. 4, 92–3.

3   Bonn's Weimar

Peter C. Caldwell

The experience of the Weimar Republic's failure directly influenced the formation of Germany's second democracy, the Federal Republic of Germany. The actors who shaped the Bonn Republic actively compared Weimar and Bonn. The "Weimar analogy" discussed in this volume was not an abstraction; it was real and present for them as a lesson and a trauma. Looking at "Bonn's Weimar" allows us to see how an historical analogy works in practice, and to make several general arguments about the way the analogies work.

First, there was never just one Weimar analogy. The Weimar Republic's failure was too complex and the result of too many causes to provide an unambiguous response to the question: "Why do democracies fail?" This chapter argues that underneath the singular term "Weimar analogy" lies a multitude of different explanations for why it failed and why that matters for other democracies. A study like this can only begin to list such causes, which Sebastian Ullrich has pulled together in his lengthy book on *The Weimar Complex.*[1] The analogy with Weimar poses a question more than providing an answer for the failure of democracy.

Second, making analogies between the Weimar Republic and another democracy – in this case, the Bonn Republic – served the function not of fully explaining either case, but of indicating general parallels or likenesses between situations. The Weimar analogy should be understood, I argue, as a rhetorical tool for thinking through the implications of democracy's failure. Once we understand analogy as a tool, we can better get at the ways in which it functioned in different communicative contexts and appreciate analogy making as a rhetorical strategy for making sense of complex phenomena. Literary devices such as analogy are indeed justifiable and useful forms for communicating about the meaning of historical events, while focusing attention on the lasting fears, hopes, and challenges that they present.[2]

This chapter illustrates these two more general points by looking at four moments when the Weimar analogy was important for thinking about how to form a new German democracy after World War II. First, it describes the big, "world-historical" pronouncements about the meaning of Weimar's failure for modernity and democracy writ large, in the years around 1945. Second, it shifts to the closed-door discussion of the Herrenchiemsee Convention, at which political and administrative leaders developed specific arguments about the proper form of a constitutional democracy after Weimar. In essence, they were translating the big pronouncements developed in the first section into concrete, constitutional form, and in so doing they clarified the contradictory implications of the different Weimar analogies for democratic thought. The third section turns to the discussion of voting laws at the Parliamentary Council in Bonn, the body that drafted the new German constitution in 1948–9; here, the Weimar analogy helped to orient conversation toward the problems to be addressed, as well as operating strategically, in the sense of being brought in to justify institutional arrangements that would favor a certain political party over others. And the fourth section describes how the practical discussion around writing the constitution developed into one of the first serious historical debates about why Weimar failed, the confrontation between the social historian Werner Conze and the political scientist Karl Dietrich Bracher. At its heart was a question implicit in the Weimar analogy, which has structured historical discussions ever since: Was the failure of Weimar the result of the actions of irresponsible parties in the age of the masses, or was it the result of the machinations of elites seeking to evade democratic controls? How one answers this question helps to explain what the "Weimar analogy" means for one's argument.

The chapter concludes with the argument that analogies persist in contemporary discussions about the threat to democracy. They do not persist because of poor or sloppy reasoning, but because they pose hard questions, articulate the stakes of the questions in the emotional terms (fears and hopes) that underlie them, and lead to discussions about the uncertain future of democracy, in ways that detailed historical accounts and statistical correlations cannot.

1945: How Not to Be Like Weimar

The term "analogy" does not point to direct, causal relationships so much as it indicates possible, or even probable, outcomes of certain situations. Argument by analogy suggests that like conditions can produce like results. Analogies, in other words, suggest what could happen; their value lies in permitting people to have some sense of likely developments in a contingent social and political situation. In this sense, analogies have a similar function to correlations, which express the probable coincidence of specific factors. Both are ways to reduce complexity in the face of an open, contingent, and complex future. There is a big distinction between an analogy and a correlation, of course. Analogies tend to invoke a constellation of factors that threaten to recur, though never in the same form, a notion perhaps best expressed in the term commonly used to describe the "Weimar analogy" in contemporary German: *Weimarer Verhältnisse* or "Weimar conditions." Correlations, by contrast, aim to isolate specific factors or variables across different cases, in order to express the overall probability of their recurring, despite the many dissimilarities across cases. Both, however, seek to reduce complexity in order to help the observer to grasp the relative chance of certain conditions' recurrence. The term "complexity" is important in this connection. Situations are never directly replicable in history, even in one country over the course of a few decades – such as Germany in 1920–50.

This first section looks at the way representatives of different political traditions thought of Weimar's fate as an example of the big challenges of the modern world, whether in democratic, liberal, or conservative terms. They were *big* analogies, asking what Weimar's failure meant for Germany's future – and indeed for Western civilization as a whole. These were hardly timid theses; indeed, they tended to be arguments about the need for radical change, rather than arguments about how to tinker with constitutional rules to produce better outcomes.

Leading intellectuals from right-liberal and conservative traditions connected the end of the Republic and its replacement by a populist dictatorship with the threat of mass democracy and worship of power in modernity. In 1948, for example, Gerhard Ritter (1888–1967), already established before 1933 as one of the leading historians of the postwar period, connected the German dictatorship with longer democratic traditions. Ritter was himself directly involved with both the Freiburg Circle of Ordoliberalism and Carl Goerdeler's plot to assassinate Hitler; he was jailed at the end of the Nazi regime, but, unlike others in Goerdeler's circle, escaped execution. After the war, Ritter connected National Socialism to the idea of popular sovereignty itself, to the idea of an omnipotent popular will and an infallible rationalism, drawing a line from 1789 to 1933: in a way, he created an analogy between Weimar/Hitler and the French Revolution/Terror, which was the problem to be faced after 1945. Democratic conditions undermined democracy. His frankly antidemocratic rhetoric fit with the German Protestant and liberal tradition of the late nineteenth century and would be echoed in conservative and Christian democratic rhetoric of the time (and also in the arguments of Leo Strauss, described by William Scheuermann in this volume [Chapter 7]).[3]

The German economist Wilhelm Röpke (1899–1966) and the intellectual historian Friedrich Meinecke (1862–1954), both connected with political liberalism, similarly stressed the apotheosis of the state in the modern age of the masses, culminating in what Meinecke in 1946 called "the German catastrophe." For Meinecke, as for Ritter, the problem lay in modernity; Germans were not the only ones in modern times to develop an "intoxicated craze for power," but they were the ones who produced the most dangerous example of power-oriented, Machiavellian politics. Meinecke was a liberal reformer (he supported the left-liberal Friedrich Naumann's attempt to combine the "national" and the "social" in order to tame the "demonic" nature of the mass-democratic modernity that ended up in the "satanism" of National Socialism, and coined the term *Vernunftrepublikaner* to describe his acceptance of the Weimar Republic); a supporter of a strong executive power during the Republic; and not least a nationalist. He retreated from political life under National Socialism. Meinecke sought internal, spiritual sources for German rebirth, not unlike Ritter. He seemed to argue that forgetting the foundational traditions of German idealism laid the foundations for a destructive democratic and industrial modernity.[4] Just a year before, in 1945, the economic liberal Röpke, a follower of Smith and Ricardo, blamed the catastrophe on a Germanic and neo-Prussian worship of power that led to more political parties, giant cartels recognized by the state, massive welfare systems, imperialism, and a monopoly capitalism that meant ever more centralized state control and ever less individual freedom. The roots of the evil lay in the era before 1914, when monopoly capitalism, giant concerns, and mass culture replaced liberal egalitarianism and a human scale of thinking. Like Meinecke and Ritter, Röpke connected Germany's failure with the more general rise of the masses in the West.[5]

All three described, in different ways, the perils of modernity, characterized by a democracy of the masses, a gigantic and growing state colossus, and political parties. They tracked a continuity from Weimar to Hitler (and reaching back into the nineteenth century), relating the breakdown of democracy to an inherent flaw in mass democracy itself. If the problem lay in the masses, then the response had to be found not just in political institutions but in how society was arranged, in developing and reinforcing a sense of public decency, in popular political education: hence Röpke's advocacy of an economic liberalism aimed as an integral, human-oriented, competitive economic order; hence Meinecke's advocacy of Goethe reading groups.

Perhaps because he was more directly involved in politics, the left-liberal Theodor Heuss (1884–1963) praised the Weimar Republic for its basic rights and its constitutional structure. In this sense, he was not critical in the same way that Meinecke had been: It should be recalled at this point just how fractured and contradictory the liberal tradition in Germany actually was. Heuss had been part of the left-liberal grouping around Friedrich Naumann that had called for a democratic transition before 1918, and thereafter supported the Republic; he would become a leading figure in the postwar debates on the Basic Law, and he played a critical role in the discussions of the Parliamentary Council in 1948–9. Heuss was clear: The Weimar Republic was destroyed by those who *rejected* parties, pluralism, and democracy, and the German people were all too willing to be enslaved by the Nazis. The question was not how to tinker with a basically sound, liberal constitution, but how to overcome the elements of German culture that allowed antidemocrats to undermine the Republic – and the people to accept their victimhood passively.[6]

Further left, both Social Democrats and Communists viewed the social structure as the ultimate cause of Weimar's demise. In the stilted words from 1947 of Stalinist economist Fred Oelssner (1903–77), "a small group of powerful masters of firms and finance who control billions" had taken down the democracy; to avoid similar conditions and results in the future, a resolute people's democracy had to resist the reconstruction of capitalism. Notably, Oelssner's rhetoric, repeating the Stalinist position of the war years, relieved non-elites in Germany of responsibility for what had happened.[7] By contrast, the Social Democratic leader Kurt Schumacher (1895–1952) stressed in 1945 the way in which National Socialism had, with the help of big capitalists and imperialists, undermined the values of republic, socialism, and the nation with its lies, its appeals to base nationalist instincts, and its offer to workers that they become "masters by virtue of their superior race."[8] For left-leaning liberals and Social Democrats, it was important not to allow the old elites once more to undermine support for democracy and democracy itself. The Communists were more direct, calling for direct control by popular democracy, empowered by its party, to repress the social strata that had destroyed democracy before: a dictatorship in the name of democracy.

We do not find a single "Weimar analogy" among the postwar intellectuals; rather, we find multiple *big* theories of why National Socialism had come to power in 1933–4, each describing a different set of structures and characteristics leading to catastrophe – each, in other words, describing the similar situations that needed to be avoided in a successful democratic state. Notably, only one of the examples I have brought up here made the German people into simple victims who could be trusted to create a new democracy – and that exception came from the Marxist-Leninist tradition, which in practice had little trust in the people and whose most powerful leaders thought of democracy as party dictatorship.

Conceptualizing the Basic Law: Voting Laws, Parties, and Stable Regimes

Analogies like these oriented people toward the big challenges of modern German history, or indeed of modernity. Such general orientations became problematic when applied to concrete political situations, because concrete political moments are complicated, concrete, and not replicated. Relating the German dictatorship *in general* to 1789 and radical democracy, for example, runs into the conceptual problem that, *in the specific case*, the conservative leaders Hindenburg, Papen, and Hitler all rejected the tradition of democratic revolution. Specificity mattered for those seeking concrete lessons from the Weimar experience for a new, democratic German constitution.

When, in July 1948, the minister-presidents of the individual *Länder* of the British, French, and US zones of occupation were asked to send representatives to the former monarchical palace at Herrenchiemsee in Bavaria to outline the basic principles of a new, West German constitution, they were not asked to overcome the democratic tradition since 1789, but to figure out what specifically needed to be done to create a viable new German democracy. Despite sincere attempts to find a basic consensus about the new democratic order at Herrenchiemsee, distinctly different notions appeared concerning what had led to the end of the democracy in Weimar. Underlying assumptions appeared about political parties (opportunistic factions manipulating the masses or necessary forms for organizing political positions?) and the executive (a source of stability or an implicit threat to democracy?). Later commentators made light of the way that "everyone" knew that voting laws and President Hindenburg were the cause of Weimar's downfall.[9] That criticism neglects the way in which the very general discussion of "Weimar conditions" gave way to a specific description of what mechanisms led to the end of the Republic. Discussion of the matter had already begun in the context of creating the *Länder* constitutions – usually stressing the need for a decentralized federalist legislative to counter Nazi centralization.[10] Now the delegates had to work out the specific constitutional challenges of what later scholars saw as a kind of Weimar trauma.[11]

The specific context of the Herrenchiemsee Convention helps to explain the way in which the Weimar analogy worked in its deliberations.

It was not a convention called by the western German *Länder*, which did not have the right or the power to start talking about a constitution for Germany. The military authorities in the western zones of occupation were the ones to set the process in motion toward creating a separate western German state, for economic reasons (to overcome the inefficiencies and costs of divided economies) as well as for the diplomatic and geopolitical goal of creating a western German state firmly rooted on the US and western European side in the nascent Cold War. Despite the perceptions of many Germans at the time and since, the Western Allies did not dictate the content of the Basic Law. The Frankfurt Documents of 1 July 1948 opened up the way for a new constitution under three basic conditions: that the constitution establish a democratic government; that it be federalist in nature, recognizing the individual *Länder*, which had already been created in 1946–7; and that it guarantee individual rights and freedoms.[12] It is in fact difficult to imagine a postwar German constitution constructed by non-Nazis as a refutation of National Socialism that would *not* be in some form democratic, federalist, and outfitted with basic rights. The guidelines set by the Frankfurt Documents were generally in accord with the positions of the major political parties (partially excluding the Communists) after 1945 in the West. But precisely in their vagueness (which covered different positions among the Western Allies), the requirements created an uncertainty among Germans about whether their plans would be accepted by the military authorities. That uncertainty was an underlying context to the entire discussion. But at the same time, the Berlin Blockade, which began on 24 June 1948, focused both Western Allies and the German *Länder* on international relations and the potential for war with the Soviet Union. That fact gave the German minister-presidents and *Land* assemblies more leeway at Herrenchiemsee.[13] Allied interference in the constitution-making process ended up limited to specific topics such as the degree of federalism in the new state – which, far from showing a concerted Allied influence revealed instead the profound differences between a France interested in a decentralized and weak German state and British and US policy more focused on creating a viable bulwark against the Soviet Union.[14] In short, the Basic Law was a German product, not imposed on Germany by the Western Allies.

In one very important way, though, the Allies did set the preconditions for the discussion of how to create a new democracy: by removing leading National Socialists from public life, they enabled the new anti-fascist parties – from Communist and Social Democrat to Free Democrat and Christian Democrat, along with several smaller parties – to set the parameters of discussion, starting with the new governments and constitutions of the *Länder*. Each minister-president of each *Land* in the western zones named a single voting delegate to the Herrenchiemsee conference (accompanied, of course, by legal and political advisers). Those under the American occupation, which had pushed early for new constitutions at the *Land* level, were more likely to have clear conceptions of what a new, democratic constitution for all of Germany might look like; those of the British zone were administrators, and less attuned to constitutional discussions; and those from the French zone were more preoccupied with the often arbitrary rule of the French occupation authorities. All held positions of authority only with the permission of the military occupiers. Not all were party leaders or even constitutional experts.

Of the eleven voting representatives at Herrenchiemsee, all but two were close to the parties of the Weimar-era democratic coalition of Social Democracy, Center, and German Democrats.[15] These included two representatives who had actively opposed the Nazis before and after 1933, calling for armed resistance; these were Fritz Baade and Hermann Brill – both had been involved in the councils movement in 1918–19 and Brill was a former inmate at Buchenwald. Two intellectually leaning politicians who were central to forming West German postwar political culture were there as well: the brilliant Social Democratic lawyer Carlo Schmid, a student of SPD (Sozialdemokratische Partei Deutschlands – German Social Democratic Party) jurist Hermann Heller in Weimar; and Adolf Süsterhenn, lawyer for the Center Party in Weimar, proponent of Christian Socialism and advocate for limiting state power following the principles of Catholic natural law.[16] Absent at Herrenchiemsee were the right-wing defenders of dictatorship, advocates of centralized authoritarian rule, and high-profile apologists for National Socialism, including Carl Schmitt, Otto Koellreutter, and their students (with the exception of Theodor Maunz, whose background was not widely known at the time, and who was marginal to the discussions).[17] Also absent were the émigré intellectuals such as Carl Friedrich, Ernst Fraenkel, Karl Loewenstein, and Franz Neumann.[18] While they certainly played a role in rebuilding a democratic political culture in West Germany, the ideas that they expressed (e.g., the militant democracy described by Jan-Werner Müller in this volume (Chapter 9) or Franz Neumann's conception of the radical potential of party democracy as discussed by Peter Breiner (Chapter 4)) were already under discussion in the Weimar Republic, and known to the representatives in Herrenchiemsee and later Bonn.

Weimar's end hung like a shadow over the entire discussion, in ways that could have derailed it. Fritz Baade of Schleswig-Holstein, for instance, described the parliamentary vote on the Enabling Act of 23 March 1933, which suspended basic rights and handed the power of issuing emergency decrees directly to Hitler, as a "purely criminal act" carried out in the presence of the Nazi stormtroopers.[19] Liberal and Center Party delegates had voted for the Enabling Act. Baade carefully returned to the events later to describe how Center Party delegates came to him in tears on 23 March, after having been forced to affirm the bill by threats of physical violence. He carefully avoided party-political attacks in the discussion.[20] As this example shows, behind closed doors, the Herrenchiemsee representatives tried to cooperate across party lines against a common enemy. But the deeper they delved into the technical constitutional rules that had contributed to democratic collapse, the more apparent it became that they understood differently what had led to fascism.[21]

Indeed, the Enabling Act invoked by Baade was not just a moment in the process of the Nazi accumulation of power; it was the result of many factors that could challenge any potential democracy, any one of which could require rethinking constitutional rules. These included: a splintered party landscape; the constitutional power of the president to name a chancellor, to approve emergency decrees, and to dissolve parliament if it opposed his decision; the turn after 1930 toward an authoritarian system intended to sideline parties; Papen's use of emergency powers to carry out a coup d'état against Prussia, smashing *Länder* resistance to the Nazis; and, most importantly, the transformation of presidential emergency decrees into non-parliamentary means for issuing laws. The sheer number of factors reveals the complexity and contingency of the Republic's end, and the challenges confronting the founders of West German constitutional democracy.

The representatives drew several different lessons from these historical events. The German Reichstag was paralyzed after 1930, as were many parliaments on the level of the *Länder*, by a coalition of parties that declared no confidence in the existing government but could not agree on a new one. The delegates generally accepted the recommendation that parliament be permitted to remove a chancellor and government only if it approved another government in its place: the so-called *positive vote of no confidence.*[22] The delegates also agreed that the *president should not be directly elected* and should be more of a symbolic than a political figure.[23] Also generally accepted was the requirement that parties adhere to the notion that political organizations opposed to the principles of a *"free and democratic basic order"* should be dissolved by a militant democracy; they agreed that a new constitutional court (i.e., neither parliament nor government) should enforce that rule. And, as noted, the delegates all affirmed a certain autonomy of the *Länder*, although there was a broad range of views on what this might look like in practice.[24]

These elements of the constitutional draft would find their way into the final version of the Basic Law, suggesting an underlying agreement about why Weimar failed and how to guard against a similar failure in the future. But a closer examination of the discussion, even in the consensus-oriented Herrenchiemsee Convention, shows that it was more complicated and controversial. Which aspects of Weimar's failure were systematic, and which contingent? What was the root cause of the failure – too much democracy or too little? As the delegates at Herrenchiemsee began to discuss the organization of the new constitution, their attempts to remain polite and consensus-oriented at times threatened to collapse over the question of what Weimar's failure meant for a new West German constitution.

Fritz Baade made his argument in a way that one might not expect from a member of the Social Democratic Party, which had promoted proportional representation as a response to the unequal voting laws of the Empire.[25] He expressed the hope that Germany could develop the kind of senators in a second assembly representing the *Länder* that he had seen while in the United States: "the type of older politician," who "has a certain amount of independence in his own party."[26] Advocating such independence implied a conception of the political party quite different from the Weimar-era Social Democratic tradition, which had stressed party unity based on Marxist theory. His arguments sounded almost like John Adams's defense of a natural aristocracy of older, experienced men standing above the parties – and this from a former leader of the councils in the German Revolution of 1918.[27] Most striking was the way Baade's words could imply a criticism of parties for representing splinter groups rather than the common good, exactly the criticism that many liberals and conservatives made of Social Democracy in the Republic. It is unclear why and when Baade developed this position, but it is clear that his political ideas were not dictated by the party. His Social Democratic colleague Carlo Schmid (himself not always following the SPD script) quietly corrected Baade's point a few minutes later: Parties were "necessary if one really wants to form an organized will of the people" through democratic processes.[28]

Did proportional representation strengthen party discipline and party bureaucracy at the cost of the ability of the polity to function? Or did it ensure inclusion of all major social voices, a key substantive criterion for democracy? Baade seemed to imply that political parties themselves created the unstable conditions that ultimately led to Weimar's collapse. His rhetoric was surprisingly close to that of the Bavarian delegation, which arrived at Herrenchiemsee with a fully elaborated constitutional draft that seemed intended to limit party power. That draft gave the president the right to name the chancellor with the agreement of the Bundestag and Bundesrat. Initiative to form the government lay with the president, which sounded like a revised version of the semi-presidential system. The chancellor would then hold that position for the full duration of the legislative session, and not be removable by a parliamentary vote of no confidence. The constitutional draft stated that the chancellor "must resign if the political conditions make a trusting [*vertrauensvoll*] cooperation with Bundestag and Bundesrat impossible," but left it up to the chancellor to determine whether such a state obtained. Likewise, if the Bundestag was unable to agree upon a chancellor four weeks after convening or four weeks after a chancellor's resignation, the president had the right to name a chancellor and ministers with the agreement of the Bundesrat.[29] This proposal was not, then, for a constructive vote of no confidence, but rather to deprive parliament of the ability to remove the chancellor, and to provide a second path – one that was presidential and relied on the "reservoir of legality" of the *Länder* – for maintaining a stable government.[30]

The Bavarian proposal brought into focus the very different understandings of what the core problem of Weimar democracy was. Joseph Schwalber, the Bavarian interior minister, framed the issue in stark terms:

> It is a question of whether we make the federal government dependent on the prevailing mood of the parliament, whether we want to make it the plaything [*Spielball*] of the political parties in the present and coming hard times, or whether we shouldn't rather build in an element of stability [*Stabilitätsfaktor*] that offers a guarantee for sober governmental work over the long term for the good of Germany.[31]

He echoed the conservative rhetoric of a government standing above the parties – exactly the rhetoric of a conservative chancellor unattached to a party, like Hans Luther in 1925–6. It also reflected the rhetoric of stable community and harmonious social order so often present in Catholic social theory.[32] For Schwalber, the experience of Weimar showed the need for a strong president . Otto Küster (1907–89), a lawyer for the Christian Democratic government in Württemberg-Baden, declared that it was time to make an irresponsible parliament "impossible" through some rule that could bring an obstructive parliament to reason. The German people, he declared, were disgusted by parliament: "[W]e must spare the people such charades," which just "alienate people from politics."[33] One can read these utterances as fallbacks into the antiparty sentiments of the Weimar Republic (as Schmid did). But Küster was also a committed antifascist. There can be little doubt that his harsh words about the political parties were aimed at consolidating rather than harming German democracy, at providing limits to legislative power and parties in the interest of community, an important idea for so many involved in the formation of Christian democracy in Europe. The attempt to avoid the threat of parties to democracy thus led an antifascist conservative to a model that enabled the government to operate with a great deal of independence from parliament using a language that, intentionally or not, paralleled the antiparliamentary language of Weimar conservatives.

The Social Democrat Schmid turned the argument around: Making governments more independent in fact distanced them from the people. Governments should be chosen by the people, and the people were represented in parliament, by parties. Without that parliamentary and party support for governments, the logic of parliamentarianism, the government would abandon the foundations of democracy. Certainly stability was important to a political system, Schmid argued, but other values, including democracy, were as well. At heart, Schmid wondered whether the arguments being made against parties revealed the deeper problem of German political culture, with its roots in the monarchical constitutionalism of the nineteenth century.[34]

In a democracy, a government did not stand above the people and their particular interests; the "'government' is not something in itself, but rather governance through certain men, who for their part represent certain interest groups," Schmid remarked. Tensions among the masses, if they could not be resolved by parliament, could turn into a revolution. Precisely because parliamentarianism was more dynamic, precisely because it connected parties with government and made governments less stable, it permitted the struggle among interests to be fought within institutions rather than in the streets. Schmid realized full well that parties could act in an improper way, but he considered that requiring a constructive vote of no confidence would solve that problem *within* a parliamentary framework.[35]

There was a gulf between Schmid's position and that of Claus Leusser (1906–66) of the Bavarian Interior Ministry, who had developed the draft constitution under discussion – Schmid seeking a means to force parties to act responsibly; the delegation from the Bavarian Christian Social Union (CSU) essentially viewing political parties as an inherent threat to democracy (a position by no means shared by many in the leadership of the Christian Democratic Union (CDU), not least Konrad Adenauer). Schmid stressed that parties representing divergent interests were necessary to argue problems out. Repressing differences in the name of a higher unity was, by implication, antidemocratic.[36] Or, as Baade said more directly, the German people's distrust of parliament, a "typical form of political thinking" across "broad layers of our generation in Germany and in Italy," led either to monarchism or to fascism. The solution, Baade repeated, was majority voting rather than proportional representation (a position with which Schmid sympathized).[37]

The discussion began with an agreement on all sides to avoid the conditions that led to the collapse of the Weimar Republic, and therefore led to fascism; there is no doubt about the antifascist consensus in the room. Nor was there disagreement about the way in which a positive vote of no confidence could increase political stability. The process of discussion revealed deeper disagreements about the nature of party democracy itself. While representatives from all parties could view the parties as a potential source of disorder, those from the CSU at Herrenchiemsee sought to limit party power while the Social Democrats sought ways to push parties to fulfill their democratic role better by articulating clear positions and taking responsibility for a functional and legitimate government.[38]

The discussion of rule by emergency decree revealed a similar divide. That discussion began, again, with apparent consensus: After the experience of rule by a president directly elected by the people who usurped power, there seemed to be little support for recreating a strong presidential regime, especially one that included extensive emergency powers. Carlo Schmid, making an argument that reached across party lines, argued for a president whose role was largely to represent the nation through symbolic acts in the name of the entire nation.[39] His idea dovetailed well with the Bavarian constitutional draft, which saw the president elected by the Bundestag and Bundesrat, not directly. For Bavarian federalists, of course, a directly elected president threatened the existence of the Länder.

The Bavarian draft constitution outfitted the federal chancellor and his government with the power to issue emergency decrees in response to parliamentary failure, although granting the Bundestag the power to suspend such decrees, limiting the duration of decrees, and requiring consultation with the Bundesrat.[40] The subcommittee's report on the emergency decree power justified it with reference to the threat posed by parliament to democracy if it failed to pass legislation. In the event of an emergency, the executive's "right to issue an emergency decree [Notverordnungsrecht] has to be of assistance."[41]

Criticism of this position came from within the Bavarian delegation. Hans Nawiasky (1880–1961), a longtime lawyer for the Bavarian

People's Party and after 1945 for the dominant Christian Socialists, complained that the government was granted the right to issue emergency decrees with the force of parliamentary laws.[42] Nawiasky argued that such misuse of executive power had already begun with Brüning in the Weimar Republic (notably a Center Party politician), and that the Enabling Act of 23 March 1933 marked a continuation of this practice. A colleague from Bavaria responded that such emergency legislation was only necessary if parliament was obstructive or hindered from assembling; Nawiasky pointed out that Hitler had used precisely the same argument about parliamentary obstruction to take emergency measures before the Enabling Law.[43] Küster and Anton Pfeiffer (1888–1957, a co-founder of the CSU in Bavaria in 1945) protested that someone in the government had to act when parliament failed; Schmid responded that they were granting the government the role of a "deus ex machina" that in fact contributed to parliamentary dysfunction.[44] At issue for Schmid was a "latent disease" of democracy that only full responsibility would cure, the willingness to give speeches to the masses (a *Fensterreden* in German) instead of working for compromises within parliament.[45]

The later Parliamentary Council would, after much discussion, set aside plans for extensive emergency powers in the event of parliamentary paralysis, perhaps because of Konrad Adenauer's personal objections or perhaps because of the objection of the occupation authorities; but that would take place in a different context, far more directly influenced by the leadership of the political parties. The Parliamentary Council could not ignore another role for emergency powers implied by the constructive vote of no confidence. Their solution to the problem of parliamentary paralysis was found in Article 81 of the Basic Law, which permitted the government to approve laws rejected by parliament if the Bundesrat approved and with the agreement of the president. The special powers of the government could be invoked only once during the government's term and could not be extended; furthermore, the legislation could not violate the constitution. This solution excluded the president from playing the leader above the parties, as happened in the Weimar Republic; it kept the parties in parliament from paralyzing the government, and indeed pressured them to act responsibly; and it set clear limits to emergency ordinances that remained unclear in the Weimar Constitution. Some on the right criticized the Parliamentary Council for limiting the ability of the government and president to respond to "real" crises; some of the left viewed Article 81 as a means of dramatically increasing the government's power and creating a *Kanzlerdemokratie*. Article 81 was controversial, not least because it was responding to two very different notions of what paralyzed Weimar democracy.[46]

Analogies as Party-Political Weapons: Debating Voting Rules in the Parliamentary Council

Avoiding the fate of Weimar democracy meant avoiding the conditions that led to such horrendous results – in other words, thinking about how analogous conditions created analogous results. An analogy with Weimar could also serve to justify party interests, however. The discussion of a new voting law for western Germany, despite the many concerns about the way in which proportional representation worked in the Weimar Republic in both Herrenchiemsee and Bonn, was in fact largely driven by party interests.[47] The delegates to the Parliamentary Council were named not by the minister-presidents of the individual *Länder* but by political parties. Their representation at the Parliamentary Council corresponded to their relative strength in *Land* elections. They remained in close contact with their party leaderships. The party leadership was fully aware that voting rules would affect their relative power in the new parliament, and indeed carefully calculated how different voting systems would affect their standing. For many in the CSU, a "first-past-the-post" system in 1948 seemed risky, given recent losses to the radical federalist Bavarian Party; only later were they able to assume an absolute majority in the Catholic south. In other western *Länder*, meanwhile, Christian Democrats faced the possibility of being a minority party excluded from power in a first-past-the-post voting system.[48] The Social Democrats, meanwhile, would have profited from a relative majority system in their strongholds, but would have been closed out of power for the long term in the less urban parts of the south. This uncertainty – and the SPD's longer-term identification with proportional representation – led them to be friendlier to proportional representation. Nonetheless, some SPD leaders, such as Schmid and Baade, in line with criticisms from the right wing of Social Democracy at the end of the Republic and in exile, preferred the relative majority system. SPD, CDU, and CSU were all, then, internally divided on the matter of voting.[49] The smaller parties – the conservative German Party, the centrist Center Party, and the Communists – would probably have been thrown out of parliament under a relative majority system (although the German Party still favored it). The national liberal Free Democrats (FDP) could have profited from a majority system only if that system required an absolute majority and runoff elections, which would have made a third party like the FDP kingmakers in some regions.[50] Party interests played an important role in the Parliamentary Council's difficult negotiations on voting laws, and party considerations (regional versus central as well as considerations of voting trends) affected official party positions much more than principle.

Indeed, there is something unreal about the discussion on voting laws in the Parliamentary Council, since it is so clear that the real discussion was taking place elsewhere, among party leaders behind closed doors.

To consider this to be a merely cynical party calculation is to do an injustice to the main actors. This partisan focus is part and parcel of democracy, and not some kind of aberration: Parties are about power, yes, but that power is about how to further substantive aims that the parties think are right. Parties are also about gathering votes – they cannot ignore the sentiments of their potential voters, who were indeed part of a lively parallel discussion about voting rules in 1948–9. For this reason, reports by voting rights experts had little effect on the actual discussion. In a report on the history of voting laws, the aging constitutional and administrative lawyer Richard Thoma (1874–1957), for example, noted that a simple relative majority system was rejected in so many countries largely because it excluded significant voices from representative assemblies. His report also empirically dismantled the argument that proportional voting necessarily led to a host of parties and that a simple majority vote would necessarily produce a two-party system. Majority voting had produced a complex multiparty system in Germany and across continental Europe both before 1914 and after 1945; a plethora of parties was not simply the result of proportional voting. Nor, he argued, did a two-party system necessarily lead to more freedom of individual delegates; indeed, the development of party whips in both Britain and the United States proved otherwise. Thoma certainly saw the value in limiting the development of extremist parties, but that, he pointed out, was a different question entirely.[51] His presentation was technically and empirically precise, and directly undermined the notion that a simple change to a relative majority system would lead to a stable, two-party political world. His proposal for a mixed system involving both proportional representation and direct election of representatives, already developed in the Weimar Republic, would eventually win the day. Not, however, because of his argument, but because of party interests.

The chair of the voting law subcommittee, Gerhard Kroll (1910–63) of the CSU, was perhaps the exception to this characterization of the committee's work. And in his refusal to think strategically, he actually became something of a problem. Kroll ignored the information provided by Thoma. Instead, he argued – or rather asserted – that parliamentary government was impossible with proportional representation. He argued that proportional voting systems necessarily led to rule by emergency cabinets on the part of the executive. "This is a parliamentarianism that dissolves itself," he proclaimed. The *only* alternative, according to Kroll, was a relative majority system of voting, which would produce two party blocks, CDU/CSU and SPD, both with clear worldviews and able to take on parliamentary responsibilities. Small parties would, he suggested, be all but eliminated.[52] Kroll was supported in this point by the expert testimony of Hans Luther (1879–1962), who had served as an "unpolitical" or rather non-party chancellor under President Hindenburg in 1925–6 with a partially technocratic cabinet. Like Kroll, Luther argued that proportional representation led to splintered parties based on interest groups, only interested in bargaining (*Kuhhandel*) rather than governing. Furthermore, proportional voting for party lists resulted in the ideological radicalization of parties, a deformation of the list of people elected (Luther singled out for special criticism the practice of putting women, who would have trouble getting elected directly, in the third position on party lists), and in general an abdication of leadership. For Luther the result was necessarily rule of a chancellor (he held up Brüning for praise) and some version of Article 48, the clause of the Weimar Constitution that provided the president with emergency powers. Luther, like Kroll, presented a story of how proportional representation, interest groups, and political parties destroyed Weimar democracy from within: "Weimar voting law bears a considerable share of the blame for the terrible Hitler disaster."[53]

It is notable how Kroll made use of a general analogy – proportional representation would have a similar function in West German democracy as it did in Weimar democracy – not to further and deepen discussion, as took place at Herrenchiemsee, but to halt compromise. Kroll did so out of a fundamental and even dogmatic belief that he was right. Indeed, Kroll became a problem for both Christian Democratic parties precisely because he argued out of conviction rather than party interest. He was "inflexible and unproductive" in his defense of a simple first-past-the-post voting system, just as the Christian Democrats were concerned about maintaining a voice in industrial areas. Indeed, his party remained divided over the issue behind closed doors, for pragmatic reasons.[54] CDU and CSU representatives on the subcommittee repeated Luther's argument as the debate went on, and they rejected versions of Thoma's 1924 proposal for a system that combined proportional and direct voting as well as the FDP's ideas for an absolute majority, but apparently for strategic reasons.[55] The subcommittee on voting spun its wheels throughout the fall of 1948, making little progress.

Indeed, the leading intellectual lights of the Parliamentary Council moved away from viewing voting rights as the key problem of Weimar. Already in September, as noted above, Theodor Heuss openly questioned whether the Weimar Constitution in general was the cause of

Weimar's failure: That explanation was Hitler's, he said pointedly, and served antidemocratic ends. In the eighth plenary session, on 24 February 1949, Heuss noted that many democracies functioned well with proportional representation, defended lists as a way of bringing qualified people into parliament, and noted just how few women were present under Anglo-American majority voting systems. Carlo Schmid likewise stressed that key to any parliamentary democracy was not a stable majority but public discussion and compromise, and criticized CDU representative Heinrich von Brentano for wanting to shock the German public by implementing a foreign voting system that would kill off smaller parties just when broad public support for German reconstruction was necessary. And the great outsider Heinz Renner (1892–1964), a Communist, asked the hard question: Would Hitler, whose party received the largest votes of any party in 1932, not have come to power more easily with a majority voting system?[56]

Social Democrats, Communists, and the small Center Party were finally able to produce a modified proportional voting system that satisfied both small parties and larger parties like the SPD, but the CDU/CSU refused to accept the solution. Not because they had a better plan, or because they were in principled opposition. Indeed, they remained divided, which partly explains why they removed the inflexible Kroll from the subcommittee. (A few years later, Kroll would make public his support for an antiliberal and antidemocratic, corporatist constitution in the tradition of Salazar and Franco.[57]) In a meeting of the party faction on 16 February 1949, Konrad Adenauer proposed supporting a majority voting system precisely so that the proposal would be defeated: "That can be exploited later for election propaganda."[58] The SPD proposal furthermore dropped the requirement of a five percent hurdle for a party to be represented, revealing just how little the "Weimar analogy" mattered according to which proportional representation led to splinter parties and paralysis. The majority opposing the five percent hurdle now stressed the need to integrate all elements of German society that recognized the "free democratic basic order" into the polity, to aid in national reconstruction.[59] In any case, the military occupation authorities rejected the plan for ambiguous reasons on 2 March 1949, suggesting instead that each *Land* should develop its own voting laws, a plan that would have been beneficial especially to the CDU/CSU, as Adenauer clearly saw.[60] This suggestion made for general confusion. A renewed attempt by the Parliamentary Council to propose a law failed to gain the two-thirds vote that the military governors declared necessary, and also ran up against further Allied opposition (and Allied infighting, as the French sought to slow the process down). In the end, the occupation authorities handed the decision back to the minister-presidents of the *Länder*, who approved a mixed proportional/majority voting system supported by the SPD, FDP, and Communists with minor changes. Under the influence of the military governors, these parties reintroduced the five percent hurdle, which would have the effect of weakening small parties and hindering the formation of new parties.[61] The Parliamentary Council did not decide on the voting system; the minister-presidents did.

This system with variations has held in the Federal Republic ever since, and, certainly, the Federal Republic stands as an example of successful democratization. But it would be hard to make a direct causal connection between these two points: It is not clear that the specific voting system they adopted consolidated democracy. It is also not clear that the voting system hindered the development of what would become by the 1980s a four-party system, and by 2021 a six-party system. To be blunt, the specific voting system eventually approved was not the result of a careful examination of *the* Weimar analogy, but the result of extensive party-political negotiations under the conditions of occupation – informed by assessments of Weimar but not completely determined by them. When push came to shove, the analogy with Weimar voting laws was a tool rather than a guide.

From Analogy to Historical Analysis: The Bracher–Conze Controversy

The previous sections have described two different kinds of use of the Weimar analogy to describe the potential failures of postwar German democracy: The first described fears about constitutional democracy in general (what happened in Weimar is likely to happen again under mass democracy or class society); the second and third articulated in more precise ways the fears and hopes about the shape of democratic institutions in the Basic Law. This final section shifts to a different kind of argument by analogy, one that involved a turn back from the arguments about the Basic Law to a careful, scholarly description of why Weimar failed. The debate took place between Werner Conze and Karl Dietrich Bracher, and it remains foundational for historical and political arguments today. In several articles published in the half decade after the Basic Law's approval, Conze, an innovative social historian who had been involved with the National Socialists, argued that the Weimar Republic self-destructed as a result of a dysfunctional relationship between mass parties and parliament that was potentially inherent in modern democracy. Bracher, a younger political scientist who studied at Harvard University after the war and was deeply committed to liberal democracy, argued in 1955, on the basis of much the same evidence, that the Republic was destroyed by its opponents, not least the president and his chancellors, who aimed to transform the democratic constitution into an authoritarian one. Notably, neither was directly involved with the end of the Republic: When Hitler took power, Conze was in his early twenties and engaged in historical research on Germans in Eastern Europe (hardly a pro-republican historical topic in the early 1930s!), while Bracher was only eleven years old.[62]

Bracher noted that the Basic Law had made three basic corrections to the Weimar political system: "limiting presidential power, extending and modifying the party-based parliamentary state, and strengthening the government." "The question is," he continued, "whether the assessment of the crisis situation of 1930–33 holds true," and, in particular, whether the narrative of a breakdown (*Versagen*) of the multiparty system of 1930 was true or whether it was a "legend."[63]

His main opponent, Conze, was one of the methodological innovators in post-1945 German history, who contributed both to the development of structural social history and to Reinhart Koselleck's pathbreaking encyclopedia of the change of key concepts in the social sciences over five centuries, the *Geschichtliche Grundbegriffe*. Conze had made use of anti-Semitic and Nazi rhetoric in works from 1937–9 that racialized social policy and sought to justify mass expulsions or transfers of non-German ethnic groups. These parts of his scholarly biography were not really addressed until the 1990s, after his death.[64] After 1945, Conze argued that the crisis beginning in 1930 reflected a structural shift from liberal parliamentarianism to mass democracy, which had transformed political parties and led to the necessity of a strong executive above a fragmented society . Bracher, by contrast, argued that the crisis reflected conscious decisions of elites on the right to sideline parties and to create an alternative constitutional system based on presidential rule by emergency decree. The Conze–Bracher debate worked out in detail for the first time the contrasting diagnoses of the conditions that brought about the end of Weimar democracy that were only implicit at Herrenchiemsee and in the Parliamentary Council.[65]

Conze's thesis about the structural change of the political system in the era of mass democracy was pretty much identical to Carl Schmitt's 1923 *Crisis of Parliamentary Democracy* (as well as opinions across the spectrum of right-liberal to conservative opinion during the Weimar Republic).[66] Political parties had become tools of interest groups dependent on mass voting in order to maintain their power, and therefore unable to enter into the stable coalitions necessary for a stable government. According to Conze, the two main parties necessary for Hermann Müller's Grand

Coalition of 1928–30, the SPD and the right-liberal German People's Party (DVP), were beholden respectively to the trade unions and to heavy industry. On Conze's account, the SPD was an especially problematic party, because it combined a pro-democratic, parliamentary stance with an extremist worldview focused on class struggle. The SPD's mid-1920s strategy of seeking "economic democracy" (a vague term encompassing everything from more codetermination at the firm level, to more union rights, to planning and regulation), according to Conze, was a radical turn back to class conflict that made compromise with the DVP difficult or impossible. These parties' aim was to "usurp" the state (Conze used the term in scare quotes) for their own aims, which made it impossible to form a stable government. The Weimar Republic therefore had to fail as a parliamentary democracy, long before Hitler was on the horizon as a serious contender. In its place would arise a president standing above the parties, guiding a "stable state based on civil servants" (*stabilen Beamtenstaat*). Conze drew that model explicitly from the form of constitutional monarchism that prevailed before 1914 in Germany. An "inner necessity" rooted in mass democracy would lead to the replacement of the "party-state" with a "presidential republic."[67] Using the language of this volume, we might say that Conze pointed out a structural aspect of Weimar that by analogy still held in the Bonn Republic.

Bracher's magisterial *Dissolution of the Weimar Republic* (*Die Auflösung der Weimarer Republik*) of 1955 addressed the same events and structures that Conze did; indeed, like Conze, he did not blame the end of the Weimar Republic on either the Versailles Treaty or the Great Depression, though both, of course, played a role in the rhetoric of actors at the time. Like Conze, Bracher saw the tensions between SPD and DVP – i.e., between "capital and labor, monopoly economy and interventionist state" – as central to the process of dissolution. But unlike Conze, Bracher did not describe the transition to presidential rule as necessary. The motives of the actors mattered for Bracher, especially those seeking to replace parliamentary democracy with some form of authoritarian and corporatist dictatorship. Certainly, the SPD made a mistake in breaking with the Grand Coalition over unemployment benefits, but its attempts to alter the relationship between labor and capital were part of a democratic process, not a break with democracy. For Bracher, the SPD's support for economic democracy did not mark an exit from the democratic ground rules. The strategy on the right to bring in a "strong man" who could rule without parliament did.[68] Implicitly, the calls for a strong executive in the early years of the Federal Republic threatened by analogy the crisis that brought down Weimar.

According to Bracher "freeing" the president from the parliament, creating a kind of ersatz Kaiser on the model of constitutional monarchism, broke his connection to the political parties, which organized the people. The effect was to weaken both the president and the parties, creating the conditions for radical parties to grow.[69] In short, Weimar did not fail because of parliamentary democracy in the age of the masses, as Conze seemed to say, but because of the conscious decisions of a bureaucratic and social elite to rely on Article 48 (emergency decrees) and Article 25 (the right to dissolve the Reichstag) to evade parliamentary control. The political leaders involved in this game were President Hindenburg, Chancellor Papen in 1932 – and also Chancellor Brüning in 1930, whose centralization of the state around a strong man armed with emergency decrees lay the foundations for Hitler's rule. It was not political parties and too much democracy that led to the fall of the Republic, but "essentially the power of authoritarian, bureaucratic conceptions of order to persist and to seduce," directed precisely against the trade unions, the "party-state," and parliamentarianism itself.[70]

The Conze–Bracher debate marked the beginning of solid scholarship about the end of the Weimar Republic.[71] Both Conze and Bracher also presented models for how a modern democracy ended. Conze's model focused on the internal tensions in any modern (by which he also meant capitalist) society: Factions (parties) based on individual interests and articulated worldviews would usurp the state, use it to defend their own interests, and render it unable to defend the common good. Students of Carl Schmitt agreed, and questioned whether the Basic Law provided a strong enough executive to resist the interests organized in a plurality of parties, external threats, and the immanent threats of modernity itself.[72] These arguments found their counterparts on the left, especially after 1970: those who took up the arguments of the 1920s about how a society based on class conflict eventually required rule by a man claiming to stand above parties, on the model of Marx's account of Napoleon Bonaparte III.[73] Bracher's argument, meanwhile, led to the debate on Brüning's role in the transformation of Weimar democracy toward authoritarianism in 1930, which still continues today. At the heart of his work was the question of what conditions led political elites to seek to transform a multiparty state into an authoritarian system: social factions that paralyzed democracy and opened the door to dictatorship, or long-term mentalities of certain social groups – for Bracher, members of the military, the old nobility, civil servants, and heavy industry.[74]

Bracher and Conze shifted from drawing potential outcomes from generally similar conditions to examining the specific structures and individual decisions that led to the final years of crisis of Weimar democracy. And they came up with very different narratives that echoed the narratives already evident at Herrenchiemsee and at Bonn. Certainly, the Basic Law reflected the historical experiences of Weimar, but two different sets of "Weimar conditions" were under discussion. The constructive vote of no confidence was either intended to strengthen the chancellor and therefore singular, executive leadership in the face of irresponsible and self-serving parties, the foundation of the *Kanzlerdemokratie* attacked by the democratic left during Adenauer's long reign, *or* it was intended as a nudge to parties to enhance their ability to play the leading role in a pluralist democracy. The president was certainly deprived of many of his powers, and no longer elected directly in a national vote, *or* these powers shifted over to the chancellor and the government, notably outfitted with the power to enact emergency administrative decrees with the force of law should parliament seek to paralyze the government (Article 81). The article was intended either to empower the chancellor in a state of emergency (while, of course, setting clear legal limits to such action, something that Article 48 of the Weimar Constitution had failed to do), *or* to advise the parties in parliament not to abuse their powers. And, in the end, was the lesson that small splinter parties had paralyzed Weimar and made it unstable, thereby necessitating some kind of rule that would hinder small parties' formation, a Weimar lesson for the founders of the Federal Republic at all? The Parliamentary Council had rejected the rule that parties had to gain five percent of the vote to be represented; that rule was approved only by the minister-presidents of the *Länder*, in a murky process no doubt involving consultation with the Allied military governments. The five percent hurdle is hardly the story of a clear lesson learned by the Parliamentary Council, which ended up putting the principles that democracies should be inclusive and dynamic first. There were certainly lessons embedded in the Basic Law, from the assertion that basic rights would apply to all governmental activity, including legislation, to the affirmation of a new constitutional court. But the point is, the actual process of "learning from Weimar" was far messier and ambiguous than the story of "lessons learned" suggests.[75]

Conclusion: On the Persistence of Analogies

The story of the Republic's end no longer seems so simple. Indeed, in a short book about current crises of democracy, the political scientist Adam Przeworski stresses the complexities and contingencies of the story of the Weimar Republic. By extension, one might assume that Weimar's peculiarity and particularity make it a particularly bad case of analogical reasoning. "The collapse of the Weimar democracy" might be "widely used as an omen," but little more; and Przeworski seems to doubt whether the facts support even that claim.[76]

But this essay has made a somewhat different argument. Analogies differ from correlations. Correlations serve to show, on the basis of aggregated experiences, the probable connection of certain variables to certain outcomes. Thus, as Przeworski notes, the US has lasted so long as a democracy (in the most minimal sense, as a country with regular elections in which leaders can be removed) that it has a statistically tiny chance of experiencing a mortal crisis of democracy.[77] Analogies, however, are not probabilities in this sense. They describe general patterns that facilitate the articulation of fears and hopes in an uncertain and contingent world. Out of these general anxieties can arise the specific questions that guide research – and feed back into the more general question, but in a less vague, more specific way. Both Conze and Bracher contributed to a specific historical narrative and raised general questions that resonate beyond their specific context. Do political parties have a tendency to function in ways that actually harm democracy, making it necessary for a charismatic leader to govern? Does strong executive leadership serve as a tool to destabilize democracy and reduce the power (and responsibility) of parties? These are both useful political questions in a world of populist leaders and technocratic managers, parties dominated by interest groups, and experts interested in maintaining their own power.

Bracher applied his analysis to what he saw as continuations of German antidemocratic traditions: on the far right, certainly, but also, and especially, on the part of the New Left and the Greens, both of them critical of parliamentary representation and both calling for more "direct democracy."[78] The jurists Conze cited viewed parties (not extremist parties, but parties) as a threat to political order; they continued to be cited through the 1970s, and, in the unsettled times after German unification, they experienced a renaissance, especially on the far right.[79]

Current discussions about Alternative for Germany (Alternative für Deutschland or AfD), meanwhile, have continued to bring these parallels into discussion. The AfD itself is a right-populist party, and in this sense a party that claims the right to represent the real nation in opposition to existing parties, which it views as part of a corrupt system of particular interests separate from the people. The AfD's embrace of Donald Trump was a way of attacking Chancellor Angela Merkel and a parliamentary system that the AfD deemed unable to deal with a real crisis. A little-noticed plank of their 2017 platform calls for a directly elected president, with much more power, expressing a yearning for a German Trump. And yet, the Weimar analogy is a bit different today than in the founding years of the Federal Republic. The AfD is considered a problem because of its right-radical, *populist* content; after 1945, it was the democratic, *non-populist* and interest-based parties that were seen as the problem by conservative as well as not so conservative politicians, and Hitler's rise as a kind of aftereffect. If anyone, it is the AfD that is echoing (perhaps unknowingly) the conservative critique of parties that lies just below the surface of much post-1945 political rhetoric. As far as I can tell, the AfD itself has not invoked "Weimar conditions."[80]

Analogies are useful tools for a present condition whose future is unknown. They are not the same as scholarly arguments; their value lies in a different field, in articulating fears. The steps toward authoritarianism and then dictatorship in the German case were many, and they derived from a number of specific causes in specific, contingent moments. An analogy about Weimar is not really about these specific causes and moments. It is about conditions and processes in general: the possibility that mass democracies might also produce a strong executive, for example, or the possibility that elites shift power to a strong executive whom they can better influence and control, or the possibility (as per the AfD) that political parties might "endanger our democracy" by forcing gender studies on innocent students.[81] Tendencies, conditions, climates – these are vague words that might better express our fears and hopes than causes or correlations.

Most German historians today tell a complicated story of the end of the Weimar Republic, which relies neither on specifically *old* elites, nor on the outcome of World War I, nor on the Great Depression to explain the vacuum allowing Hitler to rise. The process toward authoritarianism involved extremist parties pressuring responsible ones, responsible parties forced into extremist positions, conscious strategizing by elites about how to exclude certain parties from power, manipulation of the law and the judiciary to reach certain ends, cultural and intellectual currents focused on the idea of "crisis," and not least ideologies of national community.[82] There is no single cause of collapse. Przeworski therefore rightly cautions us against using the Weimar Republic's collapse to say anything in general about the current crises of democracy across the world. But at the end of his book, Przeworski describes a step-by-step, contingent, and yet coherent process in which a leading political party conspires with an unscrupulous right-wing leader to undermine the legislative branch, cast doubt on the legitimacy of democratic government, diminish the independence of the judiciary, and install authoritarian rule.[83] Despite the different institutions and different contexts, one cannot but hear in his words an analogy with the dissolution of the

Weimar Republic. Analogy enters the picture when correlations provide little guidance about a threatening future.

The Weimar analogy served at the start of this chapter as a way to articulate the fear that democracy could end up in the same kind of violence, dictatorship, and disaster as occurred after 1933. In the discussions about the formation of a new West German democracy, that general fear became articulated as different diagnoses of what went wrong, and therefore different notions of how to form a "safe" democracy. But analogies could also be used strategically (in Habermas's sense) to further particular interests, in the sense of being invoked not to get at the heart of a problem but to gain an immediate advantage.[84] Last but not least, the Weimar analogy, as it broke down into contradictory arguments, facilitated scholarly discussion. Analogies are not sharp and precise tools. That doesn't make them useless; indeed, it might make them useful tools in developing discussions about complex and traumatic events.

Notes

1 Ullrich pulls together the many "lessons" of Weimar democracy in great detail. Sebastian Ullrich, *Der Weimar-Komplex: Das Scheitern der ersten deutschen Demokratie und die politische Kultur der frühen Bundesrepublik 1945–1959* (Göttingen: Wallstein, 2009).

2 The reference is to Richard Rorty's approach to contingency and situatedness in discussion of self and society and the need for literary analogies as ways to think life problems through. Richard Rorty, *Contingency, Irony, and Solidarity* (New York: Cambridge University Press, 1989). Dorothy Noyes brought up the connection to the work of Kenneth Burke in the conference that led to this volume; indeed, lurking behind the scenes in this chapter is Hayden White's work, which was so heavily influenced by Burke. Hayden White, *Metahistory: The Historical Imagination in Nineteenth-Century Europe* (Baltimore: Johns Hopkins University Press, 1973).

3 See, e.g., Gerhard Ritter, *Das deutsche Problem: Grundfragen deutschen Staatslebens gestern und heute* (Munich: Oldenbourg, 1962 [1948]), p. 44: "With the transformation of the old authoritarian state into the democratic people's state and with the expulsion of the churches from the center of life, the way toward the modern total state was opened." See Gabrielle Metzler, *Der Staat der Historiker: Staatsvorstellungen deutscher Historiker seit 1945* (Frankfurt: Suhrkamp, 2018), pp. 59–62, 75–8, with further references. On Ritter's past, see especially the sympathetic portrayal by Klaus Schwabe and the more critical commentary in Thomas A. Brady, Jr., "Change and Continuity in German Historiography from 1933 into the Early 1950s: Gerhard Ritter (1888–1967)" in James Van Horn Melton, ed., *Paths of Continuity: Central European Historiography form the 1930s to the 1950s* (New York: Cambridge University Press, 1994), pp. 83–117.

4 Friedrich Meinecke, *The German Catastrophe*, trans. Sidney B. Fay (Cambridge, MA: Harvard University Press, 1950). See Jonathan B. Knudsen's critical "Friedrich Meinecke (1862–1954)" and Ernst A. Breisach's response in Van Horn Melton, *Paths of Continuity*, pp. 49–81. More recent literature has been even more critical of Meinecke: e.g., Metzler, *Der Staat der Historiker*, pp. 62–7. But compare Ullrich, *Der Weimar-Komplex*, p. 105. Ullrich, I think correctly, stresses Meinecke's optimism about whether the Weimar Republic could have survived had it not been for a handful of elites, especially Hindenburg, who undermined it.

5 One example of many is Wilhelm Röpke, *The German Question*, trans. E. W. Dickes (London: Allen and Unwin, 1946).

6 See especially Heuss's speech to the Parliamentary Council plenary session of 9 September 1948, in *Der Parlamentarische Rat 1948–1949: Akten und Protokolle* (Boppard am Rhein: Boldt, 1975ff.), vol. IX, pp. 103–5 (hereafter cited as *Parl. Rat*); this was a more widespread interpretation among liberals: see Ullrich, *Der Weimar-Komplex*, pp. 99–101.

7 Fred Oelssner, "Der Imperialismus," *Neues Deutschland*, 31 January 1947, p. 3; on Oelssner in context, see Catherine Epstein, *The Last Revolutionaries: German Communists and Their Century* (Cambridge, MA: Harvard University Press, 2003).

8 Kurt Schumacher, speech of 6 May 1945, to Social Democratic leaders in Hannover, in Kurt Schumacher, *Reden-Schriften-Korrespondenzen 1945–1952*, ed. Willy Albrecht (Bonn: Dietz Nachf., 1985), pp. 203–36, especially pp. 208–10. The centrality of a democratic nationalism is stressed in *Kurt Schumacher und seine Politik*, ed. Haus der Geschichte der Bundesrepublik Deutschlands (Berlin: Argon, 1996).

9 Thus the historian Alfred Grosser, cited in Erhard Lange, "Der Parlamentarische Rat und die Entstehung des ersten Bundestagswahlgesetzes," *Vierteljahrshefte für Zeitgeschichte* 20 (1972), p. 292, note 44.

10 See especially Bettina Blank, *Die westdeutschen Länder und die Entstehung des Grundgesetzes: Zur Auseinandersetzung um die Frankfurter Dokumente von Juli 1948* (Munich: Oldenbourg, 1995); Michael F. Feldkamp, *Der Parlamentarische Rat 1948–1949* (Göttingen: Vandenhoeck und Ruprecht, 1998), pp. 13–18.

11 Especially Rudolf Morsey, "Die Debatte um das Staatsoberhaupt 1945–1949" in Eberhard Jäckel, Horst Müller, and Hermann Rudolph, eds., *Vom Heuss bis Herzog: Die Bundespräsidenten im politischen System der Bundesrepublik* (Stuttgart: Deutsche Verlags-Anstalt, 1999), p. 58. This image of a trauma was ubiquitous, as noted by Ullrich, *Der Weimar-Komplex*, pp. 17–18.

12 Document reproduced in *Parl. Rat*, vol. I, pp. 30–6; Feldkamp, *Der Parlamentarische Rat*, pp. 18–21. For the US international politics context, see Erich J. C. Hahn, "The Occupying Powers and the Constitutional Reconstruction of West Germany, 1945–1949" in *Cornerstone of Democracy: The West German Grundgesetz, 1949–1989*, German Historical Institute Occasional Paper 13 (Washington, DC: German Historical Institute, 1995), pp. 7–36.

13 At the same time, the conflict with the Soviet Union raised the question of whether Germany would remain divided, something that the Western

occupation authorities were more willing to countenance than the Germans. See Wolfram Werner, "Einleitung," *Parl. Rat,* vol. III, pp. xxii–xxiii; Werner, "Einleitung," *Parl. Rat,* vol. V, p. xxv; Carlo Schmid's carefully considered argument presented on 8 September 1948, in *Parl. Rat,* vol. XI, pp. 21–45.

14 The process did indeed give Bavarian and other advocates of an extreme federalism an advantage in the discussions, but the positions existed already in Germany, independently of the military authorities, so it is hard to call federalism an imposition from outside. For more detailed discussion, see Blank, *Die westdeutschen Länder und die Entstehung des Grundgesetzes,* Part III; see also Schmid's description of the lack of a German majority for either extreme solution, a German confederacy based on *Land* sovereignty or a more centralized state on the model of Weimar, in Carlo Schmid, *Erinnerungen* (Munich: Scherz, 1979), pp. 325, 369–70, 376–7.

15 Feldkamp, *Der Parlamentarische Rat,* p. 29; more generally, Ullrich, *Der Weimar-Komplex,* pp. 196–203. One exception was Justus Danckwerts (1887–1969), an administrative expert named by Lower Saxony active in the Republic, under fascism, and in postwar Germany. See Peter Bucher, "Einleitung," *Parl. Rat,* vol. II, pp. xix–xx. The other was Theodor Kordt, who was both a member of the Nazi Party and involved in a resistance movement: Bucher, "Einleitung," *Parl. Rat,* vol. II, pp. xxviii–xxix.

16 Bucher, "Einleitung," *Parl. Rat,* vol. II, pp. xvi–xix, xxi–xxiii, xxvi–xxviii. On Süsterhenn's often theologically inspired (and divisive) interventions, see Christoph von Hehl, *Adolf Süsterhenn (1905–1974): Verfassungsvater, Weltanschauungspolitiker, Föderalist* (Dusseldorf: Droste, 2012), pp. 364–425. On Brill, see especially Renate Knigge-Tesche and Peter Reif-Spirek, eds., *Hermann Louis Brill (1895–1959)* (Wiesbaden: Thrun, 2011).

17 Hans Lietzmann's argument that Carl Schmitt's ideas infused the founders of the Federal Republic is not convincing. None of the arguments that he brings up are original to Schmitt: The liberals' focus on presidential authority comes from Hugo Preuss and Max Weber, the idea of a Bundesrat combines both eighteenth-century ideas of a higher assembly with ideas of *Land* representation common to the ideas of John Adams, among many others, and the Constitutional Court's defense of a "free democratic basic order" is, first, positivized, second already present in Weimar-era legislation protecting the Republic, and third in any case anathema for Schmitt's presidentialism. Cf. Hans Lietzmann, "Vater der Verfassungsväter? Carl Schmitt und die Verfassungsgründung in der Bundesrepublik" in Hans Lietzmann and Klaus Hansen, eds., *Carl Schmitt und die Liberalismuskritik* (New York: Springer, 1988), pp. 107–18.

18 See especially Udi Greenberg, *The Weimar Century: German Émigrés and the Ideological Foundations of the Cold War* (Princeton: Princeton University Press, 2016), with further references.

19 *Parl. Rat,* vol. II, p. 93. Notably, Baade went on to compare Nazi rule to that of the Allied occupation authorities.

20 *Parl. Rat,* vol. II, p. 427. The subterranean arguments about Catholicism and National Socialism played in the background of the Parliamentary Council, where the leading constitutional thinker Adolf Süsterhenn (Rhineland-

Palatinate) was pushed aside as chair by Anton Pfeiffer, because of the former's proximity to authoritarian church circles and his acceptance of National Socialism in 1933 (followed by a growing distance from the regime by the mid-1930s): see von Hehl, Adolf *Süsterhenn*, pp. 62–102, 392–3, and the documentation of the role of the church hierarchy against the Center in Ernst-Wolfgang Böckenförde, "German Catholicism in 1933: A Critical Examination" (1961), reprinted in *Religion, Law, and Democracy: Selected Writings*, trans. Miriam Künkler and Tine Stein (New York: Oxford University Press, 2020), pp. 77–103.

21 That they focused on constitutional rules is obvious, since that was their job. Volker Otto's criticism of the Herrenchiemsee conference as involving a "one-sided conception of the constitution," namely the "constitution as instrument to provide order," thus strikes me as off base. See Volker Otto, *Das Staatsverständnis des Parlamentarischen Rates: Ein Beitrag zur Entstehungsgeschichte des Grundgesetzes für die Bundesrepublik Deutschland* (Dusseldorf: Droste, 1971), p. 37.

22 This conception was already addressed and developed in the Weimar Republic at both *Land* and national levels. See especially Christoph Gusy, *Die Weimarer Reichsverfassung* (Tübingen: Mohr/Siebeck, 1997), pp. 133, 229, 449. This concept of a constructive vote of no confidence was notably central to the Social Democrats' attempt, under Prime Minister Otto Braun, to save German democracy by stabilizing Prussia – a democratic notion of Prussia's "mission" to save Germany, as pointed out in the famous book by Hagen Schulze, *Otto Braun, oder Preussens demokratische Sendung* (Frankfurt: Propyläen, 1977), chapter 6.

23 The liberal representative from Bremen, Theodor Spitta, a former Democrat, was nearly alone among the delegates in supporting a strong president on the Weimar model: Werner, "Einleitung," *Parl. Rat*, vol. II, p. xxvi, citing Spitta's 1960 memoirs. Others in the FDP leadership also harbored this support for a presidential system: see Schmid, *Erinnerungen*, pp. 365, 383. On Heuss, see Wolfgang Wiedner, *Theodor Heuss: Das Demokratie- und Staatsverständnis im Zeitablauf* (Ratingen: Henn, 1973), pp. 130–56, especially p. 138. Fears that an unstable parliament would require a strong president could be found across the party spectrum: Peter Rütters, "Direkte Wahl des Bundespräsidenten: Sehnsucht nach präsidentieller Obrigkeit?," *Zeitschrift für Parlamentsfragen* 44 (2013), pp. 276–95; Morsey, "Die Debatte."

24 This is summed up in Feldkamp, *Der Parlamentarische Rat*, p. 31; Martin Borowski, "The Beginnings of Germany's Federal Constitutional Court," *Ratio Juris* 16 (2003), p. 159.

25 Erhard H. M. Lange, *Wahlrecht und Innenpolitik: Entstehungsgeschichte und Analyse der Wahlgesetzgebung und Wahlrechtsdiskussion im westlichen Nachkriegsdeutschland 1945–1956* (Meisenheim am Glan: Anton Hain, 1975), pp. 223–32.

26 See Feldkamp, *Der Parlamentarische Rat*, pp. 70–2, 103–4.

27 *Parl. Rat*, vol. II, p. 146 (Baade). Notably, Carlo Schmid had similar thoughts about a senate: Schmid, *Erinnerungen*, p. 344.

28 *Parl. Rat*, vol. II, p. 152 (Schmid); the language comes directly from Hermann Heller's political writings. The critique of parties was part of a longer discourse, reaching from the far right to liberals such as Max Weber, about the danger of democracy to the national interest.

29 The Bavarian draft reproduced in *Parl. Rat*, vol. I, pp. 1–52, here Articles 49 and 51 (pp. 19–20); see *Parl. Rat*, vol. II, pp. 157–8 (Leusser). Leusser and Hans Nawiasky developed the draft.

30 This was clearly noted in the further elaboration of the plan: *Parl. Rat*, vol. II, pp. 282, 297–8 (report of the subcommittee); pp. 404–5 (comment by Gustav von Schmoller).

31 *Parl. Rat*, vol. II, p. 158 (Schwalber).

32 There is a sympathetic reading of Luther in connection with antiparty politics in Hans Mommsen, *The Rise and Fall of Weimar Democracy* (Chapel Hill: University of North Carolina Press, 1996), pp. 191–7.

33 *Parl. Rat*, vol. II, p. 163 (Küster).

34 *Parl. Rat*, vol. II, pp. 164–5 (Schmid). For this argument, see Kurt Sontheimer, *Antidemokratisches Denken in der Weimarer Republik: Die politischen Ideen des deutschen Nationalismus zwischen 1918 und 1933* (Munich: Nymphenburger Verlags-Handlung, 1962).

35 *Parl. Rat*, vol. II, pp. 166–68 (Schmid).

36 *Parl. Rat*, vol. II, pp. 167, 169 (Schmid).

37 *Parl. Rat*, vol. II, p. 171 (Baade).

38 Notably these different reform ideas and different motivations were already present in the Weimar Republic, and were extensively debated in the 1946–7 constitutional conversations in the southern states: Ullrich, *Der Weimar-Komplex*, pp. 178–9, 213–17.

39 At first, however, Schmid denied that such a position could even be considered so long as Germany was occupied by foreign military powers; such a position would lack majesty: *Parl. Rat*, vol. II, p. 125.

40 *Parl. Rat*, vol. I, p. 22 (Article 57 of the Bavarian draft); *Parl. Rat*, vol. II, p. 328, para. 55 of the Herrenchiemsee working draft. This proposal fit with a broader range of thought, reaching from the conservatives and liberals into the SPD, in favor of emergency powers. On the broader discussion, see especially Karrin Hanshew, *Terror and Democracy in West Germany* (New York: Cambridge University Press, 2012), pp. 43–52.

41 *Parl. Rat*, vol. II, p. 281.

42 *Parl. Rat*, vol. II, pp. 326, 419–20 (Nawiasky).

43 *Parl. Rat*, vol. II, pp. 421–2 (Küster and Nawiasky); see also Nawiasky's historical description of the misuse of emergency laws before 23 March in Hans Nawiasky and Claus Leusser, *Die Verfassung des Freistaates Bayern vom 2. Dezember 1946* (Munich: Biederstein, 1948), pp. 267–73. Nawiasky was not, however, opposed to a much stronger president, and he directly influenced the Bavarian constitution in this respect, as noted by Ullrich, *Der Weimar-Komplex*, p. 222.

44 *Parl. Rat*, vol. II, p. 422 (Schmid).

45 *Parl. Rat*, vol. II, pp. 424–5 (Schmid).

46 Hans Luther had already laid this problem out clearly on 5 October 1948, before the voting law committee – calling, however, for the retention of

Article 48: *Parl. Rat*, vol. VI, pp. 173–4. See especially Friedrich Karl Fromme, *Von der Weimarer Verfassung zum Bonner Grundgesetz: Die verfassungspolitische Folgerungen des Parlamentarischen Rates aus Weimarer Republik und nationalsozialistischer Diktatur* (Tübingen: Mohr/Siebeck, 1960), pp. 123–30. It is notable how the entire section on emergency decrees was subject to extensive revision, becoming longer and longer – before being mostly removed from the constitutional draft (see the draft documents dealing with the original Article 11 in *Parl. Rat*, vol. VII). See also Hanshew, *Terror and Democracy*, pp. 51–2. Article 81 is a complex document trying to solve multiple problems simultaneously; it also has been of little practical relevance in the constitutional history of the Federal Republic. Christoph Schönberger, "Parlamentarische Autonomie unter Kanzlervorbehalt?" *Juristen-Zeitung* 57 (2002), pp. 211–19.

47 It was unclear what powers the Parliamentary Council had to create voting laws within the framework created by the military governors, an issue that would return as the Basic Law itself was approved in April–May 1949, as noted below. On the complex debate, see Lange, *Wahlrecht und Innenpolitik*, part 2; Lange, "Der Parlamentarische Rat," pp. 285–7; *Parl. Rat*, vol. II, p. 368 (Küster).

48 Schmid, *Erinnerungen*, p. 396. See also Süsterhenn's speech at the first plenary session, clearly stating the CDU's support for a relative majority system: *Parl. Rat*, vol. IX, p. 59. Lange, however, notes the many different positions in the CDU/CSU as a whole, based on regional considerations – especially with the challenges of the CSU's losses in early 1948 – and that Kroll was not entirely in line with his party: Lange, "Der Parlamentarische Rat," pp. 293–5. In much greater detail, see Lange, *Wahlrecht und Innenpolitik*, pp. 189–223, especially p. 344. For how the division on voting laws remained for the entire period, see Rainer Salzmann, ed., *Die CDU/CSU Fraktion im Parlamentarischen Rat: Sitzungsprotokolle der Unionsfraktion* (Stuttgart: Klett und Cotta, 1981), pp. 26–7, 35–6, 76, 542.

49 The parties were also acutely aware of the divisions: the CDU/CSU faction estimated that there was a 20:7 majority among SPD representatives in favor of proportional voting, and considered Baade a "fanatical adherent of majority voting" (Süsterhenn): Salzmann, *Die CDU/CSU Fraktion im Parlamentarischen Rat*, pp. 36, 464.

50 Lange, "Der Parlamentarische Rat," pp. 295–8; Lange, *Wahlrecht und Innenpolitik*, pp. 231–58, 290–7 (on the dramatic shift to proportional representation among liberals such as Heuss after 1948); Werner, "Einleitung," *Parl. Rat*, vol. VI, pp. xxvii–xxx. Schmid is clear about the way arguments about voting laws were a reflection of party interests: Schmid, *Erinnerungen*, pp. 396–7.

51 *Parl. Rat*, vol. VI, pp. 4–26.

52 *Parl. Rat*, vol. VI, pp. 37–40.

53 *Parl. Rat*, vol. VI, pp. 164–85. Luther praised parties – but only responsible ones, which he thought could be produced only through relative majority vote. Notably authoritarian populist leaders have often been elected by relative majority votes, as more recent examples in Mexico, the United States, and Venezuela show, a point that did not come up in the discussion.

54 See his description in Werner, "Einleitung," *Parl. Rat*, vol. VI, pp. xiv–xv; Rudolf Uertz, "Gerhard Kroll (1910–1963): Landrat, Bayern," biography on the Konrad-Adenauer Stiftung website at www.kas.de/c/document_library/get_file?uuid=b09d4634-80d7-11d6-3fa2-b1af5b8f5199&groupId=252038; Metzler, *Der Staat der Historiker*, pp. 67–71 (connecting him to the conservative Abendland organization).

55 See, for example, Kroll's statement before the Parliamentary Council's plenary session of 21 October 1948: an "excess of formal freedom" helped tyranny to power in the case of the Weimar Republic: *Parl. Rat*, vol. IX, pp. 288, 290; see also comments by Brentano (CDU), on pp. 327–32, claiming that Hitler could not have achieved power without proportional representation, and that totalitarian systems come out of such systems. Kroll did eventually propose a system that would involve roughly 86 percent of representatives to be elected by relative majority and 14 percent by proportional vote: Lange, *Wahlrecht und Innenpolitik*, p. 348.

56 Plenary session of 24 February 1949: *Parl. Rat*, vol. XI, pp. 333–4 (Schmid), 335–9 (Heuss), 349–50 (Renner). Heuss himself, like many in the SPD as well, had shifted from support for majority voting to proportional upon considering the effects on his Free Democrats: Joachim Radkau, *Theodor Heuss* (Munich: Carl Hanser, 2013), p. 311. On Renner's role in the Parliamentary Council, see Günter Gleising, *Heinz Renner: Eine politische Biographie* (Bochum: RuhrEcho, 2000), chapter 6.

57 Gerhard Kroll, *Grundlagen abendländischer Erneuerung: Das Manifest der abendländerischen Aktion* (Munich: Neues Abendland, 1951).

58 Salzmann, *Die CDU/CSU Fraktion im Parlamentarischen Rat*, p. 403.

59 See especially the arguments of Helene Wessel (Center) against any such limit, especially in the first elections to the new representative assembly, in *Parl. Rat*, vol. VI, pp. 385–6 (28 October 1948), 443 (2 December 1948), 653–4 (1 February 1949).

60 Lange, "Der Parlamentarische Rat," pp. 303–5; Lange, *Wahlrecht und Innenpolitik*, pp. 362–80. Lange notes also the different explanations for the military's decision, in particular the French attempt to slow the process of state-formation and put a lid on national parties. As Adenauer pointed out to party members, if CDU/CSU *Länder* implemented a relative majority system, then SPD *Länder* would have to do so as well to avoid diffusing their votes; the CDU/CSU position developed in part with the help of a "mathematician committee" that calculated as precisely as possible how many votes would be gained under different systems. The military governors were quite likely unaware of these possible effects.

61 *Parl. Rat*, vol. VI, pp. xxxii–xxxvi; *Parl. Rat*, vol. IX, p. xxix; Feldkamp, *Der Parlamentarischer Rat*, pp. 89–93; Benz, *Auftrag Demokratie*, pp. 436–9; Lange, "Der Parlamentarische Rat," pp. 315–18; Lange, *Wahlrecht und Innenpolitik*, pp. 381–407; Rudolf Morsey, "Die letzte Krise im Parlamentarischen Rat und ihre Bewältigung (März/April 1949)" in Dieter Schwab et al., eds., *Staat, Kirche, Wissenschaft in einer pluralistischen Gesellschaft* (Berlin: Duncker und Humblot, 1989), pp. 393–410.

62 Of the many accounts of this often veiled debate and its political and scholarly contexts, see especially Thomas Etzemüller, *Sozialgeschichte als politische*

Geschichte: Werner Conze und die Neuorientierung der westdeutschen Geschichtswissenschaft nach 1945 (Munich: Oldenbourg, 2001), pp. 108–11; Metzler, *Der Staat der Historiker*, chapter 5; Ullrich, *Der Weimar-Komplex*, pp. 583–613.

63 Karl Dietrich Bracher, "Parteienstaat, Präsidialsystem, Notstand: Zum Problem der Weimarer Staatskrise," *Politische Vierteljahresschrift* 3 (1962), p. 213. On Bracher, see especially Horst Müller, "Karl Dietrich Bracher zum Gedenken," *Vierteljahreshefte für Zeitschichte* 65 (2017), pp. 103–13.

64 See especially Götz Aly, "Theodor Schieder, Werner Conze oder Die Vorstufen der physischen Vernichtung," putting them in the same group with other intellectuals who provided the "scholarly" background for genocide, and the critical but more differentiated tone of Wolfgang Mommsen, "Vom 'Volkstumkampf' zur nationalsozialistischen Vernichtungspolitik in Osteuropa: Zur Rolle der deutschen Historiker unter dem Nationalsozialismus," both in Winfried Schulze and Otto Gerhard Oexle, eds., *Deutsche Historiker im Nationalsozialismus* (Frankfurt: Fischer, 1999), especially pp. 163, 172–8, 187, 192, 204, 210.

65 It was also, of course, a debate about the entire tradition of German historical writing, in particular its tendency to close itself off from social science interventions and to put the "state" at the center of the story. Notably, however, both Bracher and Conze were engaged in this transformative work – Bracher in moving from the hypostatized state to rules, processes, and interests in government; Conze in his consistent focus on the transformation from agricultural to industrial, rural to urban societies. A good reading of Conze – filling in the blank spaces – in Irmline Veit-Brause, "Werner Conze (1910–1986): The Measure of History and the Historian's Measures" in Van Horn Melton, *Paths of Continuity*, pp. 299–343; on Bracher's methodology, see Ullrich, *Der Weimar-Komplex*, pp. 595–8.

66 Carl Schmitt, *The Crisis of Parliamentary Democracy*, trans. Allen Kennedy (Cambridge, MA: MIT Press, 1988), first German ed. 1923. The critique of "parliamentary absolutism" and party rule preexisted Schmitt's work and was popular across the right: see Ullrich, *Der Weimar-Komplex*, pp. 167–77, with further references.

67 Werner Conze, "Die Krise des Parteienstaates in Deutschland 1929–30," *Historische Zeitschrift* 178 (1954), pp. 48, 52–7, 66, 68, 74. Notably, the trade unions had attempted (and failed) to introduce aspects of "economic democracy" into the Basic Law during the Parliamentary Council's proceedings, and the question of how much codetermination was controversial in the first years of the Federal Republic; it is hard not to see Conze's negative view of the SPD in the Weimar Republic as applying to his understanding of the party in the Federal Republic. For context, see Wolfgang Benz, *Auftrag Demokratie: The Gründungsgeschichte der Bundesrepublik und die Entstehung der DDR 1945–1949* (Berlin: Metropol, 2009), pp. 390–2; Peter C. Caldwell, *Democracy, Capitalism, and the Welfare State: Debating Social Order in Postwar West Germany, 1949–1989* (New York: Oxford University Press, 2019), chapter 2.

68 Karl Dietrich Bracher, *Die Auflösung der Weimarer Republik: Eine Studie zum Problem des Machtverfalls in der Demokratie* (Stuttgart: Ring, 1955), pp. 192–5, 262, 267–9, 271.
69 Bracher, *Die Auflösung*, pp. 222–3, 274; cf. Conze, "Die Krise des Parteienstaates," 56, for his positive model of the German Empire, and his defense of the Empire in his review of Bracher's *Die Auflösung* in *Historische Zeitschrift* 183 (1957), p. 381.
70 Bracher, "Parteienstaat," pp. 215–24.
71 Cf. the review essay by Erdmann written before Bracher's book appeared: Karl Dietrich Erdmann, "Die Geschichte der Weimarer Republik als Problem der Wissenschaft," *Vierteljahrshefte für Zeitgeschichte* 3 (1955), pp. 1–19 – none of the works cited there are part of contemporary discussions, while Bracher and Conze are. On Erdmann's statist conservatism, see Ullrich, *Der Weimar-Komplex*, pp. 573–7, 585–8; see also the analysis of Hindenburg's authoritarian personality *and* the statist, antiparliamentary, and anti-SPD politics it entailed, especially the portrait in Horst Müller, *Die Weimarer Republik: Demokratie in der Krise* (Munich: Piper, 2018), pp. 69–97.
72 On the critics, including Werner Weber, Ernst Forsthoff, and Rüdiger Altmann, see Hanshew, *Terror and Democracy*, pp. 52–7. Carl Schmitt notably praised Conze's work on Weimar in a letter to Conze from 1960 quoted in Jan Eike Dunkhase, *Werner Conze: Ein deutscher Historiker im 20. Jahrhundert* (Göttingen: Vandenhoeck und Ruprecht, 2010), pp. 222–7, with further references.
73 See the essays in Michael N. Dobkowski and Isador Walliman, *Radical Perspectives on the Rise of Fascism in Germany, 1919–1945* (New York: Monthly Review Press, 1989), with further references.
74 Dunkhase, *Werner Conze*, p. 224.
75 For a recent example, see Claire Greenstein and Brandon Tensley, "Why Does Germany Have Boring Politics? Good Institutions Thwart Radicalism," *Foreign Affairs*, 17 May 2017, www.foreignaffairs.com/articles/germany/2017-05-17/why-does-germany-have-boring-politics.
76 Adam Przeworski, *Crises of Democracy* (New York: Cambridge University Press, 2019), pp. 39–51.
77 Przeworski, *Crises of Democracy*, p. 133.
78 See, e.g., Karl Dietrich Bracher, "Problems of Orientation in Germany's Liberal Democracy" in *Turning Points in Modern Times: Essays on German and European History*, trans. Thomas Dunlap (Cambridge, MA: Harvard University Press, 1995), pp. 246–8. Michael Stolleis presents a far less alarmist view of the same period, stressing the way in which the Greens revealed the German political system's capacity for renewal: Michael Stolleis, *Parteienstaatlichkeit – Krisensymptome des demokratischen Verfassungsstaats?* Veröffentlichung der Vereinigung der Deutschen Staatsrechtslehrer, vol. 44 (Berlin: de Gruyter, 1986), pp. 8–45.
79 Jan-Werner Müller, *A Dangerous Mind: Carl Schmitt in Post-War European Thought* (New Haven: Yale University Press, 2003).
80 Christian Thoma, "Panikwort W.," *Frankfurter Rundschau*, 8 February 2019, www.fr.de/kultur/timesmager/panikwort-11742766.html; see also Rütters, "Direkte Wahl."

81 Alternative für Deutschland, *Programm für Deutschland* (2017), 9 ("Macht der Parteien beschränken"), 40 ("Gender-Ideologie ist verfassungsfeindlich"), www.afd.de/wp-content/uploads/sites/111/2017/06/2017-06-01_AfD-Bundestagswahlprogramm_Onlinefassung.pdf.
82 See, e.g., Ursula Büttner, *Weimar: Die überfordete Republik* (Stuttgart: Klett-Cotta, 2008); Andreas Wirsching, Berthold Kohler, and Ulrich Wilhelm, eds., *Weimarer Verhältnisse: Lektionen der Weimarer Republik für unsere Demokratie* (Stuttgart: Reklam, 2018); Müller, *Die Weimarer Republik*, pp. 287–91, which stresses the combination of a surreptitious presidentialism and multiple ideological attacks on the notion of democracy itself.
83 Przeworski, *Crises of Democracy*, pp. 188–91.
84 That said, even this strategic use of an analogy might be used sincerely, for example if one believed, as many in the CDU/CSU did, that the Social Democrats would undermine democracy.

4 The Paradigmatic Example of Weimar and Postwar Political Science
The Case of Otto Kirchheimer

Peter Breiner

> ... all political concepts, images, and terms have a polemical meaning. They are focused on a specific conflict and are bound to a concrete situation: the result (which manifests itself in war or revolution) is a friend–enemy grouping, and they turn into empty and ghostlike abstractions when this situation disappears.
>
> Carl Schmitt, *The Concept of the Political*[1]

> The Marxist theory of the state could never therefore be harmonized with a mode of understanding that took as the departure point for political and constitutional discussions the a priori knowledge of matters of state and society beyond and independent of concrete social experience.
>
> Otto Kirchheimer, "Verfassungsreform und Sozial Demokratie" [Constitutional Reform and Social Democracy][2]

The émigré political scientists and theorists of public law from Weimar brought a perspective to the United States that often translated oddly once it was imported into American political science. This chapter focuses on one of the most significant of these émigrés, the great Weimar émigré political scientist Otto Kirchheimer, and the way in which he translated his account of the constitutional crisis of the Weimar Republic into mainstream political science. Kirchheimer, as is well known, was deeply steeped in the political debates over the Weimar Constitution, as a theorist of constitutions, party politics, and parliaments and as a fiercely committed democratic socialist. For him, the Weimar Republic became an exemplar of the potential (though unrealized) of combining "constituent power" based on popular sovereignty with a democratically elected parliament directly transmitting the popular will. However, it also became an exemplar of an unresolvable tension between, on the one hand, a liberal constitutional framework with no clearly defined principle of sovereignty, and, on the other, capitalism along with its attendant struggle of classes and the political parties through which that struggle took place. Among the many dilemmas the Weimar Republic represented for him, the most significant one was what a socialist party committed to democracy should do when the other parties and classes defect from a liberal democratic constitutional framework.

Through multiple articles, Kirchheimer laid out how in the absence of a will by the socialist parties to impose a socialist version of popular sovereignty in conjunction with a representative parliament, constitutional decision-making would be displaced to the executive, the administration of the state, and the courts, opening the way to dictatorship. The fundamental problem that Weimar raised for him was how to produce a form of political opposition in which these outcomes could be avoided and in which a democratic socialist state might be advanced.

Once in America, Kirchheimer became a major political scientist of parties, parliaments, and political opposition, but political science neatly retranslated his major work into support for a liberal democratic model in which political competition among parties, political elites, and interest groups produced a regime that was self-correcting and de-ideologized despite the fact that Kirchheimer understood his work to be raising the old Weimar questions under new postwar conditions.

This chapter seeks to examine how Kirchheimer constructed his account of the struggle of the Social Democratic Party of Germany to redirect the Weimar Constitution into a model of socialist democracy and how the outcome of this failed struggle contained in Weimar provided him with an exemplary lesson on how the logic of liberal democracy could spawn a shift of authority to administration and the courts and eventually to dictatorship. At the core of this account is Kirchheimer's insistence that constitutions must be understood in terms of the sociology of power within which these constitutions must operate rather than as an exclusive focus on a priori legal structure and reform. With this account in mind, I also examine how American political science turned Kirchheimer's powerful left criticism of the logics of liberal democracy based on the Weimar example into support for that very political form by redefining the Weimar example itself into a dangerous warning of what can happen if we do not accept a liberal pluralist regime. This move left the force of Kirchheimer's criticism and the complex meaning of the Weimar example blunted, though still relevant. Focusing on Kirchheimer's continuous preoccupation with sustaining a left political opposition against its neutralization by the liberal parliamentary state, we see a continuity between his Weimar work and his influential postwar political science, even though this work was often reinterpreted in a way that was at odds with its meaning. At the end, I argue that his original argument forged in the crucible of the Weimar Republic continues to have the critical force that American political science had so attenuated.

The Weimar Republic as Paradigmatic Example

In discussing the way in which Kirchheimer's interpretation of the Weimar example carries over into his postwar political science and its peculiar reception in the United States, I am not treating Weimar as a constitutional problem of the rule of law, as does William Scheuerman;[3] nor am I contextualizing his critical arguments on the Weimar Constitution within the intertwined dialogue among the social democratic public law theorists seeking to insert a robust concept of popular sovereignty into its constitutional structure, as does Peter Caldwell.[4] Both of these scholars have mapped out these debates with acuity and force. Rather, I am treating the Weimar Republic as political theorists (and political scientists) of this period and thereafter treated it: as a paradigmatic example that teaches political lessons on the deficiencies of liberal democracy and parliamentary procedure within the routine business of party politics. What I mean here by a paradigmatic example is the deployment of an historical example for constructing political conjunctures and providing political foresight. Paradigmatic examples are similar to the way in which political analogies function to guide (and also obscure) future choices, as indeed was the case of Weimar, as Peter Caldwell points out in his chapter (Chapter 3). But I would like to specify one characteristic of a paradigmatic example that moves beyond being a mere analogy, even one used authoritatively.

A paradigmatic example, as I use it here, reverses the relationship between a generalization and its instantiation. This means that the example becomes the source of both the characteristics of the generalizations drawn from it, especially with regards to present dangers and opportunities for future action, and predictions of future political developments. Analogies draw similarities between cases that share certain determinate characteristics but not others. Paradigmatic examples contain all the relevant characteristics the theorist wants to emphasize. They contain the lessons for the present or the future. Examples of this kind may be stylized – indeed, they most often are – including over-emphasizing, and even distorting, certain features of the situation or period at the expense of others in order to generate prudential lessons for the future. But this does not render examples of this kind any less authoritative or useful. On the contrary, the example may generate a particular arrangement of political forces or political ideas that are only potentially present and may factually be at odds with the actual present. In this way, the paradigmatic example allows counterfactual judgments to be drawn regarding possibilities for action that were overlooked or not taken advantage of. In fact, paradigmatic examples, precisely because they are a stylized perspective on an historical case, allow us to see a particular political arrangement or a particular alignment of political-ideological forces as containing counterfactual possibilities that an immersion in the case in all its complexity might obscure.

What interests me here in treating the Weimar Republic as a paradigmatic example is the way in which political thinkers stylized its political-ideological field of conflict – especially in the alignment of political-ideological forces and institutions – and constitutional arrangements to draw political lessons for the revival of politics in a situation in which the very possibility of politics was threatened. The Weimar Republic is a unique case of political theorizing because writers and commentators on its constitutional form, politics, and culture already knew in the midst of it that it would be a paradigmatic example from which to draw lessons for the future. But, not surprisingly, they differed markedly on what it was an example of.

Here, I focus on the case of the political scientist, Otto Kirchheimer, and the way his construction of the Weimar political conjuncture through a critical account of its constitution and its parliamentary system becomes a paradigmatic example from which at least four intertwined political lessons are derived. First, precisely in contrast to its constitutional framework in which a parliament of incompatible political forces prevents democratic legislation, the Weimar Constitution allows Kirchheimer to offer a potential model of what a genuinely democratic socialist form of constitution might look like – one that connects a popular will to a parliament that legislates.

Second, it allows him to show how the failure to forge a political opposition (of the left) when one or more of the parties to a democratic constitution are antidemocratic unleashes a hidden logic in which a constitutional equilibrium of incompatible political forces shifts all political power and decision-making to the state administration and the courts with eventually dictatorship as its default outcome. As we will see, modern liberal democracy is not immune from this logic.

Third, the Weimar conjuncture as constructed by Kirchheimer allows him to demonstrate that ultimately constitutions embody a particular form of society and embody a decision for that society; therefore, viewing them purely through the logic of public law overlooks the entwinement of constitutions with their sociological setting and the relation of law to distributions of social power. This relationship explains why what seems to be a negotiated compromise among sharply disagreeing parties can lead to either the loss of legislative authority as an expression of a public will or a dissipation of political mobilization of citizens.

Finally, the politics of the Weimar Republic becomes, again by its negative example, an illustration of what a proper political opposition of the left would look like tested against different constitutional arrangements.

I argue here that Kirchheimer's version of the Weimar example seeks to break through two conflicting but influential contemporaneous examples: first, and most significantly, that of Carl Schmitt, for whom Weimar is the occasion to intensify a politics of extremity in order to recover the struggle for sovereignty among irreconcilable political principles – in particular, the principles of democracy, liberal parliamentarism, and dictatorship – from their collapse into the anodyne compromises of parliamentary democracy; second, though less direct, that of Karl Mannheim, for whom the Weimar political-ideological conjuncture provided an opportunity for trying to forge a political science enabling dialogue among the contending positions. In this case, Kirchheimer uses Mannheim's account of political ideology to criticize Schmitt's existential view of political principles but ignores Mannheim's aim of using it to construct the Weimar field of conflicting and incommensurable political ideologies so that they all might gain insight from one another over the features of political reality they share in common and to which they are blind.[5]

I further argue that Kirchheimer's Weimar-forged alternative to these two conflicting exemplars of Weimar politics did not end in 1945. Rather, it continued to inform his influential postwar political science of parties and political opposition. This work, I argue, used the lessons he drew from the Weimar exemplar to criticize the forms of de-ideologized party politics and loss of contentious mass mobilization typical of postwar liberal democratic regimes – regimes that, ironically, mainstream political science cheerfully took to be a positive escape from the dreaded example of the politics of Weimar. Indeed, I argue that mainstream postwar political science mistakenly incorporated Kirchheimer's rigorously critical political science – especially his famous notion of the "catch-all party" – into their claims that modern competitive party and pluralist political systems had successfully overcome the debilities of Weimar polarization. However, at the end we will see that Kirchheimer's critical interests in the forces of depoliticization and the loss of opposition have robustly survived this redefinition. Indeed, his Weimar lesson on how liberal democratic constitutions can turn into their very opposite without a proper form of political opposition continues to resonate in the present.

Act I: Clearing Ground – Replacing Schmitt's Weimar Example Using Mannheim

As part of forging his own account of the authoritative meaning of both the Weimar Constitution and the Weimar political-ideological field, Kirchheimer takes aim at one of the most authoritative accounts of the larger meaning of the politics of Weimar – that of his teacher and mentor Carl Schmitt – while deploying the theory of ideology of a more kindred spirit seeking to forge a new political science of competing political ideologies, Karl Mannheim. Carl Schmitt posed the greater challenge, as Kirchheimer incorporated into his own account of a constitutional political science his teacher's concept of sovereignty as a decision while rejecting Schmitt's fundamental claim that parliamentary democracy is a self-contradictory concept both in principle and in practice because it is merely a legal form of political process lacking any claim to legitimacy.[6] Viewed through its existential rather than political-sociological origins, Schmitt claims, the legitimacy of parliamentary institutions rests on the liberal principle of openness of discussion and balanced opposition, along with legislation issuing from argument and counter-argument immune from the influence of popular will. The existential principle of democracy, by contrast, is based on the unitary, homogeneous will of the people expressed through the arbitrary decision of the majority, which requires the exclusion of minorities.[7]

Schmitt forges this principle of radical democracy from a very stylized account of Rousseau's general will in which popular sovereignty lacks debate or any internal principles that shape decision-making outside of majority rule. For Schmitt to combine these two existential principles into a constitutional legal form of "parliamentary democracy" is a dilution of both into professional politics and routine bargaining. The Weimar Constitution, for Schmitt, is the paradigmatic example of this dilution of the conflict among fundamental political principles of legitimacy into a constitutional form of legality bereft of any substantive claim to legitimacy.[8] This conclusion rests on Schmitt's methodological claim that the conceptual contradiction in the constitution – liberalism versus democracy – is necessarily a contradiction in the reality of its functioning.[9]

In "Remarks on Carl Schmitt's 'Legality and Legitimacy,'" Kirchheimer attacks this claim about the Weimar Constitution from many angles. But his central argument rotates around restoring the *potentiality* within that constitution for rendering compatible the principles of popular sovereignty and parliamentary democracy – even if in other writings he demonstrates that the reality of its functioning, an irresolvable struggle between bourgeois and socialist democracy, teaches us very much the opposite. Against Schmitt's notion of democracy as requiring a homogeneous society of equal individuals producing a homogeneous popular will based simply on the (arbitrary) will of the majority, Kirchheimer argues that this formula misunderstands the relation of majority rule and political freedom. Majority rule in a democracy requires an equal distribution of political rights among citizens – the right to vote and the right to equal access to public office – and is only intelligible if it is connected to the enjoyment of political freedom as an agreement between the uncoerced "will formation among citizens" and the will of government. The rights that Schmitt associates with liberalism against democracy – freedom of the press, opinion, assembly, and association – are enabling rights to democratic will formation.[10] No such notion of "democratic will formation" reflected in the will of the government is to be found in Schmitt, Kirchheimer maintains, because Schmitt associates democracy with equality but not with the political freedom enjoyed by equal citizens.

Kirchheimer then shifts his attack from Schmitt's conflicting existential principles to the Schmittean empirical claim that democracy cannot be realized in a heterogeneous society because, in such a society, democratic will formation leading to universal laws applying to all citizens is impossible. Kirchheimer argues that this claim is empirically not true. In some countries, despite class conflict and contending political ideologies, it is still possible through the equalization of political rights of citizenship to produce democratic will formation. In other states, however, the very demand for homogeneity when tied to nationalism can be and is used to limit the electorate to a portion of the nation, leaving out classes and groups that ostensibly do not belong.[11]

More importantly, Kirchheimer invokes against Schmitt Mannheim's famous redefinition of ideological false consciousness as the existence of political ideas that are not adapted to major changes in social structure but instead either harken back to a world that no longer exists or project a world not yet in existence. Schmitt's notion that democracy needs homogeneity both seeks a return to conditions long superseded by sociopolitical developments and projects into the future conditions that are not yet realized or realizable.[12] Mannheim's concept of false consciousness as the tendency of political ideologies to fail to make a realistic assessment of possibilities in a "changed and dynamic reality" and to overstate what is possible serves Kirchheimer well in undermining Schmitt's claim that democracy, as a matter of realism, requires homogeneity, and thus genuine democracy under the Weimar Constitution is impossible.[13] Using Mannheim, Kirchheimer is able to make the claim that Schmitt's dichotomy between democracy as a homogeneous popular will and parliament as a kind of Burkean realm of free and unconstrained debate based on the best argument represents a set of political ideas that are maladapted to a dynamic sociological and historical reality. He thus replaces Schmitt's claim that modern parliaments with conflicting political parties represent a dissipation of the existential struggle between two completely incompatible principles of politics – democracy and liberalism – with a sociological testing of principles in which popular sovereignty and parliamentarism representing the majority can be made constitutionally compatible – even if the Weimar Constitution failed to realize this potentiality.[14]

With the Mannheim standard in mind, Kirchheimer is now able to answer Schmitt's various empirical objections to the democratic credentials of the Weimar Constitution: first, Schmitt's claim that a state providing legally binding substantive material standards on schools or economic provision leads to instability and fragmentation; second, that parliaments cannot be democratic because elections to them do not give every citizen an equal chance to be part of the majority; and third, in light of these two objections, parliaments and direct democracy as the exercise of popular sovereignty are incompatible.[15] It is this last claim that Kirchheimer finds to be a thorough mischaracterization of the potential of the Weimar Constitution and of parliamentary democracy in general. First off, he argues that the state provision of social rights (in juristic language, "material legal norms") enhances the political rights of all citizens. Second, and even more significantly, he argues that if we understand the principle of equality to include the equal enjoyment of political rights through a democratic model guaranteeing one person one vote and unconstrained admission of all candidates and parties to the electoral arena, there is no fundamental distinction between "the unmediated expression of the popular will" and the norms of parliamentary decision-making, as Schmitt had argued.[16] With these constitutional criteria of will formation linking citizens to representative institutions, parliament and direct democracy are merely structurally "different organizational forms of the same type of organizational legitimacy." Thus, Kirchheimer concludes, the founding principles of the Weimar Constitution – the process of public discussion and voting as well as parliamentary discussion and decision-making – are both expressions of "constituent power."[17] This continuity between popular sovereignty and parliamentary decision-making reconciles democratic legitimacy with constitutional legality. Moreover, it is now adapted to the very heterogeneous political reality that, for Schmitt, must irrevocably sever democracy from parliamentarism and legitimacy from legality.

This vindication of the democratic claims of parliamentary democracy in the founding principles of the Weimar Constitution represents only the first act of Kirchheimer's reframing of the Weimar example. It allows Kirchheimer to eliminate Schmitt's attempt to render Weimar as a paradigmatic example of why parliamentary democracy represents both the failure of democracy and the failure of parliaments to live up to the existential demands of "the political." The second act introduces the sociological dynamics of the political struggle that leads to the failure of Weimar's democratic potential. In this account, he reverses course and incorporates Schmitt's famous argument that all constitutional forms require some agent to impose a principle of sovereignty. In agreement with Schmitt, he now understands this notion of sovereignty as indeed an irrevocably existential feature of political reality.

Act II: Kirchheimer's Version of the Weimar Political-Constitutional Conjuncture – Constitutions as Social Power and the Failure of the Left to Claim Political Sovereignty

Writing as a committed left democratic socialist, Kirchheimer now takes the Weimar Constitution and its political institutions in their actual rather than potential functioning. In their actual functioning they appear as paradigmatic of a self-defeating logic *within* existing liberal constitutional forms. And he finds this more general logic precisely in the unique historical failure of the Weimar Constitution to make good on its potential claim to combine political legitimacy through popular sovereignty with its legal structure. The constitution's lack of support from the political parties and interests that its legal structure was meant to adjudicate based on some governing principle of sovereignty, its attempt to contain the irreconcilable class interests of the bourgeois and the working classes as players within both its parliamentary institutions and the social structure outside of parliament, and the existence of a dictatorial moment within its procedures reveal for Kirchheimer a logic of politics always already present within even the seemingly more secure liberal states. And, in this case, following his mentor Schmitt, he seems to argue that we need an exceptional or extreme moment like that of Weimar to examine the functioning – or, more accurately, the failure – of sovereignty within ordinary functioning liberal constitutional states. This extreme moment of liberal constitutional fragmentation and breakdown also reveals a simultaneous crisis within the workers' movement and its parties.[18] Indeed, he understands this constitutional failure as a failure of the left to move from seeking constitutional reform to political opposition and eventually making a claim to political sovereignty.

Writing toward a political future that could have been but did not take place – recall his fusion of popular sovereignty with parliament – Kirchheimer treats the tensions within the Weimar Republic between its political functioning and the social forces seeking to operate within its structures as the paradigmatic example of a liberal constitution whose failure to solve the problem of political legitimacy should have forced the left to pivot from defending the constitution to learning to becoming a unified political opposition to it. Unfortunately, he argues, it was a lesson it failed to learn, allowing the dictatorial moment of sovereignty within liberal democracy to turn into outright dictatorship. His inquiry treats the constitution as a potential arena for the working class and its parties to make gains in their conflict with the bourgeois class through parliamentary legislation buttressed by the claim to represent genuine popular sovereignty. But the Weimar Constitution also serves him as the exemplar for the undermining of this possibility, because, following Schmitt, it never made a "decision" on who would have sovereignty or on the principle of political *Herrschaft* under which that sovereignty would be exercised. This problem for Kirchheimer appeared in two sequential forms: in the constitutional structure itself and in the political dynamics of the constitution within parliaments and between political parties.

As for the constitutional structure, Kirchheimer claims that every well-constructed constitution has to be the expression of a collective will that aspires to realize a collective consciousness seeking to master the necessities of a given historical reality and to free itself from them. And, for Kirchheimer, this development of a will to mastery or rule is a function of "the maturity of class consciousness."[19] Viewed this way, constitutions potentially are the harbingers of a principle of validity governing the condition of society's development at a particular moment. However, the Weimar Constitution, for Kirchheimer, is an exemplar of the very opposite: It was never the outgrowth of a collective will, seeking to express a distinctive account of developmental realities in society. Instead, it was a compromise between two antagonistic principles of democracy: a democracy based on capitalism and a democracy based on socialism. It thus never made a "decision" on whether the constitution would realize a capitalist or socialist democracy. Unlike Schmitt's and Mannheim's portrait of Weimar – as a struggle of multiple existential principles or incommensurable political ideologies respectively – Kirchheimer claims that the struggle of principles and the question of ultimate power in the Weimar Constitution was suspended, and in turn the political-ideological struggle remained unresolved between *two* principles and *two* groupings: the principle of capitalist private ownership and the principle of common ownership under socialism – that is, the working class and bourgeoisie. "The decision about which of these principles would have the ultimate decision on political rule [*das wirkliche herrschende Prinzip*] was left to the future."[20]

In the place of such a decision as to who and what principle would have ultimate sovereignty, on Kirchheimer's reading the constitution produced a "catalogue of basic rights" pulling in multiple directions – some justifying private ownership, some justifying the socialization of enterprises and land ownership.[21] This distinctive combination of a concatenation of rights and warring classes ending in a political stalemate and the absence of a principle of sovereignty becomes on his reading a paradigmatic example of the logic of the liberal state in general and the role of a unified political opposition of the left to overcome this logic in a new concept of democracy in particular.

These arguments, which are distributed through his many writing from the Weimar period, are pulled together in a distinctively intensified form – even a stylized form – in his influential piece from 1930: "Weimar – And What Next?" ("Weimar – Und Was Dann?").[22] It is in this work that he controversially reshapes the distinctive particularities of the Weimar Constitution, as a political and social arrangement, into a paradigmatic example of the deficiencies of liberal democracy understood from a democratic socialist viewpoint. And as the title suggests, he tries to address the dilemma of what to do now given that the constitution has become an empty shell of itself.

Curiously, more recent commentators have criticized this account of liberal democracy for embracing a Schmitt-inspired notion of socialist homogeneity as an answer to liberal failure, while others have criticized him for not deriving the logic of democracy from the contradictions of capitalist accumulation.[23] However, without his emphasis on socialism as a foundation for democracy and his emphasis on the generalizability of the political logic of the Weimar example, the argument loses its force. Here, I emphasize his democratic (socialist) criticism of liberal democracy at the core of the argument.

The strategy of this work is to appear to be a simple inventory of the different aspects of the Weimar Constitution. But every particular function that appears to be rooted in the German case and in German history is bent in the direction of a more general lesson regarding the space for political action within a liberal parliamentary democracy with a capitalist economy. Weimar appears merely as a case in which the operation of these lessons was intensified and tested over a very short and compressed timespan – it becomes a paradigmatic example precisely because it does *not* fit the model of an ideal functioning parliamentary democracy representing a popular will.

Kirchheimer begins his examination of Weimar by immediately treating it as a particular case of the more general problem: While present-day democracies are defined by the granting of universal suffrage, the latter does not make a state democratic. On the contrary, "the decisive problems of democracy are social in character."[24] Quoting Marx, he argues that real democracy is the equalization of social power in conjunction with universal suffrage, which is short-circuited under capitalism. Making no reference to Weimar at all, Kirchheimer then quotes the Austro-Marxist Max Adler to the effect that political democracy as rule by the people does not speak to the "economic power relationships" that under capitalism have come to determine whether modern constitutional states are democratic or not. Kirchheimer then updates Rousseau in arguing that political democracy as majority rule can be democratic *only* through a thorough realization of "social democracy" defined as a socialist community:

The principle of majority rule is comprehensible only with reference to that social homogeneity which incorporates the principle of a democratic value community in our time. Only in a society with a Socialist social structure do majority decisions not imply doing violence to those who are outvoted; here majority decision means only the application of attested technique for settling differences over which means are technically the best ones for achieving the principles which are adhered to by all.[25]

What provides the constitutional justification for dictatorial powers in constitutional regimes is the prevention of the demands for this translation of political democracy as universal suffrage into social democracy defined as decision-making over societal means using universal suffrage and the rights and institutions that attend to it. That is, given the threat of the equalization of social power within production and through cooperation in society, the famous Article 48 of the Reich Constitution granting the president emergency powers to suspend parliament and deal with threats to the political order is not a peculiarity of the Weimar Constitution but a necessary feature of all capitalist democracies that guarantee *only* universal suffrage. On this argument, liberal parliamentary democracy contains a logic of democracy as universal suffrage entwined with a logic of dictatorship when universal suffrage leads to a claim within parliaments to intervene in the prerogatives of capital. But the point at which one turns into the other is a contingent matter for each "bourgeois political democracy," Kirchheimer argues.

He then turns to the structure of the parliament under the Weimar Constitution. Interestingly, Kirchheimer does not address the parliament of Weimar as suffering a unique problem due to its late appearance historically. Rather, as we have already seen, he implicitly attacks Schmitt's stylization of the nineteenth-century parliament as occupying the role of a body of equal representatives selected by property ownership and engaged in open discussion and rational decision-making in opposition to radical democracy. Against Schmitt's already exaggerated picture, Kirchheimer argues that the unity of this model has dissolved in the twentieth century as parliament has now become an arena for economic power blocs; this applies in particular to capital and labor, which, through the vessel of political parties, have used parliamentary procedure to conduct a class struggle through peaceful means.[26] Likewise, elections are merely mathematical registers of that class struggle.[27] Kirchheimer's point is that the Weimar model is merely the inheritor of this development, not the result of some historical anomaly of its late development.

In discussing the basic rights (*Grundrechte*) of the Weimar Constitution, he once again subtracts the distinctive way in which the Weimar Constitution treats them from a more general discussion of the tension between such unconditional rights and the principles of democracy. Universal rights became instead a concatenation of group rights distributed according to the political power of each group. Equality under the law became a tool for legitimating inequality of property – a typical criticism of formal equality upholding substantive inequality insofar as it requires no redistribution or rectification. But Kirchheimer then draws a general point from the inadequate distribution and application of rights in Weimar:

In the early liberal era it [equality before the law] served as a defense against administrative arbitrariness, in the advanced capitalist period it serves as a guarantee of the existing social order, and in the socialist era it will serve to establish a basis of economic equality. It is only through clarifying its function with any given social order that the real significance of the clause of equality before the law can be revealed.[28]

Kirchheimer's point here is that a constitutional provision guaranteeing legal equality as an unconditional right depends on the way in which the social order distributes life chances and control over the production process and its products; and therefore it is the political sustenance or transformation of that order that gives substance to the legal principle. For him, the Weimar Constitution laid this point bare by *not* making a decision as to the social order, capitalist or socialist, to which its rights were to be applied: "[I]t grants equal status to capitalism, which seeks to perpetuate private property, and to socialism, which presupposes communal property. It tolerates private property but explicitly foresees the possibility of its transformation into communal property."[29] The consequence of this linkage of rights to social order, while keeping the two interpretations of rights in suspension, is that the existing social order of capitalism absorbs the right of socialization in the constitution by demanding indemnification for any expropriation of property and installing a corporatist model of relations between capital and labor unions. But again, from his socialist standpoint, Kirchheimer argues that the law guaranteeing the participation of labor via codetermination in large concentrated firms forestalled the workers ever achieving "a share in the control of the enterprises."[30] So the overall logic Kirchheimer finds here is a continuous displacement of these conflicting principles of capitalism and socialism rather than a decision as to what social order the Weimar Constitution is meant to realize.

Not surprisingly, when Kirchheimer turns to assess the functions of government in the Weimar Constitution, he discounts the relevance of the relationship of parliament to the chancellor and the cabinet, which he views as generic to most parliamentary systems that form governments. As with the application of rights, and even more so with the structure of the parliament, he argues, the exercise of governmental power is largely a "mirror" of ongoing "social relationships"; this is a recurrent point in all of his writing. This means – in an argument similar to arguments made today about corporate heads as unaccountable decision-makers over the economy – that economic policy and trade are increasingly determined by leaders of industry and production, rendering decisions more often than not at odds with the populations of the country.[31] Kirchheimer famously labels this area "the sphere of management" in which governments must adapt to "the laws of the existing capitalist order," a functional area in which government becomes responsible for decision-making made in the economy in response to the capitalist market. However, internally, governments also have authority over what he calls "the sphere of distribution." In exercising this function, governments must reconcile the conflicting demands of economic organizations with a particular focus on the shifting power relationships between capital and labor, but including all organized associations of economic actors.[32]

Not only do these two functions constrain what governments can do but they also circumvent shifts taking place during elections. The result is that the political success of a party of the working classes in parliament that would influence the sphere of distribution toward greater autonomy is reined in through the dependency of the sphere of distribution on the sphere of management. Hinting at his earlier argument that formal

political equality as universal suffrage under a liberal state within capitalism also has a dictatorial element built into it, Kirchheimer ominously
concludes that "the continuation of these tensions [between economic
power and distributive political functions] for the future is impossible.
No state can permanently sustain such disproportionalities."[33]

Only at the end of "Weimar – And What Next?" does he bring the
variety of general features of the liberal democratic state he has found in
the Weimar Constitution to bear on the distinctive problem of the relation of elections, parliament and the asymmetrical power relations
between capital and labor as they operate within the Weimar constitutional framework. In pursuing the political implications of the
Weimar Constitution as exemplar of the decay of parliament as the arena
for the pursuit of the class struggle, Kirchheimer does not separate its
formal legal structure from society and its power relations or from social
solidarity or a lack thereof. Instead, he argues that, just like any constitution, it should either be regarded as "an unconditional political decision" for a particular form of society or it signifies an (unstable)
"compromise of multiple political forces."[34] Indeed, in "Weimar – And
What Next?" he argues that every constitution that represents a transition
to a new political form, as was the case with the Weimar Constitution,
announces a program of action for the realization of a new social order.
However, the Weimar Constitution lacked any such program of action
and was in no position to provide one.[35] It was, in effect, a shell in which
completely incompatible and incommensurable conceptions of society
and politics were collected. And this rested on the fact that (in
Schmittean terms) it was a constitution without any "decision" as to
who had sovereignty. Instead, apart from all the different parties it was
intended to contain, he views it, as already mentioned, as representing an
impossible attempt to mediate between two conceptions of society:
bourgeois society and socialism.

Thus, in its unique weaknesses, the Weimar Constitution – viewed less
through a legal lens than as a political arrangement trying to contain the
political conflict between labor and capital – lays bare, for Kirchheimer,
*the inner logics of liberal democracy that better functioning versions of this
regime tend to hide.* And this logic contains both the possibility of the
parties of capital defecting from support for the democratic features of
this model, leaving social democracy to uphold the constitution against
its opponents, or of dictatorship filling the vacuum left by the failure to
solve the problem of sovereignty. Indeed, the transition to dictatorship
could be found in the emergency powers of Weimar that shifted the
decision-making power in the political system over the legitimacy of
parties and labor disputes from parliament to the state bureaucracy.[36]

The fragility of liberal democracy without a politically viable socialist alternative lies exposed.

Act III: The Problem of Left Opposition – Breaking the Stalemate and Seizing the Moment, Exercising Political Will

Already in his articles of 1929 "Das Problem der Verfassung" (The Problem of the Constitution) and "Verfassungswirklichkeit und politische Zukunft der Arbeiterklasse" (Constitutional Reality and the Political Future of the Working Class), Kirchheimer reveals that his examination of the Weimar Constitution is not ultimately a defense of the rule of law; rather, it is a criticism of the failure of political will on the part of the German Social Democratic Party seeking to buttress a failed (bourgeois) constitution. Rather than make a "decision" to meet the demands of the moment, the majority of the party sought to uphold the status quo of a failed constitutional arrangement, even to the point of tolerating a dictatorship while other parties defected.[37] In his most stinging criticism, he accuses the Social Democrats of having "underestimated the significance of the will as a factor in the construction of a constitution."[38] Having seen everything that was promising in the Weimar Constitution dissolve, he argues (again as a committed democratic socialist), the lesson they should have drawn is "that only through an act of will can the space be created to bring a constitution that will realize a socialist reality."[39] "We must again learn how to will," he concludes. And this entails not trying out different means of constitutional reform, such as a direct election of the executive or appeals to popular referenda, but rather seeking "continuous cooperation of the social forces of a planned transformation of social relations," given, as argued in "Weimar – And What Next?," that every new constitution is also a plan for a distinctive social order.[40] And he ends that piece with the claim that "a socialist politics based on a knowledge of the grave fact that the gulf between these positions [polity and economy within the functioning of democratic constitutional institutions] is indeed unbridgeable would not seek to evade the problem by providing the mere appearance of a solution."[41] Here, he entwines a unified political opposition with a new constitution based on popular sovereignty flowing out of a demand for socialist society – his defense of both popular sovereignty and parliament as "constituent power" is now tied to democratic socialism.

Kirchheimer's commitment to a socialist democracy in which the constitution combined parliamentary democracy with an active popular will (including citizens engaged through elections and mobilized in political parties and parliaments) and a democratization of the economy as the counter to the chronically irresolvable contradictions of the Weimar political arrangement is not left behind in his postwar political science of mass politics, parties, parliaments, and, above all, "political opposition." On the contrary, it directly informed these inquiries – and indeed it is hard to understand them without this political commitment in view. However, political science of the postwar period to the 1970s absorbed Kirchheimer's Weimar-informed political inquiries into the very concept of a consensual self-correcting notion of democracy devoid of the political-ideological conflict that he saw deeply embedded in the liberal constitutional framework. And, as we will see, the postwar political science account of a post-ideological politics was informed by its own inverted version of the Weimar example.

The Odd Misinterpretation of Kirchheimer's Postwar Political Science: The Lesson of the Weimar Example versus American Political Science

Kirchheimer's post-Weimar and postwar work is almost obsessed with the way in which changes in the relation of electorates, political parties, and parliaments have contributed to the decline of political opposition. Indeed, in his later work he foregrounds the features of this decline as a general problem for modern politics. While he is not always explicit about this, the concept of political opposition serves as a kind of proxy for the failure of social democracy to demonstrate political will and to organize a political opposition of the left that would form a majority front across society at the very moment when the parties of capitalism and the traditional forces in Weimar defected from the constitution in favor of dictatorship. It also serves as a proxy for his recurrent invocation (against Schmitt) of the lost potential for a constitution in which the socialist project was tied to an identity between the political will of citizens possessing equal political rights and parliaments as the replication of that political will. In other words, in the background of Kirchheimer's political science is the shadow of the failure of the left during Weimar to stave off what he saw as the dictatorial features within the constitution's liberal frame and to introduce a genuine parliamentary democracy reflecting a popular will. Indeed, this failure haunts much of his later work. In the foreground are to be found the multiple ways in which left political parties are thwarted by banks, political cartels, and the evolution of mass-ideological parties into catch-all aggregations.

Thus, in his post-Weimar article of 1944 on "Changes in the Structure of Political Compromise," Kirchheimer draws attention to a particular form of constitutional compromise to be found in twentieth-century mass democracies in which creditors (our modern bond vigilantes *avant le lettre*) and the independent central banks of most governments "become a transmission belt for the financial community [that] can be profitably used to hold the government and parliament in check."[42] This veto of the banks leads to a chronic political cycle whenever left governments come to power: Specifically, the electorate puts a party or a coalition of the left into power; the government develops a fairly limited program of social reform only to face a sudden crisis of confidence among the holders of government bonds and currency accounts; the government is therefore unable to take on long-term loans to support its policies; then the head of the central bank chastises the politicians who offered the reform, and a new set of politicians takes their place who will submit to the demands of banking and the reforms are forgotten.[43] Bankers view their demands upon governments to pursue deflationary policies instead of public provision as "correcting the popular will."[44] Again, the shadow of the forward thrust of socialist democracy through parliamentary government is thwarted through a displacement of decision-making power to the central bank.

A liberal democratic version of this financial veto of the popular will in mass democracies consists of a compromise among large organizations in a pluralist state in which citizens gain participation only as part of one of the large partners to the compromise.[45] Here, we get a replay of the Weimar example in post-Weimar conditions – except that instead of two opposing classes without a constitutional principle of sovereignty to decide on their conflicting concepts of society, we have a series of negotiated compromises among parties of capital and labor as well as the largest social groups. In this political arrangement, a majority will is thwarted less by banking than by a corporatist agreement between large social and political organizations and interest groups, capital and labor being among the most important. The system of rights, property rights, religious guarantees, and rights of free speech and association serve to protect the largest social groups and uphold the status quo without the intervention of the banking veto.

In his influential article "The Waning of Opposition in Parliamentary Regimes," Kirchheimer directly addresses the logic by which parliaments in mass democracies suffer a decline in political opposition in one of two ways, both of which signal a decline in the power of parliaments of the old kind in which traditional parties with clients fight out their differences within established rules. The first kind, typical of *fin de siècle* socialist parties, rotates around "parties of principle" that criticize as useless the dominant conservative and liberal parties for whom the "rules of the game" allow them to alternate between government and opposition to the exclusion of all outsiders. These parties of principle make a claim to form an alternative government and thus test the claim of actual institutional parties to support parliamentary supremacy. This promising form of political opposition, however, is thwarted because the established parties abandon the parliamentary game and form a political cartel, dividing the offices among themselves while labeling the party of principle – for Kirchheimer a proxy for the socialist left – disloyal to the system.[46] And so the supporters of the party of principle are effectively disenfranchised. The second way in which political opposition is thwarted takes its cue from the previous one and consists of the parties from the outset establishing a political cartel. This model distributes cabinet, administrative, and even zones of electoral competition to make sure that the vote is distributed among the cartel members with all other votes rendered irrelevant. All policy and legislation are worked out by members of the cartel. And the cartel becomes increasingly intertwined with state institutions. The result is that the struggle between state intervention and pro-market policies is kept within very narrowly negotiated bounds. This approach obstructs from the outset both the classical competition of two established parties in parliament and the rise of parties of principle.[47]

These paths of decline in political opposition and political competition, Kirchheimer argues, cannot be reversed, because all parties in the present postwar conjuncture are forced to mobilize a variety of occupational groups with middle-class aspirations. The result is that parties seek to harmonize and homogenize the interests of their members internally. And individuals are increasingly homogeneous as part of the mass society of consumers. Hence parties lose their political-ideological definition as it becomes risky to become an ideologically defined opposition party.[48] At this point, we would seem to be far away from the polarized world of Weimar as the paradigmatic example of an underlying logic thwarting a political will of the left to finally generate a fusion of constitutional democracy and socialism, but for one thing: The concept of political opposition in this account is increasingly offering another paradigmatic example of a failed moment with potential dangers in the absence of a political will to change it. After all, Kirchheimer is not abandoning that standard by which he is judging these developments – the degree to which the working class has been integrated into the European party system and the degree to which it has a voice through a political party and ultimately becomes the driving force of popular sovereignty.

We can see this in Kirchheimer's most influential article, one with the anodyne title "The Transformation of the Western European Party

System" (1966). In this article, he famously polarizes the "catch-all party" against the "mass integration party," arguing that the former is steadily displacing the latter in modern liberal democratic politics, resulting in an overall decline in "political opposition."[49] This transition refers to a transformation both in party organization and in its political ideology, but the imperatives of the former shape the latter rather than the other way around. For Kirchheimer, the various barriers to political opposition that he laid out in his previous work ushered in the necessity for all parties in the postwar period to expand their audience in order to win "immediate" electoral success at the cost of having their principles win out in the long run – the original aim of working-class parties. In particular, and this has become a staple of political science, the catch-all parties seek to homogenize the different categories of voters through programs that benefit all of these groups. They focus on issues beyond individual group interests and avoid issues that would spawn group conflict. The rise of welfare states and collective bargaining regimes shift the burden of party success to political leaders. And partisan ideologies containing clear political goals become one of an array of means to mobilize voters to be used or not used as need arises.[50] Indeed, the party itself becomes something of a brand to be marketed in the place of its political ideology.[51] The political-ideological distinctiveness of the political party is diluted. Instead of intensifying the relationship between the party and its members and the classes and statuses within society that it fought for, the political leadership of the catch-all party loses touch with its members. In turn, the party and the party leadership seek to sustain themselves within the system of political competition rather than transform that system in a political-ideological direction. Since the aim is to get into office and stay there, elections become a way of gaining momentary support from a variety of groups rather than organizing the citizens into a political constituency.[52] The result for the citizens is a rather loose relation to the parties that they support; this differs from the earlier mass integration party that mobilized citizens for their protection, to protest policies, and to realize fundamental principles based on class or mass in opposition to denominational parties.[53] Kirchheimer warned that this vacuum is filled by personality-driven politics in which political leaders become the source of party support.

Now, one may see this famous article as simply another version of the "end-of-ideology" thesis applied to political competition in modern Western liberal democracies, so typical of sociology and political science from the 1950s to the early 1970s.[54] And, indeed, Kirchheimer's famous article on the rise of the catch-all party was seen this way. But when viewed through the Weimar example of his previous work, he is clearly speaking of a dissipation of the political left, and, as we will see, of the displacement of the constituent power of both popular sovereignty and parliaments to a distant and uncertain future. After all, the frame of this article is based on a comparison with the period after World War I when the members of governments throughout Europe would not allow working-class mass parties into government despite the fact that they had played by the rules of electoral democracy. This exclusion politicized the following of these parties, and the parties themselves sought to mobilize that following for the struggle for political power. This struggle was given new stimulus by the tendency of the bourgeois parties to ally with the bureaucracy and the military to prevent any opening to the working classes.[55] Here we are back at the struggle and the logic of Weimar in which social democracy opted to defend a constitution from which the other parties had exited when a political will based on a mobilized integration party was needed to make a decision in favor of a democratic socialist principle of sovereignty as the basis for constitutional legality.

Thus, when Kirchheimer speaks of the decline of political opposition, the transformation of the mass integration party into the catch-all parties of the present, he is not thinking of the revival of right-of-center conservative parties, many of which were well entrenched in the post–World War II period, often in political cartel arrangements.[56] Rather, political opposition is clearly still identified with the left, a left that had failed to unify against the dictatorial tendencies in the formally pluralist constitution of Weimar. In his postwar articles, Kirchheimer lays out a variety of tendencies leading to the decline of political opposition, but they all warn of new political vacuums that could be created through the dissipation of political-ideological parties and political-ideological conflict: in particular, the rise of political cartels on the one side and citizens detached from the political contest on the other. The upshot is a politically alienated citizenry, politically demobilized, oscillating between estrangement from and anger toward the electoral system, representative institutions, and the functioning of governments.[57]

Weimar and Postwar American Political Science

Curiously, political science viewed as a beneficial development Kirchheimer's account of the politically de-ideologized catch-all party whose leaders were geared toward each other and sought political office through short-run cobbled-together programs, as opposed to parties that mobilized their members and supporters for the sake of a long-range and durable social transformation. They understood this account not as the harsh criticism Kirchheimer intended but as consonant with the end-of-ideology view of modern democratic politics. The curious translation of Kirchheimer's Weimar-driven understanding of the decline of political opposition into the model of the pluralist, ideologically depolarized system of consensual party competition is poignantly typified in the comments he received when he turned in his draft of "The Transformation of the Western European Party System" to Joseph LaPalombara for the book LaPalombara and Myron Weiner were editing, *Political Parties and Political Development*.[58] Skeptical that the "catch-all" concept could apply to all modern European political parties, LaPalombara cautioned Kirchheimer to specify the countries to which it applied because there was a whole list of countries – among them Italy, France, and Germany – for which it was not true. He also claimed that Kirchheimer needed to "demonstrate this decline rather than assume it." And in response to the claim that the mass-class party attained more integration of its members (in the party) than the catch-all party that was primarily interested in winning elections and recruiting voters, LaPalombara asked Kirchheimer to lay out the "phases in development" that moved parties "from one kind of functional performance to the other." Hoping that Kirchheimer would frame his whole account of parties within a functional analysis of their integration into "the political system," LaPalombara dismissed Kirchheimer's partisan judgment on the diminished worth of the catch-all party compared to the mass-class integration party that attended to its members demands and their struggle to participate in constitutional regimes: "The point is that what is a central interest to us is not so much the evaluation of the party systems per se but, rather, how these changes in turn affect other changes or developments in the broader political system."[59]

Kirchheimer's response was cordial and deliberately diffident. But he did not relent. In fact, he responded that in his revision he would indeed apply the catch-all term to Italy, France, and Germany. To the request that he integrate his analysis of the two kinds of parties according to their various functions in "the political system," in keeping with the attempt at the time of comparative politics to integrate all comparative studies under a functionalist model of the political system at large, he responded revealingly:

[A]s to your more general remarks in re [sic] to the broader political system – the deeper trouble is that I am not much of a functionalist and have already made too many concessions to the functionalist fad in the body of the paper. This will be a somewhat limiting factor in my attempt to make you more happy – while still conserving those critical thought patterns which are vital to my way of thinking.[60]

Clearly, LaPalombara fails to understand – or at least wants to misunderstand – the overall driving interest in Kirchheimer's account of the decline of the mass-class integration party into the catch-all party; nor does he understand that Kirchheimer has no interest in contributing methodologically to reducing political developments to a functional model integrating all aspects of politics into something called "the political system." Above all, Kirchheimer takes as irrelevant the attempt to mute his overall criticism of modern competitive party systems that issues from this article. Without directly referring to it, it is obvious in this exchange that, for Kirchheimer, the immediate driving interest of the article is the damage being done to both modern democratic regimes and their citizens by the disappearance of mass-class-based parties that mobilized the citizens as large social groups and classes to make comprehensive demands and enable them to become fully fledged participants in the constitutional political system.

Indeed, in response to an earlier letter from LaPalombara, Kirchheimer makes explicit that he has no brief for the catch-all party as it functions well only in the selection of leaders, and that he is "old-fashioned enough to think that class-mass parties have been more steady and reliable political formations."[61] In referring to his critical thought patterns in the later letter, he is explicitly using the long-range developments in political parties and parliaments to criticize contemporary developments, all from the same standpoint. Thus, behind not just this article but the whole range of his postwar inquiries we still see his earlier political commitment as a democratic socialist and the shadow of the failure of the Social Democratic Party in Weimar to tie its role as a integrative party of the working class to political will. The present he describes is an inverse mirror of that world, but the problem of tying a will of the masses to a political party that puts the deficiencies of capitalism on the agenda and of striving for a democratic socialist notion of a constitutionalism and the rule of law is still operative behind this work.

This curious reception of one of Kirchheimer's most influential works in political science is indicative of a larger inversion of the Weimar example in American political science. What Kirchheimer sees as a dangerous development in democracies, especially in the relation of parties to their followings due to the political alienation produced by the structures of political compromise and the catch-all party, American political science of the postwar period sees through the lens of Weimar, at least until the 1970s, as well as from the opposite optic: namely, the decline of opposition and political ideology bespeaks the disappearance of the polarization of politics away from the dangers represented by the Weimar Republic. Mainstream American postwar political science, especially of the dominant behavioral and functionalist strands, saw the Weimar Republic as a specter haunting consensual competitive party systems supplemented by pluralist interest groups. The Weimar Republic served as the paradigmatic example of all that was dangerous to modern stable democracies: high participation, polarized parties, class conflict, mobilized citizens in a world where cleavages coincided with class and status, and lack of support for the rules of party competition.[62] In particular, the Weimar Republic's high rates of political participation were cited as prima facie evidence for viewing low rates of citizen participation as a sign of democratic stability. Typical was the argument of Seymour Martin Lipset:

> The belief that a very high level of participation is always good for democracy is not valid. As the events of the 1930s in Germany demonstrated ... an increase in the level of participation may reflect the *decline* of social cohesion and the breakdown of the democratic process; whereas a stable democracy may rest on the general belief that the outcome of an election will not make too great a difference in society.[63]

In short, the authority of the Weimar example provided political science with the grounds for supporting citizen apathy side by side with competing political elites, both in parties and in government, buttressed by survey research claiming that political elites – not the citizens – were preservers of the "rules of the game." The problem for political science was "socializing" the parties and political elites to this model.

Here, I merely cite a number of further examples of the way in which the Weimar counterexample provided political scientists with generalizations to the effect that the real problem for the sustenance of democratic politics is socialization of political elites to the rules of the game in a system based on party competition to win over a politically passive electorate. In his contribution to his edited volume *Political Oppositions in Western Democracies* from 1966 – a book dedicated to the memory of Otto Kirchheimer – Robert Dahl interprets the collapse of the Weimar Republic as the result of the fact that "neither the middle classes nor the working classes *underwent a sufficient period of tutelage in the politics of parliamentary democracy* before the responsibilities of operating a republic were abruptly thrust upon them."[64] In his later book *Polyarchy* (1972), Dahl references Weimar as an exemplar of a political system in which universal suffrage was granted so suddenly that there was not enough time for "the arts of competitive politics [to be] mastered and accepted as legitimate *among the elites*," and so parties failed to undergo the process of socialization to the rules of party competition.[65] And "because the rules of the political game are ambiguous and the legitimacy of competitive politics is weak, the costs of suppression may not be inordinately high" and so the process of party competition will soon end in a "hegemony ruled by one of the contestants."⁶⁶ Here there is no struggle between capital and labor through competing political parties; no competing concepts of what democracy, in particular a democratic constitution, should be; no constitutional frame that failed to make a decision as to what kind of society it was advancing; and no party that had to maintain the system while also needing to display an organized act of will to form a new democratic constitution based on a broad and inclusive concept of popular sovereignty. Furthermore, in the model of democracy for which Weimar is the counterexample, the democratic agency of parties and citizens is not thwarted by the formation of political party cartels, financial vetoes of the policies of elected left governments, or political alienation produced by catch-all parties that have given up on mobilizing an integrated following within society. The Weimar example for Dahl is all about the lack of socialization of *elites* and parties to the rules of the game, leaving the citizens as spectators.

Gabriel Almond in his influential book *Comparative Politics* (1966) makes a more unusual claim regarding the lesson of Weimar and subsequent Nazi dictatorship: While invoking the standard view of the Weimar Republic of "insecure ... national identity" and party fragmentation leading to fascism, he then claims that their combined effect on the politics of postwar Germany was to produce a citizenry that did not support its political institutions and instead supported government only as long as it delivered the goods. This contrasts with the longstanding socialization to democracy in England, in which the parties, their followings, and the political elites were integrated into the rules of the game. And the reason why support for democratic institutions was weak in Germany, according to Almond, was that "a historical background of discontinuity and trauma has resulted in a political culture lacking in deep and stable system commitment and loyalty."⁶⁷ Here, everything rotates around a functional relationship between political culture and system loyalty. Against these examples, one can see why LaPalombara saw Kirchheimer's refusal to give up on generalizing his critical account of the decline of political opposition through the catch-all party to all industrial democracies as a problem for a political science seeking the sources of functional integration.

Kirchheimer's Explicit Critique of American Political Science: Consensus, Class, and the Criticism of Pluralism

But Kirchheimer also launched a more explicit criticism of the Weimar-inflected consensus view of competitive party democracy based on plural groups so central to postwar political science. In one of his very last articles, "Private Man and Society," he explicitly attacked the claim that both the concept of "consensus" and the concept of "pluralism" should be conceived as the source of political stability in postwar Western democracies.

He directly attacks the concept of "consensus" as support for the rules of the game in modern democratic regimes, arguing that political science substitutes the passive term of consensus as submission to the rules of party competition for the active term that distinguishes democracy as based on "the common will" of the citizens. Consensus, he argues, fails to address the distinctive process through which individuals acquire a capacity to participate in the general affairs of the state "as a part of a body of citizens not as particular individuals," so that "their particular wills embrace the state as their common affair."[68] This notion of democracy was already articulated in his famous Weimar argument on "Remarks on Carl Schmitt's 'Legality and Legitimacy,'" in which he sought to show against Schmitt how democracy as popular will ("democratic will formation") and parliamentary democracy based on formal constitutional procedures were compatible, even in a heterogeneous society.[69] The concept of "consensus," he points out, hides the multiple conflicts between rich and poor, powerful and not powerful. Also, it papers over the significance of the findings of quantitative political science that, in fact, agreement between political elites and the population at large, especially in supporting the major premises of the political system, is extremely weak.[70]

While mainstream (American) political science claimed that part of the stability of the modern democratic system rested on the fact that professional – in particular, political – elites supported the democratic values of liberty and equality, even if ordinary citizens did so halfheartedly at best and not at all at worst, Kirchheimer argued, this apparent source of stability was in fact the result of a serious flaw in these self-same systems: namely, a fundamental reduction of active citizens to consumers. The loss of liberty over both the political system and citizens' work environment was now channeled into their identification of liberty with consumption.

While no longer speaking of a distorted parliamentary system with irreconcilable class-based parties in which the German Socialist Party is potentially the one driving force for creating a responsive democratic constitution, as in the Weimar writings, Kirchheimer describes the new postwar democracy as inhabited not simply by a vast mass of private consumers but simultaneously by what he calls "the executant class," a combination of blue-collar and white-collar employees whose jobs are "circumscribed" by "strict subordination" devoted to a "single phase" of a specialized division of labor.[71] And within this work situation, enterprises offer different balances of competition and cooperation depending on differences in "initiative, security, and status." Some executants enjoy more mobility, many less. But within this balance, individuals remain privatized within the workplace while the main activity of life is focused on the family and consumption.[72] For Kirchheimer, what is lost in this displacement of liberty to family and consumption is "collective workers' action against management" and ultimate control over the workplace.

Even the modern constitutional welfare states, including those based on social citizenship in which the state and unions secure social rights and a living wage, merely reinforce this channeling of the executants into the pursuit of private rewards and away from connecting their personal experiences to social equality in a just society based on mutual respect; here, Kirchheimer is still invoking the aims of democratic socialism.[73] Against this backdrop, "consensus" as understood by postwar political science becomes a cover for loss of control over the conditions of work and production as well as loss of control over conditions for democratic decision-making in a nominally democratic state based on competing political elites and parties. Conformity within inequality in work and politics replaces political and social engagement.

For Kirchheimer, the claim of postwar (American) political science that a plurality of groups within society can serve as an intermediary between individual citizens and the state is equally suspect. In an implicit nod to his distinction between the mobilization and the catch-all party, Kirchheimer claims that only unions and religious organizations can actually serve as intermediary forms of participation between a large number of citizens and the state and press social problems on the political agenda. The vast variety of organizations pursuing very partial interests does not function as "intermediary powers" between state and individual except in the narrowest sense. Indeed, viewing the mass of citizens as "executants," as he defined them above, Kirchheimer points out that the plural interest groups of society simply reinforce the separation of this class from engagement with political institutions and the problems affecting the wider society. And here again, the exemplar for this channeling of individual members of intermediate organizations into private life is to be found in the Weimar Republic:

[T]he Weimar Republic had an untold multitude of associations of this hobby type which quickly took to the prescribed brown coloring in 1933. Intensive participation in hobbies – often another form of escapism from political reality – left the people stranded in their political ignorance just as it left the country without a government enjoying sufficient political backing by intermediary social organizations.[74]

With the Weimar lesson now in the foreground, Kirchheimer argues that plural associations encourage their members to separate themselves from politics, leaving them uninformed about political institutions and creating a comfort zone in which the shared pursuit of private interests encourages a withdrawal from public ones; the result is that the associations undermine constitutionally legitimate democratic political institutions rather than link the citizens to them. In the Weimar case, these plural associations became a means of fascist integration. In the postwar model they serve to discourage the "executant classes" from involving themselves in protests or participation in national-level politics.

Clearly, the lessons of the Weimar example inform Kirchheimer's overall criticism of postwar mainstream political science: They are present in his attack on what political science calls "consensus" from the vantage point of the failure to realize a parliamentary state based on genuine popular sovereignty and an economy based on the democratic socialist aim of employees collectively controlling their workplace. They are explicitly present in his criticism of both "consensus" and "pluralism" for channeling individuals away from public engagement and toward a depoliticized private life. And yet, paradoxically, his criticism here – part of his overall criticism in his postwar works on the loss of political opposition – describes a moment that seems to be the polar opposite of the Weimar case, one in which democracy seems placid and depolarized. But just beneath the surface of that democracy is a cauldron of displaced political opposition: That is, Kirchheimer's account is constructed from the vantage point of a potential political opposition that has not been channeled into private consumption and has overcome a life of fragmented and depoliticized group participation offered to subordinate citizens as compensation for inhabiting different parts of the "executant class."

Conclusion: A Renewed Relevance for Kirchheimer's Weimar Example?

When we compare Kirchheimer's Weimar to the Weimar of political science, what we see is not simply two conflicting approaches to the role of citizens, parties, parliaments, and political opposition in mobilizing the citizens to participate in and against these political institutions, but also two paradigmatic examples with their mutually opposed stylized characteristics teaching widely differing lessons about action and the opportunities for future action in modern politics. The latter tries to efface the lesson of the former in the name of a political science aimed at finding at all costs the functional requisites of political stability. The former seeks to find the sources of political opposition through ideologically mobilized parties that will force modern parliamentary democracies to live up to their democratic credentials as opposed to the dissipation of politics into political cartels and catch-all parties. And, as with the Weimar example, Kirchheimer is still seeking an entry point within this political conjuncture of the democratic socialist aspirations so central to his version of the Weimar paradigm.

The question that remains is whether Kirchheimer's latter, thicker version of the Weimar example and its post-Weimar lessons still contain lessons relevant to a political science of contemporary politics. I would suggest that there are at least three. First, Kirchheimer's Weimar-inspired account of the decline of political opposition in postwar political conjuncture has more recently provided an explanation of how social democratic parties submitted to neoliberal programs of austerity at the cost of expanding social rights and mobilizing a new following. In this case, social democratic parties finding themselves unable to produce majorities through the catch-all model decided not to go back to being opposition parties and instead opted to go into political cartel arrangements with their conservative opponents while claiming that they were merely responding to the imperatives of the global market.[75] Rather than fight against, they embrace the veto of finance over comprehensive redistribution.

Second, in particular in the United States, we are seeing a replay of a constitutional crisis reminiscent of, even if not identical with, Kirchheimer's version of the crisis of the Weimar constitutional arrangement. In one of his most acute criticisms of the attempt to reform the dysfunctions of the Weimar Constitution through the resort to constitutional law [*Staatsrecht*], Kirchheimer asks: What are we to do when we have a constitutional arrangement in which one or more of the parties within the democratic system is not "willing to recognize the basic democratic institutions if those institutions are likely to limit their aspirations to rule and guarantee a space to their political opponents" – or, indeed, they aim to destroy democracy?[76] The result, he points out, will be the emergence of fractured constitutional structures in which the parties and their followings represent two different types of constitution – a democratic representative version and an authoritarian makeover of existing constitutional procedures, leading to a shift of legislative power to the courts, economic decision-making to central banks, increased reliance on the state administration for order, and, above all, the potential for opportunistic political leaders to offer an authoritarian regime to break through this stalemate.

Kirchheimer already saw in Weimar how the steady decline of parliaments as representatives of the people and internal parliamentary dysfunction provided an occasion for individual political leaders to offer to break the deadlock extralegally. He later demonstrated the catch-all party separating itself from involving citizens could have the same result within postwar liberal democracy.[77] This potential outcome in conditions of intense political deadlock leading to constitutional deadlock will only be exacerbated, Kirchheimer argues, if we view the problem as a matter of constitutional reform and public law rather than the relations of power that sustain this impasse. The latter requires us to assess the probabilities of a new order for the state and whether there is an agent that can bring it about.

Third, and last, if the other two lessons are salient for political theory and political science, we are back to Kirchheimer's dilemma generated through the Weimar example and running through all of his subsequent work: What counts as effective political opposition, and under what circumstances can it shape a defective political arrangement into a genuinely democratic state in which political will formation among citizens and the legal structure coincide? This problem, which is at the core of Kirchheimer's Weimar example, is still front and center.

Notes

1 Carl Schmitt, *The Concept of the Political,* expanded ed. (Chicago: University of Chicago Press, 2007), pp. 30–1.
2 Otto Kirchheimer, "Verfassungsreform und Sozialdemokratie" in *Funtionene des Staats and der Verfassung Zehn Analysen* (Frankfurt: Suhrkamp, 1972), p. 79.
3 William Scheuerman, *Between the Norm and the Exception: The Frankfurt School and the Rule of Law,* Studies in Contemporary German Social Thought (Cambridge, MA: MIT Press, 1994).
4 Peter C. Caldwell, *Popular Sovereignty and the Crisis of German Constitutional Law* (Durham, NC: Duke University Press, 1997).
5 Karl Mannheim, *Ideology and Utopia; an Introduction to the Sociology of Knowledge,* trans. Louis Wirth and Edward Shils, International Library of Psychology, Philosophy, and Scientific Method (New York: Harcourt, Brace, 1936), pp. 154, 163–4.
6 Carl Schmitt, *The Crisis of Parliamentary Democracy,* trans. Ellen Kennedy, Studies in Contemporary German Social Thought (Cambridge, MA: MIT Press, 1988), pp. 4–5, 13.
7 Ibid., pp. 35–46.
8 Otto Kirchheimer, "Remarks on Carl Schmitt's 'Legality and Legitimacy'" in William Scheuerman, ed., *The Rule of Law Under Siege: Selected Essays of Franz L. Neumann and Otto Kirchheimer* (Berkeley: University of California Press, 1996), p. 64.
9 "Daher wird implizit von Schmitt die Annahme gemacht, daß der Widerspruchshaftigkeit eines politischen Ideensystems das einem

bestimmten Normsystem zugrunde liegt, eine 'nichtfunktionierende' Wirklichkeit bei der Anwendung dieses Normsystems entpspreche – eine Begriffsrealistches Element seiner Theorie." Otto Kirchheimer, "Bemerkungen zu Carl Schmitts 'Legalität und Legitimität'" in Wolfgang Luthardt, ed., *Otto Kirchheimer von der Weimarer Republik zum Faschismus: Die Auflösung der Demokratischen Rechtsordunung* (Frankfurt: Suhrkamp, 1972), p. 113.

10 Kirchheimer, "Remarks on Carl Schmitt's 'Legality and Legitimacy,'" p. 65.

11 Ibid., p. 68.

12 Ibid., pp. 68–9.

13 See Mannheim, *Ideology and Utopia*, pp. 95–7.

14 In light of his subsequent account of the Weimar Constitution as a frame for the struggle between bourgeois and socialist democracy without either claiming sovereignty, Kirchheimer chooses not to incorporate the context of Mannheim's application of his evaluative concept of ideology or "false consciousness." This context was the Weimar conjuncture of political ideologies ranging from bureaucratic conservativism, to traditionalist conservatism, to liberalism as a procedural account of political competition to Marxism, and finally to anarchism and fascism – a position Mannheim associates with Schmitt. Kirchheimer avoids invoking this construction of the Weimar political field of incompatible and incommensurable political ideologies all unmasking the blindness of their opponents' understanding of political reality but blind to their own. He furthermore ignores Mannheim's claim that these warring political ideologies are nevertheless capable of engaging in dialogue, because, in Mannheim's words, they are "experiencing the same reality" and thus the "present structure of society makes possible a political science that will not merely be a party science, but a science of the whole." Mannheim, *Ideology and Utopia*, pp. 99, 149. See Peter Breiner, "Karl Mannheim and Political Ideology" in Michael Freeden, Marc Stears, and Lyman Tower Sargent, eds., *The Oxford Handbook of Political Ideologies*, Oxford Handbooks in Politics and International Relations (Oxford: Oxford University Press, 2013), pp. 38–55.

15 Kirchheimer, "Remarks on Carl Schmitt's 'Legality and Legitimacy,'" pp. 70–82.

16 Ibid., pp. 78–82.

17 Ibid., p. 86.

18 See Alfons Söllner, *Geschichte und Herrschaft, Studen zur Materialistischen Sozialwissenschaft 1929–1942* (Frankfurt: Suhrkamp, 1979), p. 86. Söllner views Kirchheimer as well as Franz Neumann as the emblematic political theorists of the left for whom the Weimar Republic represented the exemplar of the intertwined crises of liberalism and the socialist labor movement.

19 Otto Kirchheimer, "Das Problem der Verfassung" in Luthardt, *Otto Kirchheimer von der Weimarer Republik zum Faschismus*, p. 64.

20 Otto Kirchheimer, "Verfassungswirklichkeit und Politische Zukunft der Arbeiterklasse" in Luthardt, *Otto Kirchheimer von der Weimarer Republik zum Faschismus*, pp. 71–2.

21 Ibid., p. 72.

22 Otto Kirchheimer, "Weimar – And What Then? An Analysis of a Constitution" in Frederic Burin and Kurt Shell, eds., *Politics, Law, and Social Change: Selected Essays of Otto Kirchheimer* (New York: Columbia University Press, 1969), pp. 33–74. For the political writings of the Weimar period, see Otto Kirchheimer, *Von der Weimarer Republik zum Faschismus: Die Auflösung der demokratischen Rechtsordnung*, ed. Wolfgang Luthardt (Frankfurt: Suhrkamp, 1976); Otto Kirchheimer, *Funktionen des Staats und der Verfassung*, ed. Günther Busch (Frankfurt: Suhrkamp, 1972).
23 Scheuerman, *Between the Norm and the Exception*, p. 8. For a summary of critics on the left who accused the argument in "Weimar – And What Next?" of overemphasizing the political logic over the logic of capital accumulation and class conflict, thus leading to a social democratic acceptance of a pluralistic liberal democratic state, see Wolfgang Luthardt's introduction to Kirchheimer, *Von der Weimarer Republik zum Faschismus*, pp. 8–9.
24 Kirchheimer, "Weimar – And What Then?," pp. 38–9.
25 Ibid., p. 40.
26 Ibid., pp. 50–1.
27 Ibid., p. 46.
28 Ibid., pp. 53–4.
29 Ibid., pp. 55–6.
30 Ibid., pp. 57–9.
31 Ibid., p. 62.
32 Ibid., pp. 62–3. Kirchheimer subsequently mentions that the rule of law through compulsory arbitration procedures can allow governments to shift the distributive function to various quasi-judicial tribunals within the state administration. But he concludes, in keeping with the claim that formal institutions are vessels for already existing power relations, that "it is solely the actual political and economic power relationships which determine the directions and form of administrative activity" (ibid., p. 47).
33 Ibid., p. 65.
34 Wolfgang Luthardt, "Bemerkungen zu Otto Kirchheimers Arbeiten bis 1933" in Luthardt, Otto Kirchheimer von der Weimarer Republik zum Faschismus, p. 12.
35 Kirchheimer, "Weimar – And What Then?," p. 72.
36 Otto Kirchheimer, "Legality and Legitimacy" in Scheuerman, The Rule of Law Under Siege, pp. 64–98. In effect, the unresolved problem of who exercised legitimate sovereignty within the legal structures of a class-divided parliament led to "a dictatorial alteration of the constitution" beyond legality (ibid., p. 51).
37 Kirchheimer, "Verfassungswirklichkeit und Politische Zukunft der Arbeiterklasse," p. 76.
38 Ibid., p. 76.
39 Kirchheimer, "Das Problem der Verfassung," p. 68.
40 Otto Kirchheimer, "Die Verfassungsrform" in Luthardt, Otto Kirchheimer von der Weimarer Republik zum Faschismus, pp. 106, 112.
41 Kirchheimer, "Weimar – And What Then?," p. 74.
42 Otto Kirchheimer, "Changes in the Structure of Political Compromise" in Burin and Shell, Politics, Law, and Social Change, pp. 134–5.

43 Ibid., p. 134.

44 Ibid., p. 138.

45 Ibid., pp. 141–2.

46 Otto Kirchheimer, "The Waning of Opposition in Parliamentary Regimes" in Burin and Shell, Politics, Law, and Social Change, pp. 298–300.

47 Ibid., pp. 301–5.

48 Ibid., pp. 311–13, 315.

49 Otto Kirchheimer, "The Transformation of the Western European Party System" in Burin and Shell, Politics, Law, and Social Change, pp. 346–71.

50 Ibid., pp. 354–7.

51 Ibid., pp. 361–2.

52 For an elaboration of this outcome for producing a class of politicians who live in world of governing networks rather than as agents of their parties, their members, and their supporters, see Peter Mair, *Ruling the Void: The Hollowing of Western Democracy* (London and New York: Verso, 2013).

53 Kirchheimer, "The Transformation of the Western European Party Systems," pp. 368–71.

54 Seymour Martin Lipset, *Political Man* (Garden City, NY: Doubleday, 1963); Daniel Bell, *The End of Ideology: On the Exhaustion of Political Ideas in the Fifties.*, revised ed. (New York and London: Free Press, 1965); Raymond Aron, "The End of the Ideological Age" in *The Opium of the Intellectuals* (New York: W. W. Norton, 1955), pp. 295–305.

55 Kirchheimer, "The Transformation of the Western European Party Systems," pp. 352–3.

56 See Otto Kirchheimer, "Germany the Vanishing Opposition" in Burin and Shell, *Politics, Law, and Social Change*, pp. 319–45.

57 See Otto Kirchheimer, "Private Man and Society" in Burin and Shell, *Politics, Law, and Social Change*, pp. 453–78.

58 Joseph Lapalombara and Myron Weiner, eds., *Political Parties and Political Development* (Princeton: Princeton University Press, 1966).

59 Letter from Joseph LaPalombara to Otto Kirchheimer, 14 February 1964, in "Otto Kirchheimer Papers 1929–1972" in the *German and Jewish Intellectual Émigré Collection*, M. E. Grenander Department of Special Collections and Archives, University at Albany, State University of New York (SUNY Albany).

60 Letter from Otto Kirchheimer to Joseph LaPalombara, 22 February 1965, SUNY Albany.

61 Letter from Otto Kirchheimer to Joseph LaPalombara, 20 July 1964, SUNY Albany.

62 "A stable democracy requires a situation in which all the major political parties include supporters from many segments of the population. A system in which the support of different parties corresponds too closely to basic social divisions cannot continue on a democratic basis, for it reflects a state of conflict so intense and clear-cut as to rule out compromise. Where parties are cut off from gaining support among a major stratum, they lose a major reason for compromise." Lipset, *Political Man*, pp. 12–13.

63 Ibid., p. 14, emphasis in the original. Interestingly, Kirchheimer cites Lipset in the article on "The Transformation of European Party Systems" but offers

these features of modern political competition negatively as signs of a danger-ous decomposition of parties and political opposition. For a critique of the Lipset view, see Carole Pateman, *Participation and Democratic Theory* (Cambridge: Cambridge University Press, 1970), p. 2.

64 Robert Dahl, "Some Explanations" in *Political Oppositions in Western Democracies* (New Haven and London: Yale University Press, 1966), p. 365, emphasis added. Curiously, further on he sees the problem of the Weimar Republic as a failure of the pre-Weimar voting system to integrate the working classes and middle classes; this meant that, once the Republic was founded, class resentment rendered it susceptible to crisis. Interestingly, unlike Kirchheimer, he makes no mention of the German Socialist Party as a democratizing force, or Weimar as an exemplar of a struggle over capitalist versus socialist conceptions of a democratic constitution, or the problem of a parliament so polarized that it ultimately ceded decision-making power to the executive, the state bureaucracy, and the courts, leaving constitutional reform a dead end. For Kirchheimer, Weimar was all about an effective political opposition from the left that could produce a new democratic constitution and a new state, not a problem of integration. See Kirchheimer, "Verfassungsreform und Sozialdemokratie," pp. 93–8.

65 Robert A. Dahl, *Polyarchy: Participation and Opposition* (New Haven and London: Yale University Press, 2008), pp. 38–9, emphasis added.

66 Ibid., pp. 38–9.

67 Gabriel A. Almond and G. Bingham Powell, *Comparative Politics: A Developmental Approach* (Boston, MA: Little, Brown & Co., 1966), p. 319.

68 Kirchheimer, "Private Man and Society," p. 453.

69 Kirchheimer, "Remarks on Carl Schmitt's 'Legality and Legitimacy,'" pp. 67–9.

70 Kirchheimer, "Private Man and Society," pp. 454–5.

71 Ibid., p. 459.

72 Ibid., pp. 460–1, 463.

73 Ibid., pp. 464–5.

74 Ibid., p. 470.

75 See Mark Blyth, "Globalization and the Limits of Democratic Choice: Social Democracy and the Rise of Political Cartelization," *Internationale Politik und Gesellschaft / International Politics and Society* 6, no. 3 (2003).

76 Kirchheimer, "Verfassungsreform und Sozialdemokratie," pp. 81–2. Here, Kirchheimer points out that the collapse of a parliamentary democracy into a series of warring parties when one of the parties is not willing to accept constitutional limits to its pursuit of power is a chronic problem and not unique to Weimar: "After all, experience teaches that the best possible of constitutions can lose its democratic character through deformation processes that a transformed social substratum in the political order [*Staatsordnung*] unleashes" (ibid., p. 82). Also see Kirchheimer, "Legality and Legitimacy," p. 51.

77 See Andre Krouwel, "Otto Kirchheimer and the Catch-All Party," *West European Politics* 26 (2003), pp. 32–3. Krouwel points out that, in two unpublished papers, Kirchheimer put particular emphasis on the fact that as catch-all parties offer only symbolic participation to citizens and as political

parties and organizations became separated from their followers, power would flow increasingly to political leaders who would leverage their popularity in superseding constitutional legality for their own ends. The seeming contrast that political science drew between the example of Weimar and the example of present party politics starts to diminish once we view Kirchheimer's account of Weimar as a paradigmatic example offering lessons for future politics.

5   Swedish Social Democracy and Weimar
Engineering the Democratic Population with the Myrdals

Ludvig Norman

This chapter applies and further develops discussions on analogy and lesson-drawing in an analysis of what Weimar meant to social democracy in Sweden. Swedish social democracy often serves as a paragon of a Scandinavian model for societal and political organization, well known as an example in the postwar era of charting a course that sought to balance a regulated economy and a comprehensive welfare state with the existence of a free market. Less is known, especially in an Anglo-American context, about how and to what extent social democratic ideas as they emerged in Sweden were shaped by interpretations of the country's tumultuous surroundings in and around the time of World War II, by the collapse of Weimar, and by the rise of totalitarian regimes.

As several of the contributions to this volume demonstrate, the lessons drawn from Weimar in the postwar reconstruction of Europe were often articulated by people whose lives had been fundamentally affected by democracy's collapse and the rise of fascism. This was true for the German émigrés who ventured to the UK and US and whose experiences shaped their political outlooks, some of which, as other chapters in this volume demonstrate, became highly influential.[1] It also shaped politicians on continental Europe – not least in Germany – some of whom had endured the Nazi regime, experiencing life changing traumas, and who were later tasked with constructing the postwar democratic system.[2] The emergence of various lessons drawn from Weimar and the analogies that would later be mobilized to make sense of the present were, at least in the initial decades after its collapse, deeply colored by the individual experiences of those who formulated them.

After the war, Jean-Paul Sartre published a short text articulating precisely the gulf between those who had experienced war and occupation and those who had not. He captured the distance created by this radical difference in life experiences and described the difficulty of bridging this "abyss" with words.[3] Weimar's collapse has in many contexts come to symbolize the starting point for the continent's journey into totalitarian war. It has been mined for clues regarding which problems and weaknesses, not least those inherent in democracy itself, could help explain these fateful developments. My aim in this chapter is to explore the following questions: What role did Weimar play in a setting, like Sweden, where such experiences were, by and large, absent? How was the societal and political breakdown that fomented the rise of the Nazis interpreted in a context that was in this sense unique in Europe at this time? And how did it shape social democratic thinking in this context?

To address these questions, this chapter engages with the writings of two prominent intellectual architects of the Swedish welfare state, Alva and Gunnar Myrdal. The Myrdals played a pivotal role in outlining wide-ranging social programs in the 1930s, in significant parts centered on how to address the problem of the country's shrinking population, but also concerned with fostering an enlightened and democratic population.[4] Their efforts in this period, along with those of other prominent social democratic thinkers, supply the basis of my analysis of how Weimar came to influence social democratic political thought in Sweden.[5]

The engagement with the Myrdals, focusing on their work in the 1930s and 1940s, helps explore two primary themes: first, how "Weimar" in the sense of democracy's collapse was interpreted and shaped social democratic thinking at crucial junctures in the 1930s and onward. The particular focus on the Myrdals is motivated by the fact that they were intimately involved in providing the rationales for some of the broad government social reform programs of this era. In addition, Alva and Gunnar Myrdal were less shaped by everyday political considerations, allowing for an analysis of more freely articulated ideas, identifying problems of their time, and mapping out how to address them.

My thesis is that Swedish social democracy, especially in the period after 1930, was infused by a sense Swedish exceptionalism. The sense of exceptionalism created a situation where the rise of totalitarianism in Europe, specifically Nazism in Germany but also dictatorial Communism, in a far-reaching sense became understood as occurring elsewhere, on a different branch of history. Weimar did come to represent a cautionary tale even here, but primarily as a manifestation of what happens if irrationality is allowed to shape social engineering. As such, democratic collapse and chaos were treated as external threats, and not something that would emerge from tensions intrinsic to democracy itself, and certainly not in Swedish democracy. In this sense, Weimar's collapse and the rise of Nazism served as an affirmation of the course taken by social democrats during the interwar years.

This leads to a second and more general point regarding analogical reasoning and lesson-drawing in politics. Analogies function not only to draw negative or positive lessons. Lesson-drawing as a way to establish radical difference may also play an important role in politics. Weimar has often worked as an instrument to diagnose social and political ills in particular societies. What the Swedish case helps illustrate is how analogies can also work to identify certain problems as entirely foreign. I try to show how this use of analogies as externalizing certain problems may be associated with its own consequences.

In Sweden, these consequences, I argue, took the form of a certain degree of blindness that reduced the scope for critical self-reflection. The self-image of an avant-garde in democratic social reform allowed certain aspects of social democracy, bolstered by its self-perceived rationality, to proceed without much in terms of limits of what could be achieved through state intervention. While the Myrdals charted an extremely progressive course for Swedish society, they also embraced and developed the rationale for more troubling aspects of the welfare state regime – in particular, the wide-ranging sterilization program aimed at parts of the population deemed undesirable and of "substandard quality." My argument is that their failure to see the parallels with the racial politics of fascism can in part be explained by understanding the sense of exceptionalism that characterized aspects of social democratic thinking.

The chapter proceeds by outlining the general political context in which the Myrdals' ideas became influential in the 1930s, focusing specifically on the social democratic lessons drawn from Weimar. By then engaging with some of their most influential works from this period, I seek to address the question of how the Weimar lesson manifested itself in their vision of a democratic population program. This leads to a discussion on more troubling aspects of this program: the eugenic perspective underlying their advocacy for forced sterilization of individuals who risked adversely affecting the quality of the population. The chapter concludes with a discussion on the more general insights regarding analogy and lesson-drawing that we can glean from this case.

Swedish Social Democracy and the Weimar Lesson

Lessons drawn from democracy's collapse in Weimar Germany, articulated by social democrats, liberal and conservatives alike, converged around the idea that democracy needed to shift from the politics of the masses toward more constrained notions of democracy.[6] There was a pervading sense that politicians could not be trusted with all aspects of politics, an idea that came to the fore both in discussions on how to devise democratic constitutions but also in discussions on international cooperation, in particular in Europe.[7] Mechanisms were put in place to short-circuit excessive polarization and exploitation of the emotional and irrational masses by opportunistic politicians.[8]

Social democrats in the Nordic countries took a slightly different, and often a far less stringent, constitutional perspective on democracy. An illustrative example can be found in the work of Alf Ross, a Danish constitutional lawyer and political thinker. His reflections, published at the end of the war, paint an image in stark contrast to the constrained notion of democracy.[9] He offered a perspective less focused on democracy's perceived inherent weaknesses. Where thinkers like Löwenstein saw the notion of democratic "romanticism" as futile, Ross instead underlined the need for creating enthusiasm, not least among the young, for democracy.[10] More importantly, however, Ross emphasized the importance of science and expertise at the base of politics. This was an aspect that also permeated political thinking in other Nordic countries, notably Sweden. Rather than keeping the masses at bay, they needed to be educated and involved in the workings of democracy.

In one sense, Swedish social democrats made similar analyses of democracy's fall in Weimar as did social democrats elsewhere.[11] They identified Weimar's collapse as a result of underlying social conditions, unemployment, and economic insecurity for large swaths of society, conditions pushing them toward the extremes, in either the revolutionary communist guise or that of National Socialism. However, their perspective on how to protect democracy also exhibited differences from these lessons. Social democratic thinkers in Sweden focused more specifically on *uncertainty* as the element that had the most detrimental effect on society, rather than economic disparities or poverty in itself.[12]

Like elsewhere, the great economic crisis of the late 1920s had negative effects in Sweden. However, during the 1930s the social democratic government was able to implement far-reaching programs of social reform that helped bolster the development of a society characterized by both prosperity and relative social equality. A significant aspect of these social reforms was that they were intimately associated with a specific notion of democracy, one that encompassed the broader conditions needed for a democracy to function properly.

In contrast to many contemporary European societies in the 1930s, Sweden experienced far less social and political polarization. Instead, social democracy established itself as a dominating force in Swedish politics from the 1930s onward. In the early 1930s, the social democratic workers party Socialdemokratiska Arbetarepartiet (SAP) started to consolidate its hold on

Swedish politics, receiving more than 41 percent of the votes in the 1932 elections and close to 46 percent in 1936, gaining its own parliamentary majority in 1940. Thus, while democracy foundered and fascist dictatorship took hold in Germany and elsewhere, the Swedish social democrats embarked on an unparalleled period of government power.[13] Sweden emerged largely unscathed from World War II and continued its rapid process of modernization and social reform that had picked up steam in the 1930s; three decades of unbroken social democratic hegemony followed, interrupted only in the 1970s. So, what lessons did it draw from Weimar? What role did the analogy with the Weimar Republic's collapse play in this apparent exception in the European context?

One possible answer is that Swedish society should be treated as a wholly negative case for the Weimar analogy: Lessons that were formulated on the basis of the Weimar Republic's collapse simply did not figure prominently in the context of Swedish political thinking.[14] Early on in the twentieth century, the SAP had committed itself to democracy, and it took a far more pragmatic position in terms of forging political coalitions across "class borders" than many of its European counterparts.[15] At the time of the Weimar Republic's collapse, the SAP was already well on its way to establishing itself as the single most dominant force in Swedish politics. The "third way" of Scandinavian politics is largely, as is well known, a way to navigate the thorny territory between democracy and the market without succumbing to either complete state capture of the means of production or laissez-faire capitalism.[16]

Weimar, in the sense of democracy's downfall, thus did not provide the same cues for Swedish social democrats as it did in other European countries. Specifically, the protective notion of democracy that emerged elsewhere, informed by the perceived dangers associated with the emotional and irrational masses, did not seem to inform Swedish social democracy.[17] However, it would be inaccurate to argue that democracy's downfall in Weimar Germany and the rise of totalitarian fascism did not affect political thinking among Swedish democrats, and in Sweden more generally. But, rather than a cautionary tale that could be applied directly to Swedish society, it seemed rather to play the role of affirming Swedish exceptionalism and the sense that Sweden had been able to embark on a parallel and rational path to modernity.

Toward Modernity with the Myrdals: Democratic versus Totalitarian Solutions to the "Population Problem"

Alva and Gunnar Myrdal were two of the preeminent intellectual figures of Swedish social democracy from the 1930s onward. While both were members of the Social Democratic Party and served in formal political roles at different times, it is through their practically inclined scholarly work that they became perhaps most well known and influential.[18] Alva Myrdal's ideas in particular supplied the ideational groundwork and had a far-reaching impact on the structure of important social reforms of the Swedish welfare state, especially those concerned with policies aimed at the family, housing, and child-rearing.[19] She was also an important voice for the entry of Swedish women into the workplace and a very public figure, not only in the Swedish public sphere. Both she and her husband stand out as internationally facing public intellectuals who published books and scholarly articles in Swedish as well as in English for an international audience, and as such they also became important proponents of the Swedish model of societal organization.[20]

A key aspect of the Myrdals' intellectual project was their reliance and deep faith in rationality and the social sciences as the necessary basis for social reform. Throughout, their arguments are accompanied by data on everything from popular attitudes, consumption patterns of different types of foods, and nutritional data for different social groups, to housing, apartment sizes for families in different income brackets, and so on. As a whole, their project was steeped in a deep faith in rationalism and science as the basis on which democratic society should be built. It is also on this basis that they contrasted their ideas for social reform from those that emerged in societies where the reliance on science had given way to nationalism and irrationality.

What is interesting in relation to this volume's focus on lessons of Weimar is that key works by the Myrdals relating to social challenges facing Swedish and European societies, as well as the US, were written in the 1930s and 1940s. These works also focused on issues that were of great concern elsewhere in Europe, not least in Germany – namely, dwindling birthrates. Their approach to address this issue was, however, driven by different political impulses than those dominating in other parts of Europe at the time, and emerged in direct contrast to reform programs implemented elsewhere. Their works are thus a fruitful starting point for a discussion on how the collapse of German democracy and the rise of totalitarian ideologies in Europe shaped Swedish social democratic ideas.

A key concern for the Myrdals – and, indeed, for politics more generally at this time – was the so-called population question, and it was through addressing this question that they came to formulate a wide-ranging program for social reform that touched on almost all aspects of social life. Their key work on this topic, *Kris i befolkningsfrågan* (*Crisis in the Population Question*), published in 1934, became hugely influential and has continued to spur discussion throughout the postwar era in Sweden. It is often seen as perhaps the clearest statement of a form of social engineering that, in part, came to characterize the Swedish social democratic state.

The primary problem that the Myrdals addressed in *Kris i befolkningsfrågan* was the declining number of births of Swedish people. Sweden had the world's lowest birthrate for the whole period from 1923 to 1934.[21] The concern with this problem was not specific to Sweden but had come to the fore in several European countries. Scholars and politicians across Europe were wrestling with the fact that new births were going down and populations were aging.[22] In Sweden, the question gained considerable political attention, resulting in public investigations and a government commission tasked with providing solutions.[23] It was through the prism of this society-wide problem that the Myrdals defined a particular path for democratic social reform.

In the Myrdals' view, many of the policies suggested elsewhere were driven by irrational, conservative, and nationalistic concerns that did not deal adequately with the core issues and, above all, did not correspond well to the challenges faced by societies that were now fully entering the modern era. This concerned, in particular, Germany, the clearest example of a country where "all sorts of unsubstantiated speculative biological cheap insights" underpinned the spreading of "racial and class barbarity."[24] However, the Myrdals did not see this as specifically tied to the rise of the Nazis but as a consequence of a society that had more generally drifted away from a rationalistic path. A partial explanation for the rise of Nazism, they argued, was that this unfortunate country had for "two generations lacked a critical social scientific research of an international standard."[25]

The Myrdals were driven by the aim to define a social policy for families as an alternative to those of totalitarian states.[26] An emphasis on voluntarism, science-based advice, and education in combination with creating the conditions for economic security is contrasted with efforts, not least in Germany, to invoke duty and allegiance to the state, religion, or race as motivations to produce more children.[27] Alva Myrdal in particular treated efforts to deal with the population question as part of a necessary adaptation for a society that had entered a modern phase but where antiquated institutions developed for the mores and functional needs of previous eras still lingered.

A prime example was the family and, in particular, the role of women in the family. The key problem here consisted in the difficulty of adapting a family institution inherited from previous "production periods" to modern economic and social life.[28] In particular, compared to agrarian society, the direct economic function of women in the home had been largely taken away and children increasingly represented an economic burden rather than an asset for families.[29] This necessitated a fundamental rethinking of the family as an institution, and, with that, of the relation between the state and the family.

Thus, rather than seeking to safeguard the traditional conception of the family, Alva and Gunnar Myrdal used this new perspective on the family as a starting point for an intensely progressive and far-reaching program for social reform. The population question was to be treated as a society-wide problem and it was thus up to society as a whole to create the conditions that would make it rational for families to have children. One may moralize as much as one desires, the Myrdals argued, but if the fundamental factors discouraging people from having children are left unaddressed, all efforts will be in vain.[30]

Apart from this pragmatism, there was also a certain teleological tinge to their arguments as they held that demands for both efficient and costly social policies, along with a restructuring of production in a socialist direction, would emerge as a result of the "rising political and social enlightenment among the broad masses."[31] A key notion was that "we are approaching a time where one will generally find it unreasonable that each person should so completely carry the economic burden for one's own children."[32] It could also be expected, they held, that as children became increasingly rare the necessary solidarity from the rest of society for supporting economic benefits for families would be ensured.[33]

While the tone of the Myrdals' arguments in relation to the population question may seem decidedly socialist, their ideas were initially met with skepticism from the far left.[34] The perception was initially that their approach was similar to the efforts of Nazi Germany to strengthen the birthrate to "provide cheap labor and cannon fodder for the bourgeois state."[35] Their ideas found a more enthusiastic reception among social democrats and also among some conservatives who had been engaged with the population question, although from a more pronounced nationalistic perspective.[36] However, the Myrdals' vision was neither nationalistic nor an attempt to fill factory floors or battlefields. Rather, it was seen as a necessary means to continue the path as a democratic society in modernity.

Contrary to what some have argued, there is, however, little evidence for the notion that the Myrdals were seeking to put in place a system of exclusively means-tested policies of "in kind" benefits aimed at the most vulnerable.[37] Rather, a highly universalist position emerges from Alva Myrdal's writing on the population problem.[38] Writing during the war, she reflects on what will be needed when the war ends and freedom and progress again have a chance to flourish. Then democracy will have to "fulfill its social obligation. Political freedom and formal equality will not be enough; real democracy, social and economic democracy, will be exacted."[39] In such a democracy, unceasing reforms to decrease the impact of all major insecurities – old age, sickness, disability, unemployment – will be needed.[40]

There are clear parallels between the Myrdals' treatment of the population question and the notion of the social democratic "people" encapsulated in the notion of *Folkhemmet*, the People's Home, that became a key concept for Swedish social democracy and which continued to serve as an important reference point during much of the postwar period. The People's Home signified healthy and well-functioning society characterized by social and political equality and individual freedom, but with a fundamentally collectivist ethos. When considered against the backdrop of the Nazi regime's emphasis on the German *Volk*, it might seem surprising that the notion of the People's Home could not only be pursued after the war but become such an important aspect of Swedish social and political identity, even invoked in contemporary Swedish politics.[41] However, this notion of the people emerged as an alternative to the thick organicist notion of the people. The early Marxist revisionism of the SAP had allowed it to venture beyond an exclusive focus on class, instead using "the people" as its most important reference point. In doing so it used elements found among political forces on the nationalist right, but it was able to marry to these its own programs of social reform and the betterment of conditions for the many, with ideas of "people" and "nation" that elsewhere had been captured by fascism, and by the Nazis in particular. "The people" in the political discourse of the social democrats, however, instead mirrors more inclusive and universalist ambitions equating the People's Home with that of the "citizens' home."[42]

The notion of the People's Home does not figure prominently in *Kris i befolkningsfrågan*. Yet, the book's treatment of the population question clearly highlights in a similar way how the notion of people and population could be discussed without reference to any thicker notion of national culture. The Myrdals were outspoken in their criticism of nationalism. An example of this is how *Kris* discusses the possibility of addressing the declining numbers of births through immigration. While the Myrdals agree that this would in essence be a rather practical solution, they also note that people in general can be expected to oppose solving the population problem in this way. Reactions, especially from the working class, as employers push wages down, are likely to be strong, especially in a context of high unemployment.[43] They also note with disappointment that, even among academics and student associations, reactions "which speak from the darkest narrowmindedness" against the acceptance of academics and culture workers who had been driven out of dictatorial countries by race or religion.[44] The Myrdals adopted a more pragmatic position. They "loathed" national borders but also noted that their dissolution was not within reach in the current reality.[45]

Swedish Exceptionalism: The Myrdals and Democracy

Although at various points the Myrdals highlight narrowminded and conservative impulses in Swedish debate, Sweden's exceptionalism is an important through-line in their work and one that is important for understanding its relation to the collapse of democracy, in Germany in particular. What emerges here is a complex picture in which Sweden is depicted as the epitome of a decent, humble, and unassuming society but also one that has boldly ventured out on a different branch of history than those embarked on by many contemporary societies. At the same time, great emphasis is being put on actively fostering the democratic population, improving it in various ways, preparing it for the challenges of the modern era. A highly collectivist notion of the democratic society emerges. However, it is at the same time anchored in the view that collective solutions should be devised so as to balance the goal of the most efficient and rational use of the population with that of individual freedom.[46]

When looking at their work from the perspective of Weimar lessons, and the implications of those lessons for democracy, it is striking how much it differs from the otherwise pervading sense that Weimar's collapse supplied general lessons on the fragilities inherent in democracy. Weimar lessons came to inform new perspectives on constitutional law and on the organization of party systems, often focused on the potential fragilities of democratic politics. Swedish social democrats were not blind to these problems. However, the decidedly constitutional tinge of post-Weimar debates, extending further after World War II, found little resonance in the Myrdals' political vision. Their model of democracy was similar to those of other social democratic thinkers in the Nordic countries, such as Alf Ross, in that it diverged from the notion that the people, understood as the masses, should be kept at arm's length from politics.

The Myrdals' discussions on democracy exhibit a notable absence of references to constitutional mechanisms or to democratic institutions or procedures. In general, their work contains very little on how the democratic system could be protected from internal threats, antidemocratic political movements, irrational masses, or opportunistic politicians. Neither Alva or Gunnar were constitutional lawyers or political scientists, so, to an extent, their focus on economic and social issues rather than constitutional ones is not surprising.[47] However, in many instances the trust in the rationality and decency of ordinary people that permeates their work supplies a stark contrast to much of the political thinking that had been informed by the collapse of Weimar democracy.

The Myrdals' notion of "social engineering" and the Scandinavian model of the welfare state have at times been associated with a paternalistic, overly intrusive social model: a way to organize politics where citizens are regarded as unable to freely choose the best course of action.[48] There are indeed elements of this in their approach. In aspects of Alva Myrdal's work in particular there seem to be no limits to the areas in which the state could assist and educate citizens, from what foods to consume to how to best furnish the family home.[49] However, a closer reading reveals that the Myrdals' position is far less consistently paternalistic than is sometimes thought. Their vision of democratic society was not one that took its cues from thinkers focusing on the fragilities of an open democracy, core ideas in the standard lessons taken from Weimar's fall. The widespread notion that the openness of the democratic system in Germany had been exploited for undemocratic ends was notably absent in their discussions.

On the contrary, a key aspect of their view on democracy was that citizens needed to be afforded the conditions necessary for active participation in politics and that this required creating possibilities for spending a portion of one's leisure time on civic duties.[50] In Sweden, Alva Myrdal argued, adult education and a widespread habit of political participation had made "practically the whole general public competent to take part in public discussions."[51] The masses' reasonableness and willingness to educate themselves and take on various roles, whether on councils and in municipal institutions or in the national parliament, are highlighted as ideals characterizing Swedish society.[52] This perspective on democratic society thus emerges in sharp contrast to perspectives that saw Weimar's collapse as evidence supporting the untenability of democracy as a mass movement.

In their assessment of Swedish democracy, the internal tensions and fragilities that others had identified as inherent aspects of democracy were nowhere to be found. In their works published during the war, they recognize the possibility that their country, like many of their neighbors, might come under attack. However, faced with the possibility of invasion and war, they adamantly argued for the soundness of their democratic vision of Swedish society. Writing in the preface to *Nation and Family* in

1940, Alva Myrdal expresses her fear that the democratic government in Sweden may have perished before the book is published, but she adds: "Our house may be burned, but this will not prove there were basic faults in its construction."[53]

In this context, Alva Myrdal's position on how Swedish society should prepare itself for a possible invasion is further indicative of this perspective. Together with another prominent member of the Social Democratic Party, Sonja Branting-Westerståhl, she authored a memo in 1940 presented to the party's executive committee. There, the authors outlined their strategy in terms of mobilizing society's democratic forces in the event of an invasion. Resistance was to be mobilized through forceful slogans and fundamental tenets outlined in condensed versions of the SAP's program.[54] It would also spread information about the Nazis' tactics to prevent collaboration with the invaders.[55] Myrdal's faith in the power of democracy and the necessity of grounding it as broadly as possible across society thus also became part of the ways in which she envisioned its protection.

Their perspective in this regard was founded on the view that Sweden, by fortuitous historical circumstance but also skillful maneuvering on the part of its political leaders, had allowed a democratic mindset to firmly take root in its population. Part of the explanation was that this was a society that had been spared the scars that fundamentally shaped European societies in the interwar years. This is elaborated specifically in *Kontakt med Amerika* (*Contact with America*), published in 1941, where the Myrdals lay out arguments of why the rest of Europe had been drawn into destructive conflict while Sweden had managed to stay outside.[56] Here, they identify the single most important factor in the consequences of the First World War, which Sweden was largely able to escape. They outline these effects in terms of widespread cultural destruction with far-reaching negative consequences for intellectual and political thinking. In conjunction with this argument, they also point to the "selective mass murder" of large parts of the best of a young generation in many European countries, a generation that Sweden was able to keep and that emerged unscathed in the interwar years.[57] Equally important, they highlight, was the psychological damage to the decimated and culturally damaged generation who survived, and who rose to power in the interwar years, in Germany in particular.[58]

Irrespective of the Myrdals' self-perception regarding the exceptionalism of Swedish society, it is an inescapable fact that Sweden occupied a highly unusual position during the 1930s and during the war. For Sweden, it was a period of wide-ranging social reform and also a period when social democracy ruled with broad popular support, seemingly removed from the extreme forms of polarization that characterized many societies on continental Europe. The country's exceptional status was not a point that escaped Alva Myrdal; the sense that Sweden charted a unique, and indeed exemplary, course permeates her writings. In a text published in 1941 as part of a collection of works addressing Swedish democracy entitled *Vår plats bland nationerna* (*Our Place Among the Nations*), Myrdal provides an overview of the assessments of observers from other countries, including the Anglo-American sphere and France as well as Germany.[59] Here, she quotes a US observer who, she argues, captures the sentiment in the Anglo-Saxon world in relation to Sweden, stating: "In a world where the return to dark and bloody primitivism is so likely, the appearance is certainly welcome of this sound people, who know the limits as well as the great opportunities for creating a society for all people."[60]

This text stands out, not only because it propagates a particular way of organizing politics and society, but also because it is devoted entirely to how others see Sweden and its accomplishments.[61] This disposition, the sense that Sweden was finding a unique way of dealing with the transition to modern society, also permeates the Myrdals' treatment of the population question and their effort to engineer a democratic population program. Throughout *Kris* and *Nation and Family*, references are made to the unique traits of Swedish society while carefully avoiding essentialist or organicist notions of the nation.

The Myrdals' understanding of democracy was a substantive one. It was a notion that went beyond minimalist procedural understandings of democracy; instead, for the Myrdals, democracy had to do with building a society populated by democratic citizens, fostered into a disposition that balanced individualism and collectivism, and where the state would be ever present to create the conditions for the flourishing of individuals and their health, and with that the flourishing of society as a whole. The goal in an educated democracy, Alva Myrdal argued, is that "citizens look upon all public activity as a huge citizens' cooperative."[62] For the Myrdals, the conditions for achieving this were present in Sweden more than anywhere else.

The Blindness of Boundless Rationality: Creating Difference through Analogy

So far, we have seen that lessons taken from Weimar's collapse in terms of their implications for Swedish democracy differed from lessons drawn in many other contexts. If anything, democracy's downfall and the rise of Nazism in Germany served to bolster the Swedish sense of exceptionalism. The Myrdals held the conviction that a strict adherence to rationality and science and a fundamental commitment to democracy placed Swedish society on a different historical trajectory than the totalitarian states they recurrently criticize in their work. Their democratic population program was thus designed in contrast to an undemocratic one.[63] This contrast, however, does not figure as lessons that need to be heeded to avoid disaster; rather, it confirmed that the Swedish path was the correct one. The "Weimar lesson" in this sense functions as a way to create distance and difference, rather than self-reflection. For the Myrdals, it can even be argued that this sense of exceptionalism became associated with a degree of blindness in terms of the ability to reflect critically on their own ideas. In particular, the conviction that the population program they outlined was in all its aspects driven by democratic concerns and based on accurate science appears to have made them blind to how parts of their proposed social reforms relied on the same type of radical disregard for the individual and an overriding concern with the population and the proper functioning of society that they criticized as part of totalitarian population programs.

These aspects came to a head with a key element of the population program for which the Myrdals were strong advocates: the sterilization of those deemed to adversely affect the quality of the "human material" of which the population was made up.[64] As outlined above, their treatment of the population question included a wide range of issues. It is thus important to underline that, while the sterilization policy was considered highly important, it was also only one of a multitude of social policies deemed necessary. For the purposes of the discussions in this chapter, the sterilization question, however, is highly pertinent, especially as a way to highlight how the self-perception of Sweden as a rational, democratic, and science-based exemplar seemed to have shielded the Myrdals from deeper reflection on the moral implications of this type of intervention.

For the Myrdals, the use of sterilization for eugenic or social reasons to ensure that individuals deemed unfit as parents were prevented from reproducing was part and parcel of "the democratic population policy." Its broader rationale deserves a longer quote:

When society is helping some parents to get better conditions for their children and is helping others to avoid children they do not want to have, there is no wonder that society also sometimes wants to dictate that some children should not be born. Such a desire, at least in a democratic state, will only appear in connection with eugenically doubtful parentage.[65]

The use of forced sterilization to prevent procreation was primarily to be directed toward "feebleminded" and "asocial" individuals. In the same way that the transition into modernity and the introduction of new modes of production required reconsidering ingrained social institutions such as the family, sexual morality, and work, modern society also placed much higher demands on the "quality" of individuals.[66] More and more spheres of society are rationalized, consequently leaving less and less room for "substandard" individuals.[67] Vigorous social policies directed at the "moderately feebleminded" and "insane," as well as those with "bodily defects," would be needed to integrate them as much as possible as productive members of society.[68] However, society would still be left with a portion of the population that would require a "radical culling of highly unfit individuals through sterilization."[69]

The Myrdals pay a great deal of attention to the possible problems with such interventions. The core difficulty they identify, however, is of a less ethical kind; rather, it mainly concerns the state of existing knowledge regarding what is hereditary and what is not. Ideally, they argue, one would like to root out all traits of "lesser worth" – physical and mental – from the population, including "feeblemindedness and insanity, physical diseases and poor predispositions in character."[70] Uncertainty in discerning what is caused by genetics and what is caused by the environment, however, set limits on the application of sterilization as a tool. The scope of its application, however, could be widened in view of advances in the science of heredity and also for "social-pedagogical" reasons, which related to assessments of unsuitability of the family environment to raise children.[71]

The question that emerges is how the Myrdals could defend these ideas, obviously failing to see what in hindsight appears as a clear link to the racial theories of the Nazis in terms of refining the population and maintaining and increasing the quality of the "human material" that forms part of the "population stock."[72] Here, as in other aspects of their program, the Myrdals trust in science to relieve them from the grave ethical problems associated with this outlook on society. There is indeed a striking absence of any ethical discussions throughout their treatment of these issues. In places they do concede that there are sections of society where compulsory sterilization cannot be defended. Often the reason for this, however, is that it is difficult to scientifically isolate the effect of hereditary factors and thus what should instead be treated by interventions to provide better living environments. The emphasis is thus more clearly placed on the efficiency of measures rather than on their proportionality in relation to any ethical considerations. In fact, the Myrdals lament the fact that the "weeding out of unsuitable child-rearers by restricting their freedom to reproduce will not be as complete as one would wish," leaving society, even in the best of worlds, with a multitude of cases where children need to be "separated from unsuitable parents and their harmful environmental influence."[73] They also have few qualms with regard to the further possible extension of the sterilization tool.

This point comes up specifically in discussions about individuals who are deemed competent in the eyes of the law but who nonetheless are considered unsuitable as parents. There, the Myrdals argue, doctors and social authorities should work actively to convince those individuals to accept voluntary sterilization. They go on to argue that if this should prove ineffective, the law should be made stricter to also include competent individuals in the framework of both compulsory and voluntary measures.[74] Consistently, the Myrdals avoid discussing ethical concerns, instead relying on what approach is likely to achieve the goals of a growing population of a quality required for modern society.

A reliance on rational science for their eugenic arguments also underlies their position against the racial theories practiced in Germany, which the Myrdals denounce categorically. They go to great lengths to criticize "racial and class biological population doctrines" and lament the inadequacies of the German social sciences in the interwar period, which, they argue, could have helped counter racial and class fanaticism.[75] They criticize what they refer to as "superficial and uncritical assumptions of racial biology" that are proliferating and which have found new political expressions.[76] Their arguments are equally critical of the popular notion of the time that "substandard" individuals were especially numerous among the lower classes, and that, as such, society's class structure should be seen as a reflection of the distribution of particular inherited traits.[77] The core of their position is that social groups, such as classes or "races," are not naturally given biological units.[78] Until proven otherwise, these units are expected to contain "a constant proportion of imbeciles and morally deficient or otherwise hereditarily encumbered individuals."[79] Applied to individuals, however, they regard social eugenics as having far more purchase and as a necessary aspect of the democratic population program.

As a reader of these texts from a contemporary standpoint, the harshness of the language through which the necessity of these policies is explained is disturbing. This particularly concerns passages where the Myrdals underline the importance of not showing "leniency" and of ensuring the strict implementation of the rules of forced sterilization in order to have the most effect.[80] What emerges is how the Myrdals are able to bolster their position as being borne out by science and rational adaptation to shifting demands created by society's modernization. Alva Myrdal points specifically to how the Scandinavian countries are fortunate to have achieved such close collaboration between social science and politics, resulting in a "rationalistic democracy."[81]

As researchers focusing specifically on the history of eugenics and the emergence of race biology have shown, it is important to note that eugenics and racial biology were an international research paradigm that engaged researchers in many European countries and the US.[82] The Swedish Institute for Racial Biology at Uppsala University was a forerunner to many similar research centers in other countries, including Germany.[83] Ideas regarding race and the application of racial theories to society and politics were thus widely spread in the first decades of the twentieth century, and while these theories certainly came to shape politics, not least under the Nazi regime, as part of a scientific research field they were not initially wedded to any particular ideological program. Rather, these ideas were embraced by politicians on the right as well as on the left, although in slightly different ways, ways that also depended on the political context in which these ideas took hold. For instance, Porter compares debates on eugenics in the UK and Sweden, demonstrating how debates in the UK mapped ideas of eugenics onto the class system, while in Sweden they took a different turn, instead pointing to the lack of evidence that deficiencies were especially common in certain social classes.[84] Therefore, our assessment of the Myrdals' position on these issues also needs to take into account the specific context in which they developed their ideas. This was a context in which arguments about racial hygiene had yet to be fundamentally discredited.

A key point is that their position was characterized by their deep confidence in the ability of rationality and science to alleviate political problems; this seems to have short-circuited much of the ethical debate one might have expected to appear in these discussions. Rationality and a fundamental commitment to democratic values are seen to characterize the Swedish people as well as permeating the Swedish state. Nowhere in the Myrdals' work is there any discussion of the concern that aspects of the population program, and specifically the sterilization policies, would risk disproportionally affecting vulnerable or marginalized groups. There is a notable absence of discussions on control mechanisms, such as review boards or the like, that could be put in place to oversee the program's implementation.[85] They are careful to underline that sterilization is far from being a panacea to deal with the problem of individuals of "lesser worth." However, they set limits on the application of this instrument only in relation to its perceived efficiency and not in relation to any ethical problems.

Ensuring a Population of High Quality in Practice

The Swedish government enacted sterilization laws in 1934 and further on in 1941.[86] Under these laws, which were in force from 1935 until their termination in 1975, approximately 63,000 people were sterilized.[87] The law adopted in the 1930s was further reinforced in 1941, widening its remit to also include voluntary sterilization. At the end of the century, the Swedish government issued public inquiries into the laws and their application; these also formed part of discussions on the possibility of economic compensation for victims of wrongdoing under these laws.[88] Government investigations of the program have shown that an overwhelming majority of sterilized individuals (93 percent) were women. While a portion of interventions were made forcibly, against the expressed will of the individual, many were also done voluntarily. However, the voluntary aspect was often seriously compromised. It was common for individuals to be actively persuaded to undergo the procedure, a practice that was explicitly encouraged by the Board of Health, which issued guidelines for the law's implementation.[89] Sterilization was also sometimes introduced as a condition for release from state institutions or to be granted an abortion.[90]

The legislation identified indicators that motivated sterilization under the law as medical, eugenic, or social. The focus was thus both on characteristics that were deemed hereditary, such as "feeblemindedness," and indicators that captured the social circumstances in which individuals found themselves. Social indicators included if individuals were seen as unfit as parents in view of their mental capacities, but also if they led an "asocial lifestyle" – among other things, the latter would include being an alcoholic or a prostitute, or even if their social circumstances included asocial elements, such as an alcoholic husband.[91] Studies of applications for sterilization found a noticeable overrepresentation of individuals designated as "*tattare*," a term commonly used at the time for travelers.[92] Accounts taken from sterilization applications demonstrate that perceived eugenic and social indicators were often intermingled in assessments. This was especially the case when dealing with individuals from the group designated "*tattare*" or "*zigenare*" ("gypsies"); these individuals were routinely deemed asocial and feebleminded in applications to the Board of Health.[93] In general, the term widely used – "feeblemindedness" (*sinnesslöhet*) – was a highly ambiguous medical term, including a range of rather ill-defined characteristics that were deemed to make individuals unsuitable parents.[94]

Alva and Gunnar Myrdal were far from the only ones advocating for sterilization laws to be applied to the "feebleminded" and "asocial" individuals deemed to negatively affect the population's "quality," and they were not directly involved as legislators at the time of the introduction of such laws. They were, however, two of the policy's perhaps most notable and well-known intellectual proponents. The question that animates the chapter's account of this aspect of their work is how they were able to deal with what one could see as a clear dissonance between the sterilization instrument and their "democratic population program." There are, of course, many possible reasons for this. An important reason, highlighted above, was the general ideational context in which social eugenics had been established, especially during the 1920s, as a highly regarded and legitimate scientific paradigm. The perspective developed in this chapter, I argue, supplies additional clues.

The Myrdals were convinced that, in some sense, Sweden had been able to venture on a path toward modernity that was unique, especially in a European context, in its ability to solve the tensions arising during the course of this broad societal transition. While they repeatedly emphasized the importance of a critical and science-based disposition, their writings also exude a fundamental lack of self-reflection in terms of considering the possible limits of the program they were advocating. Their general position on Sweden as an exemplar of rational democratic social engineering seems to have shielded them from questioning some of the more troubling aspects of their approach to the population question.

Conclusions

As we note in the introduction to this volume (Chapter 1), Weimar can be seen as the paradigmatic historical lesson of the twentieth century, reappearing with renewed strength as a device to make sense of the social and political developments of our present. The contributions to this volume deal in different ways with how Weimar as an analogy and as a set of political lessons has shaped and continues to shape political thinking in various contexts. This chapter's engagement with Swedish social democracy highlights an aspect of the Weimar lesson that has received less attention. The conventional lesson drawn from the collapse of democracy in Weimar has led thinkers and politicians to reconsider democracy in terms of a more disciplined and constrained form of politics. This protective notion has often been rooted in the perceived dangers associated with mass politics and the inherent fragilities of democratic procedures, easily exploited by those who would like to demolish democracy from within. The starting point of my argument in this chapter was that these lessons were far less prominent in the Swedish case and that the Weimar analogy has had a much weaker grip on the Swedish political imaginary, especially among social democrats.

However, rather than conclude that the Weimar lesson had no place in the outlooks of Swedish social democratic intellectuals, I have sought to show that it fulfilled a rather different role in Sweden than it did in many other European countries. Studying social democratic ideas in this context in the 1930s onward from the perspective of the Weimar analogy helps illustrate aspects of social democracy in Sweden that are less often acknowledged, especially by international observers. This concerns in particular the sense that Sweden had conceived a uniquely effective solution to the problem of devising a democratic society by dealing head on with the monumental shift toward modernity, without triggering the violent convulsions that were evidenced elsewhere. This indicates the outlook we find in this aspect of social democratic discussion in the interwar years and beyond: Sweden, due to its fundamentally democratic character, while serving as an example to the world, had little to learn from others about how to successfully organize society. The Weimar lesson then informed this outlook, especially in the works of the Myrdals, as a way to create a sense of difference and as bolstering the notion of Swedish exceptionalism, a society venturing successfully on a different historical path than those of its neighbors.

My argument is that this made Sweden – and the Myrdals in particular – blind to the deeply problematic aspects of their social program and the social eugenic outlook that underpinned the sterilization of those deemed to negatively affect the population stock. The insistence that these measures, as well as the program as a whole, were driven by fundamentally rational democratic concerns, and as such were categorically different from those developed in Germany, seems to have closed the door on more critical self-reflection on this issue. Importantly, the deep faith in a rationalistic planning of society supplied a counterpoint to the perceived irrationalism of the racially informed population policies of Nazi Germany and seemingly helped obscure the parallels that we today can identify in the Myrdals' arguments for maintaining a population of "high quality."

For the purposes of this volume, the engagement with the Myrdals' works illuminates a more general point regarding historical examples and analogies in politics. For the Myrdals, analogies and lesson-drawing did not work primarily to highlight similarity. Rather, they worked as a device to reinforce a self-perception of difference, and, by implication, as a shield against seeing parallels between the policies they advocated and those they criticized.

Notes

The author would like to thank Paula Blomqvist for constructive comments on an earlier draft of this text as well as those provided by the other contributors to this volume.

1 See contributions by William Scheuerman (Chapter 7) and Peter Breiner (Chapter 4) in this volume.

2 See contributions by Douglas Webber (Chapter 2) and Peter Caldwell (Chapter 3) in this volume.

3 Jean-Paul Sartre, "Paris under Occupation," *Sartre Studies International* 4, no. 2 (1998 [1945]), pp. 1–15.

4 Jenny Andersson, "Choosing Futures: Alva Myrdal and the Construction of Swedish Future Studies, 1967–1972," *International Review of Social History* 51, no. 2 (2006), pp. 277–95; Thomas Etzemüller, "Die Romantik des Reißbretts: Social Engineering und Demokratische Volksgemeinschaft in Schweden: Das Biespiel Alva und Gunnar Myrdal (1930–1960)," *Geschichte und Gesellschaft* 32, no. 4 (2006), pp. 445–66; Thomas Etzemüller, *Alva and Gunnar Myrdal: Social Engineering in the Modern World* (Lanham, MD: Lexington Books, 2014); Walter A. Jackson, *Alva and Gunnar Myrdal in Sweden and America, 1898–1945* (New York: Routledge, 2021); John Holmwood, "Three Pillars of Welfare State Theory: T. H. Marshall, Karl Polanyi and Alva Myrdal in Defence of the National Welfare State," *European Journal of Social Theory* 3, no. 1 (2000), pp. 23–50; Jay Winter, "Socialism, Social Democracy and Population Questions in Western Europe: 1870–1950," *Population and Development Review* 14 (1988), pp. 122–46.

5 It is well beyond this chapter to provide an account of the longer and multifaceted history of social democracy in Sweden, which, of course, involved many influential actors. For an account with more comprehensive ambitions, see Sheri Berman, *The Primacy of Politics: Social Democracy and the Making of Europe's Twentieth Century* (Cambridge: Cambridge University Press, 2006).

6 The emblematic works for this view are the two articles authored by Karl Löwenstein in 1937 outlining the contours of a "militant democracy." Karl Löwenstein, "Militant Democracy and Fundamental Rights I," *American Political Science Review* 31, no. 3 (1937), pp. 417–32; Karl Löwenstein, "Militant Democracy and Fundamental Rights II," *American Political Science Review* 31, no. 4 (1937), pp. 638–58; cf. Anthoula Malkopoulou and Ludvig Norman, "Three Models of Democratic Self-Defence: Militant Democracy and Its Alternatives," *Political Studies* 66, no. 2 (2018), pp. 442–58.

7 David Mitrany, *A Working Peace System* (Oxford: Oxford University Press, 1943); Ludvig Norman, "Democracy's Fragility and the European Political Order: Functionalism, Militant Democracy and Crisis" in R. N. Lebow and L. Norman, eds., *Robustness and Fragility of Political Orders: Leader Assessments, Responses and Consequences* (Cambridge: Cambridge University Press, 2022); Cornelia Navari, "Functionalism Versus Federalism: Alternative Visions of European Unity" in Philomena Murray and Paul Rich, eds., *Visions of European Unity* (Boulder, CO: Westview Press, 1996), pp. 63–92; Ludvig Norman, "Defending the European Political Order: Visions of Politics in Response to the Radical Right," *European Journal Social Theory* 20, no. 4 (2017), pp. 531–49.

8 Löwenstein, "Militant Democracy and Fundamental Rights I."

9 Alf Ross, *Why Democracy?* (Cambridge, MA: Harvard University Press, 1952); Originally published in Danish: Alf Ross, *Hvorfor Demokrati?* (Copenhagen: Munksgaard, 1946).

10 Ross, *Why Democracy?*

11 Alf Ahlberg, *Tysklands ödesväg: Varför segrade nationalsocialismen?* [*Germany's Path of Destiny: Why Did National Socialism Win?*] (Stockholm: Natur och Kultur, 1934). See contributions by Webber (Chapter 2) and Caldwell (Chapter 3) in this volume for analyses of how German social democrats analyzed Weimar's fall and the rise of Nazism.
12 Sofia Näsström, "Democratic Self-Defense: Bringing the Social Model Back In," *Distinktion: Journal of Social Theory* 22, no. 3 (2021), pp. 376–96.
13 The SAP maintained consistent electoral support in the decades after the war at levels between 44 percent and 50 percent and remained in government power until the election of 1976. This level of electoral support needs to be understood in the context of the Swedish parliamentary system of proportional representation, where majorities of a single party tend to be more uncommon. Nicholas Aylott, "The Party System" in Jon Pierre, ed., *The Oxford Handbook of Swedish Politics* (Oxford: Oxford University Press, 2015), pp. 152–67.
14 A simple keyword search in Google Scholar comparing the number of hits when using the Swedish spelling of the Weimar Republic (*Weimarrepubliken*) and the German (*Die Weimarer Republik*) supplies an indication that this was the case, the German garnering 241,000 results and the Swedish a mere 594. Even adjusted for population size, this illustrates a vast difference between the extent to which Weimar figures in the scholarly debates of the respective countries.
15 Aylott, "The Party System," p. 154.
16 Rudolph Meidner, "Our Concept of the Third Way: Some Remarks on the Socio-Political Tenets of the Swedish Labour Movement," *Economic and Industrial Democracy* 1 (1980), pp. 343–69.
17 Näsström, "Democratic Self-Defense."
18 Gunnar Myrdal entered parliament for the Social Democratic Party during short stints in the 1930s and 1940s. While the party embraced many of the ideas developed by Alva Myrdal, it first showed little interest in extending opportunities for formal roles in the party. After the war, she served as a diplomat and ambassador. Lars Lindskog, *Alva Myrdal* (Stockholm: Sveriges Radios Förlag, 1981). While a member of the SAP from 1932, she served as a parliamentarian for the party only between 1962 and 1970. From the late 1940s, Myrdal's engagements were increasingly international, holding senior positions in the UN, focusing in particular on social issues. The couple also worked in the US, where Gunnar worked on and published an influential study on US race relations. Gunnar Myrdal, *An American Dilemma: The Negro Problem and Modern Democracy* (New York: Harper and Brothers, 1944). Alva Myrdal, during this same period, published *Nation and Family: The Swedish Experiment in Democratic Family and Population Policy* (New York: Harper and Brothers, 1941), published in Swedish as *Folk och familj* (Stockholm: Kooperativa Förbundets Bokförlag, 1944).
19 While the Myrdals were influential intellectual figures, it should be noted that not all social democrats were equally convinced that the social issues championed by, in particular, Alva Myrdal were of such primary importance. As Yvonne Hirdman recounts, Gustav Möller, an influential social

democratic politician and minister of social affairs for an astoundingly long tenure of nineteen years (1932–51), argued that the principal focus should be placed on the labor market, and not on social reforms aimed at the family. Yvonne Hirdman, *Att lägga livet till rätta* (Stockholm: Carlssons, 1989). Bo Rothstein has argued in a similar vein that key figures in the Social Democratic Party were skeptical toward the ideas of these "social engineers" and that the population question was a less prominent issue at the time. Bo Rothstein, "The Moral, Economic, and Political Logic of the Swedish Welfare State" in Pierre, *The Oxford Handbook of Swedish Politics*, pp. 69–84 .

20 The discussion here is primarily based on works published by Alva and Gunnar Myrdal in the 1930s and 1940s, in particular on the following works: Alva Myrdal and Gunnar Myrdal, *Kris i befolkningsfrågan* [*Crisis in the Population Question*] (Stockholm: Albert Bonniers Förlag, 1934); Alva Myrdal, *Nation and Family*; Alva Myrdal and Gunnar Myrdal, *Kontakt med Amerika* [*Contact with America*] (Stockholm: Albert Bonniers Förlag, 1941); Alva Myrdal, *Något kan man väl göra: Texter 1932–1982*, selected by Cecilia Åsa and Yvonne Hirdman (Stockholm: Carlssons, 2002); Hirdman, *Att lägga livet till rätta*.

21 Alva Myrdal, *Nation and Family*, p. 26.

22 Allison McIntosh, "Population Policy in Western Europe: Responses to Low Fertility in France, Sweden, and West Germany," *International Journal of Politics* 12, no. 3 (1982), pp. 3–100.

23 Population Commission, *Slutbetänkande avgivet av Befolkningskommissionen* [*Final Report of the Population Commission*] (Stockholm: Statens Offentliga Utredningar, 1938), p. 57. Gunnar Myrdal, who was a parliamentarian in the 1930s for the social democrats, was part of the commission. Several of the ideas outlined in *Kris i befolkningsfrågan* were transposed here into more concrete policy proposals.

24 Myrdal and Myrdal, *Kris i befolkningsfrågan*, p. 78.

25 Ibid.

26 Ibid.; Arthur Montgomery, "Befolkningskommissionen och befolkningsfrågan," *Ekonomisk Tidskrift* 41 no. 3 (1939), pp. 200–21, here p. 212.

27 Alva Myrdal, *Nation and Family*, p. 110.

28 Myrdal and Myrdal, *Kris i befolkningsfrågan*, p. 113.

29 Ibid., pp. 113–14.

30 Ibid., pp. 174–5.

31 Ibid., p. 116.

32 Ibid., p. 188.

33 Ibid.

34 Ann-Katrin Hatje, *Befolkningsfrågan och välfärden: Debatten om Familjepolitik och nativitetsökning under 1930- och 1940-talet* [*The Population Question and Welfare: The Debate on Family Policy and Increased Nativity in the 1930s and 1940s*] (Uddevalla: Bohuslänningens AB, 1974).

35 Ibid., p. 16.

36 Ibid., p. 19.

37 Cf. Rothstein, "The Moral, Economic, and Political Logic of the Swedish Welfare State."

38 Here, it seems that Rothstein misinterprets Myrdal's support for "in kind" benefits as an argument for primarily means-tested, rather than universal, benefits. In contrast, in both *Kris i befolkningsfrågan* and *Nation and Family*, Myrdal makes the case for free schooling, abolishment of private schools, free school lunches, and the provision of subsidized housing available to all. She also highlights the stigmas associated with means-tested benefits, emphasizing the need to create a comprehensive system that would alleviate the economic burdens of childrearing. Myrdal and Myrdal, *Kris i befolkningsfrågan*, pp. 200–2. See also Alva Myrdal, *Nation and Family*, p. 345; cf. Rothstein, "The Moral, Economic, and Political Logic of the Swedish Welfare State," p. 73.

39 Alva Myrdal, *Nation and Family*, pp. v–vi.

40 Ibid., p. 119.

41 Here, it is important to highlight the struggle of the meaning of "the people" and the *Folkhemmet* that had already occurred and in which the social democratic understanding of the idea had in many ways won over the organic theory of the state. See Hans Dahlqvist, "Folkhemsbegreppet: Rudolf Kjellén vs Per Albin Hansson," *Historisk Tidskrift* 122, no. 3 (2002), pp. 445–65. It is also notable that the contemporary resurgence of far-right populism has again brought this struggle to the fore, with the far right appropriating the concept to underpin chauvinistic political welfare programs. See Christian Norocel, "Populist Radical Right Protectors of the Folkhem: Welfare Chauvinism in Sweden," *Critical Social Policy* 36, no. 3 (2016), pp. 371–90.

42 Dahlqvist, "Folkhemsbegreppet," p. 459; Per Albin Hansson, "Folkhemmet, medborgarhemmet" in Anna Lisa Berkling, ed., *Från Fram till folkhemmet: Per Albin Hansson som tidningsman och talare* (Solna: Metodica Press, 1982), p. 227.

43 Myrdal and Myrdal, *Kris i befolkningsfrågan*, pp. 105–7.

44 Ibid., p. 110.

45 Ibid., p. 107.

46 Alva Myrdal, *Nation and Family*, p. 102.

47 Gunnar Myrdal was an economist and Alva Myrdal studied psychology and statistics.

48 Hirdman, *Att lägga livet tillrätta*; Ingegerd Troedsson, *Den Kommenderade Familjen: 30 år med Alva Myrdals familjepolitik* [*The Commanded Family: 30 Years with Alva Myrdal's Family Politics*] (Stockholm: Timbro, 1999).

49 Alva Myrdal, *Nation and Family*, p. 230.

50 Ibid., p. 58.

51 Ibid., p. 27.

52 Ibid., p. 376.

53 Ibid., p. v.

54 Alf W. Johansson, *Per Albin och Kriget: Samlingsregeringen och utrikespolitiken under andra världskriget* [*Per Albin and the War: The Coalition Government and Foreign Policy during the Second World War*] (Stockholm: Tidens Förlag, 1984), p. 435; Klas Åmark, *Att bo granne med ondskan: Sveriges förhållande till nazismen, Nazityskland och Förintelsen* [*Living Next Door to Evil: Sweden's Relations to Nazism, Nazi Germany and the Holocaust*] (Stockholm: Albert Bonniers Förlag, 2011), p. 670.

55 Johansson, *Per Albin och Kriget*.
56 Myrdal and Myrdal, *Kontakt med Amerika*.
57 Ibid., p. 12.
58 Ibid., p. 13.
59 Alva Myrdal, *Vår Plats Bland Nationerna* in Elsa Cedergren et al., eds., *Diskussion om Demokratin* (Stockholm: Albert Bonniers Förlag, 1941).
60 Marquis W. Childs, *This Is Democracy: Collective Bargaining in Scandinavia* (New Haven: Yale University Press, 1938), quoted in Myrdal, *Vår Plats Bland Nationerna*, pp. 54–5.
61 It could be added that this form of positive international attention to Sweden remains a popular theme in Swedish news reporting, featuring not least in Swedish news media's reporting of its unusual approach to dealing with the COVID-19 pandemic.
62 Alva Myrdal, *Nation and Family*, p. 148.
63 The notion that democratic society and scientific progress were inextricably linked also comes out in Ross's discussions on the future of democracy, where he even goes as far as to say that many of the political conflicts that mar the present will dissolve as scientific solutions emerge that can effectively address them. Ross, *Why Democracy?*
64 Alva Myrdal, "The Swedish Approach to Population Policies: Balancing Quantitative and Qualitative Population Philosophies in a Democracy," *Journal of Heredity* 30, no. 3 (1939), pp. 111–15; Leo Lucassen, "Brave New World: The Left, Social Engineering, and Eugenics in Twentieth-Century Europe," *International Review of Social History* 55, no. 2 (2010), pp. 265–96; Alberto Spektorowski and Elisabet Mizrachi, "Eugenics and the Welfare State in Sweden: The Politics of Social Margins and the Idea of a Productive Society," *Journal of Contemporary History* 39, no. 3 (2004), pp. 333–52; Gunnar Broberg and Mattias Tydén, "Eugenics in Sweden: Efficient Care" in Gunnar Boberg and Nils Roll-Hansen, eds., *Eugenics and the Welfare State: Norway, Sweden, Denmark and Finland* (East Lansing: Michigan State University Press, 2006), pp. 77–150.
65 Alva Myrdal, *Nation and Family*, p. 212.
66 Myrdal and Myrdal, *Kris i befolkningsfrågan*, p. 206.
67 Ibid., p. 215.
68 Ibid.
69 Ibid., p. 218.
70 Ibid.
71 Ibid., p. 219.
72 Ibid., p. 217; Alva Myrdal, *Nation and Family*, p. 121.
73 Myrdal and Myrdal, *Kris i befolkningsfrågan*, p. 220.
74 Ibid., p. 220.
75 Ibid., p. 78.
76 Ibid., p. 191.
77 Ibid., p. 73; cf. Dorothy Porter, "Eugenics and the Sterilization Debate in Sweden and Britain before World War II," *Scandinavian Journal of History* 24, no. 2 (1999), pp. 145–62.
78 Myrdal and Myrdal, *Kris i befolkningsfrågan*, p. 66.

79 Ibid., p. 224.
80 Ibid., p. 222.
81 Alva Myrdal, *Nation and Family*, p. 100.
82 Paul Weindling, "International Eugenics: Swedish Sterilization in Context," *Scandinavian Journal of History* 24, no. 2 (1999), pp. 179–97.
83 Peter Weingart, "Science and Political Culture: Eugenics in Comparative Perspective," *Scandinavian Journal of History* 24, no. 2 (1999), pp. 163–77, here p. 166.
84 Porter, "Eugenics and the Sterilization Debate."
85 In the legislation adopted in 1934 and later reinforced in 1941, applications for sterilization needed to be approved by the Swedish Board of Health. As government investigations have shown, however, rather than serving as a control mechanism, the Board and its director during the 1940s were strong advocates of sterilization and gave wide remit for its application by doctors. Government of Sweden, *Steriliseringsfrågan i Sverige 1935–1975: Historisk belysning* [*The Sterilization Question in Sweden 1935–1975: Historical Account*] (Stockholm: Statens Offentliga Utredningar, 2000), pp. 37–41.
86 Government of Sweden, "Lag den 8 Maj 1934 om sterilisering av vissa sinnesjuka, sinnesslöa eller andra som lida av rubbad själsverksamhet" [Law of 8 May 1934 on Sterilization of Certain Insane, Feebleminded or Others Suffering from Deranged Mental Activity]; Government of Sweden, "Lag om sterilisering, given Stockholms slott den 23 maj 1941" [Law on Sterilization], p. 282.
87 Government of Sweden, *Redogörelse för steriliseringsfrågan i Sverige åren 1935–1975 och regeringens åtgärder* [*Account of the Sterilization Question in Sweden 1935–1975 and the Actions of the Government*], Regeringens skrivelse 2000/01:73, available at https://data.riksdagen.se/fil/B27C45BD-1F80-4963-AAC2-E89892E6486E (accessed 8 March 2022).
88 Government of Sweden, Steriliseringsfrågan i Sverige 1935–1975: Historisk belysning, p. 20.
89 Public Investigation of the Swedish Government, SOU 1999:2, p. 13.
90 Government of Sweden, *Steriliseringsfrågan i Sverige 1935–1975: Historisk belysning*, p. 46.
91 Ibid., p. 177.
92 Ibid., p. 240.
93 Ibid., p. 241; see also Åmark, *Att bo granne med ondskan*, p. 367.
94 Public Investigation of the Swedish Government, SOU 1999:2, p. 12.

6   Our Past, Weimar's Present
Democracy's Defense and the Inversion of an Historical Lesson

Amel Ahmed

We live in uncertain times. Across the globe, political systems are in a state of flux. Institutions long taken for granted now produce unexpected results. And centuries-old coalitions, both within and between states, are fraying. As we seek to understand the current moment of political upheaval and structural change, public discourse increasingly turns to history as a source of theoretical insight and pragmatic guidance. A steady stream of books and articles have warned us about the impending collapse of the liberal order. And many draw on the experience of interwar Europe and the case of Weimar Germany in particular to support their analysis. This includes both traditional scholarly work and more publicly engaged scholarship, to say nothing of the numerous op-eds and journalistic engagements with the topic.[1]

The interest in Weimar is not new, of course. Within the fields of comparative politics, and particularly within the study of political development, there exists a significant body of scholarship that engages with the history of Weimar.[2] Indeed, the field of democratization studies has its roots in the study of Weimar and postwar debates about the fate of democracy in this pivotal case. Subsequently, it has been common to reach into the history of Weimar whenever democracy seems imperiled.[3] In this field-defining historical case, we have sought to understand the consequences of party fragmentation, the role of civil society, the structural foundations of democratic survival, and other dynamics that might help us navigate the contemporary political landscape.[4] These works draw on a vast historiography on German political development, which has engendered fierce theoretical and methodological debates regarding questions of German exceptionalism, as well as the continuities and discontinuities of the German Reich.

Engagement with the history of Weimar in the public sphere today, however, has become largely untethered from these rich traditions of scholarship, along with their disagreements, ambiguities, and ongoing controversies. Many publicly engaged scholarly works, seeking to seize the rhetorical force of Weimar's lessons, have turned to highly stylized narratives that are guided explicitly by contemporary threats to democracy. Certainly, history is often read with the goal of better understanding the present, but the challenges of such an endeavor are numerous and have themselves been the subject of much scholarly debate. From Marc Bloch's warning that history directed toward specific political objectives can itself become a form of "propaganda" to Foucault's declaration that these efforts can produce only a "history of the present," historians of various intellectual traditions have warned of the pitfalls of putting history in service of the present.[5] At a minimum, it can limit our ability to understand history on its own terms, leading to flaws of interpretation and empirical errors. At an extreme, as the editors of this volume warn, such an approach can subvert historical understanding altogether, pre-formulating lessons and imposing historical interpretations that justify them. The lessons come first and "history" second.

In this analysis, I address myself to several recent works that have sought to harness the lessons of Weimar to offer guidance to ailing democracies around the globe. Utilizing a Weberian evaluation of ideal types, I examine the model of democracy and democratic defense employed within these accounts. I argue that what they offer as a general or universal model of democracy defense comes to reflect in its construction a very particular model that emerged in the postwar context of Cold War competition. It was a reaction to the perceived weaknesses of Weimar, to be sure, but, more than this, it was driven by Cold War imperatives, intended to produce a political outcome rather than a political process. Specifically, this was a model of democracy defense aimed at strengthening the influence of domestic actors aligned with the West, and diminishing the influence of those aligned with the East, and one that came to rely heavily on a tactical view of democracy preservation. It is often associated with Joseph Schumpeter's minimalist definition, which reduced democracy to a method of managing elite competition, but in fact this model was never purely procedural, but rather it had a very concrete substantive vision associated with the economic and political goals of the West.[6] It is better understood as a defense of *political democracy*, a particular postwar creation offered as an alternative to social democracy.

Today, this Cold War model of democracy defense dominates much thinking on democracy preservation. Long past the point at which the reasons that gave rise to it have disappeared, the same model now returns in recent works on Weimar's lessons. But unmoored from its historical particularity, it appears as a universal and has been presented as such in recent works. The lack of reflexivity with respect to this model, I argue, presents serious analytical problems in that it distorts the history of

Weimar from which these works purport to draw. Further, and perhaps more significantly, these analytical flaws quickly become political pitfalls. By offering this historical model as a universal, these works both misconstrue the terrain of the political fight and miss opportunities to appeal to those who may support democracy but may seek more radical outcomes beyond the confines of political democracy. Accounting for the historical particularity of this vision helps to reveal important elements of the problems faced by contemporary democracies. It may also help to open up space for a revisioning of democracy that would serve as the basis for a more robust democratic defense.

Reflexivity and Historical Understanding: A Weberian Analysis

The analysis here centers reflexivity as a key component of historical understanding. To guide the inquiry, I rely primarily on a Weberian perspective, utilizing an evaluation of ideal types. Weber's unique position within the philosophy of the social sciences makes his approach especially suited to the present analysis. His critique of objectivity in the social sciences stands as one of the most foundational statements on the topic. Inspired largely by what he saw as the unreflexive use of "history's lessons," he sought to demonstrate the perspectival nature of historical narratives, maintaining that they were infused at every turn by the scholar's value orientations, cultural dispositions, and theoretical priors. In the context of imperial Germany, he challenged the ways in which history's lessons had been mobilized by both the left and the right. His interventions hinged on the insight that both the conservatives and the Marxists offered historical narratives that were, in his view, particular and political in nature, but both presented them as universal and objective, even scientific.[7]

For Weber, however, this perspective did not lead to a disavowal of history or of history's lessons. While fully appreciating the challenges of historical understanding, the obstacles imposed by one's own subjectivity, and the perspectival nature of all historical accounts, Weber still believed (or perhaps hoped) that it was possible to learn from history. This position set him apart within the great epistemological battles of the nineteenth century, and it sets him apart still.[8] These debates pitted proto-positivist, neo-Kantian perspectives against non-positivists of various persuasions who came to identify with the "cultural sciences."[9] Within these debates, Weber joined the non-positivists in their critique of objectivity. But, unlike others who saw in the critique an insurmountable obstacle to historical understanding, Weber offered an alternative mode of reading history that rested on reflexivity rather than objectivity. This is perhaps the element of his approach that makes it most helpful for the current inquiry – his was an internal critique in that he did not see the attempt to offer lessons from history as illegitimate, as did many others in the non-positivist camp. However, he maintained that reflexivity about the particularity of one's perspective was an essential condition of historical understanding.

Weber himself, of course, never used the term "reflexivity." Rather, he offered the concept of *verstehen*, which is typically translated as "understanding," but in Weber's usage came to represent a mode of reflexive understanding that does not seek to negate but to foreground the scholar's own subjectivity.[10] This mode of analysis accepts the historian's subjectivity to be an inescapable reality, and offers transparency about this subjectivity as the standard of scientific rigor. In this respect Weber's epistemology bears many similarities to some modes of ethnographic research.[11]

Formalizing the practice of reflexivity is precisely what he aimed to do with the evaluation of "ideal types," an approach that he offered as an answer to the problem of objectivity in the social sciences.[12] He maintained that all historical analysis involved some form of conceptualization or abstraction that is essentially a creation of the scholar, heuristic models that prime our expectations and our adjudication of historical facts. The evaluation of ideal types was meant to make transparent the hidden models that lurk in our scholarship.[13]

The real danger, for Weber, was not that these mental models would enter into historical inquiry, but that, without a sense of reflexivity, they would become an invisible part of the analysis, invisible even to the historians themselves. Without an evaluation of the concepts we bring to bear on our investigations, historical inquiry becomes entirely self-referential: We get out what we have put in, although we take it to be evidence of something external to ourselves. It is a rather extreme form of confirmation bias that threatens to undermine the very possibility of learning from history.

While ideal type analysis is typically associated with Weber's sociological work, I rely here on the approach employed in his historical writings. Weber's approach was in fact first designed for historical research and only later applied to sociological analyses. It was with the evaluation of ideal types in *The Protestant Ethic and the Spirit of Capitalism* that he was able to illustrate the historical particularity of "rational economic man" and the inadequacy of this mental model for explaining the actions of the early Calvinists.[14]

Animated by a similar Weberian sensibility, my goal in this analysis is to understand the model of democracy defense employed in recent works that seek to harness Weimar's lessons. The goal is to understand this model in its historical particularity, the conditions of its emergence, the purposes it was meant to serve, and limitations of its application. This exercise, similar to what Fred Schaffer has described as "locating," proceeds from the understanding that, while certain concepts such as democracy, liberalism, and egalitarianism may exist as universalist abstractions, when we draw on them, we access them in a particular form, often relying on what is familiar or what Clifford Geertz referred to as the "experience near."[15] In the analysis that follows, I offer an evaluation of the model of democracy defense employed in recent works on threats to contemporary democracies, with the goal of elucidating the particular form that appears in these work and why it matters for the lessons they draw from history.

Democracy's Defense: A Tactical View

In this section, I address myself to several works in the recent wave of publicly engaged scholarship that draw on the history of Weimar to offer lessons to ailing democracies across the globe. This includes *Hitler's First One Hundred Days* by Peter Fritzsche; *Death of a Democracy* by Benjamin Hett; *How Democracies Die* by Steven Levitsky and Daniel Ziblatt; *On Tyranny* by Timothy Snyder; and *How Fascism Works* by Jason Stanley. As analogy, as metaphor, and as warning, Weimar's lessons are used in these works to promote modes of thought and action that would fortify democracy against its detractors. These works, all penned by esteemed historians and social scientists, are rendered with an air of urgency, and while the styles differ depending on their specific audience, they present the history of Weimar as having very specific lessons for democracy defense writ large and for the current context of the United States and Western Europe in particular. While importantly engaging the public on these topics, I contend that the ways in which Weimar's lessons have been constructed and mobilized hold hidden and underappreciated pitfalls that may limit the reach and efficacy of their purported lessons.

One thing that comes across very vividly in these works is the highly tactical view of democracy defense they employ. This begins with their framing of the problem and motivation for the inquiry. In the contemporary context, many identify 2016 and the election of Donald Trump as a pivotal moment, with the potential to determine the fate of democracy in the United States. According to Levitzky and Ziblatt, by electing "a president with dubious allegiance to democratic norms," Americans failed the first test of democratic viability.[16] While they acknowledge that "norm erosion," one of the key dangers to democracy in their view, began long before Trump, they still identify his election as the defining moment. Stanley identifies Trump's 2016 "America first" campaign platform as the revival of a fascist strain of American politics that had been dormant since the 1930s.[17] And Hett weaves together the Trump election and the Brexit vote, representing a similarly pivotal point in Europe, as signaling a turn toward populism and as a general cause for alarm.[18]

In their efforts to draw insights from the experience of Weimar Germany, they similarly train their analytical gaze on Hitler's ascent to power. Many begin with his assumption of the chancellorship. Several focus in particular on the appointment of the Papen cabinet in 1932 and Papen's calamitous miscalculation in supporting Hitler's rise.[19] Fritzsche focuses even more narrowly on Hitler's first 100 days.[20] Thus, in the construction of the problem, both past and present, the danger begins with the rise of a populist demagogue advancing a xenophobic program and overtaking vital democratic institutions. Ongoing pressures from various economic crises may have created an opening and conditions favorable to such demagoguery, but the threat essentially comes from an individual and the resources they can mobilize.

Given that, at the time of their writing, aspiring autocrats had already emerged in the US and Europe, this may seem like a logical starting point. However, the threat identified in these works, it is argued, goes beyond this historical moment. According to Levitzky and Ziblatt, "extremist demagogues emerge from time to time in all societies, even in healthy democracies."[21] Synder similarly identifies an ever present danger, drawing a line from Greek and Roman democracy, through the American Founding, and finally to twentieth-century Europe, and stressing that the threat of tyranny is constant and pervasive in democracy.[22]

The threat is an endemic one precisely because of democracy's openness, allowing aspiring autocrats to gain power through its very institutions. Hett maintains that "Hitler had destroyed the democratic system by having his party compete successfully within that system until he was strong enough to bring it down."[23] Levitzky and Ziblatt also maintain that the threat from within makes the institutions of democracy especially vulnerable, as today "[d]emocracy may die at the hands not of generals but of elected leaders – presidents or prime ministers who subvert the very process that brought them to power."[24] Snyder similarly warns of the naïve view that "the rulers who came to power through institutions cannot change or destroy those very institutions."[25] Stanley maintains that the threat is not only that institutions will be dismantled but that they can be coopted and made to serve undemocratic ends. Pointing to the *Gleichschaltung*, or Nazification of the German state, he describes the process by which "the institutions of the German government gradually became 'Nazified,' moving from liberal democratic organizing principles to National Socialist ones."[26]

The threat from within is a recurring theme across these works, a threat that is all the more dangerous because those with autocratic aims will also claim democratic credentials, making the work of democracy defense not only one of resisting the aspiring autocrats, but also one of knowing decisively who they are. Some address this challenge explicitly. Levitzky and Ziblatt offer four criteria that may help in this determination – all cogent criteria but still vulnerable to the ambiguities of democratic contention.[27] The first, for example, asks about the "rejection of or weak commitment to the democratic rules of the game." However, given the endogeneity of these rules and the fact that they can be changed, it still offers little guidance as to whose democratic rules should be defended. Others, such as Snyder, forgo the question altogether, allowing the reader to assume that they will know who the tyrant is, and also that they are the democrats.

The construction of the problem is important because it guides the construction of the solution toward tactics aimed at containing the demagogue. Each of these works goes to great lengths to impress upon the reader the evitability of the demagogue's success and the need for tactical action to thwart their continued rise. In the historical context of Weimar, many of these narratives focus on the actors around Hitler who could have prevented his rise, but sat idly by as he accumulated power. Hett faults the conservative elites who, despite finding Hitler contemptable, supported him for political gain.[28] He guides the reader through a highly detailed account of Hitler's first year, chronicling several efforts to resist the Nazi takeover. This included a plan by Edgar Jung to infiltrate the NSDAP (Nationalsozialistische Deutsche Arbeiterpartei or National Socialist German Workers' Party), aborted schemes for Hitler's assassination, and efforts to convince President Hindenburg to turn against Hitler and seize emergency powers. Each failed, according to Hett, due to a lack of unity among conservative elites.

Fritzsche similarly focuses on the failure of the political class to check extremism, stressing that, even after Hitler's rise, his success was highly contingent.[29] He tells us: "There was nothing inevitable about Hitler's appointment on January 30, 1933, or self-evident about Germany's Nazi future. There was no crowd at the Brandenburg Gate or march on Berlin to push the National Socialists to power. The National Socialists were not riding a wave of newfound popularity."[30] This all, he maintains, was transformed in the first 100 days as the Nazis succeeded in uniting a public that had been deeply divided under the Weimar Republic.

Without disputing the claim that Hitler's rise was avoidable, what is important here is that this construction helps to bolster a highly tactical view of democracy's defense, stressing that, even after the demagogue's appearance, it is still possible to thwart their rise. What is needed is a unified democratic defense. For some, this defense comes from the broader society. Snyder's treatise is focused on citizens' ability to resist. He offers twenty theses meant to alert the reader to the dangers around them and their role in arresting those dangers. Similarly, Stanley maintains that his purpose in writing the book is to expose fascist tactics, "providing citizens with the critical tools to recognize the difference between legitimate tactics in liberal democratic politics on the one hand, and invidious tactics in fascist politics on the other."[31]

For others, it is elite coalitions that are necessary and were absent in Weimar. According to Fritzsche, faced with the rapid rise of the NSDAP, "the other parties might have been expected to form a coalition to protect the constitution and preserve law and order. But German politics didn't work that way."[32] Without a unified opposition, the Nazis easily won over a fragmented society through propaganda campaigns waged in the street and in the media; a society that was too divided to defend democracy somehow united to support fascism. For Levitzky and Ziblatt, the focus is primarily on political elites, and especially parties, as critical gatekeepers. In cases where democracy has survived challenges from extremists and demagogues, they argue, it is because parties "make a concerted effort to isolate and defeat them." They maintain that, within the political class, "[u]nited democratic fronts can prevent extremists from winning power, which can mean saving democracy."[33]

While one cannot dispute the importance of pro-democracy actors in times of regime challenges, the lessons that are drawn for the present context rely on a tactical rather than structural view of democratic preservation. Democracy's defenders are asked to take up strategies to block the demagogue's rise, but they are not obligated by these accounts to address the deeper structural issues. This, after all, is an enduring challenge according to these accounts; demagogues can appear at any time and the threat of tyranny is endemic. The message that comes across most forcefully in these studies is that democracy's defense requires, first and foremost, a unified pro-democracy coalition. Further, democracy's survival rests on this coalition's ability to defeat extreme political forces, preferably before they emerge on the political scene but even after.

What is most striking about this model of democracy defense is how very particular it is. It is particular not only in the sense of centering a particular form of liberal and Schumpeterian democratic ideals, as many critics have pointed out,[34] but also in its articulations of an *historically particular* understanding of democracy defense that originated in the circumstances of postwar Europe. In part a reaction to the fall of Weimar, but more a creature of Cold War imperatives, the idea of a pro-democracy coalition fending off extremists on the left and the right has its roots in this period and was intended to diminish the influence of fascist remnants, but more so communists and even social democrats who threatened the ascendent liberal order. In the next section, I examine the emergence of this model of democracy defense and how it came to reconfigure democracy in a tactical battle to preserve the liberal capitalist consensus domestically as well as internationally.

Democracy Defense and Cold War Imperatives

The model of democracy and democratic defense found in recent works drawing on Weimar has been described as liberal and Schumpeterian, and it is that. But it represents a particular variant of each. It is a model rooted in the postwar political and economic consensus known as the liberal international order, alternatively referred to as the Cold War order,[35] and one that came to rely heavily on institutions as the guarantor of peace, both domestic and international. Democracy in this view had certain liberal features, but it was very distinct from the liberal democracies of the prewar period; in fact, in many respects it was highly illiberal.[36] It was understood as a form of "political democracy," a framing that came into use in the postwar period to distinguish these political systems from social democracy, which connoted more participatory and egalitarian ends.

Although political democracy came to be closely associated with procedural definitions focused on elite competition, the most important and distinctive feature of these democracies at the time had to do not with a political process, but with a specific political outcome: strengthening domestic actors aligned with the West, and diminishing the influence of those aligned with the East. These efforts became increasingly focused on finetuning the mechanisms of democracy – regulations of party competition, the design of electoral systems, and so on – as a means of securing victories for political forces, typically center-right coalitions, aligned with the West and especially with liberal capitalism. The express goal of these efforts was to engineer a system that would allow for competition, but keep it within specific parameters, which meant excluding more radical political forces along with their visions of democracy.

Many of these transformations transpired in the decade after the Second World War, which saw ongoing domestic struggles within the beleaguered democracies of Western Europe. These struggles were not between democrats and non-democrats: The decisive victory of the Allied forces ensured that democracy had no serious competitors in the political system. Rather, the struggles were waged among democratic actors over conflicting democratic visions. In these contests, Christian Democratic parties, which in several countries emerged as the dominant political force in the postwar period, became the face of government and the main champions of the ascendent liberal democratic capitalist order. In opposition were the various parties of the left, primarily communists and social democrats critical of the emerging capitalist order, and advancing a vision of social democracy stressing egalitarian rather than liberal principles.[37]

Of course, social democratic parties would come to play an important role in the postwar period as well, especially in Northern Europe. However, in the countries most vital for the geostrategic interests of the Allied forces – particularly Germany, Italy, and France – the left was heavily scrutinized and its democratic credentials continually questioned. This was especially true of communist parties, but also of social democratic parties depending on their position vis-à-vis the liberal capitalist order. It was only in instances where social democrats had moderated their position and accommodated themselves to the emergent liberal international order that they were welcomed into government and into the fold of the democracy defense coalition. This was true, for example, of the French Section of the Workers' International (SFIO), which played a critical role in the postwar reconstruction and campaign for democracy defense in France. And it was true of the German Social Democratic Party, but only after the party's shift in platform in 1959 to embrace a more accommodationist outlook toward the capitalist order.[38] The shift followed a decade of decline in electoral politics, and, perhaps more importantly, a ban on the Communist Party in 1956 which left it without its main partner in opposition.[39]

The imperatives of Cold War competition and the need to consolidate support for the liberal capitalist order meant that these domestic contests had important international consequences. Postwar Germany, divided between East and West, became the epicenter of this fight. The period of Allied occupation between 1945 and 1955 saw the most intense pressure and intervention from the West to structure politics in the new German state. Konrad Adenauer, first chancellor of the German Federal Republic and head of the Christian Democratic Union (CDU), famously opined that the Cold War was as much a domestic as an international conflict.

In this conflict, the West, and especially the United States, was heavily invested in German affairs and came to forge strong ties with the Christian Democratic right. For the United States, Germany was key to stabilizing the emerging liberal order and sustaining an environment where capitalism could thrive. And the Christian Democrats were key to that.[40]

Fortifying the center-right coalition required both ideational and institutional innovation. While the left advanced a radical vision of democracy which centered popular sovereignty, the right embraced a conservative vision in which representative bodies were the primary vehicle of democratic governance and the guarantors of democratic stability. The left put its faith in mechanisms of participatory and direct democracy, the right in parliamentarism.[41] In this contest, the left was at a decided disadvantage given the disillusionment of postwar politics with the principle of popular sovereignty, and the high disregard in which "the will of people" was held. In the words of Karl Loewenstein, the German émigré who returned after the war to establish political science as a discipline in the German academy, "the peoples whose madness brought the world so near to ruin" could not be entrusted with the power to govern, unless they "undergo a long course of reform and probation."[42]

The right took advantage of such sentiments to question the democratic credentials of the left and to enlist the public in a movement for democratic defense, which required the defense of pro-democracy, pro-capitalist, center-right governments aligned with the West. The same partners on the left who, just a few years earlier, had helped to establish the new democratic constitution were now portrayed as "the enemy within." Not only in Germany but throughout Western Europe, the right warned that communist and social democratic parties could not be trusted to defend democracies in light of their associations with and perceived sympathies toward the Soviet Union.[43]

In this context, defending democracy meant defending the parliamentary majorities of center-right governments.[44] Along with the CDU bloc in Germany, the "third force" in France and "democrazia protetta" in Italy presented themselves as coalitions of democratic defense.[45] All were supported by the United States and figured prominently in its foreign policy agenda of uniting the Western bloc and safeguarding the liberal international order.[46] Importantly, the same tactical view of democracy defense expressed in contemporary works can also be found in these postwar struggles. Democracy was to be secured by a pro-democracy coalition that would keep extreme views at bay and protect democracy from the ever present threats within it.

To secure parliamentary majorities, these coalitions relied not only on appeals to voters, but also on a host of institutional safeguards that were introduced in the early stages of party system formation to weed out extreme parties.[47] These included, for example, the addition of a threshold for elections to the German parliament and the switch to the two ballot system, both introduced in 1953.[48] The 5 percent threshold would impose a high barrier to entry for smaller parties and the two ballot system would reduce the proportionality of representation, also hindering the access of smaller parties.[49] Both were strongly opposed by the Social Democrats and their partners on the left, and both passed with the support of the Christian Democrats' center-right coalition.[50]

This period is often associated with the rise of the idea of militant or defensive democracy, whereby decision-making was increasingly moved away from elected bodies toward bureaucracies and courts, and aggressive measures were taken to root out anti-systemic forces with the use of party bans and restrictions on organization. But the transformations of this period were not just about the move away from popular representation. Alongside this, there was a concerted effort to reconfigure the institutions of representation themselves in order to safeguard the position of center-right coalitions of "democracy defense," and to fortify the new liberal democratic capitalist order against its detractors on the left.[51] Ironically, the same power-consolidating institutional changes we now associate with the populist challenges to contemporary democracy were first employed in the postwar period to secure the liberal order, internationally and domestically, against "extreme opinion," which included much of the left.

The Science of Democracy Defense

This institutional turn on the question of democracy's defense found ample support in wider reform circles and especially in the academy. The locus of these activities was the Inter-Parliamentary Union (IPU), a consortium originally established in 1889 to advance the cause of parliamentarism, but which in the 1950s was given renewed purpose as parliaments came to take center stage in the emerging model of democracy defense.[52] The United States, which previously had a very limited presence in the IPU, in the postwar period would come to take a leading role. Hosting the 1953 meeting in Washington, President Eisenhower welcomed the delegates, stressing the importance of the organization in promoting "the peaceful role of Parliaments." Parliaments, according to Eisenhower, were to "constitute a forum for political discussion which

needed for democracy defense and that such a coalition might have saved Weimar. What is overlooked is that there was in fact a robust pro-democracy coalition in Weimar. It is often referred to as the Weimar Coalition. It included the Social Democrats, the Catholic Center Party, and the Left Liberals, and at times also expanded to include the Liberal Party in a Grand Coalition. The problem was not that they were not united over democracy, but that democracy was all that united them. On matters of policy, they were often divided and found it difficult to govern, which opened the door to executive encroachment on several occasions.

The idea that Weimar's pro-democracy coalition fell apart is often linked to the decision of the Catholic Center Party and the Liberal Party to break with the Social Democrats in 1930.[68] However, the decision of these two pivotal parties to break off and form a center-right coalition was not unusual; they had done this many times before.[69] In fact, throughout the Weimar Republic, governments moved between what was referred to as a center-left "Grand Coalition" and a center-right "Bourgeois Coalition," or a coalition of the non-socialist bourgeois parties. Each of these coalitions hinged on the movement of the two parties of the center. Yes, the decision of these parties to break with the Social Democrats in 1930 proved highly consequential, but it did not signal a decisive breakdown of the pro-democracy coalition as much as an effort to identify a viable policy coalition to respond to the economic crisis. In fact, the Weimar Coalition reunited in 1932, belatedly realizing the dangers posed by the rise of the Nazis, but unable to stop them due to the coalition's diminished numbers.

Another potential source of democracy defense, we are told, may come from the right. Hett, for example, tries to identify points of resistance to Hitler among conservatives, perhaps communicating a desire to see such resistance from conservatives today. Even after the Weimar Coalition had been diminished, and even after Hitler had been appointed chancellor, he maintains that there were significant opportunities on the right to block his rise, opportunities lost due to a lack of unity. However, in his efforts to demonstrate the possibilities and ultimate failure of a conservative resistance, he elides the fact that Weimar's conservatives were not democrats. They participated in the political system but never accepted democracy.[70] Had they succeeded in resisting Hitler, the outcome would very likely have been autocracy.

Related to this, any narrative of democracy defense that begins with the Nazi takeover in 1932–3 is confounded by the fact that Weimar was already a semi-presidential system with heavily curtailed representative government and had been since 1930. While it is true that Hitler used a constitutional act, Article 48, to permanently dissolve parliament, it had effectively been suspended for three years before this point. Then chancellor and head of the Center Party, Henrich Brüning, had invoked Article 48 in 1930 to pass a budget. Unable to assemble a government majority, he ruled mostly through presidential decree after that point. Papen inherited and continued the semi-presidential system.[71] In 1932, mobilizing a pro-democracy coalition among political elites would have required first undoing these measures.

Beyond the structure of the conflict, actors' understanding of it was also quite different from what is portrayed in this model of democracy defense. The very notion of tyranny, which may obviously point in one direction to a contemporary audience (and even that is questionable), could have implicated a wide array of actors and ideologies in Weimar. Asked to resist an unnamed tyranny, the citizens of Weimar might have been just as likely to turn on the Social Democrats as they would on the Nazis. Even the idea of preserving democratic norms, which is clearly integral to contemporary democracies, makes little sense in Weimar. In a democracy of fourteen years, norms were never very strong, politics was never very civil, and guardrails were scarcely to be found.

The point here is not to quibble with these issues of historical interpretation. Rather, it is to illustrate that it is hard to see Weimar in the solutions they offer. The model of democracy defense these works purport to draw *from* Weimar very likely would not have worked *in* Weimar. It comes from a different place and was designed for a different fight, one that we now read back onto Weimar. The lack of reflexivity about the model employed in these works not only produces errors of historical interpretation, it also jeopardizes the very possibility of learning from history. As Weber warned, such an analysis becomes highly self-referential. We take out what we have put in, but understand it to be evidence of something external to ourselves.

The dangers, however, are not just academic. The inversion of these historical lessons presents serious challenges for politics as well, as it obscures part of the problem and what might be needed to enact a robust defense of democracy in the current context. This gets to the real "So what?" of it all. The lack of reflexivity with respect to the historical particularity of this model of democracy defense not only leads to a backward reading of Weimar; it also inhibits a forward reading of our own democratic context and a revisioning of democratic defense more appropriate for our times. The postwar model of democracy defense, rooted in the geostrategic imperatives of Cold War competition, advancing centrist coalitions, and leaning in to an institutional understanding of political democracy that is stripped of its social and participatory elements, emerged in a particular historical time to serve a particular historical purpose. Whether or not one ever accepted these Cold War imperatives as legitimate, most would accept that today they are obsolete. Yet the repertoires of democracy defense they set in place continue to dominate political thought. What is more, this model of democracy defense has been naturalized to such an extent that today it appears and is offered in these works as universal, along with the vision of political democracy it is meant to defend.

In asserting the universality of this model, such works exclude alternative visions of democracy that could be vital for the very democratic rejuvenation they seek. While their target seems to be an authoritarian style of populism emerging on the right, their tactics would also exclude potential allies on the left. This is a more serious limitation as it is those who might seek more radical or participatory, but still democratic, outcomes who may most fruitfully be enlisted in the effort to halt the progress of autocratization in these polities. Engaging such perspectives requires a revisioning of democracy and democratic defense that interrogates the inheritances of Cold War repertoires as well as their assumptions.

Perhaps the most pressing question that emerges for the contemporary context is whether political democracy must continue to travel a separate path from social democracy. The choice to separate the two – a choice that, it must be stressed again, was driven by Cold War politics – is arguably the source of many of democracy's present-day woes. Many have noted the "social" roots of recent populist challenges. As Sheri Berman has argued, these movements tap into social grievances that persist long after the political forces of the old European left have been vanquished.[72] Certainly, there is much more to the populist insurgence, but the vacuum left by the decline of social democratic forces and their visions, particularly in Europe and Latin America, has been central to many accounts.[73] Moreover, the social grievances which today animate much democratic discontent have enabled democratic claims-making by populist movements on both the left and the right.

The role of social grievances in bolstering populist movements is acknowledged within much of the recent scholarship employing the Weimar analogy. But the conditions that have brought it about are also naturalized. For example, Hett and Snyder both attribute the crises of democracy, past and present, to "globalization" and the failed promise of progress. According to Snyder, publics responded "to the real and perceived inequalities it created, and the apparent helplessness of the democracies in addressing them."[74] However, globalization and the liberal order in which it is embedded are taken to be largely exogenous to the problem. Both authors concede that liberal democracy was ill equipped to handle the challenge of rising inequality; however, the possibility that it may have contributed to the problem is not seriously considered. Globalization and its pathologies are taken to be natural vulnerabilities of liberal democracy.

Even critics of these works have accepted aspects of their universalizing tendencies. Peter Breiner has critiqued them for failing to recognize the cyclical nature of the conflict between liberal and egalitarian visions of democracy.[75] His framing aptly captures the tensions we continue to see between the substantive and the procedural, the political and the social, and between liberalism and egalitarianism, but the temporalities of cyclical conflict suggest an undifferentiated continuity. There may indeed be a cyclical nature to this struggle, but such temporalities elide the very particular nature of this instantiation of the conflict between liberalism and egalitarianism. A greater sense of the historical particularity of the postwar confrontation – that it was a clash between a specific set of liberal goals and a conflicting set of egalitarian objectives – might offer greater grounding to the current moment and open up room for political creativity. There is no doubt that the struggle between liberalism and egalitarianism has enduring qualities, but that does not eliminate the possibility for new formulations and novel configurations of democracy's defense.

Reading Weimar for the Present

What does it mean to read the history of Weimar in the twenty-first century? Certainly, we read history for the purpose of understanding the present, deriving whatever lessons we can for our current circumstances. But some histories are more challenging than others. Weimar is a place that did not exist until after it ended. As the editors of this volume note, the term "Weimar Republic" did not come into use until after the Second World War. In a multitude of ways, its history has been colored by our knowledge of what came after. This has inhibited a grounded understanding of actions and motivations, at times subverting history to present-day concerns and shaping it to contemporary objectives.

The reality is that we cannot but read history backward. However, as I have argued in this chapter, the practice of reflexivity can lend greater clarity to such a reading. A reflexive approach might lead us to examine why we return to Weimar, what we are looking for, and how that shapes what we find. Ideally, it would allow for some elements of a forward reading of history, one in which actors operate in a context where the future is uncertain and filled with possibility. This reflexivity might enable different historical lessons; it would certainly suggest that there are multiple lessons one can take from the history of Weimar.

In this chapter I have aimed to offer a reflexive evaluation of an ideal type – the model of democracy defense employed in recent publicly engaged scholarship drawing on the lessons of Weimar. These works rely on a model of democracy defense that is offered as universal, but, as I argue, in its construction it comes to reflect a very particular model of democracy defense that emerged in the postwar context of Cold War competition. It was a model of democracy defense that aimed at preserving *political* democracy, a particular postwar creation, related to but distinct from both liberal and elite democracy.

The lack of reflexivity with respect to this model of democracy defense, I argue, presents serious analytical problems in that it distorts the history of Weimar from which these works purport to draw. Further, the lack of reflexivity introduces significant political pitfalls that may undermine the very goal of democracy preservation. By offering this historical model as a universal one, these works both misconstrue the terrain of the political fight and miss opportunities to appeal to those who may support democracy but may seek more radical or participatory outcomes beyond the confines of political democracy. Accounting for the historical particularity of this vision helps to reveal important elements of the problem faced by contemporary democracies. It may also help to open up space for a revisioning of democracy that would serve as the basis for a more robust democratic defense.

Notes

1 For traditional scholarly works on the subject, see Hermann Beck and Larry Eugene Jones, eds., *From Weimar to Hitler: Studies in the Dissolution of the Weimar Republic and the Establishment of the Third Reich, 1932–1934* (New York: Berghahn Books, 2019); Sujit Choudhry, "Resisting Democratic Backsliding: An Essay on Weimar, Self-Enforcing Constitutions, and the Frankfurt School," *Global Constitutionalism* 7, no. 1 (2018), pp. 54–74; Ellen Kennedy, "Constitutional Failure Revisited" in Mark Graber, Sanford Levinson, and Mark Tushnet, eds., *Constitutional Democracy in Crisis* (New York: Oxford University Press, 2018). For engaged scholarship, see Benjamin Hett, *Death of a Democracy* (New York: Henry Holt, 2018); Steven Levitsky and Daniel Ziblatt, *How Democracies Die* (New York: Penguin, 2018); Burt Neuborne, *When at Times the Mob Is Swayed: A Citizens Guide to Defending Our Republic* (New York: The New Press, 2019); David Runcimann, *How Democracy Ends* (London: Basic Books, 2018); Timothy Snyder, *On Tyranny* (New York: Tim Duggan Books, 2017); Jason Stanley, *How Fascism Works* (New York: Penguin, 2018); Tom Ginsburg and Aziz Huq, *How to Save a Constitutional Democracy*

(Chicago: University of Chicago Press, 2018); Peter Fritzsche, *Hitler's First One Hundred Days* (New York: Basic Books, 2020). Other, more journalistic, accounts include Madeleine Albright, *Fascism: A Warning* (New York: Harper Collins, 2019); Robert Gerwarth, "Weimar's Lessons for Biden's America," *Foreign Policy*, 6 February 2021; Matthew Rosa, "Joe Biden, Donald Trump, and the Weimar Republic: History's Dark Lessons," *Salon*, 6 June 2021; Andrea Kluth, "Even Without a Red Wave, This Could Now Be Weimar America," *Bloomberg*, 9 November 2022; Christopher Browning, "How Hitler's Enablers Undid Democracy in Germany," *The Atlantic*, 8 October 2022; Andrew Port, "Embracing Democracy: The Storming of the US Capitol and Mixed Lessons of Weimar Germany," *Public Seminar*, 21 January 2021.

2 Particularly influential has been the tradition of comparative historical analysis, which has seen several fruitful engagements with the history of Weimar. The early works of Barrington Moore and Alexander Gerschenkron showcased a macro-historical approach. Realist in their methodology, such works often took for granted actors' motivations, seeking instead to unearth the deep structural movers of political development. Later generations have both critiqued and refined these methods, adopting contextualist methodologies, and seeking grounded explanations based on actors' situated understanding of the conflict.

3 Daniel Bessner, "The Ghosts of Weimar: The Weimar Analogy in American Thought," *Social Research: An International Quarterly* 84, no. 4 (2017), pp. 831–55.

4 From the classical works of Schumpeter to the debate between Lipset and Moore on the structural determinants of democracy, Weimar has often played a starring role, both in our conceptualization of democracy and in our theoretical claims about democratization. Joseph Schumpeter, *Capitalism, Socialism, and Democracy* (New York: Taylor and Francis, 2010 [1942]); Seymour Martin Lipset, "Some Social Requisites of Democracy: Economic Development and Political Legitimacy," *American Political Science Review* 53, no. 1 (1959), pp. 69–105; Barrington Moore, *The Social Origins of Dictatorship and Democracy* (Boston, MA: Beacon Press, 1966).

5 Marc Bloch, *The Historian's Craft* (Manchester: Manchester University Press, 1992); Michel Foucault, *The Order of Things* (London: Routledge, 2002).

6 Against classical visions of democracy that relied on representation of the will of the people, Joseph Schumpeter's 1942 treatise defined democracy as a method of government, an "institutional arrangement for arriving at political decisions in which individuals acquire the power to decide by means of a competitive struggle for the people's vote." Schumpeter, *Capitalism, Socialism, and Democracy*, p. xiii.

7 Marxian historical materialism in particular presented itself as scientific in its approach to history. In its use of abstractions to develop universal categories, it claimed to transcend the particularity of specific contexts and offer universal history. See Amel Ahmed, "What Can We Learn from History?: Competing Approaches to Historical Methodology and the Weberian Alternative of Reflexive Understanding," *Polity* 54, no. 4 (2022).

8 This included both the *Methodenstreit* within the field of economics and broader debates about the place of objectivity in historical analysis. See Fiona Maclachlan, "Max Weber within the *Methodenstreit*," *Cambridge Journal of Economics* 41, no. 4 (2017), pp. 1161–75.

9 Richard Lebow, "Weber's Search for Knowledge" in Richard Ned Lebow, ed., *Max Weber and International Relations* (Cambridge: Cambridge University Press, 2017).

10 Weber was not alone in making use of the concept of *verstehen*. Among his contemporaries, Wilhelm Dilthey and Georg Simmel also developed this idea in their works. However, his conceptualization was distinctive in two important respects: First is the view that any causal explanation of social action must be based in an empathetic understanding of the motivations of actors; and second is the claim that an accounting of the historians' own conceptual and theoretical priors is necessary to achieve this understanding. William Tucker, "Max Weber's *Verstehen*," *Sociological Quarterly* 6 (1965), pp. 157–65.

11 Jan Kubik, "Ethnography of Politics: Foundations, Applications, Prospects" in Edward Schatz, ed., *Political Ethnography: What Immersion Contributes to the Study of Power* (Chicago: University of Chicago Press, 2009), 23–52.

12 Hans Henrik Brunn and Sam Whimster, eds., *Max Weber: Collected Methodological Writings* (London: Routledge, 2012).

13 Thomas Burger, *Max Weber's Theory of Concept Formation* (Durham, NC: Duke University Press, 1976), p. 119; Patrick Jackson, *The Conduct of Inquiry in International Relations* (London: Routledge, 2011); Lebow, "Weber's Search for Knowledge," pp. 55–6.

14 Max Weber, *The Protestant Ethic and the Spirit of Capitalism* (London: Routledge, 1992 [1905]). On this as an evaluation of an ideal type, see Ahmed, "What Can We Learn from History?," pp. 760–1.

15 Frederic Schaffer, *Elucidating Social Science Concepts: An Interpretivist Guide* (London: Taylor & Francis, 2015), p. 55; Clifford Geertz, *Local Knowledge: Further Essays in Interpretive Anthropology* (London: Basic Books, 2008 [1983]), p. 57.

16 Levitzky and Ziblatt, *How Democracies Die*, p. 8.

17 Stanley, *How Fascism Works*.

18 Hett, *Death of a Democracy*.

19 Levitzky and Ziblatt, *How Democracies Die*, pp. 14–15.

20 Fritzsche, *Hitler's First 100 Days*.

21 Levitzky and Ziblatt, *How Democracies Die*, p. 7.

22 Snyder, *On Tyranny*.

23 Hett, *Death of a Democracy*, p. 216.

24 Levitzky and Ziblatt, *How Democracies Die*, p. 3.

25 Snyder, *On Tyranny*, p. 24.

26 Stanley, *How Fascism Works*, p. xix.

27 Levitzky and Ziblatt, *How Democracies Die*, pp. 23–4.

28 Hett, *Death of a Democracy*.

29 Fritzsche, *Hitler's First 100 Days*.

30 Ibid., p. 6.

31 Stanley, *How Fascism Works*, p. xxxii.

32 Fritzsche, *Hitler's First 100 Days*, p. 3.

33 Levitzky and Ziblatt, *How Democracies Die*, p. 26.

34 Peter Breiner, "End of Democracy or Recurrent Conflict: Minimalist Democracy, Legitimacy Crisis, and Political Equality" in Ned Lebow and Ludvig Norman, eds., *Robustness and Fragility of Political Orders* (Cambridge: Cambridge University Press, 2022); Jan-Werner Müller, *Democracy Rules* (New York: Farrar, Straus and Giroux, 2021); Jedediah Purdy, "Normcore," *Dissent Magazine*, Summer 2018.

35 G. John Ikenberry, *Liberal Leviathan: The Origins, Crisis, and Transformation of the American World Order* (Princeton: Princeton University Press, 2011); Daniel Deudney and G. John Ikenberry, "The Nature and Sources of Liberal International Order," *Review of International Studies* 25, no. 2 (1999), pp. 179–96; John Mearsheimer, "Bound to Fail: The Rise and Fall of the Liberal International Order," *International Security* 43, no. 4 (2019), pp. 7–50.

36 This included, for example, prohibitions of anti-systemic parties, both fascist successor parties and communists who identified strongly with the Soviet Union. On the peculiar character of these polities vis-à-vis liberalism, see Jan-Werner Müller, "Beyond Militant Democracy?," *New Left Review* 39 (2012).

37 Pepijn Corduwener, *The Problem of Democracy in Postwar Europe: Political Actors and the Formation of the Postwar Model of Democracy in France, West Germany and Italy* (London: Taylor & Francis, 2016); Martin Conway, *Western Europe's Democratic Age: 1945–1968* (Princeton: Princeton University Press, 2022); Jan-Werner Müller, *Contesting Democracy* (New Haven: Yale University Press, 2011).

38 Carl Hodge, "The Long Fifties: The Politics of Socialist Programmatic Revision in Britain, France and Germany," *Contemporary European History* 2, no. 1 (1993), pp. 17–34; Talbot Imlay, "Exploring What Might Have Been: Parallel History, International History, and Post-War Socialist Internationalism," *International History Review* 31, no. 3 (2009), pp. 521–57.

39 This shift paved the way for the Social Democratic Party to join a coalition with the Christian democratic CDU in 1966. It was the first time in the postwar period that the Social Democrats were in government and the first time since Weimar that they were part of a Grand Coalition with Christian Democrats. Mark Ruff, "Building Bridges between Catholicism and Socialism: Ernst-Wolfgang Böckenförde and the Social Democratic Party of Germany," *Contemporary European History* 29, no. 2 (2020), pp. 155–70.

40 Deborah Kisatsky, *The United States and the European Right, 1945–1955* (Columbus: Ohio State University Press, 2005).

41 Patrick Major, *The Death of the KPD: Communism and Anti-Communism in West Germany, 1945–1956* (London: Clarendon Press, 1998).

42 Karl Loewenstein, *Political Reconstruction* (New York: Macmillan, 1946), pp. 402–3.

43 Rosario Forlenza, "The Enemy Within: Catholic Anti-Communism in Cold War Italy," *Past & Present* 235, no. 1 (2017), pp. 207–42.

44 Pepijn Corduwener, "Democracy as a Contested Concept in Post-War Western Europe: A Comparative Study of Political Debates in France, West Germany, and Italy," *Historical Journal* 59, no. 1 (2016), pp. 197–220.

45 Irwin Wall, *The United States and the Making of Postwar France, 1945–1954* (Cambridge: Cambridge University Press, 1991); Chiarella Esposito, *America's Feeble Weapon: Funding the Marshall Plan in France and Italy, 1948–1950* (Westport, CT: Greenwood Press, 1994); Silvio Berardi, *Five Years of Edera: The Italian Republican Party in Search of a New Identity (1943–1948)* (Rome: Edizioni Nuova Cultura, 2017).

46 Kisatsky, *The United States and the European Right*.

47 In Germany, some of these mechanisms such as party bans were introduced under occupation and carried over to the Republic after 1949, but others were innovations.

48 Germany's mixed electoral system combined seats allocated within single-member districts with seats allocated through party list proportional representation. Originally, the two were reconciled to ensure proportionality. The decision in 1953 was to separate the two ballots and have them operate independently. Without reconciliations, the element of proportionality was lost. Peter James, *The German Electoral System* (London: Taylor & Francis, 2017).

49 The combination of measures reduced the number of effective parties in parliament from ten to six, and the split ballot allowed the CDU, which dominated in the majoritarian portion of the balloting, to sweep to a landslide victory in 1953. See Eckhard Jesse, *Wahlrecht zwischen Kontinuitaet und reform: eine Analyse der Wahlsystemdiskussion und der Wahlrechtsaenderungen in der Bundesrepublik Deutschland, 1949–1983* (Dusseldorf: Droste, 1985), pp. 117–20; Dieter Nohlen, *Wahlrecht und Parteiensystem* (Leverkusen: Leske & Budrich, 1986).

50 Susan Scarrow, "Political Parties and the Changing Framework of German Electoral Competition" in *Stability and Change in German Elections: How Electorates Merge, Converge, or Collide* (London: Praeger, 1998).

51 Daniel Rogers, "Transforming the German Party System: The United States and the Origins of Political Moderation, 1945–1949," *Journal of Modern History* 65, no. 3 (1993), pp. 512–41.

52 Léopold Boissier, "L'Union Interparlementaire et sa Contribution au Développement du Droit International et a l'Établissement de la Paix" in *Collected Courses of the Hague Academy of International Law*, Volume 88 (London: Brill, 1955).

53 Summary record of Interparliamentary Conference, Washington, DC, 1953.

54 The Commonwealth Parliamentary Association and the Assemblée Parlementaire de la Francophonie emerged in the postwar period as leaders of the effort to promote parliamentarism. Although not a member of either, the United States regularly sent delegation to the Commonwealth meetings, and occasionally to the Francophonie. The strategic interests of US foreign policy were at the center of its support for these associations. Wayne Morse, chair of the US delegation, wrote to then Vice President Richard Nixon in 1958 that "[t]hese Conferences are invaluable for the tole they play in bringing about international understanding and promoting peace." Wayne Morse, "Letter of Transmission" in *Report of the Delegation Appointed to Attend the Commonwealth Parliamentary Association Meeting in New Delhi, India,*

168 Amel Ahmed

December 9–10, 1957 (Washington, DC: US Government Printing Office, 1958).

55 Viscount Stansgate, "The Interparliamentary Union," *Contemporary Review* 1026 (1951), pp. 32–324; Ivo Rens, "L'Union interparlementaire entre le passé et l'avenir," *Montecitorio* 10–11 (1963), pp. 5–14.

56 André de Blonay, "The Inter-Parliamentary Union and Patterns of World-Wide Parliamentary Cooperation," *Journal of Constitutional and Parliamentary Studies* 1, no. 3 (1967), pp. 7–14.

57 See, for example, Michel Ameller, *Parliaments: A Comparative Study on the Structure and Functioning of Representative Institutions in Fifty-five Countries* (London: Inter-Parliamentary Union, 1962). Several editions of these comparative studies were published in the 1960s.

58 For a register of publications, see Inter-Parliamentary Bulletin: Official Publication of the Bureau of the Inter-Parliamentary Union (Geneva: The Bureau, 1964).

59 Karl Bracher, *Die Auflösung der Weimarer Republik* (Stuttgart: Ring-Verlag, 1955).

60 Karl Bracher, "Problems of Parliamentary Democracy in Europe," *Daedalus* 93, no. 1 (1964), pp. 179–98.

61 For an important account of how Cold War politics reconfigured the academy and especially the field of political science, see Ido Oren, *Our Enemies and Us: America's Rivalries and the Making of Political Science* (Ithaca, NY: Cornell University Press, 2003).

62 Gerhard Loewenberg, "Parliamentarism in Western Germany: The Functioning of the Bundestag," *American Political Science Review* 55, no. 1 (1961), pp. 87–102; John Hess, *A Survey of German Parliamentarism* (Berkeley: University of California Press, 1958); Charles Foster and George K. Romoser, "Parliamentary Reform in West Germany," *Parliamentary Affairs* 21, no. 1 (1967), pp. 69–74; Rudolf Heberle, "Parliamentary Government and Political Parties in West Germany," *Canadian Journal of Economics and Political Science / Revue Canadienne de Economiques et Science Politique* 28, no. 3 (1962), pp. 417–23.

63 Udi Greenberg, *The Weimar Century: German Émigrés and the Ideological Foundations of the Cold War* (Princeton: Princeton University Press, 2016), pp. 175–6.

64 Harold Lasswell, "The Developing Science of Democracy" in Leonard D. White, ed., *The Future of Government in the United States: Essays in Honor of Charles E. Merriam* (Chicago: University of Chicago Press, 1942).

65 John Gunnell, *Imagining the American Polity: Political Science and the Discourse of Democracy* (University Park: Penn State University Press, 2015); Martin Conway, "Democracy in Postwar Western Europe: The Triumph of a Political Model," *European History Quarterly* 32, no. 1 (2002), pp. 59–84.

66 William Carpenter, "Review of Capitalism, Socialism, and Democracy by Joseph A. Schumpeter," *American Political Science Review* 37, no. 3 (1943), pp. 523–4.

67 Lipset, "Some Social Requisites of Democracy," p. 71.

68 Giovanni Capoccia, *Defending Democracy: Reactions to Extremism in Interwar Europe* (Baltimore, MD: Johns Hopkins University Press, 2005).

69 This is documented in numerous historical accounts. Especially helpful are William Patch, *Heinrich Brüning and the Dissolution of the Weimar Republic* (Cambridge: Cambridge University Press, 2006); Larry Eugene Jones, *German Liberalism and the Dissolution of the Weimar Party System, 1918–1933* (Chapel Hill: University of North Carolina Press, 2017).

70 See Daniel Ziblatt's important analysis on the role of conservative parties in preserving democracy in interwar Europe, and on the weakness that prevented German conservatives from taking on such a role. Daniel Ziblatt, *Conservative Political Parties and the Birth of Modern Democracy* (Cambridge: Cambridge University Press, 2017).

71 Patch, *Heinrich Brüning and the Dissolution of the Weimar Republic*, pp. 36–8, 50–4.

72 Sheri Berman, "Populism Is a Symptom Rather than a Cause: Democratic Disconnect, the Decline of the Center-Left, and the Rise of Populism in Western Europe," *Polity* 51, no. 4 (2019), pp. 654–67.

73 Cas Mudde and Cristobal Kaltwasser, eds., *Populism in Europe and the Americas: Threat or Corrective for Democracy?* (Cambridge: Cambridge University Press, 2012); Roberto Frega, "The Fourth Stage of Social Democracy," *Theory and Society* 50 (2021), pp. 489–513; Sheri Berman and Maria Snegovaya, "Populism and the Decline of Social Democracy," *Journal of Democracy* 30, no. 3 (2019), pp. 5–19.

74 Snyder, *On Tyranny*, p. 12.

75 Breiner, "End of Democracy or Recurrent Conflict."

7   Weimar on the Potomac?
Leo Strauss Goes to Washington

William E. Scheuerman

Recent scholarship has tried to make sense of the political ascendancy of Donald Trump and other authoritarian populists with recourse to the Weimar Republic and its tragic fate.[1] That literature often draws parallels between the political and social conditions that enabled Trump and those that debilitated interwar German democracy.[2] Its contributors typically aim to warn liberal democracy's defenders of the burgeoning authoritarian threats. My main focus here lies elsewhere. Little attention has been paid to how right-wing intellectuals who supported Trump have relied heavily on so-called lessons from the Weimar Republic to undergird their own authoritarian choices. This tendency is especially pronounced among a vocal group of Trump partisans who trace their intellectual genealogy to the influential German Jewish émigré political philosopher Leo Strauss (1899–1973).[3] Although Trump and his presidency excited little enthusiasm among American intellectuals, Straussian lawyers and political scientists, many of whom are affiliated with the right-wing Claremont Institute (at California's Claremont McKenna College), represented a striking exception to the intellectuals' overwhelmingly anti-Trumpian mood. Their politically charged, methodologically limited, and in many ways misleading narrative about Weimar's decline has played a pivotal role in justifying their political preferences. Their redeployment of Weimar reminds us that stories about its legacy can be instrumentalized to serve authoritarian as well as anti-authoritarian purposes.

Strauss's self-described "Claremonster" disciples immediately "appreciated and gave intellectual legitimacy," as one of them has bragged, "to the populist revolt against the politically correct contempt of the ruling class," a revolt they supported by energetically buttressing Trump's

The author would like to thank the volume editors, Peter Breiner, and Peter Caldwell for helpful suggestions, as well as Alexander Somek and Fabio Wolkenstein for the opportunity to present at the Vienna Legal Theory Workshop, where the paper gained from extensive feedback.

cause.[4] They transformed the Institute's core publications, *Claremont Review of Books* and *The American Mind*, into pro-Trump ideological organs, served in a number of official and semi-official capacities for Trump in Washington, DC, and played a major role in seeking to overturn the November 2020 presidential election results and abet the attempted 6 January coup.[5] Most controversially, longstanding Claremont affiliate John Eastman worked aggressively alongside Rudy Giuliani to halt Congress's tallying of electoral college votes by drafting a memo to then Vice President Michael Pence outlining how he might successfully do so.[6] Eastman and other so-called Claremonsters have since expressed little remorse about their efforts to derail democracy.

The central role of the Straussians at Claremont in enabling Trump has now been documented in excruciating detail by astute political commentators.[7] Crucial for our purposes here is how the Straussians make use of Weimar's legacy. In this vein, Harvard-trained political theorist and Trump enthusiast Charles Kesler, the Claremont Institute's leading figure and editor of *Claremont Review of Books*, notes in his post-2020 election postmortem that "[e]very republic eventually faces what might be called the Weimar problem. Has the national culture, popular and elite, deteriorated so much that the virtues necessary to sustain republican government are no longer viable?"[8] Reminiscent of crisis-plagued Weimar, the US is undergoing a "cold civil war," with two diametrically opposed visions of the constitutional order engaged in a life-or-death battle for supremacy. According to Kesler, Americans mistakenly assumed that "revolutionary challenges" to their political existence had come to an end with the Soviet Union's demise.[9] In reality, domestic liberals and leftists at home have been waging a successful war to supplant the founders' original constitutional vision, firmly rooted in unchanging natural right, with a novel left-leaning progressive system whose ascent would mean complete victory for moral relativism and nihilism. A core element of that new order, Kesler and his allies claim, is an unchecked administrative state exercising tyrannical power.[10] Even Joe Biden represents a revolutionary figure actively cooperating with the politically "woke" mobs that have occupied streets and are apparently bent on transforming America's civil war from "cold" to "hot."[11]

Although Kesler expresses caveats about Trump's personal foibles, he praises the former president's "courage in defense of one's own."[12] Admittedly, the Trump Administration was "a mess," yet, fortunately, "competent people [including, of course, many Claremonsters] eventually were found" to work alongside him.[13] "In his confidence in America's principles and in the ultimate justice of the people ... Trump resembles those brave conservatives" – including Clarence Thomas, the

Claremonsters' favorite Supreme Court justice – now resisting the administrative state and dangerous, left-wing "guilt-mongering" about race and gender.[14] Alas, Trump's failure to gain a second term means that the US remains in crisis, with no satisfactory answer to the "Weimar problem" in view. Other Claremonsters appear to share Kesler's bleak assessment.[15]

Kesler is hardly the only recent Straussian to identify contemporary parallels to a so-called Weimar problem. Strauss's pro-Trump firebrands offer an especially fierce version of the general narrative, yet a previous generation of his followers similarly saw historical analogies between a decadent, crisis-ridden Weimar Republic and the US. In a 1989 lecture revealingly entitled "The Reichstag is Still Burning," Harry V. Jaffa – the Claremont Institute's founder, one of Strauss's politically most pugnacious followers,[16] and dean of so-called west coast Straussianism – pilloried US universities and liberal academics for succumbing to relativism and nihilism, disastrous trends that allegedly paved the way for political violence (e.g., destructive acts by Black Power militants on 1960s college campuses, an obsession among many Straussians).[17] Allan Bloom's bestselling *The Closing of the American Mind*, a popularization of key Straussian ideas, tied 1960s campus violence at Cornell University (where Bloom taught before migrating to the University of Chicago) to "the German experience" and, especially, prominent intellectual figures (e.g., Martin Heidegger and Max Weber) who had been imported into the US. What the US campus import ignored, Bloom insisted, was that the Germans' "theoretical critique of morality" had not only entailed relativism and nihilism but also invited Nazism's ascent.[18]

Bloom's book was filled with quick summaries of difficult thinkers. Yet even for a mass readership unfamiliar with Heidegger or Weber, its main point was obvious enough: Unless the American Republic reversed course and again embraced the political and moral truths of natural right as expounded by Plato and Aristotle, it was doomed to repeat Weimar's fate. The pessimistic Bloom seemed unsure about the prospects of success. Yet, he was convinced that "[l]iberalism without natural rights," with its inattention to "the fundamental principles or the moral virtues that inclined men to live according to them," was the chief culprit behind American decline.[19] Conveniently, Bloom's preoccupation with relativism and nihilism simply ignored the decidedly *moralistic* contours of so much liberal-left and progressive politics in the United States.[20]

In this chapter I explore how this relatively commonplace diagnosis among Strauss's disciples has its roots in his own critical, yet more complex, view of Weimar's lessons for postwar liberal democracy. As many commentators have already noted, the German Jewish Strauss was traumatized by Weimar's destruction. His views about that destruction's sources decisively shaped his work after he fled Europe and became postwar America's most influential conservative political theorist, ensconced at the prestigious University of Chicago.[21] The story of how Strauss's ideas morphed into the crudely partisan ideology of the Claremonsters, however, turns out to be at least as messy as the Trump Administration they celebrated. To make sense of it, we will explore how US-based Straussians came to endorse expansive notions of executive power, a trend that has culminated in the embrace of a view of Donald Trump as a redemptive political figure tasked with returning a decadent republic to its original, morally superior bases in natural right. By briefly revisiting Strauss's Weimar-era dialogue with Carl Schmitt, I highlight the tragic and arguably farcical character of the Straussian enthusiasm for Trump. Eager to ward off a repeat of Weimar's fate, some Straussians are now embracing an authoritarian presidentialism with parallels to Schmitt's political vision for Germany. Despite genuine divergences from their master's original Weimar-inflected narrative, elements of contemporary Straussian political analysis can be directly linked to theoretical lacunae that plagued Strauss. In particular, Strauss's longstanding preference for ideational or *geistesgeschichtliche* (spiritual and/or intellectual-historical) analysis meant that he always sidelined more systematic modes of historical, political, and social analysis. That methodological limitation, with even more troublesome political consequences, has plagued many of his followers and paved the way for their Trump partisanship.

Weimar's Lessons: Back to Classical Natural Right?

Strauss exploded onto the American intellectual scene in 1953 with *Natural Right and History*, a provocative critique of modern Western political philosophy that rapidly became required reading among academic political theorists.[22] Both Western political thought *and* practice had lost their bearings by rejecting natural right as expounded by Plato and Aristotle, Strauss's heroes and, he insisted, still the West's most impressive sources of philosophical and political wisdom. In Strauss's nostalgic retelling, classical political philosophy relied at its best on a teleological view of nature conceived as a source of universally valid moral distinctions. Classical natural right constituted an eternal, transcendent philosophical truth, with the idea of nature providing a firm basis for both morality and a sound, albeit undeniably hierarchical, political and social order. To be sure, Strauss rejected any mechanical return to Plato or Aristotle, or an interpretation of their ideas as offering easy templates for reform. In part because of its deeply hierarchical and anti-egalitarian contours, classical "[n]atural right would act as a dynamite for civil society"; consequently, any real-life reapplication would need to dilute it.[23] Nonetheless, *Natural Right* insisted unambiguously on the ancients' superiority vis-à-vis modern thinkers, many of whom spoke the language of natural right yet had robbed it of its normative kernel.

Even when subsequently modifying some elements, Strauss's overall narrative represented a dramatic *Verfallsgeschichte* (story of inevitable decline), in this case one triggered by modern political thinkers (i.e., Niccolò Machiavelli and Thomas Hobbes) who rejected ancient ideas of a permanent natural right, along with its somewhat modified manifestations within medieval Christianity (e.g., in Thomas Aquinas). In Strauss's creative rereading of Machiavelli, Hobbes, John Locke, Jean-Jacques Rousseau, and others, modern political thinkers divorced natural law "from the idea of man's perfection," replacing the praiseworthy classical aspiration for a fully good order committed to the cultivation of virtue and pursuit of moral duties with individual rights and the modest quest for self-preservation.[24] The liberal Locke, for example, built on "'the low but solid ground' of selfishness or of certain 'private vices.'"[25] Locke demoted nature to nothing more than "worthless materials," objects of human manipulation and creativity, conceived in individualistic and ultimately subjective terms.[26] Painting with an exceedingly broad brush, *Natural Right and History* then traced how the rejection of classical natural right paved the way for moral relativism. Stated bluntly: Modern political thought invited a reduction of matters of right and wrong to arbitrary subjective preferences and thereby nihilism, or "the view that every preference, however evil, base, or insane" is in principle "as legitimate as any other preference."[27] Absent a creative retrieval of the great lessons of classical antiquity, relativism and nihilism meant that the political scene would unavoidably be "darkened by the shadow of Hitler" and other dictators.[28] Only classical natural right, it seemed, could guard against political barbarism, though precisely how it might be recovered remained a matter of legitimate intellectual and political disagreement.

Not surprisingly, Strauss's dramatic and sometimes apocalyptic view of modernity has been subjected to widespread criticism. For our purposes here, it suffices to underline its more conventional traits, at least within the broader context of twentieth-century German thought.

At mid-century, many others on both the right and the left from German-speaking Europe were offering competing *Verfallsgeschichten*; many made parallel calls for reviving natural law as an antidote to totalitarianism's alleged roots in positivism and/or moral relativism.

Finally, many engaged in what we might describe as a chiefly intellectual or spiritual diagnosis of real-life political and social trends.[29] *Natural Right and History*, in short, represented a strikingly conventional and identifiably *central European* intervention, albeit one with some unusual traits. John Gunnell has accurately observed that, for Strauss, the crisis of modern political thought was always *simultaneously* a crisis of modernity, despite the fact that he had little to offer "in the way of concrete institutional and ideological analysis" of modern society.[30] To understand modernity's crisis, one turned to *Geistesgeschichte* (spiritual and/or intellectual history), not history, the social sciences, or social theory. Indeed, throughout his long career, Strauss was always hostile to and dismissive of the social sciences, which he interpreted as building on the quicksand of modern moral relativism.[31] To the extent that the crisis of modernity necessarily entailed a crisis of liberal democracy, Strauss's view of it was similarly "ideational" in structure.[32] On one reading, it imputed astonishing political influence to *intellectuals*: Their ideas, after all, were allegedly responsible for modernity's ills.[33] In this vein, *Natural Right* offered a rather unsympathetic reading of Locke, whom Strauss interpreted as modern liberalism's foundational figure, and thus, by implication, an illuminating source of real-life liberal pathologies.[34] Why worry about the messy intricacies of real and existing liberal democratic institutions and practices if Locke provided a master key for understanding them? Like Carl Schmitt (whom Strauss knew from Weimar Germany), Strauss was convinced that one could deconstruct liberal practice by dissecting liberalism's intellectual tensions. As in Schmitt's *Geistesgeschichtliche Lage des heutigen Parliamentarismus* (Spiritual and/or Intellectual Situation of Contemporary Parliamentarism), doing so meant offering a highly stylized intellectual history that downplayed some key dissonant notes.[35] It similarly tended to reduce the analysis of political and social life to creative – and sometimes rather idiosyncratic – exegeses of major thinkers and their "great books."

Nonetheless, embattled conservative US political theorists in the 1950s and 1960s, confronted with political science's "behavioral revolution" and the discipline's growing hostility to political philosophy, latched onto Strauss's writings: Here was a way for them to relate the teaching of canonical political thinkers and texts directly to momentous political events. Even better perhaps, here was an approach that justified resistance to influential contemporary left-leaning liberals (e.g., John Dewey) and their many offspring, who were even more remote from the lessons of classical antiquity than Hobbes or Locke. No wonder that Strauss's ideas soon reached broader conservative audiences and made their way into prominent journals, such as the *National Review*.[36]

Strauss's hostility to Locke and to others he depicted as central to liberalism presented genuine dilemmas for his postwar US disciples, far more eager than Strauss to demonstrate their patriotic credentials. Before turning to that part of the story, however, we need to consider how Strauss's interpretation of Weimar shaped his critique of liberal democracy.

The opening paragraph of *Natural Right* ominously warned that the US risked following precisely the path the Germans had taken, with all of its well-known catastrophic consequences: It was in Germany that even the most minimal remnants of a desirable notion of natural right had been most systematically eliminated.[37] Weimar democracy, Strauss suggested, represented a laboratory of sorts for contemporary liberalism's decadent – that is, relativistic and nihilistic – variants.[38] Within contemporary Germany, influential liberal figures not only radicalized the worst tendencies of modern natural right but were no longer even capable of paying lip service to it. In case his readers remained unsure about his target, Strauss openly reprimanded the prominent interwar German-speaking left-liberal Hans Kelsen for embracing moral relativism as a necessary complement to liberal democracy.[39] Modern liberals such as Kelsen viewed the "abandonment of natural right not only with placidity but with relief."[40] By rejecting moral absolutes and natural right, they could no longer distinguish between those views or political positions deserving of toleration, and those from which liberal democracy would need protection: Natural right's decay meant tolerance even for those bent on destroying liberalism and toleration itself.

Kelsen's unabashed relativism, however, was always an outlier in the universe of Weimar political and social thought, whose key figures were more commonly committed, like Strauss, to traditional and indeed conservative moral views.[41] This is probably why Strauss's diagnosis proceeded to zero in on Weber, a universally respected figure whose value relativism and call for a delineation of facts from values Strauss took as evidence of the decadence of liberalism, generally, and of German liberal democracy, specifically. On Strauss's harsh and sometimes misleading reading, Weber had suggested the dangerous idea that "genuine choice, as distinguished from spurious or despicable choice, was nothing but resolute or deadly serious decision," in the process obscuring the boundaries between his professed liberal commitments and political irrationalism: "Excellence now means devotion to a cause, be it good or evil."[42] Although Schmitt made no appearance in *Natural Right*, the book could easily be read as implicitly endorsing the view that Weber's liberalism had invited Schmitt's (fascistic) decisionism. In response to those who might respond by emphasizing Weber's liberal political proclivities and his ethic of responsibility, Strauss countered: "We cannot take seriously this belated insistence on responsibility and sanity."[43] Strauss's book could also be interpreted as implicitly endorsing Schmitt's view that relativistic liberalism (and figures such as Kelsen) had impeded a proper defense of the Weimar Republic during its final days.[44]

Strauss's subsequent writings applied this harsh assessment of deca- dent Weimar liberalism to postwar democracy, with Strauss regularly reminding his mostly US audience of its myriad perils. The attack on Kelsen and Weber was relaunched, for example, against Isaiah Berlin, whose value pluralism Strauss interpreted as demonstrative of the present-day political crisis and its origins in the fact that liberalism had "abandoned its absolutist basis and is trying to become entirely relativistic."[45] A major essay, "The Three Waves of Modernity," inter- preted the modern West in terms of a series of interrelated, unfolding, and intensifying crises, with successive conjunctures building directly on their predecessors and generating additional political and moral decay. Each could be conveniently linked to prominent philosophical figures: Hobbes and Locke undergirded a first (liberal) wave, Rousseau a second and even more decadent (socialist or communist) wave, and then Friedrich Nietzsche a third cataclysmic (fascist) wave.[46]

Predictably, the language of "crisis" (e.g., "the crisis of our time," "crisis of education," "crisis of liberal democracy") loomed large in everything Strauss wrote during the postwar decades.[47] On one reading, the intensity of his worries depended partly on contingent factors. Like many on the right, Strauss and his followers were outraged by 1960s radicalism; they sometimes seemed, as in Bloom's 1987 popular jere- miad, to abandon any lingering hope that the US could be spared Weimar's fate. At other junctures, Strauss appeared less pessimistic: The introduction to *Natural Right*, for example, praised Americans for holding onto the idea, as originally expressed in the Declaration of Independence, of unalienable natural rights, best viewed as self-evident truths.[48] Special venom, at any rate, was always reserved for the social sciences, which Strauss interpreted as irresponsibly following Weber's delineation of facts from values and the closely related idea of social scientific objectivity. Oblivious to the perils of the moral relativism it naively embraced, empirical political science "fiddles while Rome burns. It is excused by two facts: it does not know that it fiddles, and it does not know that Rome burns."[49]

A substantial scholarly literature, mostly penned by Strauss's disciples and fellow travelers, documents how the master nonetheless tried to make his peace with liberal democracy generally, and with the Anglophone democracies specifically.[50] His aristocratic classicism and rejection of core features of political modernity, in conjunction with his Weimar-inflected views about liberalism's congenital flaws, impeded any principled defense. Although he likely favored an authoritarian solution to the Weimar Republic's crisis during its final days, there is nonetheless plentiful evidence that Strauss struggled to identify grounds for what William Galston aptly calls a "qualified embrace" of postwar liberal democracy.[51] Occasionally, Strauss tentatively suggested – as in his brief comments in *Natural Right* on the Declaration of Independence – that elements of classical natural right had survived, at least in the US and perhaps in Great Britain. In a 1941 lecture on "German Nihilism" given at the New School for Social Research, he concluded his lengthy *Geistesgeschichte* of inexorable German decay with some decidedly positive comments about England's "very un-German prudence and moderation."[52] (Strauss spent his first years as a refugee from Nazism in England, whose political culture seems to have greatly impressed him.[53]) Interestingly, his sympathetic discussion of Edmund Burke in *Natural Right* oddly tried to interpret the iconic British conservative's critique of the French Revolution as based partly in classical natural right.[54] Elsewhere, Strauss observed that the framers of the US Constitution spoke not just a liberal but also a *republican* political language with ancient roots: "Let us also remember that the authors of *The Federalist Papers* signed themselves 'Publius': republicanism points back to classical republicanism and therefore also to classical antiquity."[55] Perhaps the American Republic, if its classical traits could be properly cultivated, might survive and flourish after all. The United States, to its great credit, was founded on fundamentally anti-Machiavellian principles.[56] Liberal regimes provided space for those devoted to the pursuit of moral excellence and classical education, despite their permissive egalitarianism and resulting conformist pressures.[57] Unfortunately, in contrast to other prominent refugee political intellectuals from Weimar, Strauss never systematically analyzed his adopted home or American political thought; his brief comments about US liberal democracy are scattered across a variety of publications.[58]

To his credit, Strauss occasionally challenged the idea of a direct tie between theoretical or philosophical tensions, on the one hand, and practical or real-life political crises, on the other. "The Three Waves of Modernity" concluded by asserting that liberalism's "theoretical crisis does not necessarily lead to a practical crisis, for the superiority of liberal democracy to communism, Stalinist or post-Stalinist, is obvious enough."[59] Intellectual weaknesses, it seemed, had a messier relationship to institutions and political practice than Strauss had previously inferred. In the same essay, he suggested that liberalism had not only emerged in the first and least unattractive "wave" of modernity, but also, in contrast to communism and fascism, derived "powerful support from a way of thinking which cannot be called modern at all: the premodern thought of our western tradition."[60] As we will see, his underdeveloped but suggestive comments that modern liberal democracies might rest on classical foundations were soon enthusiastically embraced by Strauss's American followers.

Given Weimar's inordinately large role in Strauss's political thinking, it remains striking that he had so little to say about its political and historical particulars. One exception is the 1965 preface to the reissue and translation of his *Spinoza's Critique of Religion*, a Weimar-era (1930) study of Spinoza's religious philosophy. Although the preface focuses on Spinoza's relevance to modern Zionism and Jewish philosophers (e.g., Hermann Cohen and Franz Rosenzweig), it includes some brief comments about Weimar liberal democracy, which Strauss describes as a "weak" and "sorry spectacle of justice without a sword or of justice unable to use the sword."[61] On his view, German Jews were wrong to place their faith in liberalism and Weimar: Liberalism can prevent political and legal but not social discrimination, because doing so would require the state to prohibit "private" discrimination. In the process, liberalism would have to abolish the private sphere and ignore the state–society divide essential to its own political identity. Yet "[s]uch a destruction would not by any means solve the Jewish problem, as is shown in our days by the anti-Jewish policy of the USSR."[62] As early as 1925, with Hindenburg's election to the presidency, Strauss claims, "everyone who had eyes to see [recognized] that the Weimar Republic had only a short time to live." Weimar's congenital weaknesses "made certain its speedy destruction."[63] The "old Germany" was still too strong; liberal democracy's opponents simply awaited an opportune moment for its destruction, which came in 1933 and was exploited by a ruthless Adolf Hitler. Dismissing the claims of "half-Marxists" who traced Weimar's weaknesses to monopoly capitalism and economic turbulence, Strauss tends to emphasize more conventional reasons for its instability, such as the injustices of the Versailles Treaty, which Germans – otherwise primed to support liberal democracy – took as a betrayal of its core principles.[64]

The 1965 preface then targets what Strauss apparently viewed as a more fundamental source of Weimar fragility: "the radicalization and deepening of Rousseau's thought" among nineteenth-century German thinkers, and a tradition of German romanticism and "dissatisfaction with modernity" that culminated in irresponsible dreams of a "third Reich" that ultimately played a role even in Nietzsche's thinking.[65]

In other words, Weimar's demise can be traced to the "second" and "third" waves of modernity and their representative philosophical figures. Here again, as so often in his writings, an intellectual or *geistesgeschichtliche* analysis, rather than recourse to systematic social or historical analysis, carried the heavy load of making sense of real-life political trends. Unfortunately, this feature of Strauss's thinking prevented him from ever properly appreciating Weimar's complexities or their possible significance for contemporary liberal democracy. Even more consequentially, it has allowed his recent US disciples to ignore how their own political preferences potentially reproduce Weimar's ugliest features.

Making the American Presidency Great Again

Many "west coast" (e.g., based at the Claremont Institute) but few "east coast" Straussians (at Harvard, Yale, etc.) joined the Trumpist bandwagon.[66] This political divide has clear intellectual roots. Strauss's more orthodox east coast followers reproduce his often qualified endorsement of liberal democracy generally, and the United States specifically. They often highlight the republic's Lockean genealogy, for example, and follow Strauss in claiming that its origins in modernity's "first wave" eventually invited relativism and nihilism.[67] Whatever its intellectual problems, that ambivalence has probably helped immunize many of them against Trump's "America First" jingoism.[68] In contrast, west coast figures such as the late Harry V. Jaffa long ago rejected such ambivalence, instead devoting their efforts to reinterpreting the US as the world's very "best regime."[69] They build on those elements of Strauss's messy oeuvre where he pointed in the direction of a more positive gloss on US liberal democracy.

The story of how Jaffa and his Claremont allies creatively tapped Strauss to ground this vastly more affirmative portrait of the American political tradition has already been explored in the scholarly literature.[70] For Jaffa and others who were committed to hard right US political views, Strauss's original pragmatic or at least cautious defense of the US republic was simply not enough: They needed an enthusiastic endorsement, and consequently they refashioned Strauss's legacy along the requisite lines. To do so, they amplified his assorted remarks about the US founding's premodern philosophical traits. As Catherine and Michael Zuckert have noted, the core of this agenda entailed "Aristotelianizing America" – that is, highlighting elements of Aristotelian political philosophy within the US political tradition and, specifically, its founding moment.[71] The US framers and subsequent iconic political figures (such as Abraham Lincoln), it turns out, were not exclusively Lockean liberals or simply products of decadent modernity's "first wave." Instead, they funneled classical antiquity and Aristotle, or at least: Aristotle interpreted along deeply anti-egalitarian lines and as Plato's most important pupil.[72] The Declaration of Independence remains the revolutionary period's greatest theoretical statement, but it should be read – far more boldly that Strauss ever inferred – as a brilliant and still unrivaled attempt to salvage classical natural right.

This reinterpretation of the US founding has long faced a skeptical reception among both Straussian and non-Straussian scholars.[73] Even if we bracket questions about its historical accuracy or intellectual merits, its political consequences seem straightforward. In a prescient 1985 critique in *National Review*, the east coast (and then Toronto-based) Straussian Thomas Pangle already warned that it risked culminating in a "new mythic Americanism." Criticizing Jaffa and also Kesler, Pangle worried about how their Aristotelian remake of America encouraged a gung-ho patriotism, even to the point of denigrating those with competing views as "un-American."[74] In fact, the west coast Straussians quickly closed ranks to embrace Trumpist hyper-patriotism. A revealing 2019 Trump speech, given at a White House ceremony rewarding the Claremont Institute with the prestigious National Humanities Medal, aptly captures the super-patriotic ideological overlap:

> As one of America's leading think tanks, the Claremont Institute has made invaluable contributions to the history of American conservative thought. Claremont educates, reminds, and informs Americans about the founding principles that have made our country the greatest nation anywhere on earth. Through publications, seminars, and scholarships, they fight to recover the American Idea – I know it well – by teaching about the Declaration of Independence, the Constitution, the writings of Abraham Lincoln (whose bedroom is right above us). The Claremont Institute helps preserve our national traditions for generations to come.[75]

However, this shared discourse of "American greatness" takes us only so far as an explanation for the west coast Straussian dalliance with Trump. First, it obscures intellectual (and personal) ties between them and their east coast brethren. Second, and even more problematically, it fails to address how an expansive view of executive or presidential power has played a crucial role among Straussians, both east and west coast. To be sure, key differences separate their competing accounts; they help us grasp why east coast Straussians often refused to join the Trumpist bandwagon. What Ken Kersch has accurately characterized as the idea of a redemptive "messianic presidency," rooted in fundamental law and natural right, has been pivotal to the *west coast* Straussians' Trumpist gambit.[76] Yet the idea of a messianic presidency represents just one version of a more general Straussian defense of an effectively all-powerful US presidency.

The main source for the Straussian defense of an institutionally dominant presidency remains Jaffa's *Crisis of the House Divided: An Interpretation of the Lincoln–Douglas Debates*,[77] a fascinating albeit peculiar reinterpretation of Lincoln. In Jaffa's narrative, Lincoln fights the good (Straussian) war against his political rival and – for Jaffa – moral relativist and demagogue, Senator Stephen Douglas. Against Lincoln's self-interpretation of his political positions as congruent with the Declaration of Independence and the framers, Jaffa construed Lincoln as *revising* the founders' Lockeanism. The surprisingly philosophical-minded Lincoln tapped elements of classical natural right to *re-found* the American polity while preserving "the central constitutive element of American nationality," interpreted by Lincoln in a strikingly Aristotelian vein.[78] Natural equality, for example, was reconnected to the idea of moral duty and a quest for virtue: Equality became "a condition *toward* which men have a duty ever to strive, not a condition *from* which they have a right to *escape*."[79] The republic's "low but solid" Lockean grounds were elevated, Jaffa inferred, by Lincoln's Aristotelian redo especially of the Declaration of Independence, which, for Jaffa, was a sturdier philosophical building block than the US Constitution.[80] As the philosopher-statesman Lincoln had apparently grasped, the republic demanded leaders "of transcendent ability and virtue," alone capable of thwarting populist demagogues who threaten its moral foundations.[81] On this view, Douglas, who defended local (white male) popular sovereignty as the best way to decide slavery's fate, represented just such a threat. The paradox, however, was that "Caesar must be encountered by one who has all Caesar's talent for domination, one who could, if he would, govern the people without their consent, but who prefers the people's freedom to their domination."[82] In short, "[m]-essianic ambition must counteract the Caesarian."[83] Fortunately, the American Republic had produced just such a sage messianic leader in Lincoln, who emerges in Jaffa's account as nothing less than a world-historical revolutionary figure who synthesized just the right mix of moral virtue, statesmanship, and grasp of Aristotelian political science.

Jaffa appears to have been irked by conservative critics who pointed out that *Crisis of the House Divided* offered a possible justification for modern presidents who might undertake an open-ended overhaul of the US constitutional order.[84] In effect, Jaffa had defended a revolutionary (or what Carl Schmitt called *sovereign*) dictatorship,[85] something that predictably alarmed more conventional conservatives who were in favor of strict ideas of constitutional government. Jaffa's long-awaited follow-up volume, *A New Birth of Freedom: Abraham Lincoln and the Coming of the Civil War*,[86] conveniently closed the gap between Lincoln and the founding, with Lincoln re-emerging as a loyal exegete of the framers, reinterpreted in a decidedly more Aristotelian light than Jaffa's initial revisionist Straussian analysis had acknowledged.[87] Lincoln remained a heroic figure, but in a US Civil War no longer depicted as a second American Revolution but instead its final anti-slavery moment. No revolutionary or sovereign dictator, Lincoln became, in Schmitt's terms, a *commissarial* dictator tasked with upholding and preserving the founding's original moral and political aims.

Jaffa's updated version of the argument failed to convince many critics. Michael Zuckert, for example, accused *A New Birth of Freedom* of "distorting the thought of the American Founders by assimilating them into the classics and Christianity to a much greater degree than is warranted."[88] Even more worrisome, the presidency remained an institutional launching pad for wide-ranging constitutional and political upheaval, and potentially a frontal assault on political developments that had (allegedly) eviscerated the framers' original, morally superior intentions. Only the superhuman Lincoln, outfitted with vast wartime executive power, at any rate, had successfully preserved the American Republic and its sound Aristotelian foundations. Given Jaffa's frequently pessimistic remarks about the contours of recent US political trends, why not seek another messianic figure of "transcendent ability and virtue" to restore the republic to its classical roots?[89] In light of relativism's continued sway and terrible perils, should Americans not hope again for a powerful president who might return the republic to its original moral basis?

Precisely this intuition has perhaps motivated Kesler and other Straussian Trump enthusiasts, who appear to share Jaffa's vision of a redemptive messianic presidency tasked with revitalizing the republic's original moral foundations. The result? The heroic yet tragic figure of Abraham Lincoln, reluctantly forced to sacrifice millions to save the union and destroy slavery, gets jettisoned for the farce of Donald Trump, a failed business executive and con artist.

Kesler tells us that, by mobilizing a mass movement in defense of the original constitutional system, Trump might have succeeded where other GOP leaders – most notably, Ronald Reagan – foundered. Like Jaffa, Kesler not only views the US founding as resting on elements of classical natural right but also hopes that heroic leadership might successfully "revive the founders' wise principles and fortify them again with prudent statesmanship."[90] Trump's chance to revitalize the republic stemmed from his role as head of a popular movement that opposed the continuing "consolidation and expansion of progressivism," something that Reagan and other GOP leaders had failed to thwart by acquiescing in the administrative state's cancerous growth.[91] "Perhaps only a genuine outsider could have smashed it."[92] Astonishingly, Trump's disdain for longstanding political mores, institutional norms, and the rule of law is simply ignored: The Claremonsters fail to mention Trump's extraordinary and arguably unprecedented illegalities.[93] Why? For Kesler, "[t]here is an old distinction – between constitutional law and the law of the Constitution – that might be repurposed here." Trump stood valiantly on the side of the latter and against the former, which has been polluted by poisonous liberal and progressive public policies and reforms. Judicial precedents that impede Trump should be interpreted as diseased products of a "second" liberal-progressive constitutional system, and thus "are not of interest to us."[94] The real threat to the republic is posed by the autocratic "administrative state," an offshoot of decadent liberalism and something never intended by the framers.

As a GOP partisan and Goldwater adviser, Jaffa already viewed his Straussian philosophical standpoint as congruent with his partisan conservative views. His present-day Claremonster offspring take things a step further: Their defense of classical natural right becomes indistinguishable from their partisan war against the administrative state and so-called "woke" politics, which they simply take as the latest evidence for contemporary America's rampant moral relativism and nihilism. At times, their embrace of a strong executive seems based less in principled institutional or constitutional considerations than in a desire for a heroic leader who embodies their own core moral (and political) values. In effect, the Straussian defense of classical natural right gets fused directly with hard right policy positions and the quest for a political superman.[95]

Nonetheless, it would be a mistake to see this in many ways astonishing defense of Trump's authoritarianism as a mere west coast Straussian idiosyncrasy. Some pieces of the bigger puzzle can be found in influential accounts of executive power from the intellectually and politically more respectable east coast Straussians Carnes Lord and Harvey C. Mansfield, Jr. The occasional overlap should not surprise us: Mansfield seems to have been brought into the Straussian fold by Jaffa, and Kesler was later Mansfield's advisee at Harvard. Michael Anton, another Claremonster and author of the explosive "The Flight 93 Election," describes Mansfield as an intellectual hero.[96]

Both Lord and Mansfield interpret the modern executive as a basically Machiavellian institution, and thus one we might expect them – as more conventional Straussians – to condemn.[97] Machiavelli, after all, was a precursor to Hobbes and Locke and unleashed modernity's pathologies.[98] However, the good news is that those who exercise executive power can still return to the wisdom of Aristotelian political science and its ideas about responsible statesmanship. The modern Machiavellian executive, it seems, can be tempered with a strong dose of old-fashioned classical learning.

A professor at the Naval War College and former director of communications for the National Security Council under Reagan, Lord intends his *The Modern Prince: What Leaders Need to Know* for a non-academic audience and especially for those considering careers in public service. Oddly, his Aristotelianism culminates, as Anne Norton has pointed out, in a defense of authoritarian presidentialism that surely would have surprised Aristotle.[99] Among his book's executive paragons are not only Lincoln and Churchill but also the authoritarian strongmen Singapore's Lee Kuan Yew and Pakistan's Pervez Musharraf. Despite expressing concerns about the fate of constitutional government and the rule of law, Lord claims that savvy modern princes need to undertake "extraordinary political action intended to remedy potentially regime-threatening developments in the legislative or judicial branches, even where this might carry some risk of overstepping accepted boundaries of executive power."[100] The executive may need to do whatever is necessary, for example, to counter the extreme egalitarianism infecting Anglophone democracies.[101]

Carnes does not follow Jaffa or the west coast Straussians: His "modern prince" is no messianic figure tasked with recovering the republic's lost soul. Nor does he romanticize an "original" constitutional compact free of the alleged excrescences of modern liberalism and the administrative state. Like Mansfield (on whom he relies), Lord worries about the "trend toward plebiscitary leadership in the advanced democracies."[102] His anxieties tend to ring hollow, however, since his book's political hero, Ronald Reagan, tapped plebiscitarianism and engaged in emotional "political pandering."[103] Plebiscitarianism and demagoguery, it seems, are congenitally left- but not right-wing phenomena. At any rate, those who share Lord's own political preferences are above them.

A parallel political and analytic tension haunts Mansfield's *Taming the Prince: The Ambivalence of Modern Executive Power*, an earlier and more erudite Straussian study of the political theory of modern executive power. Mansfield criticizes the tendency among modern US presidents to claim charisma and seek "a direct appeal to popular feeling."[104] The modern democratization of executive power conflicts with the framers' original vision. To his credit, and in striking contrast to his former student Kesler, Mansfield has forcefully criticized Trump as a dangerous populist demagogue. For Mansfield, Trump is akin to Jaffa's populist demagogue Douglas, not the heroic Lincoln. Whereas Kesler suggests that only a mass-based political outsider able to tap popular discontent might successfully retrieve classical natural right, Mansfield instead recalls the ancients' worries about demagoguery. Trump, he has argued, fits the bill: Plato and Aristotle can help us grasp the demagogic dangers he poses.[105]

Although Mansfield's position is politically more responsible than the Trump idolatry of his west coast cousins, its analytic bases remain insecure. One might obviously question, for example, how far classical Greek antiquity's ideas about popular demagoguery take us in making sense of the dynamics of present-day authoritarian populism. Does Plato's or Aristotle's image of the popular tyrant really suffice to understand Trump, Viktor Orbán, or others like them?[106] More fundamentally, as in Lord's account, Mansfield's depends on a clear delineation between responsible and (dangerous) plebiscitarian political leaders, even as his own analysis tends to blur the boundaries between them. We should not conflate east coast Straussian views of the executive with those of their west coast cousins. But the borders separating them seem correspondingly porous.

Echoing his west coast allies, Mansfield offers an affirmative reading of the founders' vision: The original idea of executive energy "best extends human choice in the capacity to set a general direction for policy now and in the future."[107] Among its exemplars, somewhat surprisingly, Mansfield names Franklin D. Roosevelt and, more importantly, Reagan. Yet *pace* Mansfield, neither can be plausibly characterized as lacking in emotional or plebiscitarian appeal, or missing what we now conventionally describe as charisma. For better or worse, both right- and left-leaning presidents in the United States, and other presidential executives elsewhere, have come to depend on mass-based plebiscitarian appeals.[108] Mansfield's main theoretical insight is that the US presidency successfully gave Lockean extralegal prerogative a *constitutional* and republican basis: Executive energy, as theorized by Alexander Hamilton, entailed outfitting the president with vast power to deal "more than any other branch with … accidents and force."[109] According to Mansfield, "[w]ithout denying the need for something like a prerogative power, that need may not be satisfied outside the Constitution."[110] Locke's extralegal emergency powers, in essence, were relocated *within* a constitutional framework and the republican office of the presidency.

Less interested than Jaffa or Kesler in attacking the administrative state, Mansfield nonetheless analogously defends the framers' original view of the presidency as the proper "guardian" of the constitutional order: "The American president was to protect the Constitution from bouts of rampant enthusiasm in the people and the legislature."[111] Only responsible executive action that takes the ideal of classical statesmanship seriously, "the modern version of Aristotle's responsible rule," can do the job of preserving the US Constitution and warding off democratic excesses.[112] Fortunately, Mansfield's worries about populism and demagoguery have kept him from endorsing Trump. Yet, his defense of the presidency as a potentially overpowering republicanized monarch, tasked with overriding "the people and the legislature," hardly seems normatively or politically appealing. Even if Mansfield refuses to embrace a messianic redemptive presidency, he justifies an executive outfitted with awesome – and arguably authoritarian – powers. Not surprisingly, Mansfield was an outspoken defender of Bush's deployment of extraordinary – and probably unconstitutional – emergency powers during the so-called War on Terror.[113] With many on the American right now supporting voter suppression and celebrating the undemocratic electoral college, his views also cohere with some hard right US political positions, even if they have spared him the political embarrassment of jumping into Trump's bed.

The right-wing but non-Straussian political theorist Paul Edward Gottfried accuses the Straussians of succumbing to a dangerous "cult of the democratic hero."[114] This seems half right: In fact, the strongmen political figures the Straussians admire are regularly depicted as doing battle with democracy and its supposed excesses. For their argument to work, however, they unconvincingly downplay the emotional, plebiscitarian appeal of "their" preferred heroic leaders (e.g., Reagan, for Lord and Mansfield). With Kesler and the west coast Straussians, in contrast, the jig is up: They openly embrace Trump's populism as a vehicle for re-establishing the original founding and natural right. Though aware that Trump lacks Lincoln's virtue and public-mindedness, they hope that he can lead the way in bringing a decadent republic, plagued by relativism and nihilism, back to its original moral and political roots. In reality, they have provided a thin ideological veneer for a presidency arguably more hostile to facts and the quest for truth than any in US history.

Leo Strauss and Carl Schmitt: Another Look

The young Leo Strauss engaged in a respectful, mutually beneficial dialogue with Carl Schmitt (1888–1985).[115] Their open dialogue abruptly ended only when Schmitt, cultivating influence with the Nazis, abruptly began to shun Strauss (and other younger Jewish scholars) in 1933.[116] Like Schmitt, the Weimar-era Strauss harbored right-wing authoritarian views. He penned a sympathetic yet incisive critique of the senior scholar's *Concept of the Political*.[117] Both later published studies on Hobbes that offered parallel readings of the seventeenth-century English thinker as a decisive source for decadent liberalism.[118] Even as late as 1941, Strauss's New School lecture on "German Nihilism," though pointedly criticizing Schmitt (alongside Heidegger, Ernst Jünger, and others) for contributing to German thought's retrograde tendencies, reiterated some of his previous words of praise for *Concept of the Political*.[119] Whatever Schmitt's other mistakes, Strauss argued, he had latently affirmed "the seriousness of [human] life," in opposition to pacifists and others seeking a world state in which the existential pathos of "the political" would simply disappear.[120] Such a world state, Schmitt had insisted (and Strauss apparently agreed), might be prosperous, interesting, and even entertaining, but no longer could be described as morally meaningful or serious. For Strauss, Schmitt's "affirmation of the political is in the last analysis nothing other than the affirmation of the moral."[121] Schmitt's view of politics, it seems, represented an understandable rebellion against the moral trivialization of human existence, a trivialization both saw as potentially culminating in far-fetched cosmopolitan political fantasies.

Echoes of Schmitt's attack on pacifism and cosmopolitanism resurface in Strauss's often acerbic postwar remarks about shared dreams among liberals and communists for a "universal and classless society" and a "universal and homogeneous state."[122] Nonetheless, Strauss's disciples are basically right to argue that he ultimately sought to gain more distance from Schmitt.[123] In this chapter I have already alluded to one source of the gap: *Natural Right and History* portrayed decisionistic moral and political theory – depicted in strikingly Schmittean colors – as complicit in the worst horrors of the twentieth century. Like its cousins, relativism and nihilism, decisionism was faulted for opening the door to German fascism. Although Schmitt' name never appears in *Natural Right*, the agenda Strauss laid out there and elsewhere in his postwar writings can be read as an implicit critical rejoinder. As a defender of classical natural law and its (alleged) moral truths, Strauss rejected Schmitt's hostile attack on so-called normativities, moral or otherwise. Schmitt's preoccupation with the "pure decision not based on reason and discussion and not justifying itself, that is, an absolute decision created out of nothingness," had to be anathema to Strauss.[124]

Many reasons nonetheless remain for why we should be troubled by Strauss's interpretation of classical natural right as a satisfactory antidote. There are, philosophically and politically, other – and, in this author's view, superior, more democratic and less illiberal – ways to respond to relativism or nihilism and their possible dangers. Revealingly, Strauss's readings of Kant, Hegel, and other major figures are often curt and underdeveloped; the paths they might offer beyond relativism and nihilism are never sufficiently explored. Strauss's followers rarely engage in systematic rather than polemical analyses of contemporary political thinkers, few of whom can be tarred as "relativists." I find many of the Straussians' remarks about Jürgen Habermas, John Rawls, and others to be limited and, frankly, crude.[125] Nonetheless, it remains the case that Strauss ultimately rejected Schmitt's ideas and tried to accommodate postwar liberal democracy.

Unfortunately, his American disciples' preoccupation with identifying political superheroes as a path to moral salvation highlights one of Strauss's own most egregious intellectual weaknesses. Their recent Trump partisanship, I have suggested, represents only the most troublesome version of an expansive vision of executive power endorsed by a number of Straussians. Hyper-presidentialism, for both east and west coast Straussians, becomes a key institutional device for countering relativism and nihilism. I have also noted how Strauss regularly favored a broad-brush rendition of *Geistesgeschichte* over systematic social or political inquiry. Not surprisingly, even when engaging Schmitt's ideas as a young scholar, Strauss seems to have been uninterested in the details of Schmitt's late Weimar political agenda – i.e., the construction of a mass-based presidential regime, in which the executive would gain vast emergency authority to pursue fundamental political and possibly constitutional change. For Schmitt, the Weimar president's sovereign and not just commissarial dictatorial powers could be justified by the office's role as a stand-in for the republic's original, constitution-making power.[126] Schmitt was no constitutional "originalist" in the present-day American sense. Yet he sought to justify an effectively all-powerful presidency by grounding its authority in the republic's original foundation: Weimar's initial revolutionary popular constituent power. Starting in 1930, Schmitt worked diligently as a prominent intellectual and adviser to right-wing Weimar's emergency presidential regimes to realize his vision. Even if Weimar failed to achieve his political and theoretical aspirations, Schmitt helped guarantee that it took on increasingly authoritarian hues.

Let me be clear: The contemporary United States is *not* Weimar. History does not, in fact, repeat itself. Trump is not Hitler. We always need to guard against facile and potentially misleading historical analogies. The highly selective fashion in which right-wing Straussians have retold Weimar's story highlights the flexible and open-ended contours of *any* attempt to posit such analogies. Their efforts also remind us of the myriad intellectual and political dangers.

In this spirit, we would do well to highlight differences between Straussian ideas of executive power and Schmitt's authoritarian presidentialism. Most obviously, Schmitt rejected the ideas of natural right on which the Straussians ground their political vision.[127] Nonetheless, it is remarkable that precisely those right-wing Straussian intellectuals so obsessed with Weimar's "lessons," and so vexed by its (alleged) relativism and nihilism, seem oblivious to the possibility that their own political agenda mirrors elements of its disturbing legacy. Like Strauss, Schmitt's contemporary disciples have little patience with the social sciences or systematic political and social analysis: They prefer to analyze history and society from the perspective of those "great thinkers" they implicitly interpret as its key driving forces. They often succumb to a crude or at least unreflective idealism. Having reproduced his methodological flaws, their vision of a redemptive authoritarian presidency sometimes seems reminiscent of Schmitt's institutional preferences. In some distinction to Schmitt, however, they embrace authoritarian presidentialism not on the basis of an analysis of its constitutional bases or institutional dynamics, but instead chiefly because they hope it can bolster their preferred moral and political agenda and thereby squelch nihilism.[128]

Strauss hoped that his quest to retrieve classical natural right might help Americans and others elsewhere avoid repeating Weimar's tragic fate. Whether or not Strauss will succeed remains an open question today, in part because his followers now seem eager to support authoritarian political outcomes that ominously recall some elements of Weimar's final days.[129]

Notes

1 See, for example, the frequent references to Weimar in Tom Ginsburg and Aziz Z. Huq, *How to Save a Constitutional Democracy* (Chicago: University of Chicago University Press, 2018); Adam Przeworski, *Crises of Democracy* (Cambridge: Cambridge University Press, 2019).

2 For example, Benjamin Carter Hett, *The Death of Democracy: Hitler's Rise to Power and the Downfall of Democracy* (New York: St. Martin's, 2019).

3 The same tendency can be seen elsewhere, for example in the writings of Patrick Deneen, a supporter of Trump and Hungary's Viktor Orbán: Patrick Deneen, *Why Liberalism Failed*, 2nd ed. (New Haven: Yale University Press, 2019), p. 181.

4 Glenn Ellmers, *The Soul of Politics: Harry V. Jaffa and the Fight for America* (New York: Encounter, 2021), p. 291. A fellow at the Claremont Institute, Ellmers celebrates its pivotal role in providing support for Trumpism.

5 Michael Anton's incendiary "The Flight 93 Election" (5 September 2016; https://claremontreviewofbooks.com/digital/the-flight-93-election) set the tone for much of the pro-Trump (and west coast Straussian) genre.

A graduate of Claremont, Anton later worked for Trump on the National Security Council. Another initially pro-Trump publication, *American Affairs*, was edited by Julius Krein, a former student of the Straussian political theorist Harvey Mansfield. Unlike the Claremont Straussians, Krein soon abandoned Trump. A number of Claremont-trained and/or Claremont-based scholars signed a prominent statement endorsing Trump: "Scholars & Writers for Trump" (28 September 2016; https://amgreatness.com/2016/09/28/writes-scholars-for-trump/). The venture capitalist Peter Thiel, an outspoken Trump supporter from Silicon Valley, also fashions himself a Straussian aficionado: see Peter Thiel, "The Straussian Moment" in Robert Hamerton-Kelly, ed., *Politics and Apocalypse* (East Lansing: Michigan State University Press, 2007), pp. 189–218. To be sure, other Straussians (e.g., William Kristol, Harvey C. Mansfield, and Michael Zuckert) have spoken out eloquently against Trump. See, for example, the important statement Kristol co-authored with left-liberals Todd Gitlin and Jeffrey Isaac: "An Open Letter in Defense of Democracy: The Future of Democracy in the United States is in Danger," *The New Republic*, 27 October 2021 , https://newrepublic.com/article/164153/open-letter-defense-democracy.

6 The memo is easily available from many media sites: e.g., www.cnn.com/2021/09/21/politics/read-eastman-memo/index.html.
7 The best discussions are: Laura K. Field, "The Highbrow Conspiracism of the New Intellectual Right: A Sampling from the Trump Years," 19 April 2021, www.niskanencenter.org/the-highbrow-conspiracism-of-the-new-intellectual-right-a-sampling-from-the-trump-years/; "What the Hell Happened to the Claremont Institute," 13 July 2021, www.thebulwark.com/what-the-hell-happened-to-the-claremont-institute/. See also Ken I. Kersch, *Conservatives and the Constitution: Imagining Constitutional Restoration in the Heyday of American Liberalism* (New York: Cambridge University Press, 2019), pp. 374–9. The Straussians' role in Washington, DC already generated a wide-ranging controversy in the context of George W. Bush's "War on Terror." Anne Norton, *Leo Strauss and the Politics of American Empire* (New Haven: Yale University Press, 2004).
8 Charles R. Kesler, *Crisis of the Two Constitutions: The Rise, Decline, and Recovery of American Greatness* (New York: Encounter, 2021), p. 376. Kesler wrote his dissertation under Mansfield before joining the Claremont faculty and "west coast" Straussians at the Claremont Institute. For a dissection of his latest book, see R. Shep Melnick, "Claremont's Constitutional Crisis," 29 March 2021, https://lawliberty.org/book-review/claremonts-constitutional-crisis/. Kesler was appointed to the Trump Administration's 1776 Commission, a committee tasked with combatting (alleged) left-wing radicalism in the teaching of US history and reasserting the republic's (unambiguously glorious, it seems) patriotic virtues. Widely criticized for its blatantly ideological agenda, the 1776 Commission included no trained historians. Its co-chair was Larry Arnn, president of the right-wing Hillsdale College, a PhD from Claremont, and one of the founders of the Claremont Institute.
9 Kesler, *Crisis of the Two Constitutions*, p. xi. Kesler's narrative taps some increasingly commonplace tropes among postwar US right-wingers about constitutional decay.

10 John Marini, *Unmasking the Administrative State: The Crisis of American Politics in the Twenty-First Century* (New York: Encounter Books, 2019). There are indeed reasons why some aspects of the administrative state should worry defenders of the rule of law. See William E. Scheuerman, "The Rule of Law and the Welfare State: Towards a New Synthesis," *Politics & Society* 22, no. 2 (1994), pp. 195–213. But the Straussians' critique is crude and heavy-handed.

11 Kesler, *Crisis of the Two Constitutions*, pp. x–xii.

12 Ibid., p. 396.

13 Ibid.

14 Ibid., p. 397. Justice Thomas's ties to the Straussians have been well documented. Prior to being named to the US Supreme Court, for example, Thomas turned to John Marini and Ken Masugi for "a crash course on the nation's founding text and its philosophical underpinnings." Corey Robin, *The Enigma of Clarence Thomas* (New York: Metropolitan Books, 2019), p. 148. More generally on the Straussians and the study of race, see Richard H. King, "Rights and Slavery: Leo Strauss, the Straussians, and the American Dilemma," *Modern Intellectual History* 5, no. 1 (2018), pp. 55–82.

15 For example, Michael Anton, "The Continuing Crisis: The Election and Its Aftermath," *Claremont Review of Books*, Winter (2020–21), https://claremontreviewofbooks.com/the-continuing-crisis/.

16 Jaffa, for example, was a speechwriter for the 1964 GOP presidential candidate Barry Goldwater. He penned the famous line in Goldwater's nomination speech: "Extremism in the defense of liberty is no vice … And … moderation in the pursuit of justice is no virtue."

17 The lecture has been reprinted in Edward J. Erler and Ken Masugi, eds., *The Rediscovery of America: Essays by Harry V. Jaffa on the New Birth of Politics* (Lanham, MD: Rowman & Littlefield, 2019), pp. 85–110.

18 Allan Bloom, *The Closing of the American Mind* (New York: Simon & Schuster, 1987), p. 317.

19 Ibid., p. 30. Bloom's main targets included college professors who had infected their students with the German (intellectual) virus. But his polemics against the academy are moderate in tone compared to what appears in more recent "Claremonster" writings.

20 I am grateful to Ken Kersch for this point.

21 On Strauss's Weimar background, see Eugene R. Sheppard, *Leo Strauss and the Politics of Exile: The Making of a Political Philosopher* (Waltham, MA: Brandeis University Press, 2006).

22 Leo Strauss, *Natural Right and History* (Chicago: University of Chicago Press, 1953).

23 Ibid., p. 153.

24 Ibid., p. 180.

25 Ibid., p. 247.

26 Ibid., p. 249.

27 Ibid., p. 42.

28 Ibid.

29 Erich Voegelin, a former student of Kelsen's from Vienna who evolved into a hardcore right-wing anti-modernist, is most pertinent here. Like Strauss, he landed in the US, taught political theory (at Louisiana State University), and influenced many conservative scholars in political science. For Voegelin as for Strauss, modernity is fundamentally a *Verfallsgeschichte* best analyzed by recourse to an historical account of key ideas.

30 John Gunnell, "Political Theory and Politics: The Case of Leo Strauss and Liberal Democracy" in Kenneth L. Deutsch and Walter Sofa, eds., *The Crisis of Liberal Democracy: A Straussian Perspective* (Albany: SUNY Press, 1987), p. 71.

31 See, for example, Leo Strauss, "An Epilogue" in Hilda Gildin, ed., *Political Philosophy: Six Essays by Leo Strauss* (Indianapolis: Bobbs-Merrill, 1975), pp. 99–130.

32 Gunnell, "Political Theory and Politics," p. 72.

33 I am grateful to Peter Caldwell for this observation.

34 Strauss, *Natural Right and History*, pp. 202–51.

35 Unfortunately, its original meaning and connotations are distorted in the English translation: Ellen Kennedy, ed., *The Crisis of Parliamentary Democracy* (Cambridge, MA: MIT Press, 1985).

36 George Nash, *The Conservative Intellectual Movement in America since 1945* (Wilmington, DE: Intercollegiate Studies, 2006).

37 Strauss, *Natural Right and History*, pp. 1–2.

38 As my colleague Michael Morgan has correctly pointed out in a conversation, this commonplace image of Weimar "decadence" can be found in many other intellectual and cultural contexts (e.g., in the recent German television series *Babylon Berlin*). It would be useful to trace its origins. Disturbingly, it reproduces elements of the Nazis' view of Weimar.

39 Strauss, *Natural Right and History*, p. 4. Kelsen had, indeed, diagnosed an elective affinity between liberal democracy and moral relativism. See, for example, Hans Kelsen, "Foundations of Democracy," *Ethics* 66, no. 1 (1955), pp. 1–101. Oddly, Strauss accused Kelsen (*Natural Right and History*, p. 4, note 2) of trying to veil his relativistic defense of democracy; in fact, Kelsen consistently remained quite forthright about it.

40 Strauss, *Natural Right and History*, p. 4.

41 Peter C. Caldwell, *Popular Sovereignty and the Crisis of German Constitutional Law: The Theory & Practice of Weimar Constitutionalism* (Durham, NC: Duke University Press, 1997); see also Peter C. Caldwell and William E. Scheuerman, eds., *From Liberal Democracy to Fascism: Legal and Political Thought in the Weimar Republic* (Boston, MA: Humanities Press, 2000).

42 Strauss, *Natural Right and History*, pp. 5–6, 46.

43 Ibid., p. 47. For a critical response to Strauss's troublesome reading of Weber, see Tzvetan Todorov, *The Morals of History* (Minneapolis: University of Minnesota Press, 1995), pp. 197–208.

44 On this feature of Schmitt's thought, see Ben Schupmann, *Carl Schmitt's State and Constitutional Theory: A Critical Analysis* (New York: Oxford University Press, 2017). Unfortunately, Schupmann does not always sufficiently recognize the depth of Schmitt's hostility to core elements of Weimar

democracy. The Weimar Schmitt hoped to "save" would have been a deeply authoritarian makeover that eliminated crucial liberal (and social) democratic elements!

45 Leo Strauss, "Relativism" in Thomas L. Pangle, ed., *The Rebirth of Classical Political Rationalism: An Introduction to the Thought of Leo Strauss* (Chicago: University of Chicago Press, 1989), p. 17.
46 Leo Strauss, "The Three Waves of Modernity" in Gildin, *Political Philosophy*, pp. 81–98.
47 Note, for example, the revealing title to Strauss's "Political Philosophy and the Crisis of our Time" in George Carey and Graham George, eds., *The Post-Behavioral Era: Perspectives on Political Science* (New York: David McKay, 1972), pp. 217–42.
48 Strauss, *Natural Right and History*, p. 1.
49 Leo Strauss, "An Epilogue" in Gildin, *Political Philosophy*, p. 129.
50 Thomas L. Pangle, *Leo Strauss: An Introduction to his Thought and Intellectual Legacy* (Baltimore: Johns Hopkins University Press, 2006); Steven B. Smith, *Reading Leo Strauss: Politics, Philosophy, Judaism* (Chicago: University of Chicago Press, 2006), pp. 156–83; Catherine Zuckert and Michael Zuckert, *The Truth About Leo Strauss: Political Philosophy and American Democracy* (Chicago: University of Chicago Press, 2006).
51 William A. Galston, "Leo Strauss' Qualified Embrace of Liberal Democracy" in Steven B. Smith, ed., *Cambridge Companion to Leo Strauss* (New York: Cambridge University Press, 2009), pp. 193–214. On Strauss's authoritarian proclivities during Weimar's final years, see Nicholas Xenos, *Cloaked in Virtue: Unveiling Leo Strauss and the Rhetoric of American Foreign Policy* (New York: Routledge, 2008).
52 Leo Strauss, "German Nihilism" [1941], *Interpretation* 26, no. 3 (1999), pp. 353–78.
53 Sheppard, *Leo Strauss and the Politics of Exile*, pp. 54–80.
54 Strauss, *Natural Right and History*, pp. 294–323.
55 Leo Strauss (with Joseph Cropsey), "Introduction" in *History of Political Philosophy*, 2nd ed. (Chicago: University of Chicago, 1972), p. 6; see also Leo Strauss, "What Is Political Philosophy?" in Gildin, *Political Philosophy*, p. 48.
56 Leo Strauss, *Thoughts on Machiavelli* (Seattle: University of Washington Press, 1958), pp. 13–14.
57 Leo Strauss, "Liberal Education and Responsibility" in Allan Bloom, ed., *Liberalism Ancient and Modern* (Chicago: University of Chicago Press, 1989), pp. 9–25.
58 In striking contrast to, among others, Hannah Arendt (*On Revolution* (New York: Penguin, 1963)) and Hans J. Morgenthau (*The Purpose of American Politics* (New York: Alfred Knopf, 1960)).
59 Strauss, "The Three Waves of Modernity," p. 98.
60 Ibid., p. 98.
61 Leo Strauss, "Preface" in *Spinoza's Critique of Religion* (New York: Schocken Books, 1965), p. 2. For an insightful discussion, see Michael L. Morgan, "The Curse of Historicity: The Role of History in Leo Strauss' Jewish

Thought," *Journal of Religion* 61, no. 4 (1981), pp. 345–63. Unfortunately, I am forced to neglect some fascinating political-theological issues – for example, how the orthodox Jewish Strauss, and even more so some of his Jewish students (i.e., Jaffa), provided an ideological basis for an interpretation of the US founding that is now being enthusiastically embraced by right-wing Christian evangelicals. Some of the issues are discussed insightfully by Kersch in *Conservatives and the Constitution*, pp. 360–83.

62 Strauss, "Preface" in *Spinoza's Critique of Religion*, p. 6. As Morgan notes, Strauss's argument about liberalism and Judaism is astonishingly "brief and a priori." Morgan, "The Curse of Historicity," p. 348.

63 Strauss, "Preface" in *Spinoza's Critique of Religion*, p. 1.

64 Ibid., pp. 1–2. One wonders if Strauss's "half-Marxists" referred to the (relatively unorthodox) neo-Marxist theories of Nazi Germany developed by Franz L. Neumann and/or Ernst Fraenkel, both refugees from Weimar whose writings Strauss likely encountered.

65 Strauss, "Preface" in *Spinoza's Critique of Religion*, p. 2.

66 This now standard categorization is both geographical and intellectual. For a discussion, see Zuckert and Zuckert, *The Truth About Leo Strauss*, pp. 228–59.

67 Bloom, *The Closing of the American Mind*, especially pp. 160–7.

68 As my colleague Jeffrey Isaac has rightly pointed out to me, at least some of the anti-Trump east coast Straussians (e.g., William Kristol) are also former neoconservatives; prominent former neoconservatives (e.g., David Brooks and David Frum) have been some of Trump's harshest and most astute critics. So the ideological background for some of the east coast Straussians who rejected Trump is complicated, in part because the nexus between Straussianism and neoconservativism is messy. Nonetheless, I think the best explanation for why most east and west coast Straussians differ on Trump revolves around competing views of US liberal democracy in general, and of the US executive in particular.

69 Harry V. Jaffe, "The American Founding as the Best Regime: The Bonding of Civil and Religious Liberty" in Erler and Masugi, *The Rediscovery of America*, pp. 121–44.

70 Zuckert and Zuckert, *The Truth About Leo Strauss*, pp. 197–27.

71 Ibid., pp. 217–27.

72 I cannot explore, unfortunately, the strengths and weaknesses of the Straussian retrieval of Aristotle, though it does seem to neglect some of his core insights. For a useful overview of Aristotle's political thought, see Bernard Yack, *The Problems of a Political Animal: Community, Justice, and Conflict in Aristotelian Political Thought* (Berkeley: University of California Press, 1993).

73 For an example of the latter, see Gordon S. Wood, "The Fundamentalists and the Constitution," *New York Review of Books*, 18 February 1988.

74 Thomas L. Pangle, "Patriotism American Style," *National Review*, 29 November 1985, pp. 30–4.

75 See "Claremont Institute Award Prestigious National Humanities Medal," 18 November 2019, www.claremont.org/press_releases/claremont-institute-awarded-prestigious-national-humanities-medal/.

76 Ken Kersch, "The Messianic Presidency in Conservative Constitutional Thought," *The Constitutionalist*, 30 April 2021, https://theconstitutionalist .org/2021/04/30/the-messianic-presidency-in-conservative-constitutional-thought/.

77 Harry V. Jaffa, *Crisis of the House Divided: An Interpretation of the Lincoln–Douglas Debates* (Chicago: University of Chicago Press, 1982 [1959]).

78 Ibid., p. 331.

79 Ibid., p. 320.

80 For an appreciative discussion, see Charles Kesler, "A Special Meaning of the Declaration of Independence: A Tribute to Harry V. Jaffa," *National Review*, 6 July 1979, pp. 850–9. As Kersch notes, "Jaffa's understandings [of the Declaration's moral and political centrality] have served as the wellspring of the contemporary conservative constitutional vision some have called 'Declarationism.'" Kersch, *Conservatives and the Constitution*, p. 55, note 82.

81 Jaffa, *Crisis of the House Divided*, p. 224.

82 Ibid., p. 225.

83 Ibid., p. 238.

84 Most importantly, Willmoore Kendall, "Sources of American Caesarism," *National Review*, 7 November 1959, pp. 461–2.

85 See Carl Schmitt, *Dictatorship*, trans. Michael Hoelzl and Graham Ward (Cambridge: Polity Press, 2014).

86 Harry V. Jaffa, *A New Birth of Freedom: Abraham Lincoln and the Coming of the Civil War* (Lanham, MD: Rowman & Littlefield, 2000).

87 See also Harry V. Jaffa, "Aristotle and Locke in the American Founding" in Erler and Masugi, *The Rediscovery of America*, pp. 5–10.

88 Michael Zuckert, "Jaffa's *New Birth*: Harry Jaffa at Ninety" in Harry V. Jaffa, ed., *Crisis of the Strauss Divided: Essays on Leo Strauss and Straussianism, East and West* (Lanham, MD: Rowman & Littlefield, 2012), p. 255.

89 Jaffa's hero worship was directed not just at Lincoln but also at Winston Churchill: Jaffa, "Can There Be Another Winston Churchill?," *Claremont Review of Books*, 12 June 1981, https://claremontreviewofbooks.com/digital/can-there-be-another-winston-churchill/.

90 Kesler, *Crisis of the Two Constitutions*, pp. xvii, 3–32. There are, to be sure, some differences between Kesler's and Jaffa's view of the founding and its ties to Aristotelianism.

91 Ibid., p. 393.

92 Ibid., p. 395.

93 For an important discussion (though one penned prior to the attempted 6 January coup), see Susan Hennessey and Benjamin Wittes, *Unmaking the Presidency: Donald Trump's War on the World's Most Powerful Office* (New York: Farrar, Straus and Giroux, 2020).

94 Kesler, *Crisis of the Two Constitutions*, p. xv.

95 The fusion is hardly unproblematic: Strauss was no critic of the modern administrative state, for example.

96 As a young high school student, Mansfield apparently met Jaffa when the latter was an Assistant Professor at Ohio State University. Mansfield's father was on the political science faculty there. Michael Anton, "Harry V. Jaffa: An Appreciation," *Claremont Review of Books* XV, no. 1 (Winter 2014–15), https://claremontreviewofbooks.com//harry-v-jaffa-an-appreciation/. I served as a teaching assistant for Mansfield twice while a PhD student at Harvard; he also served on the committee that conducted my comprehensive exams in political theory. He always conducted himself professionally in his dealings with me and other doctoral students with whom I was acquainted, many of whom were left-wingers and none of whom were Straussians.

97 Carnes Lord, *The Modern Prince: What Leaders Need to Know* (New Haven: Yale University Press, 2003); Harvey C. Mansfield, Jr. *Taming the Prince: The Ambivalence of Modern Executive Power* (Baltimore: Johns Hopkins University Press, 1989), pp. 279–97.

98 Strauss, *Natural Right and History*, p. 177–80.

99 Norton, *Leo Strauss and the Politics of American Empire*, p. 134.

100 Lord, *The Modern Prince*, p. 230.

101 Ibid., p. 2.

102 Ibid., p. xv.

103 Ibid., pp. 7, 14.

104 Mansfield, *Taming the Prince*, p. 284.

105 Harvey C. Mansfield, Jr., "The Vulgar Manliness of Donald Trump: The Greeks and Founders Feared Men Like the President, and with Good Reason," *Commentary*, 17 September 2017, www.commentary.org/articles/harvey-mansfield/vulgar-manliness-donald-trump. More recently, Harvey Mansfield, "Final Days: Trump Leaves the Scene on a Dark Note," *City Journal*, 11 January 2021, www.city-journal.org/article/final-days. See also his earlier critical comments about populism: Harvey C. Mansfield, *America's Constitutional Soul* (Baltimore: Johns Hopkins University Press, 1991).

106 Consider, for example, the major role of new informational technologies in contemporary authoritarian populism: Paolo Gerbaudo, *The Digital Party: Political Organization and Online Democracy* (London: Pluto Press, 2019).

107 Mansfield, *Taming the Prince*, p. 257, also, p. 294.

108 Juan J. Linz and Arturo Valenzuela, eds., *The Failure of Presidential Democracy* (Baltimore: Johns Hopkins University Press, 1994).

109 Mansfield, *Taming the Prince*, p. 256.

110 Ibid., p. 259.

111 Ibid., p. 285.

112 Ibid., p. 294.

113 Mansfield interpreted Bush's wide-ranging emergency powers as permitted by the office of the presidency and its requisite constitutional duties: Harvey C. Mansfield, "The Case for the Strong Executive: Now is Not the Time to Fear the Imperial Presidency," *Claremont Review of Books* VII, no. 2 (Spring 2007), https://claremontreviewofbooks.com/the-case-for-the-strong-executive/.

114 Paul Edward Gottfried, *Leo Strauss and the Conservative Movement in America: A Critical Appraisal* (New York: Cambridge University Press, 2012), p. 35.

115 For a thoughtful discussion, see Robert Howse, *Leo Strauss: Man of Peace* (New York: Cambridge University Press, 2014).

116 Sheppard, *Leo Strauss and the Politics of Exile*, p. 58.

117 Carl Schmitt, *Concept of the Political*, trans. George Schwab (New Brunswick: Rutgers University Press, 1976 [1932]).

118 Leo Strauss, *The Political Philosophy of Thomas Hobbes: Its Basis and Genesis* (Chicago: University of Chicago Press, 1952 [1936]); Carl Schmitt, *The Leviathan in the State Theory of Thomas Hobbes*, trans. George Schwab and Erna Hilfstein (Chicago: University of Chicago Press, 1996 [1938]).

119 Strauss, "German Nihilism."

120 Leo Strauss, "Comments on *Der Begriff des Politischen* by Carl Schmit" [1932] in *Spinoza's Critique of Religion*, p. 347.

121 Ibid., p. 347.

122 Leo Strauss, "Preface" in Bloom, *Liberalism Ancient and Modern*, pp. vii–xi; Leo Strauss, "Political Philosophy and the Crisis of our Time" in Carey and George, *The Post-Behavioral Era*, pp. 220–3.

123 Zuckert and Zuckert, *The Truth About Leo Strauss*, pp. 184–94.

124 Carl Schmitt, *Political Theology: Four Chapters on the Concept of Sovereignty*, ed. Tray Strong (Chicago: University of Chicago Press, 2005 [1934]), p. 66.

125 For example, to claim that for Habermas, Rawls, or many other contemporary philosophers, relativism is "unproblematic and even salutary" is nonsense. Nasser Behnegar, *Leo Strauss, Max Weber, and the Scientific Study of Politics* (Chicago: University of Chicago Press, 2003), p. 29.

126 For the pertinent texts, see Lars Vinx, ed., *The Guardian of the Constitution: Hans Kelsen and Carl Schmitt on the Limits of Constitutional Law* (New York: Oxford University Press, 2015); Carl Schmitt, *Legality and Legitimacy*, ed. Jeffrey Seitzer (Durham, NC: Duke University Press, 2004 [1932]).

127 Schmitt also interpreted the presidential regime as relying, unavoidably, on democratic legitimacy, though he viewed democracy idiosyncratically not as a quest to maximize political autonomy, but instead interpreted equality as sameness or homogeneity. Like the Straussians, Schmitt was deeply skeptical of normatively ambitious ideals of democracy.

128 Schmitt, as noted, also tended to engage in *Geistesgeschichte* and neglected systematic historical, political, and social analysis. Yet he did try to analyze, however inadequately, presidentialism's constitutional and institutional logics.

129 There are complex empirical and historical issues, to be sure, about the nexus between Weimar presidentialism and authoritarianism. For now, I simply note that critics of presidential government have often had the Weimar experience in mind. For example, Juan J. Linz, "Presidential or Parliamentary Democracy: Does It Make a Difference?" in Linz and Valenzuela, *The Failure of Presidential Democracy*, pp. 3–90; more recently, Cindy Skach, *Borrowing Constitutional Designs: Constitutional Law in Weimar Germany and the French Fifth Republic* (Princeton: Princeton University Press, 2005). On Weimar's authoritarian devolution, see Hans Mommsen, *The Rise and Fall of Weimar Democracy* (Chapel Hill: University of North Carolina Press, 1996).

8 Shadows of Babylon and Shreds of Artificial Silk

Weimar's Cultural and Political Legacies in the Contemporary Television Series Babylon Berlin

Jill Suzanne Smith

While journalists and political commentators have used mainstream media platforms to invoke the memory of the Weimar Republic, primarily as a cautionary tale regarding the fragility of Western democracies, cultural creators have revived Weimar Berlin as a center for hedonistic nightlife, sexual experimentation, and social freedom. No contemporary work has capitalized on both the titillating and dangerous allure of Weimar Berlin *and* the precarious nature of Germany's first republic more than *Babylon Berlin* (hereafter *BB*). Currently in its fourth season, the blockbuster television show written and directed by Achim von Borries, Henk Handloegten, and Tom Tykwer has reached over ten million viewers in Germany alone and has been distributed to a global audience via diverse streaming platforms such as Netflix.[1] It has won numerous awards in Germany and Europe, and it has spawned fan blogs and subreddits, computer games and Weimar-themed events. Scholars of history, cultural studies, and media studies have noted *BB*'s unique status among German-language television series, due in part to the groundbreaking funding structure that allowed it to become the most expensive European series ever made and in part to the kaleidoscopic collage style that intersplices historical events, figures, and objects with citations of art, film, literature, and music from the Weimar era to the present.[2]

Why revive Weimar for a contemporary audience? What can today's viewers learn from the series, the showrunners were asked in an interview for the Bundeszentrale für politische Bildung (Federal Agency for Civic Education), which regularly uses film and visual media as educational tools for school-age Germans on its kinofenster.de site.[3] Von Borries and Handloegten offered two key takeaways they could imagine for younger viewers: The first lesson, according to von Borries, is the appreciation for democracy and the acknowledgment that, if taken for granted, democracy can collapse. Today's "functioning society," he states, "is the best society we have ever had." Those who live in a democracy such as Germany's must defend it "with all our teeth and any weapons we have at our disposal." Handloegten homes in on a particular social group among the series' viewers: young women, who will surely find the freedoms enjoyed by women in the 1920s "astounding," especially compared to the conservative gender roles and sexual mores of the 1950s. "History," Handloegten notes, is not teleological, and "one has to be alert" to its "breaks" and backlashes. The defense of democratic freedoms, and specifically the advances made by women, emerge in the showrunners' minds as key lessons to learn from *BB*, and this chapter tests the veracity of their assumptions by focusing on how the series represents women, sexuality, and politics. It does so with the knowledge that the most obvious aspect of the series that viewers – including journalists in the German and Anglo-American mainstream press and non-specialist audience members – tend to identify is *BB*'s representation of Berlin's club culture and its erotic appeal.

Weimar Berlin was, at least in the Anglo-American imagination, the erotic entertainment capital of the world.[4] *BB*'s depiction of club culture, however, views the Weimar era through two temporal filters: the resurgence of unified Berlin as a dance club mecca shaped by the techno culture of the 1990s and the gritty post-punk alternative scene of 1970s and 1980s West Berlin.[5] As Julia Sneeringer notes in her canny analysis of *BB* from the perspective of Cold-War-era West Berlin, the 1970s also represented the first post-1945 phase of Weimar revival, with Bob Fosse's 1972 movie musical *Cabaret* and its portrait of the fictional Kit Kat Club being one of the most enduring – and troubling – renditions of Weimar culture. Reviews of *BB* in the mainstream press, both in Germany and in the Anglo-American world, with their repeated references to the series' decadence, draw explicit connections between the series and Fosse's film.[6] In so doing, these reviews perpetuate what I call "the *Cabaret* syndrome" – the idea that the so-called sexual decadence of Weimar played a key role in the Republic's end and the notion that it was even culpable in the rise of the Nazis.[7] But are Fosse's film and *BB* really so similar in their moral framing of non-normative gender roles and sexuality as somehow complicit in Nazism? I strive to answer this question by carefully reading three separate club scenes, only one of which exhibits clear features of the *Cabaret* syndrome, and two of which tell us more about how the series positions itself vis-à-vis women's emancipation and everyday reform politics in Weimar democracy. The two club scenes that resist the *Cabaret* syndrome, I argue, have less in common with the intentionally gaudy visual aesthetic of Fosse's film and its problematic political messages and more in common with Weimar-era literary texts that are more matter of fact in tone, many of which were written by women. Unlike most of the chapters in this volume, my analytical focus is on a creative cultural work, and the primary sources that *BB*'s showrunners read, heard, and viewed as they wrote the screenplay were not political policy documents from historical archives. They were films, novels, and popular songs.[8] This means that any political lessons about Weimar democracy and its demise that the showrunners might assume are evident to the series' viewers are anything but coherent. What *BB* offers viewers instead is a kaleidoscopic view of Weimar Berlin, rife with inherent tensions and contradictions. Teasing out some of these tensions and contradictions, and then relating them back to the cultural sources on which the series is built, is the project of this chapter.

New Women and Whores: Weimar-Era Fiction as Inspiration for *BB*'s Kaleidoscopic Style

Because *BB* is itself a cinematic work with an awarding-winning original score, it makes perfect sense that much of the scholarly work on the series thus far has focused on its pastiche of Weimar-era films and music.[9] This exclusive focus on the audiovisual aspects of the series, however, obscures the screenplay's own status as a literary text that creatively and extensively reworks Volker Kutscher's bestselling contemporary detective novels set in late Weimar Berlin, just as it glosses over *BB*'s clever citation of works of literature by Weimar authors.[10] The series' most obvious literary reference, the titular nod to Alfred Döblin's 1929 modernist novel *Berlin Alexanderplatz*, a book that depicts the German capital itself as the destructive Whore of Babylon, reveals itself in the unflinching depiction of traumatized veterans, petty criminals, and sexualized violence.[11] But as critics, scholars, and the series' own showrunners have argued, the Whore of Babylon is mobilized primarily as a familiar cliché associated with Weimar Berlin, one that is, at times, offset by moments of humor and hope – witty asides, entertaining song-and-dance numbers, even running jokes.[12] This "mixture of levity and threat," as I have called it in my own analysis of *BB*, characterizes the journalistic writings of Kurt Tucholsky and Gabriele Tergit and the popular late Weimar novels of Vicki Baum and Irmgard Keun.[13] Keun's 1932 novel *Das kunstseidene Mädchen* (The Artificial Silk Girl) stands out as an especially resonant intertext for *BB*, one that has been mentioned but has yet to receive sustained attention or in-depth analysis in scholarship on the series.[14] The novel's representation of club culture, permissive sexual mores, and the eighteen-year-old woman protagonist's political naiveté make it particularly rife for the interwoven analysis of

BB's depiction of erotic entertainment, the 1920s New Woman, and politics I undertake in this chapter.

As one of the bestselling books of 1932, one that was rediscovered in the 1970s and has since become widely read, taught, and interpreted by scholars and lay readers alike, Keun's *The Artificial Silk Girl* is narrated from the point of view of the teenage legal secretary Doris, who flees her humdrum job in Cologne for a life of intrigue and adventure in Berlin. She may dream of becoming a glamorous star of stage and screen (a "*Glanz*," as she repeatedly calls it), but Doris's life in Berlin vacillates wildly between financial security and precarity. At times droll and endearing, at others savvy and cynical, vapid and vindictive, Doris's narrative voice tests its readers' patience and compassion and allows them to be simultaneously sympathetic toward Doris and critically alienated from her. In this regard Doris resembles both of *BB*'s main protagonists: the police detective Gereon Rath – also a transplant from Cologne to Berlin – and the clerical worker by day and prostitute by night Charlotte Ritter (hereafter Lotte), characters who are as charming as they are flawed.[15] Keun's novel acts as a persistent and varied reference within the series, as if *BB*'s showrunners placed the book in a blender and then pasted choice pieces of it into their screenplay. To give several examples, Doris's participation in both white-collar work and transactional sex offers a clear tie to *BB*'s Lotte, and Lotte's repeated contention that her life as a sex worker and her chronic exhaustion are "*halb so wild*" (no big deal) is a quote straight from Keun's novel.[16] That said, elements of Doris's narrative are evident in other characters' storylines and plot points: Doris's brief stint as a maid and nanny, as well as her rejection of the advances of a well-known nationalist writer, aligns more closely with the storyline of Greta Overbeck, Lotte's childhood friend. Lotte's colleague and pal at police headquarters is named Doris, and when the sex worker and aspiring actress Vera Lohmann locks her rival Tilly Brooks in the dressing room to get the leading role in season three's film-within-the-film *Demons of Passion* (episode three), readers of Keun will recognize this as a scene straight out of *The Artificial Silk Girl*.[17]

There are reasons beyond those of plot and characterization, however, that cause me to read Keun's text in conjunction with *BB*. With its myriad references to popular movies, songs, and advertisements, Doris's penchant for describing everyone she encounters in purely visual terms, and her insistence that her self-authored story is written like a film, Keun's novel playfully and critically engages with Weimar's popular and consumer culture, a culture of surfaces.[18] But as a text that repeatedly enacts the processes of writing, reading, and listening, Keun's book presents these processes as ones that can disrupt the uncritical consumption of visual culture, teaching Doris – and, perhaps more importantly, the readers of *The Artificial Silk Girl* – to realize how the visible (that which the eye can behold) can be dominated and manipulated by the visual (the mediated versions of life in Weimar Berlin), as Patrizia McBride so cannily argues in her reading of the novel.[19] By referencing Weimar-era literature, the most salient of which is Keun's text, and by providing its audience with a densely textured screenplay, *BB* invites repeated listening and reading just as much as it invites repeated viewing.[20]

This act of repeated viewing, listening, and reading, I would argue, allows us to consciously acknowledge and also resist the allure of the series' glossy surface and to see beyond its most obvious references, to Döblin's Whore of Babylon, for instance, or to the literary inspiration for Fosse's *Cabaret*, Christopher Isherwood's *The Berlin Stories*. As Jochen Hung argues, Christopher Isherwood's collection of stories *Goodbye to Berlin*, published in 1939 at the height of National Socialist rule and the onset of the Second World War, "with its flighty flappers, fey gents and Nazi thugs, set the tone, with its subsequent adaptations for musical theatre and film [of which Fosse's *Cabaret* is the most famous] cementing the place this stock cast held in the popular imagination over the following decades."[21] With Keun and other literary texts as guides, I show in what follows that there are ways in which *BB* feeds the *Cabaret* syndrome, but there are also ways in which it cleverly complicates and expands the cast of stock characters on Hung's list. The self-indulgent "flighty flapper" Sally Bowles is now a street-savvy stenotypist (Lotte), who, as I show below, is more reminiscent of Vicki Baum's Flämmchen from *Menschen im Hotel* (Grand Hotel, 1929); the "fey gents" are scheming industrialists like Alfred Nyssen; the "Nazi thugs" do not appear until the penultimate episode of season two, and, when they do, they are not sitting in the audience of the cabaret. They are presented as the violent, anti-Semitic fringe group that they still were in 1929 Berlin, and they are joined – and often upstaged – by a range of other groups who work to undermine Weimar democracy from the right: industrial and military elites, veterans of the First World War, and corrupt police officials.

Keun's depiction of Weimar politics seems to align with *BB*'s own much better than *Cabaret*'s sole focus on the rise of Nazism. Perhaps the best evidence of this is a brief, witty remark Doris makes in her diary/screenplay at the start of a central sequence in the novel that has her guide the blind veteran Brenner through the Berlin streets. When Brenner's embittered wife contends that he will have to choose between her and Doris, Doris quips to herself, "Poor men, they always have to choose – Hindenburg – women – communists – women."[22] The dichotomy in Doris's comment between right-wing military elites, represented by the former Field Marshal and second president of the Weimar Republic Paul von Hindenburg, and communists as the nameless, mass representatives of the left is an apt characterization of *BB*'s dominant political paradigm that pits communists against imperialist revanchists much more often than against fascists. The vacillation in this quotation from Keun between political figures (Hindenburg) or groups (communists) and women also fits the series' preoccupation with the daily triumphs and trials of the Weimar-era New Woman and the prominent role that experiments with gender and sexuality played at the time.[23] This alternative political paradigm, as expressed through a work of popular culture, may not come much closer to giving viewers an historically accurate picture of Weimar politics, but examining the shreds of artificial silk – affordable material that stands for the increased democratization of class and gender – in *BB* might, but only *might*, just shorten the reach of Babylon's shadows of decadence and doom.

No Nazis in the Club

The final shot of Fosse's 1972 film *Cabaret* allows its viewers a glimpse of the cabaret audience in the warped mirrors that flank the stage of the bawdy Kit Kat Club. The image is distorted due to the dented surface of the mirror, but the political symbolism is easy to spot – the red arm bands with swastikas and brown shirts worn by most of the audience's men. The Nazi brownshirts who had been kicked out of the club toward the beginning of the film become, by the end, its patrons.[24] Toward the end of the fourth season of *BB*, which is set in 1931, a rowdy group of SA men takes over the series' most recognizable club, the Moka Efti. In the first three seasons, however, the few characters who are clearly marked as Nazis are never shown inside the various venues of entertainment and leisure portrayed in the series: the underground clubs Holländer and Pepita Bar, the Romanisches Café, the opulent Moka Efti. Of all these, it is the Moka Efti that acts as a point of convergence for multiple characters and storylines in the first two seasons and includes some of the series' most memorable musical numbers. In *BB*, the club is always a political space; characters meet to conspire, information is gathered, and deals are made. Some of these deals test the integrity of the Republic, but they do so without the Nazis.

The following analysis explores three separate club scenes, one from each of the first three seasons of *BB*, to show how erotic entertainment venues act as spaces for the negotiation of political, gendered, and sexual power. Lotte, *BB*'s own artificial silk girl, is a central figure in all three scenes and offers a nuanced representation of the New Woman as more than merely a fashionable image. It is through Lotte that the series celebrates women's increased social mobility, just as it also reveals how precarious and how incomplete women's sexual, economic, and political emancipation was.

A scene from season two, episode two of *BB* shows Lotte's plucky way of gaining entry to spaces usually occupied by privileged men, as she positions herself to overhear a conversation between the president of the Berlin police, Karl Zörgiebel (an historical figure), Hindenburg's personal assistant Gottfried Wendt, and the Soviet ambassador Trochin that takes place on the upper level of the Moka Efti. As Michael Sandberg and Cara Tovey have observed, "the architecture of Moka Efti upholds a stark class demarcation: the upper class occupies the balcony level of the club, the middle class the ground-level dance floor, and the working-class prostitutes the basement below."[25] Lotte is one of the only characters who is able to move between all three levels, but moving up to the balcony requires her to masquerade as a cocktail waitress and bribe some of the real waitresses with free cigarettes. The physical placement of the characters (the blocking) – the men are sitting while Lotte stands near or even at their table – as well as the camera angles used in the scene allow Lotte to occupy an elevated position as she eavesdrops. Her own power over the men must remain clandestine, however, and although she perceives herself as working undercover for the Berlin homicide division in this moment, the series' audience knows that official policework is a position she has yet to attain. Her cover is nearly blown when Ambassador Trochin recognizes her; she had in fact encountered him several days earlier at the freight train yard, as she pretended to be a newspaper reporter covering a fatal leak of phosgene gas. Trochin claims that he has "a photographic memory" and is quite sure he has seen Lotte before. Without missing a beat, Lotte shoots back in a manner that exemplifies the streetwise sarcasm of Berlin humor: "Then perhaps you've seen a photo of me." This quick and clever reply, delivered by Lotte with a coquettish glance over her shoulder, is reminiscent of a passage from one of the most popular literary works published in 1929 Berlin, Vicki Baum's *Grand Hotel*.[26]

The figure from Baum's novel who is most akin to Lotte is Flämmchen, a stenotypist who supplements her meager income with occasional work as a nude model and an escort to wealthy businessmen, and the passage is one that describes Flämmchen typing correspondence for her current employer while trying to secure a more financially lucrative arrangement with him. She does so by tempting him with the photographic image of her naked body; she says, "I'm photographed for the newspapers and so on, for soap advertisements as well ... I look very good in the nude, you know." Her strategy works; when the businessman Preysing sees one of her photos in an illustrated magazine the following day, he becomes enchanted by the "incredibly exciting" fantasy of naked Flämmchen and decides to proposition her.[27] The mixture of self-confident coquettishness with the commodified body of a woman who is both a white-collar worker and a temporary sex worker brings Baum's Flämmchen and *BB*'s Lotte together and draws readers'/viewers' attention to the forms of labor that were available to working-class and petit bourgeois women and the financial precarity that came with them.[28]

The conversation in Moka Efti to which Lotte is privy demonstrates the political "muddle" – as Sneeringer has called it – that viewers find in *BB*.[29] It turns out that the Stalinists, represented by Trochin, are on the same side as the conservative elites, represented by Wendt, who are defying the terms of the Versailles Treaty and rearming a shadow German military called the Black Reichswehr. Both characters are pushing Zörgiebel to release the quarantined train – which contains both poisonous gas and, allegedly, the gold of a slain Russian aristocratic family – and send it back to the Soviet Union. When Zörgiebel expresses his misgivings regarding their request and his astonishment that Hindenburg, via Wendt, would "not shrink from ignoring the Treaty of Versailles," Wendt threatens him with political scandal. Does the president of the Berlin police want to end his career by being associated with the murder of unarmed civilians in the *Blutmai* (Blood May), Wendt asks, just minutes after he has started the conversation by praising Zörgiebel for taking violent action against communist protesters during that same event.[30] Zörgiebel's defeated look signals what this scene conveys most powerfully: that all of the parties at the table, including the Social Democrat Zörgiebel himself, engage in antidemocratic action. The police have used excessive force against working-class protesters; the revanchists are engaged in clandestine rearmament; the communists, both the opportunist Stalinist diplomat and the Blood May casualties, are pawns in Wendt's power play, portrayed first as a legitimate political threat and then as innocent victims. This may indeed be a muddle, just as Sneeringer argues, but, she adds, it is a muddle that provokes curiosity among the viewers of streaming television who "know little about Weimar other than its descent into Nazism. So when *BB* depicts the 1929 *Blutmai* demonstration ... or the irredentist plots of the right, it informs even as it entertains."[31] And entertain it does; the showrunners never let viewers forget that this conversation takes place in a nightclub, and they frame the political machinations of Wendt, Trochin, and

Zörgiebel with a cameo performance by the British crooner Brian Ferry, who sings a Weimar-inspired, German and English rendition of the 1975 Roxy Music track "Bitter-Sweet" on the stage of the Moka Efti.[32]

The appearance of a British musician on a Berlin stage – here it is Ferry, but his presence invites associations with David Bowie, as well as US musicians such as Iggy Pop and Lou Reed, all of whom made pilgrimages to West Berlin in the 1970s – complicates any neat parallels viewers might draw between the contemporary moment and the Weimar era by filtering our experience of Weimar Berlin through evocations of 1970s and 1980s West Berlin, "whose heady mix of post-punk music, club culture, and repertory cinemas exerted a powerful influences on *BB*'s showrunners von Borries, Handloegten, and Tykwer, all of whom lived in the city during this time."[33] The West Berlin of the 1970s and 1980s was also home to political activist subcultures that were deeply distrustful of the West German state, despite its Social Democratic leadership. When we add this historical layer to the series, then the beleaguered Social Democrat Zörgiebel, caving under the pressure from both the imperialist West (Wendt) and the Soviet East (Trochin) makes perfect sense, especially to audience members who lived through the Cold War. And when we keep in mind that the 1970s was also a period of Weimar revival, with *Cabaret* being just one example of the renewed, but distorted, fascination with Weimar culture, we are cautioned to look for ways in which our own "fresh insights" regarding Weimar also lead to "fresh distortions," as André Flicker and Xan Holt argue in their investigation of Netflix's "curation of critical returns to [German] national history as well as its support of uncritical nostalgia," with *BB* as just one example.[34] While I would not go so far as to accuse *BB* of "uncritical nostalgia" for Weimar, I do think it creates numerous "fresh distortions" with which its critical viewers must contend.

One particularly puzzling distortion of Weimar's political policy regarding the regulation of sexuality comes up in season one, episode four, the episode that begins with a dramatization of the street fighting between Berlin police and communist protesters on 1 May 1929 and ends with a private deal between Lotte and Bruno Wolter, head of the *Sittenpolizei* (Morals Police). This is the second club scene I analyze, and it takes place in the Moka Efti as well, but this time in its subterranean luxury brothel. Called away from the dance floor to meet a client in the basement, Lotte is surprised to pull back the beaded curtain of her usual room and find Wolter. "Don't worry," Wolter says to set himself apart from the S&M fetishists who frequent the brothel and to underscore his role as a traditional man: "I only dance standards." Wolter, we will come to learn over the course of the first two seasons, is a member of the Black

Reichswehr and a skilled marksman who is stockpiling weapons for an attempted coup against the Republic. Anxious that he is being spied on by his colleagues in the police department, Wolter is keen to know if Gereon Rath is one of those spies. To get information on Gereon, he coerces Lotte into helping him (and to having sexual intercourse with him in the process) by threatening to register her as a prostitute with the state authorities (his own division of the Morals Police) under paragraph 361, clause 6 of the *Bürgerliches Gesetzbuch* (BGB). The screenplay has Wolter explicitly name this section of the Civil Code, revealing the writers'/directors' attention to historical detail, and yet the grounds for Wolter's extortion of Lotte in 1929 rest on a clear historical inaccuracy, considering that prostitution was decriminalized and the system of regulation dismantled, most thoroughly in Berlin, by the 1927 Law to Combat Venereal Diseases.

As historians of gender and sexuality Julia Roos and Annette Timm have demonstrated, the 1927 law was the product of years of painstaking political debate, a reform policy that, to quote Timm, "was universally accepted as a reflection of scientific ideals and social hygienic thought."[35] In terms of gender politics, the law introduced a more equitable approach to sexual health, meaning that "[l]egal measures and prophylactic policies were now no longer simply directed against women (specifically prostitutes) but would also encompass men as equal contributors to the VD problem."[36] Late twentieth-century feminist philosophers such as Laurie Schrage have argued that a social and political context that supports the decriminalization of prostitution is one that is characterized by "a robust pluralism with regard to sexual customs and practices."[37] In no other German city did such a robust pluralism thrive as it did in Weimar Berlin, where discourses on prostitution sometimes surpassed late twentieth-century debates on sex work and non-normative sexualities in their nuance and progressivism.[38] And yet *BB* remains squeamish when it comes to sex work and ambivalent when it comes to gender parity, putting Lotte in the coercive sexual relationship with Wolter and forcing her to endure repeated humiliation and violence more often than it allows her to occupy a position of strength or power.[39]

Lotte's sexual degradation because of her work as a prostitute is most blatant in the third and final club scene I examine, which takes place toward the end of season three. Despite her position as an investigative assistant for the homicide division – a position she achieves at the end of season two – Lotte still does not make enough money to help her older sister, who is poor and suffers from waning eyesight. On a tip from her friend and former lover Vera, Lotte takes a one-time job at the exclusive Club Luxor, where she is tasked with playing out the erotic fantasy of one

high-paying client. The red-wigged cross-dressing mistress of cere-
monies at Club Luxor is Edwina Morell, played with demonic campiness
by the contemporary erotic performance artist Le Pustra, who capitalizes
on the clichéd image of Weimar's sexual decadence in today's Berlin by
reviving the anarchic Cabaret of the Nameless.[40] The Cabaret of the
Nameless, a venue that invited audience members to ruthlessly ridicule
its amateur performers, was described by author Erich Kästner as "a
padded cell for the metropolis," a place that sanctioned open cruelty as a
way to let off steam. "The guests treat [the cabaret's producer] Elow
roughly. Elow treats his guests roughly. Together they treat the 'artists'
roughly," Kästner writes of the Weimar-era version of the cabaret, and
his description evokes the staged boxing matches and gleeful mockery
one finds in Fosse's *Cabaret*.[41] Indeed, Le Pustra's/Morell's white face
makeup that accentuates puckered crimson lips and dramatically lined
eyes is clearly reminiscent of Joel Grey's gender-bending, sadistic emcee
in *Cabaret*, and Le Pustra's performance is no less histrionic (even if it is
less masterful).

In stark contrast to both club scenes I have read thus far in this chapter,
the first minutes of the scene in Club Luxor (season three, episode eight)
are characterized by camera shots from above that diminish and objectify
Lotte or canted angles that signal to the audience that something is about
to go terribly wrong.[42] Once Lotte is in full costume and at the center of
the club's small stage, the camera pans slowly upward from the floor of
the stage to reveal Lotte to the series' viewers. Clad in thigh-high red
vinyl boots with laces, fishnet stockings and panties, and a pseudo-
military jacket with a plunging neckline and cinched waist, Lotte is
blindfolded and seemingly bound to a chair. Morell begins the narration
of the fantasy – "We find ourselves in the year 1917" – as a gramophone
needle crackles and Wagnerian music offers accompaniment. The
camera begins what will become an increasingly frantic movement from
character to character in this scene as the violent sexual tension mounts.
It moves from the stage, where it gives a full shot of Lotte from behind,
seemingly helpless and bound to the chair, emphasizing her role in the
fantasy as a French prisoner of war, to Morell, who is almost always shot
from below to emphasize their power in this dynamic. An extreme high
angle shot of Lotte in the chair is followed by our first glimpse of the sole
audience member, the man whose fantasy of French vanquishment
(coded here as the vanquishment of the feminine) at the hands of
German soldiers is being staged. He is a decidedly Wilhelmine figure, a
bald, monocled man in a German officer's uniform decorated with
ribbons and medals – yet another nod by the series to the conservative
military elites. Unlike the bourgeois veteran Wolter, who "only dances

standards," this member of the top military brass enjoys rapacious fantasies. As the camera brings us closer to Lotte, her mounting fear becomes
apparent as two side doors open to the stage and two rows of marching
men in tall, heavy boots and spiked Prussian military helmets (the
absurdly menacing *Pickelhaube*) enter the room. "You want to have
them ... all!" Morell shrieks, and an odd, blurred image shot at an
extreme angle shows Morell glancing upward at the customer behind
the glass, who seems to signal his approval by adjusting his monocle. The
camera then shows us the club from his perspective – a bird's-eye view of
the entire club with Lotte in the center – as the troops encircle her. Then
the camera brings us into the middle of the action, where we see the
alarm on Lotte's face as her blindfold is removed and she is surrounded
by uniformed men with rifles at their sides who proceed to kiss, grab,
fondle, penetrate, and defile her. The movement of the camera hastens as
the music crescendos, drowning out the men's groans. This scene's
cinematography, from its use of canted angles to its perpetual cuts
between the audience and the action taking place on stage, is reminiscent
of Fosse's *Cabaret*. In *BB*, the audience of one gazes curiously and
impassively upon the scene, allowing us to view the scene from his
perspective above it all, removed from Lotte's anguish, until we are
brought down to the stage level again, then back to Morell, the emcee,
who leaves the microphone with a satisfied grin, just before the camera
cuts to a tracking shot of Lotte bursting out of the club at the end of the
night, her face streaked with tears, a look of sheer disgust and anguish on
her face. I go into such painstaking visual detail here because this, of all
scenes, is the longest, most violent sex scene involving Lotte in the series
to date, a culmination of the constant interplay between sex and violence
in the first seasons of *BB*.[43] I also go into such detail because the camerawork implicates the contemporary viewer in the well-to-do client's lurid
interest in a revenge fantasy that rewrites the history both of the First
World War (the Germans conquer the French) and of women's Weimar-
era emancipation (the men conquer the women). Knowing that the
German defeat in the First World War was still being processed in
1929 may be important, as is knowing that the New Woman was an
embattled figure, but that does not mean that we must be a party to her
physical and emotional humiliation. This scene, more than any other, is a
prime example of the *Cabaret* syndrome, as it displays sexual entertainment in Weimar Berlin as always already debauched and marketed to a
politically reactionary audience.

Returning briefly to *BB*'s signature club, the Moka Efti, to the basement brothel and Lotte's extortion by Wolter allows me to reiterate a key
question: Why the willful distortion of history when it comes to the social

and sexual practices that were so central to the reform politics of the late 1920s – policy debates on issues such as prostitution, venereal disease prevention, and birth control that characterized the Weimar coalition government, a structure that was, in the spring and early fall of 1929, when the first three seasons of BB take place, still a "workable political coalition"?[44] My proposed answer: Because domestic reform politics are not what BB is interested in showing its audience, nor is it interested in presenting sexuality as a form of liberation, especially not for women. Indeed, sexuality in BB is, more often than not, a cause for shame and political vulnerability. Lotte, as I have shown, is repeatedly punished for her work as a prostitute as well as for her role as a woman who crosses boundaries into male-dominated territory or engages in queer sex (as she does with Vera in season three). Men, too, are vulnerable. Politicians and public officials from the democratic parties who engage in non-normative sex, allowing themselves to be blindfolded and humiliated by professional prostitutes in the private quarters that are located deep in the heart of Moka Efti and are home to the crime boss Edgar Kasabian (known as "the Armenian"), leave themselves open to being clandestinely filmed and then blackmailed. As Wolter exclaims as he and Gereon view the pornographic films they confiscate from Edgar and discover (unbeknownst to Wolter) that Gereon's own father, an official associated with the Catholic Center Party, is in one of them, the films could act as a "life insurance policy" for anyone who possesses them.[45] Gereon, ashamed of his own father's potentially scandalous behavior, insists that he and Wolter burn the films.

In its avoidance of German politics, particularly the politics of the centrist parties that ruled in 1929, BB recalls a particularly poignant, reflective passage from Isherwood's story "Sally Bowles." Seduced into a prolonged phase of drunken reverie by a rich American named Clive, Isherwood's first-person narrator Chris and his pal Sally find themselves standing on the balcony of the storied Hotel Adlon, where Clive is staying, peering down on the funeral of Hermann Müller, the Social Democrat who served as the Weimar Republic's chancellor in 1920 and again from 1928 to 1930. Müller died in 1931. While Clive notes the funeral procession's elegance, Sally barely gives it a glance and remarks instead on the "marvelous sunset." Her vapid observation provokes Chris to reflect on how very out of touch these two British expatriates and their American patron are. He admits, "We had nothing to do with those Germans down there, marching, or with the dead man in the coffin, or with the words on the banners."[46] As I show in the next section of this chapter, BB, too, pays little attention to German social democracy; it is portrayed, like the ailing Zörgiebel in season three, as beleaguered and depleted. Its funeral is drawing near. The political conflict between radical leftists and right-wing elites that Keun's Doris names (Hindenburg – communists) obscures the existence of a functioning democracy.

Exiting the Club: Where Democratic Hopes Reside

In the middle of *BB*'s first season, in episode five, viewers witness a meeting between the only three identifiable Social Democrats in the entire series, when Zörgiebel meets in his office with the fictional head of the Political Police, August Benda, and with the historical mayor of Berlin, Gustav Böß, who in fact belonged to the German Democratic Party (DDP) and not the Social Democratic Party (SPD).[47] All three are reeling from the bad publicity of the Blood May riots, as angry communist protesters gather and shout for justice outside police headquarters. The communist protesters outside the building known as the Red Castle grow louder, and, as they do, Zörgiebel tells Benda that he fears "the storming of the Bastille," to which Benda quickly retorts: "We are not the Bastille." His words, however, ring hollow to viewers who are already conditioned by the political power dynamic between seemingly untouchable elites (albeit from a new aristocracy made up of industrialists and military leaders) and revolutionary masses. To which side do Zörgiebel, Benda, and Böß belong? A long shot taken from the opposite end of the room from the men allows the nearly empty boardroom table to dominate the image, making the three men gathered at the end of the table seem isolated and alone. This shot is indicative of how *BB* treats the Social Democrats: They are representatives of a system under threat, and they are few and far between. As historians and cultural studies scholars alike have noted, of the everyday citizens depicted in the series, many of whom are working class or petit bourgeois, none are Social Democrats, despite the fact that Berlin remained an SPD stronghold beyond the Republic's official end.[48] As Paul Lerner argues, "*BB*'s Berlin is one of extremes ... Those extremes certainly existed, but the space between the extremes, where most people lived and died ... is largely ignored."[49] In the series, the masses are communists, the democratic leaders are forced to make deals with antidemocratic elites and therefore to hasten the demise of the Republic in order to save their own careers, and the protagonists Gereon and Lotte never express political affiliation; only their efforts to crack the case make them into unwitting republican defenders. Of the three men depicted in this particular scene, only Zörgiebel will make it – albeit limping along – to *BB*'s third season. Benda will be assassinated by two Nazi upstarts hired by Wendt, and Böß's career will be ended – as we know from history – by the Sklarek scandal. Zörgiebel stays in office only by betraying Benda in season two, episode six, undermining the investigation of the Black Reichswehr by informing Wendt of impending legal action. Hindenburg personally intervenes, and the enemies of the state go free.[50] Recalling Keun's novel again, "Hindenburg – communists" indeed.

Where do democratic hopes reside in *BB*, if not in reform policy, in venues for social and sexual experimentation, in the New Woman, in the Social Democratic leadership? Oddly enough, Zörgiebel's naming of the Bastille – and, through it, the memory of the French Revolution and the image of Paris – allows *BB*'s audience to draw French connections (pun intended) to other episodes and storylines, particularly one that involves a state visit to Berlin by the French foreign minister, Aristide Briand, in season two, episode six (the same episode that ends with Hindenburg's appearance). Placed in the series as one of the only obvious counterweights to the imperialist Hindenburg is the diplomatic relationship between Briand and German foreign minister Gustav Stresemann. A native Berliner, Stresemann may have started out his career as a conservative nationalist, but his "native pragmatism" made him increasingly convinced of the merits of Weimar democracy and the potential it had to make Germany a trustworthy political partner within Europe.[51] His work as foreign minister was one that sought to bring Germany back to the table with the Western Allies and hence to take the country out of political isolation. Together with Briand, he negotiated the terms of the Locarno Treaties in 1925, which laid the groundwork for Germany's fulfillment of war reparation payments and for the withdrawal of French troops from the Rhineland. Briand and Stresemann won the Nobel Peace Prize in 1926. With this partnership in mind, the *BB* showrunners stage a fictitious diplomatic visit centered around the two ministers' trip to the theater to see Bertolt Brecht and Kurt Weill's hit musical *The Threepenny Opera*, the very visit that Wolter and his band of Black Reichswehr troops plan to use as a venue for the ministers' double assassination. The death of the German–French diplomatic alliance, it would seem, spells the death of the Republic. Gereon is able to thwart the coup, taking action on the words of Briand, who delivers the most ardent defense of democracy as yet articulated in the series: Flanked by German reporters in front of the Theater am Schiffbauerdamm, Briand warns in French-accented yet perfect German, "There is always danger for a young democracy, but democracy is worth fighting for." This line is the only one in the series that conveys the lesson about defending democracy that *BB* showrunner von Borries points to in the interview I cite at the beginning of this chapter. The historical figure of Briand acts, too, as another point of connection between the contemporary television series and Keun's 1932 novel.

A visit by Briand, accompanied this time by the French prime minister, Pierre Laval, features as the first event that Keun's Doris witnesses when she arrives in Berlin:

> So I arrived at *Friedrichstrasse* Station, where there's an incredible hustle-bustle. And I found out that some great Frenchmen had arrived just before I did, and Berlin's masses were there to greet them. They're called Laval and Briand – and being a woman who frequently spends time waiting in restaurants, I've seen their picture in magazines. I was swept along *Friedrichstrasse* in a crowd of people, which was full of life and colorful and somehow it had a checkered feeling. There was so much excitement! ... And then the politicians arrived on the balcony like soft black spots. And everything turned into a scream and the masses ... wanted those politicians to throw peace down to them from the balcony ... And the politicians lowered their heads in a statesmanly fashion, and so, in a way, they were greeting me too.[52]

The sense of belonging to the "colorful" and "checkered" crowd, all of whom want peace, is portrayed by Keun as an urban one and as one that transcends national borders. The desire for peace and community is so strongly conveyed by this political event that it inspires Doris to become more politically aware. The man she meets at the event and peppers with political questions, however, is interested only in her eyes and in plying her with pieces of hazelnut cake. Doris exits the scene with a belly full of cake but no clearer understanding of politics. A similar feeling could apply to the viewers of *BB*; they are fed plenty of delicious images of Weimar decadence and a savory line or two (like Briand's) about the importance of defending democracy, and yet most of democracy's defenders, at least its German defenders, fight in vain and then die (like Benda in the first two seasons and Stresemann in the third).

But like the political rally that Doris attends, *BB*'s democratic horizon – like the path of the mysterious train that starts out in Russia, winds up in Berlin, and is shown heading to Paris in the final episode of season two – is not a national one; it is an urban one, and it is a decidedly European one. The historical figures of Stresemann (Berlin) and Briand (Paris) are joined by the fictional Viennese journalist Samuel Katelbach, who risks his life to write stories for the left-liberal press that expose the plots of the Black Reichswehr and the lies of the police. It is Katelbach, too, who laments the predominance of visual images in the press that makes "readers" into "gawkers."[53] The same line could apply to today's social media or sensational cable news, just as the reference to a European identity over a German national one appeals to a wide swath of contemporary Germans. Like the club scenes analyzed above that refract

Weimar history and culture through contemporary mores and concerns, as well as through 1970s and 1980s visions of Weimar such as Fosse's *Cabaret* or Ferry's jazzed-up version of "Bitter-Sweet," *BB*'s muddled political messages reveal the rather dizzying effects of cultural and historical layering. The image of Weimar conveyed by *BB*, therefore, is a multidimensional composite of Weimar, the 1970s/1980s, and today, making it nearly impossible to draw clear lessons from the historical period of Weimar itself. Relatable characters, such as the journalist Katelbach, and methods of reading that pick apart these historical and cultural layers and examine their relationship to one another, however, can offer valuable lessons with political implications. Katelbach's relentless pursuit of the truth, even at the expense of his own life, and his defense of critical reading point to an urgent message that lies beneath the glossy surface of *BB*: that we, too, can fight against the shadows of Babylon and be alert to the dangers facing our own democracies, but to do so, we must *read* – both images and text – oh so carefully.

Conclusion

As Lebow and Norman point out in their introduction to this volume (Chapter 1), Weimar's "continuing allure as an illustration of collapse and societal breakdown seems undiminished" for contemporary audiences. *BB* certainly capitalizes on the voyeuristic pleasure of watching Weimar's economic, political, and social upheavals take place as its fictional protagonists confront multiple crises, seek to avert them, and try to find their place within them. As I have shown in this chapter, the iconic space of the Berlin nightclub acts as a site for political and social negotiations and for moments of crisis, especially for *BB*'s Lotte. The first club scene shows viewers, as Handloegten hopes it would, the political possibilities of the New Woman who can gain access to a range of socioeconomic spheres. And yet by casting the politically powerful characters in this scene as men, the series also reveals the limits to women's access. By squandering the potential of a nuanced portrayal of Weimar-era sex reform discourses surrounding prostitution, birth control, and venereal health in the second club scene, *BB*'s showrunners seem to intentionally disregard the historical archival evidence of a more liberating phase for women by forcing Lotte into a coercive sexual relationship with the police official Wolter. Sexuality is rarely depicted in the series as a path to freedom; rather, it is shameful, a source of scandal, a potential weakness in the fabric of democracy. Sexual experimentation, therefore, becomes a vulnerability at best and a potentially violent threat at worst. For Lotte it is both, and in the third club scene I analyze – the one that most closely resembles Fosse's *Cabaret* – it is clearly the latter. The displacement of the Nazis from the club in the first three seasons, however, keeps *BB* at least one step removed from *Cabaret* and expands the cast of villains, or enemies of the Republic, to include conservative military and industrial elites such as Hindenburg, Wendt, and the revanchist client in Club Luxor. The beleaguered, nearly absent center, however, feeds the idea that Weimar's democracy had more enemies than supporters and hence casts doubt on von Borries's contention that contemporary viewers will be motivated to defend democracy by watching *BB*. Are both of the lessons that the showrunners von Borries and Handloegten hoped the audience of their series would learn left unlearned? For me, as a feminist literary scholar, reading *BB* for its witty citations of popular Weimar-era literature authored by women reveals that the unresolved tensions between women's liberation and limitation, between democratic defense and collapse, are perhaps the most realistic lessons we can learn from Weimar.

Notes

1 *Babylon Berlin*, directed by Tom Tykwer, Hendrik Handloegten, and Achim von Borries (New York: Netflix and Kino Lorber, 2017), on streaming series and DVD. The fourth season aired on Sky Europe in October 2022; the fifth and final season is currently in production. Netflix, however, announced in January 2024 that it would not distribute seasons four and five. On viewership in Germany and the global distribution of the series, see Florian Krauß, "Quality TV Drama with Transnational Appeal: Industry Discourses on Babylon Berlin and the Changing Television Landscape in Germany" in Hester Baer and Jill Suzanne Smith, eds., *Babylon Berlin, German Visual Spectacle, and Global Media Culture* (London: Bloomsbury, 2024), pp. 25–41. See also Juliane Blank, "Berlin, Capital of Serial Adaptation: Exploring and Expanding a Political Storyworld in *Babylon Berlin*," *Interfaces* 47 (2002), pp. 1–21, here p. 5; Hanno Hochmuth, "Mythos Babylon Berlin: Weimar in der Populärkultur" in Hanno Hochmuth, Martin Sabrow, and Tilmann Siebeneichner, eds., *Weimars Wirkung: Das Nachleben der ersten deutschen Republik* (Göttingen: Wallstein, 2020), pp. 111–25, here pp. 118–23.

2 Baer and Smith, *Babylon Berlin*; Hester Baer and Jill Suzanne Smith, "Babylon Berlin: Weimar-Era Culture and History as Global Media Spectacle," *EuropeNow* 43 (September 2021), www.europenowjournal.org/2021/09/13/babylon-berlin-weimar-era-culture-and-history-as-global-media-spectacle/; Veronika Fuechtner and Paul Lerner, eds., "Forum: *Babylon Berlin*: Media, Spectacle, and History," *Central European History* 53 (2020), pp. 845–8; Sara F. Hall, "*Babylon Berlin*: Pastiching Weimar Cinema," *Communications* 44, no. 3 (2019), pp. 308–22; Caitlin Shaw, "To the Truth, to the Light: Genericity and Historicity in Babylon Berlin," *Journal of Popular*

Film and Television 50, no. 1 (2022), pp. 24–39; Noah Soltau, "'Zu Asche, Zu Staub': Netflix Acquisitions and the Aesthetics and Politics of Cultural Unrest in *Babylon Berlin*," *Journal of Popular Culture* 54, no. 4 (2021), pp. 728–49; Kim Wilkins, "*Babylon Berlin*'s bifocal gaze," *Screen* 62, no. 2 (2021), pp. 135–55.

3 Anna Wollner, "Wir wollten erzählen, wie die Zeit vor dem Nationalsozialismus war," audio interview with Henk Handloegten, Tom Tykwer, and Achim von Borries, www.kinofenster.de/filme/archiv-film-des-monats/kf1809/kf1809-babylon-berlin-interview-tykwer-hendloegten-borries/. All subsequent quotes from von Borries and Handloegten come from this interview. Unless otherwise noted, all translations from the German are mine.

4 Colin Storer, *Britain and the Weimar Republic: The History of a Cultural Relationship* (London: Bloomsbury, 2010), pp. 9, 84–8.

5 Julia Sneeringer, "Glitter and Post-Punk Doom: *Babylon Berlin* through the Lens of 1980s West Berlin" in Baer and Smith, *Babylon Berlin*, pp. 193–207.

6 For early reviews in the press that connect *BB* with Fosse's *Cabaret*, see Noah Isenberg, "Voluptuous Panic," *New York Review of Books*, 28 April 2018, www.nybooks.com/daily/2018/04/28/voluptuous-panic/; Esme Nicholson, "Germany's 'Babylon Berlin' Crime Series is Like 'Cabaret' on Cocaine," *NPR All Things Considered*, 30 January 2018, www.npr.org/2018/01/30/581543050/germanys-babylon-berlin-crime-series-is-like-cabaret-on-cocaine?t=1591619899228. In the scholarly discourse on the series, see, for example, Fuechtner in Fuechtner and Lerner, "Forum," p. 846; Hochmuth, "Mythos Babylon Berlin," p. 117; Shaw, "To the Truth, to the Light," p. 33; Wilkins, "*Babylon Berlin*'s bifocal gaze," pp. 137, 146, 147.

7 See Smith in Fuechtner and Lerner, "Forum," p. 851.

8 On the salon evenings that the showrunners, their cameramen, and the production team held during the series' protracted development phase, see Krauß, "Quality TV Drama with Transnational Appeal," p. 36.

9 See the works cited in note 2 above, with Hall's application of pastiche to the series as particularly formative for the scholarship that followed. On music, see Abby Anderton, "Recreating the Soundscape of Weimar Berlin: Sound Technologies, Trauma, and the Sonic Archive" in Baer and Smith, *Babylon Berlin* pp. 93–103; Nils Grosch, Roxane Lindlacher, Miranda Lipovica, and Laura Thaller, "Rekonfigurationen der Weimarer Republik: Musikalische Vergangenheiten und Pastiches in *Babylon Berlin* (2018–2020)," *Archiv für Musikwissenschaft* 79, no. 1 (2022), pp. 43–60.

10 Volker Kutscher's first three Gereon Rath novels, translated by Niall Sellar, serve as inspiration for the four existing seasons of *BB*, and Kutscher regularly talks about his own literary impetus for the novels as coming from Weimar-era authors Hans Fallada, Erich Kästner, and Irmgard Keun. Kutscher, open discussion following his reading from *Der nasse Fisch/Babylon Berlin* at the Brandeis Center for German and European Studies, 3 October 2018. Volker Kutscher, *Der nasse Fisch* (Cologne: Kiepenheuer & Witsch, 2007), published in English as *Babylon Berlin* (New York: Picador, 2016); *Der stumme Tod* (Cologne: KiWi, 2009), published in English as *The Silent Death* (New York: Picador, 2018); *Goldstein* (Cologne: KiWi, 2010), published in English (New

York: Picador, 2018). *BB*'s showrunners took significant creative liberties with Kutscher's novels; in many cases, only the names of key characters and the central historical events portrayed make the connection between the works discernable. On how serial television is transforming the concept and practice of page-to-screen adaptation, see Blank, "Berlin, Capital of Serial Adaptation," pp. 1–4.

11 Alfred Döblin, *Berlin Alexanderplatz: The Story of Franz Biberkopf*, trans. Michael Hofmann (New York: New York Review of Books, 2018). Döblin's novel has recently been adapted to the film screen for the third time (following the 1931 film by Phil Jutzi and the 1980 epic miniseries by Rainer Werner Fassbinder) by the Afghani-German director Burhan Qurbani (2020). It is set in today's Berlin with an illegal immigrant from Guinea-Bissau, Francis, replacing the war veteran and recently released convict Franz Biberkopf.

12 Frank Junghänel, journalist for the *Berliner Zeitung*, draws readers to his review of *BB*'s 2017 premiere by giving it the subtitle "the big whore in top form," but he tempers his comments about the series' dark, apocalyptic side with ones about the possibilities of the Weimar era: "When everything is on the line, then everything, too, is possible." See Frank Junghänel, "Weltpremiere 'Babylon Berlin': Die große Hure in Bestform," *Berliner Zeitung*, 28 September 2017. Shaw convincingly argues that "it is not Weimar's avant-garde modernist culture which affords release … but rather … the musical number," and Lisa Zunshine notes that *BB* "resists" the generic cliché of Berlin as a "city on the edge of an abyss." Shaw, "To the Truth, to the Light," p. 35; Lisa Zunshine, "Babylon Berlin: Bargaining with Shadows," *Seminar* 58, no. 1 (2022), pp. 38–56. Co-writer and co-director Henk Handloegten, when asked in 2020 about the literary influences on the series, downplayed the role that Döblin's novel played in the writing of the screenplay, beyond the title. See Handloegten, "Ein Gespräch mit Henk Handloegten," Lecture Series on *Babylon Berlin* at the Deutsche Sommerschule am Pazifik, YouTube, 1:22:05, posted by Carrie Collenberg-González, streamed live 26 June 2020.

13 Jill Suzanne Smith, "Lotte at the Movies: Gendered Spectatorship and German Histories of Violence in *Babylon Berlin*," *Germanic Review* 97, no. 3 (2022), pp. 254–71, here p. 256.

14 Hester Baer and Jill Suzanne Smith, "Introduction" in Baer and Smith, *Babylon Berlin*, pp. 12–13; Blank, "Berlin, Capital of Serial Adaptation," p. 10; Mila Ganeva in Fuechtner and Lerner, "Forum," p. 846; see also Henk Handloegten, email to author, 9 June 2021.

15 On Gereon's characterization, see Shaw, "To the Truth, to the Light," pp. 29–30; on Lotte's status as both an endearing character and a "difficult woman," see Smith, "Lotte at the Movies," pp. 257–8.

16 Irmgard Keun, *Das kunstseidene Mädchen* (Munich: List, 2004 [1932]), p. 63. The English translation used for the rest of my citations does not do this particular quotation justice, so I refer here to the German original. See *BB*, season one, episode five and season two, episode two for Lotte's quip.

17 Irmgard Keun, *The Artificial Silk Girl*, trans. Kathie von Ankum (New York: Other Press, 2011), p. 33. The name Tilly, too, could be seen as a reference to Keun's novel, since the woman who takes Doris in when she first arrives in Berlin is Tilli Scherer.

18 Janet Ward, *Weimar Surfaces: Urban Visual Culture in 1920s Germany* (Berkeley: University of California Press, 2001). Ward mentions Keun's novel on several occasions; see pp. 85–6, 152.

19 Patrizia McBride, "Learning to See in Irmgard Keun's *Das kunstseidene Mädchen*," *German Quarterly* 84, no. 2 (2011), pp. 220–38, here pp. 221, 236.

20 For examples of the ways in which *BB* encourages viewers to repeat watching, see Smith, "Lotte at the Movies," pp. 255–7, 265.

21 Jochen Hung, "Beyond Glitter and Doom: The New Paradigm of Contingency in Weimar Research" in Jochen Hung, Godela Weiss–Sussex, and Geoff Wilkes, eds., *Beyond Glitter and Doom: The Contingency of the Weimar Republic* (Munich: Iudicium, 2012), p. 9.

22 Keun, *The Artificial Silk Girl*, p. 98.

23 On gender and sexuality in the Weimar era, see Laurie Marhoefer, *Sex and the Weimar Republic: German Homosexual Emancipation and the Rise of the Nazis* (Toronto: University of Toronto Press, 2015); Richard W. McCormick, *Gender and Sexuality in Weimar Modernity: Film, Literature, and "New Objectivity"* (New York: Palgrave, 2001); Jill Suzanne Smith, *Berlin Coquette: Prostitution and the New German Woman, 1890–1933* (Ithaca, NY: Cornell University Press, 2013); Katie Sutton, *Sex between Body and Mind: Psychoanalysis and Sexology in the German-Speaking World, 1890s–1930s* (Ann Arbor: University of Michigan Press, 2019); and the chapter on "Bodies and Sex" in Eric D. Weitz, *Weimar Germany: Promise and Tragedy* (Princeton: Princeton University Press, 2007), pp. 297–330.

24 *Cabaret*, directed by Bob Fosse (Facets Multimedia, 1972), DVD.

25 Michael Sandberg and Cara Tovey, "Liquid Space and Digital Aesthetics in *Babylon Berlin*" in Baer and Smith, *Babylon Berlin*, p. 81.

26 Vicki Baum, *Grand Hotel*, trans. Basil Creighton (Garden City, NY: Doubleday, 1931). Baum's novel served as the basis for several stage versions and eventually for the 1932 Hollywood film directed by Edmund Goulding. For a discussion of Berlin humor as coquettish, see Smith, *Berlin Coquette*, pp. 9, 20, 192.

27 Baum, *Grand Hotel*, pp. 80, 209.

28 For a more in-depth reading of Baum's novel, its depiction of commodified sex as work, and its relationship to Keun's *Artificial Silk Girl*, see Smith, *Berlin Coquette*, pp. 162–81.

29 Sneeringer in Fuechtner and Lerner, "Forum," p. 840.

30 The Blood May stands out as the key historical event depicted by the otherwise fictional series; this is the case in Kutscher's first novel as well. On the historical *Blutmai* itself, see Molly Loberg, *The Struggle for the Streets of Berlin: Politics, Consumption, and Urban Space, 1914–1945* (Cambridge: Cambridge University Press, 2018), pp. 147–8.

31 Sneeringer in Fuechtner and Lerner, "Forum," p. 840.

32 Grosch et al. give a compelling, detailed reading of the influences of Kurt Weill's music on Ferry's new version of "Bitter-Sweet" in "Rekonfigurationen der Weimarer Republik," pp. 53–6.

33 Baer and Smith, "Introduction," p. 16; see also Sneeringer, "Glitter and Post-Punk Doom."

34 André Flicker and Xan Holt, "German Netflix Culture," *Germanic Review* 97, no. 3 (2022), pp. 211–18, here p. 217.

35 Annette Timm, *The Politics of Fertility in Twentieth-Century Berlin* (Cambridge: Cambridge University Press, 2010), pp. 58–65, here p. 58; Julia Roos, *Weimar Through the Lens of Gender: Prostitution Reform, Woman's Emancipation, and German Democracy, 1919–33* (Ann Arbor: University of Michigan Press, 2010), pp. 1–2, 10, 32, 35–6, 90–5, 113, 160–2.

36 Timm, *The Politics of Fertility*, p. 61.

37 Laurie Schrage, "Prostitution and the Case for Decriminalization" in Jessica Spector, ed., *Prostitution and Pornography: Philosophical Debate about the Sex Industry* (Stanford: Stanford University Press, 2006), pp. 240–6, here p. 241.

38 Smith, *Berlin Coquette*, p. 189.

39 Smith, "Lotte at the Movies," p. 271.

40 Le Pustra brings the Cabaret of the Nameless to the stage of the newly rebuilt Moka Efti in *BB*'s season four, bringing together both of the clubs I examine in this essay. The casting of Le Pustra as a recognizable contemporary artist whose image is inextricably linked with Weimar-era Berlin is a common strategy in *BB* (and a canny marketing strategy for all parties involved), as evidenced by the casting of singer Tim Fischer as the drag queen Ilja Tretschkow, a regular act at the Holländer, and of actress and chanteuse Meret Becker as the aging film actress Esther (Korda) Kasabian. See Grosch et al., "Rekonfigurationen der Weimarer Republik," pp. 58–60.

41 Erich Kästner, "The Cabaret of the Nameless" in Anton Kaes, Martin Jay, and Edward Dimendberg, eds., *The Weimar Republic Sourcebook* (Berkeley: University of California Press, 1994), pp. 562–3, here p. 563.

42 The camerawork in the club/brothel conversation between Wolter and Lotte tends to put her on the same visual plane as him, first in a shot/counter-shot pattern that mirrors the quick back-and-forth of their negotiations and then by placing them side by side after they have clearly had sex, and by using a method of placing the speaker in focus while the other is blurred in the background.

43 Smith, "Lotte at the Movies," pp. 269, 271.

44 Peter E. Gordon and John P. McCormick, "Introduction: Weimar Thought: Continuity and Crisis" in Peter E. Gordon and John P. McCormick, eds., *Weimar Thought: A Contested Legacy* (Princeton: Princeton University Press, 2013), pp. 1–11, here p. 7.

45 *BB*, season one, episode eight.

46 Christopher Isherwood, "Sally Bowles," *The Berlin Stories* (New York: New Directions, 2008), p. 49.

47 August Benda is a fictional character modeled after the deputy police commissioner Bernhard Weiss; on *BB*'s depiction of Benda as the first season's only character who is explicitly identified as Jewish, and how Benda's

characterization differs from his historical antecedent, see Darcy Buerkle, "The City (Almost) Without Jews" in Baer and Smith, *Babylon Berlin*, pp. 160–3. This scene (season one, episode five) erroneously makes Böß a member of the SPD when he refers to the socialist newspaper *Vorwärts* as "our own party's paper."

48 See Lerner and Fuechtner, respectively, in "Forum," pp. 841–2, and my personal conversation with Julia Roos, Bloomington, Indiana, 1 October 2021.

49 Lerner, "Forum," p. 841.

50 As Eric Weitz so succinctly puts it, Hindenburg's "elections to the presidency in 1925 and 1932 were Weimar fiascoes." Weitz, *Weimar Germany*, pp. 353–4. *BB*'s showrunners managed a feat of ingenious casting by having the veteran actor Günter Lamprecht, who starred as Franz Biberkopf in Fassbinder's adaptation of *Berlin Alexanderplatz*, play Hindenburg.

51 Wolfgang Elz, "Foreign Policy" in Anthony McElligott, ed., *Weimar Germany* (Oxford: Oxford University Press, 2013), pp. 50–77, here p. 61.

52 Keun, *The Artificial Silk Girl*, pp. 60–1.

53 *BB*, season three, episode three. For a close reading of Katelbach and his tirade to the publisher of the tabloid *Tempo* in the historical context of print media in Weimar Berlin, see Jochen Hung, "Journalists and the Media as Proponents of Modern Life" in Baer and Smith, *Babylon Berlin*, p. 134.

9 Militant Democracy
A (Supposed) Weimar Lesson Revisited

Jan-Werner Müller

Recent years have witnessed a global "democratic recession" as well as what is now often, with an ugly, but entirely justified neologism, called "autocratization."[1] These trends are still not well understood; in particular, it is an open question whether one can generalize about underlying causes of these developments.[2] There is also an ongoing debate as to just how severe the reversal of democratization trends really is; some argue that the dramatic decline in the quantity and quality of democracies may in effect be due to something like measuring errors. We may have been too optimistic about democracy in the 1990s, but today we are being too pessimistic, or so at least some observers worry.[3] Not least, there is the question whether there is anything fundamentally new about the autocratic regimes that have come to power in recent years: The popular term "back-sliding" appears to suggest that we are going *back* to something already known from history; some observers – rightly, in my view – are more inclined to argue that today's authoritarians are in many respects different from their predecessors in the twentieth century.

What is beyond dispute is that references to "Weimar" and "fascism" have played an increasingly important role in trying to make sense of the present, and also to mobilize various constituencies – from elites who listen to former secretaries of state such as Madeleine Albright warning about fascism to activists who view Antifa as "an illiberal intervention that in resisting fascism does not rely on the state, the justice system or any liberal institution."[4] Related to the diagnosis of fascism (or sometimes neo-fascism), there is the question whether some of the lessons drawn in the postwar period from the failures of Weimar – especially the

This chapter draws extensively on my essay "Far-Right Populism Is Bad Enough" from *Eurozine*, available at www.eurozine.com/far-right-populism-is-bad-enough/, as well my book *Democracy Rules* (London: Allen Lane, 2021), a number of previous writings on militant democracy, and a chapter in Daniel Steinmetz-Jenkins (ed.), *Did It Happen Here? Perspectives on Fascism in America* (New York: Norton, forthcoming).

ones that inspired the creation of the legal toolkit generally known as "militant democracy" – should be central to attempts to defend democracy today (as opposed to strategies that do not rely on "any liberal institution" or any more directly political approach – be it popular-frontism or some other attempt to form coalitions against aspiring autocrats).

This chapter engages both issues, with an emphasis on the applicability of militant democracy. I argue that it is ultimately implausible to designate today's forms of autocratization as involving anything plausibly called fascism – with the possibly, and evidently not trivial, exception of the most recent iterations of Putinism. I suggest that, for the most part, we stick with the concept of far-right populism to make sense of a trend of our times – with "far-right" specifying ideological content and "populism" referring to a claim by actors uniquely to represent what they often call "the real people." This diagnosis can meet two quasi-normative criteria that have frequently been implicit in the debates around the applicability of Weimar analogies and the concept of fascism in particular: first, that a diagnosis must not create blind spots such that we no longer see the ways in which actually existing liberal democracies – and actually existing liberal democrats – might be complicit in the rise of antidemocratic actors; and, second, that diagnoses properly mobilize citizens for the defense of democracy.[5] I cannot engage these quasi-strategic considerations in great detail in the chapter, and, in any case, they should obviously not determine the choice of conceptual frames to comprehend the present all by themselves (this has arguably been the mistake of those who think that only the f-word can ever shock people out of complacency). But they are also not illegitimate to take into account.

After the brief discussion of fascism, I move on to suggest that the toolkit of militant democracy remains valuable in many ways – but that its instruments are often not well suited to dealing with today's challenges to democracy. Part of the problem we face is that at least some actors bent on undermining democracy are also engaged in the very thing that political education has often portrayed as an unqualified good: learning from history. Of course, learning from history remains important – but the unspoken assumption that only those committed to democracy ever learn from history is unwarranted. Those engaged in its destruction can also draw lessons from the twentieth century, and in particular about how to avoid situations in which militant democracy would become obviously applicable or even imperative.[6] At the very least, the toolkit would have to be developed further; more plausibly, we might think of a reorientation toward more directly political strategies. I suggest two such strategies at the end of the chapter.

Fascism or Far-Right Authoritarian Populism?

As the introduction (Chapter 1) to this volume notes, "fascism" has become ubiquitous in attempts to make sense of our present. It is helpful, I believe, to distinguish a discussion about causes and conditions (as well as historical constituencies) for fascism on the one hand and one about the characteristics of fascism on the other.[7] Clearly, one is not reducible to the other; moreover, one can possibly conclude that, while a number of contemporary political phenomena have enough of a family resemblance to historical forms of fascism to merit the application of the term, the conditions for an actual triumph of fascism are still not there. Conversely, it might be the case that our conjuncture is favorable for fascism, and that worse is to come – especially if economic conditions deteriorate and fascists were to improve their capacities for propaganda in a new media environment.

Let me start with historical conditions. As many historians have reminded us in recent years, it is impossible to comprehend the emergence of fascism (a heading under which I include Italian Fascism and German National Socialism) without taking into account two background conditions in particular: One is the experience of mass violence and death in the First World War (and its aftermath). Mussolini's celebration of *combattentismo* and "trenchocracy" appealed to a particular audience not just of veterans; the same is broadly true for the Weimar Republic.[8] The other background condition was the perception of a serious communist threat, and, irrespective of the accuracy of that perception, a reality of working-class power and broad left-wing mobilization. Fascists did not come to power in the interwar period without the collaboration of, broadly speaking, liberal and conservative elites. As Robert Paxton has pointed out: "The fascisms we have known have come into power with the help of frightened ex-liberals and opportunist technocrats and ex-conservatives, and governed in more or less awkward tandem with them."[9] Mussolini did not really march on Rome; he arrived by sleeper car from Milan, called in by the king and assorted liberal leaders who rather happily governed with him in subsequent years.

Neither condition – war experience or communist threats – obviously holds today. The military has been creeping back into the politics of seemingly consolidated democracies; and, no doubt, this is a disturbing trend (think of Brazil as an obvious example, or also the attempt by Trump to turn military men into props for his political spectacles in the summer of 2020, when, as so often with Trump, stagecraft trumped actual statecraft). But this is different from a collective experience of violence coloring political life in the way that was the case in interwar

Europe. Few people today think that mortal combat is an indispensable part of the good life, and while one can imagine all kinds of possible futures for the military (especially ones based on different technological innovations), a return of the draft would have to figure among the least likely.[10]

The question of a comprehensive threat motivating a turn to fascism is more complicated. Clearly, no revolutionary left is on the march, and there is nothing similar to the Comintern. But what hovers in the background is a post-9/11 sense that liberal democracies are endangered from without and, crucially, also from within by "radical Islamism" (or, as a number of intellectuals would claim, "Islamofascism"). Less obviously, while 9/11 and the Iraq and Afghanistan wars are hardly analogous to losing the First World War (or being frustrated by paltry gains from the war, as in post-1918 Italy), it is not implausible to see the early twenty-first century as one of humiliation for at least parts of "the West" – and to think that a feeling of victimhood can be used to mobilize for, and justify, various forms of aggression.

The far right has benefited enormously from being able to invoke this supposed threat. Not equally everywhere, of course, but the frame remains widely available; less obviously, it has been crucial in allowing the center-right (and sometimes even the center-left, as in Denmark) to mainstream far-right talking points and larger agendas.[11] One need only remember Valérie Pécresse, one-time standard-bearer of the French Republicans (the latest name for the Gaullist party), in effect legitimizing the conspiracy theory of the "Great Replacement," to see that fear of Islam – and an appeal to citizens as victims – remains part of the strategic repertoire of supposed mainstream actors.

Such forms of mainstreaming point to another background condition of fascism for which it might in fact be more plausible to imagine functional equivalents in the present: elites willing to collaborate. In the twenty-first century, no far-right figure has come to power in any North American or West European country (Italy being the, obviously not trivial, exception) without the collaboration of much more traditional elites and, more specifically, parties that would conventionally be seen as center-right. Such collaboration has been normalized in ways unimaginable not that long ago: When Austrian Christian Democrats entered a coalition with the far-right Freedom Party in 2000, Europe (or at least leading EU governments) were scandalized; when they did so again in 2017, hardly anyone bat an eye.

But then again, the far right is not the same as fascism. Which brings us from the question of causes, conditions, conjunctures, and constituencies to one about characteristics of the family of fascist phenomena.

Violence was not just a background experience for fascism; fascists also explicitly celebrated violence as a force giving meaning to individual and collective life; the latter came to be dominated by military or paramilitary regimented mass movements for a reason.[12] Mortal combat was not an occasional necessity, but an active moral choice for fascists; and it is not an accident that all fascist regimes eventually went to war (or were constructed under wartime conditions, as in Croatia). This need for expansion, confrontation, and an overall sense of dynamism, of course, also explains for some observers why fascism appeared to have a self-destructive tendency and why, in the end, it failed as a regime everywhere it was tried.[13]

It is also crucial to remember that fascism presented itself as a genuine revolution. Fascists advanced a systematic idea about how to mobilize as well as profoundly restructure society (in line with imagined racial hierarchies). Fascism is unthinkable apart from mobilized mass movements devoted to a "rebirth" of what Griffin calls an imagined "ultranation" (homogeneous and racialized).[14]

All of which is not to say that every manifestation of fascism must feature some kind of more or less coherent thought system: As is well known, the self-appointed philosophical leaders of fascism, be they Giovanni Gentile or Alfred Rosenberg, ended up being completely sidelined within the regimes. Nor is it to say that a regime will in practice, empirically, have to make good on the claim of totally dominating a collective of "new men."[15] But without anything resembling such ambitions on the part of influential actors, it is difficult to see how we can meaningfully speak of fascism. Terms like "semi-fascism," "para-fascism," "fascist tactics," and "performative fascism" invoke a family resemblance (and pocket the surplus shock value of the "f-word"), while at the same time hinting that the relatives might be so distant as in the end to have very little to do with each other.

There is a second complication in matters of conditions and content. The glorification of violence in the interwar period was inseparable from ideals of male brotherhood. As the German historian Klaus Theweleit has shown in his seminal study *Male Phantasies*, the world that men organized in militias strove for was ultimately one entirely without women.[16] Evidently, one cannot simply generalize this point; the actual regimes did not persecute women as such, but, for the most part, subordinated them in the name of natalism (a feature shared with plenty of non-fascist regimes). Still, what Virginia Woolf at the time referred to as "unmitigated masculinity" played a central role in fascism; and it still plays a role in paramilitary groups in, for instance, the US and Brazil today.[17] But, overall, the gender politics of parties and movements suspected of fascism by some today are rather different: That is not just because some have female leaders, such as Le Pen and Meloni; it is also because they mobilize women specifically by invoking rights, usually against supposedly threatening Muslim men. Highly selective feminism can be incorporated into what some scholars have called "femonationalism";[18] this is categorically different from the occasional concession to female agency one could witness in Nazi Germany and Fascist Italy.

I want to suggest that, if it is not fascism, authoritarianism is still the right designation, and far-right authoritarian populism in particular. As historians of the twentieth century have long taught us, not every dictatorship was fascist; if we lose the distinction between revolutionary fascism committed to a mobilization and reformatting of society as a whole and relatively static authoritarianism (which can also be violent, of course), we diminish our capacity for political judgment.[19]

What's more, not all authoritarianisms have the same public justification. What is particular about today's authoritarians (or aspiring autocrats such as Trump) is the claim that they, and only they, represent the people and implement its true will; this is something proponents of bureaucratic authoritarianism, for instance, would not have said. I have suggested in a number of writings that the concept of populism – and authoritarian right-wing populism in particular – can be of help here (although the word tends to misunderstandings in the American context, where, for historical reasons, "populism" is often primarily imagined as bona fide grassroots pressure on oligarchies, as defending Main Street against Wall Street, etc.).

Populism is not so much about anti-elitism, but about *anti-pluralism*: Populists hold that they, *and only they*, represent what they often call "the real people" or "the silent majority." As a consequence, they declare all other contenders for power fundamentally illegitimate. This is never just a disagreement about policies – or even values, for that matter. After all, such disputes are normal, ideally even productive, in a democracy. Rather, populists malign other politicians as traitors, as corrupt and "crooked." Less obviously, they insinuate incessantly that all those among the people who do not share their particular symbolic conception of the people – and hence do not support the populists politically – might not properly belong to the people at all. Far-right authoritarian populists ultimately reduce all political questions to questions of belonging: Trump does not answer his critics with arguments, but condemns them as un-American. The specific political business model of right-wing populists is to suggest that some people do not properly belong at all, are fundamentally illegitimate, or pose an outright threat to the integrity of the polity. But they do not openly encourage collective violence against such threats. They also do not impose an ideal of the good life on society as a whole, in the way typical of many twentieth-century authoritarians.

Still, their anti-pluralism has pernicious consequences on the ground, so to speak. My insistence that we are dealing with, in Trump's case, far-right populism, and not fascism, in no way belittles the pernicious effects of the failed businessman-turned-entertainer occupying the Oval Office.[20] Populist talk results in what Kate Manne has called "trickle-down aggression";[21] it is hardly an accident that the number of hate crimes in the US has risen dramatically, and that many Republicans are now ready to "take the law into their own hands" to defend the country against the threat supposedly posed by those who will appear to them as un-American American citizens.[22]

Far-right militias remain marginal in the US for now (unlike the RSS in India, for instance, where fascism is becoming a more plausible designation). But the "ethnic antagonism," as Larry Bartels puts it rather delicately – the de facto fear of black and brown people destroying white Christian America – keeps being stoked not just by Trump, but by plenty of more polite-sounding people in the GOP,[23] and it can pave the way for something much worse. The alternatives are not just Weimar on the one hand or democratic normality on the other. But that leaves the question whether one lesson from Weimar, forged in the fight against fascism in the 1930s – to take antidemocratic actors out of the democratic game before they can destroy democracy – is still helpful in complex contemporary circumstances.

Militant Democracy: An Obvious Lesson from Weimar?

"Militant democracy" was born in the fight against fascism in the 1930s. The core idea is that a democracy should engage in rights restrictions for the sake of defending its existence against parties (and particular individuals) bent on undermining the democratic political system.[24] These are not actors turning to violence or other forms of conduct already covered by criminal law – what applies to them is a special, in a sense political, kind of prohibition. Alternative terms – which help to clarify the underlying aspiration – are "a democracy willing to fight," as it is called in Germany, or what in Israel is known as the "defending democracy paradigm."

The example most often invoked for justifying militant democracy remains the demise of the Weimar Republic. The stylized narrative usually told is simple: The NSDAP (National Socialist German Workers' Party) stood for elections; it won popular support; once in power, it proceeded to abolish democracy – or so the story goes.

Yet this account – and the analogical reasoning based on it – tends to leave out what are hardly minor details. In particular, it is glossed over that no functioning democratic legislature authorized the effective end of democratic government. The Reichstag that voted for the Enabling Law of March 1933 could not be considered as such. Furthermore, justifications of militant democracy tend to forget that Weimar in fact had many repressive instruments for dealing with challenges to democracy, and many of them were used vigorously – the Republic saw no fewer than twenty-eight party bans, for instance. From 1923 onward, the Nazi Party was banned in the Reich, but it was allowed to be re-founded in 1925; the political police in Prussia kept an eye on the NSDAP until 1932, but never decisively weakened the party.[25] On one level, one might say, the problem was not a lack of "instruments," but a lack of consistency and, ultimately, political will.[26]

Still, the lesson for many observers at the time and in the postwar period seemed clear enough: Democracies should have legal tools to deal with existential threats by antidemocratic actors (not just fascists) abusing the "arsenal of democracy." They ought to be able to "fight fire with fire," as Karl Loewenstein, the inventor of militant democracy, had put it. More specifically, they should be able to restrict rights; in practice, this has meant, above all, the banning of political parties – restricting the rights to association – even if there is also the possibility of prohibitions applying directly to particular individuals: For instance, Article 18 of the German Basic Law holds that citizens can forfeit basic political rights. In fact, four attempts have been made to use that Article; all have been unsuccessful, either because the individuals in question were said not to pose a sufficient threat, or because they were already taken out of political circulation, so to speak, due to conduct covered by criminal law (in every single case, the person in question would have been described most accurately as a neo-fascist, devoted to violence as a way of life).

In the postwar period, militant democracy was often seen as part and parcel of an antitotalitarian stance that sought to defend the substantial values undergirding democracy, human dignity above all (which, rather than freedom, became the master value of postwar constitutions in Western Europe). In West Germany, it formed part of the state's self-understanding, condensed into the widely used formula "Bonn is not Weimar"; the Weimar analogy (or, rather, the contrast) helped elites and citizens to make sense of their politics (a function of analogies also suggested in the introduction to this volume).

Yet, as the introduction makes clear, too, analogies can also be deployed for strategic or even just tactical purposes – such as delegitimating, or even entirely eliminating, particular political actors. One of the convenient side effects of developing the doctrine of militant democracy during the Cold War was that much attention could be given to the threats from communists, effectively sidelining the Nazi past (even if fascism remained on the quasi-official list of possible threats). The de facto successor to the NSDAP was prohibited in 1953; but much more attention focused on the Communist Party, which suffered the same fate three years later (after it had defended itself with the claim that it was the real party of democrats, while the supposed "Adenauer regime" was an illegitimate imposition by Washington, DC).[27] The underlying justification was the notion of "anti-extremism," inspired by theories of totalitarianism which assume that mortal threats to democracy could emanate just as much from the left as the right. Related to this is the attendant idea of the "horseshoe theory": According to this theory, left and right extremes can converge in their antidemocratic ideas and conduct – and this thought, of course, is also based on a particular interpretation of what had happened at the very end of the Weimar Republic.

The Weimar analogy led to measures other than party bans that were widely judged to be misguided by later generations: The *Radikalenerlass*, also often called *Berufsverbot* – based on the supposed Weimar lessons that a democratic state needs civil servants loyal to democracy – enabled the firing of those suspected of harboring sympathy for left-wing radicalism in the 1970s.[28] (This measure, it should be noted, was taken by Will Brandt's government in conjunction with the federal states – proof, if any were needed, of just how much "not-Weimar" was central to the Federal Republic's collective self-understanding across party lines.)

To be sure, in unified Germany, the focus shifted much more to the right. At the beginning of the new millennium, Gerhard Schröder's government sought to prohibit the National Democratic Party (NPD) – widely perceived to be a neo-Nazi party based on *völkisch* ideology – in the wake of violent attacks on minorities. The jurists behind the attempt at banning decisively shifted away from the doctrine of anti-extremism; instead, they opted for what has been called "negative republicanism." The idea was that to remain faithful to democracy's open and experimental nature, one should be very restrained when it comes to party bans (parties, after all, are instruments for citizens to implement new political ideas); however, if a polity already had one decidedly negative experience with a particular kind of ideology, banning can be legitimate, as long as the party possibly subject to banning and the party responsible for the "negative experience" in the past are sufficiently similar.[29] Hence, lawyers sought to prove that the NPD and the NSDAP exhibited a *Wesensverwandschaft*, an essential affinity, opening themselves up to the criticisms of using historical analogies also discussed in the introduction to this book: Analogies can lead to cognitive distortions, or, worse, arguments made in bad faith to make the present look like the past in order to achieve goals for which more general and abstract arguments do not seem to succeed. Arguably, one specific reason for the strategy centered on "essential affinity" was to preempt the European Court of Human Rights rejecting a ban of the NPD; after all, the party was hardly likely to acquire executive power (one of Strasbourg's criteria for legitimate banning); yet, given the Court's doctrine of margin of appreciation – states can appeal to specific features of national history to obtain a different ruling – the idea was obviously that a ban made sense against the background of Germany's particular experience with National Socialism.

The German constitutional court never really took a stance on this doctrine, for the case had to be withdrawn before it could do so: It had become apparent that the government was using evidence against the party which had in fact been produced by state agents who had infiltrated the party. In 2017, yet another attempt to ban the NPD failed, because the constitutional court held that the party was simply so insignificant that it had no chance of getting into power anywhere (a ruling that ignored the point about local violence). At the same time, it did affirm that the party was indeed *verfassungsfeindlich* – actively hostile to the constitution – and suggested that the German parliament pass a law that would deprive parties exhibiting such hostility of financing by the state. (The law was passed; the money stopped; and, at the time of writing, the NPD is appealing.) Of course, today the situation is different in at least one important respect: Germany has seen the rise of a far-right populist party in the form of the Alternative für Deutschland (AfD). Unlike the NPD, that party has succeeded twice in entering the national parliament; in fact, from 2017 to 2021, it constituted the largest opposition party. Calls for a ban have been voiced, but skeptics worry that yet another failed ban could only make things worse, especially by reinforcing the populist frame of all against one–one against all, allowing party leaders to present themselves as martyrs and as the champions of the people, whom "the establishment" wishes to suppress at all costs.

Militant Democracy: Rationale and Applications Revisited

Militancy tends to be motivated by the thought that democracy is a form of politics uniquely at risk of self-abolition. It is, so this line of reasoning suggests, the only political system that can decide to do away with itself in a manner that is perfectly legal and legitimate. That is not really plausible, though. In theory, a monarch or a dictator could also single-handedly determine that their domination must give way to a form of democracy. The ruled may or may not obey – but that possibility also exists in a self-abolishing democracy. Less pedantic is the point that majorities must allow minorities to become majorities one day; a decision by 51 per cent to abolish the basic political rights that all had enjoyed hitherto cannot be said to be democratic in the first place. In fact, only a 100 per cent endorsement of a transition to authoritarianism would vindicate the idea that there is something inherently paradoxical about democracy (whereas the abdicating monarch or dictator is not doing anything contradictory – after all, only they had the relevant decision-making power).

For critics of the militant democracy paradigm, there is no fundamental contradiction at the heart of democracy at all – but there is one at the core of militant democracy, for the latter is said to be self-undermining. A democracy that restricts fundamental political rights to defend itself already ceases to be a democracy; the very effort to save democracy will at least harm it; diminishing political pluralism for the sake of political pluralism makes no sense. It is an illusion that fire can be fought with fire; the result will be the whole house of democracy burning to the ground. (If one looks at postwar German history, that hardly seems plausible; but it does seem plausible to say that overreactions to left-wing extremism damaged individual rooms in the building.)

For militancy to be at all plausible, there has to be an answer to the question of how threats to democracy can be identified reliably, and also a response to those who argue that any restriction of rights in the name of defending democracy in fact undermines democracy. The common way to address the first issue has been to point to courts as best placed to ascertain whether a party, or just individuals, might be intent on destroying democracy.[30] The reason is straightforward: Courts are assumed to be impartial guardians of the rules of the democratic game as such.[31] That the reality is often rather different – courts are hardly entirely above politics, and they tend broadly to follow shifts in public opinion – is a point many defenders of courts as central actors in militant democracy would concede. But they would also remind us that courts, for all their shortcomings, do not have the perverse incentives that political parties might have – namely, to use militant measures to get rid of other players in the democratic game. They also would seem to have no reason to score points with electorates by attacking vulnerable minorities or generally unpopular political views.

That leaves the question whether there is, in the end, a coherent criterion for prohibitions in cases other than what might be obviously considered fascism (with its direct promotion of violence, which is, of course, illegal anyway, hence covered by criminal law – hence not needing the "political laws" of militant democracy). The most plausible answer is this: Do political associations *systematically* deny the standing of other members of the polity as free and equal? Associations are different from individuals. Whether individuals engaged in such speech ought to face penalties is something about which reasonable people can disagree. In their defense, it is often said that they are still trying to contribute meaningfully to public debate or that we cannot ask them to obey laws unless they have had their say, even if what they say turns out to be hateful.[32]

The trouble with such leniency is that, even if those we might call for shorthand the haters do not come to power, there are still victims. Law professors might say that burning crosses in African American neighborhoods is part of democratic discourse, but the psychological burden of that act of aggression is not borne by the law professors.[33] There often are ways of articulating certain views without denying the standing of fellow citizens; the indulgent libertarianism of some free speech advocates simply liberates potential speakers from having to bother with finding such alternatives.

Those forgiving of speech can still draw the line at attempts systematically to restructure the polity in line with such speech.[34] It is one thing for someone on the proverbial soapbox – or Twitter, for that matter – to denigrate others; it is something else to form a party aimed at gaining state power to put such denigration into practice. "Systematic" or "structured" are wider concepts than just founding parties. Think of the white supremacist who step by step bought up lots in Leith, a small prairie town in North Dakota, aiming to make it a model village of racial purity.[35] The leader of the US National Socialist Movement (sic!) paid a visit; citizens from other parts of the country protested; and eventually the planner of this kind of Nazi prefigurative politics was convicted of terrorizing the town.

This story points to the difficulties of assessing the level at which a threat to democracy is really located. Neither in Germany nor in the US do openly racist parties appear to have realistic chances of occupying the federal government; but what if small parties manage to terrorize citizens locally? And if nothing happens in response, because there is no problem at the national level, the message these citizens then receive from the democratic state seems to be: "This, after all, is acceptable."

To be sure, states can also talk back at antidemocrats without restricting their rights. There are options other than silence, both-sides-ism ("very fine people" on both sides), or banning: Martin Luther King, Jr. commemorations, more civic education, official endorsements of tolerance.[36] But, at least in countries where bans are permissible, those officially opposed by the democratic state in this manner can then charge the state with apparent hypocrisy; they can say something like, "If we're really so bad, why don't you ban us? And in the meantime, don't betray your own principle of equal political chances for all contenders by employing public power to denigrate *us* in the eyes of the people."

These challenges are real. But (and this is the crucial point for a volume on Weimar legacies and Weimar analogies) many of them are also yesterday's – that is, the twentieth century's – battles. The expectation of the original theorists of militancy was that parties announce in their programs their wish to violate citizens' fundamental rights, or they are so obviously associated with violence that comparisons with twentieth-century fascism will be evident.

Very, very few parties display antidemocratic intentions or open support for violence today. We are simply not in Weimar anymore. True, as I argued earlier, right-wing populists insinuate that some citizens do not belong to the "real people," or that they are inherently suspect – but these figures also carefully hedge their rhetoric and push boundaries, rather than blatantly transgress them. Some of the de facto *völkisch* rhetoric of the German AfD is the exception here; it has justified the close surveillance of the party by a special office tasked with "protecting the constitution" – *Verfassungsschutz* – and might indeed be material that could eventually justify a ban (it is an open empirical question whether the surveillance has led the party to moderate somewhat). In general, then, the threats democracies face today are not openly announced with clearcut statements; rather, they have to fear the stealthy capture of the guardians of democracy, be they courts, watchdogs inside the bureaucracy, or election commissions.[37]

Still, courts, ombudsmen, and, for that matter, other political parties are not powerless in responding to new forms of attack on democracy. While it is hardly ever justified to take away the rights of ordinary citizens to associate (and to vote for the party of their choice), individual powerful actors might plausibly be banned from the democratic game. Think of how a Berlusconi or a Trump did not just make one-off mistakes, but exhibited a consistent pattern of seeking to undermine the rules of the game as such (which eventually justified Trump's impeachments, a political approach that did not require proof of actual criminal conduct). By contrast, suspending such figures permanently – assuming they have not engaged in criminal activity – is more of a stretch. By the same token, if a party exhibits a consistent pattern of aiming at autocratization, the case for banning is strong, even if the party does not officially endorse any antidemocratic ideas (let alone condone or promote violence).

But then there are also choices made by elites and citizens at large – as opposed to the militancy effected by courts issuing restrictions. The view that Weimar was a democracy without democrats is far too simplistic – but, of course, it does remind us of the point that citizen dispositions matter. In a number of countries, parts of civil society have mobilized against far-right authoritarian populism, demonstrating that the latter represents a loud minority (nothing wrong with loud minorities as such in democracies, to be sure). When the majority ceases to be silent, it turns out, it does not speak the language of far-right authoritarian populism. And it is important that minorities acknowledge this, too.

And elites? As Larry Bartels has recently shown, it is simply implausible, empirically, to claim that there is a "populist wave" and that masses of people are all of a sudden opting for far-right authoritarian populism; what has changed, he argues, is the conduct of, broadly speaking, conservative elites.[38] So, one might say that the interwar lesson about conservative establishments collaborating with antidemocratic actors still does hold today – except it has become easier to justify such collaboration precisely because the far right is also learning from history. Giorgia Meloni, to take the most obvious example, is not a fascist, but she does pursue policies that fit the playbook of far-right authoritarian populism (attacking minorities, trying to capture state institutions). And her conspicuous disavowals of fascism – and the absence of violence – evidently help in making her *salonfähig* (acceptable in polite society, that is). Still, elites do have a choice, and, less obviously, citizens remain in a position to determine whether they punish conservative establishments for collaborating with the far right (and for copying its rhetoric, as in the example of Valérie Pécresse).

Conclusion

I have argued that two supposed lessons from Weimar for the present – namely, that fascism can be born inside democracies and that militant self-defense in the form of party bans is the best answer to fascism – are not particularly helpful in making sense of the present; in that sense, the chapter confirms one of the major claims of this volume about the dubious or at least ambivalent character of historical analogies. My position does not assume that some countries are somehow "immune" to fascism; threats to democracy are too serious today to play parlor games with historical exceptionalism. I also concede that fascists undoubtedly exist today: Think of Golden Dawn in Greece, and consider very plausible arguments that Putinism, after early 2022 or so, exhibits some of the core characteristics of fascism – while not promising a revolution or the creation of a "new man," the Russian regime has embarked on comprehensive mobilization, indoctrination, and, not least, glorification of violence.[39]

Still, the background conditions that created fascism as a major historical force do not hold in many countries subject to the general "democratic recession." And while it is certainly possible to "de-contextualize" fascism as part of a "process of abstraction that delivers the really useful knowledge we need for today" (as Geoff Eley has put it), we also cannot ignore some of the ideational characteristics of fascism that depend on particular contexts: regimented mass movements and comprehensive mobilization of societies; cults of violence and male brotherhood, with an attendant broader gender politics; and racialized notions of what Griffin has called an "ultranation."[40]

Far-right populism certainly shows overlaps with fascism: Fascist leaders also claimed that they, and they alone, represented the people; some are connected to regimented mass movements (such as the RSS in India); and all of them are committed to reinforcing hierarchies of gender in particular. But, ultimately, the differences are more important and running together phenomena for which we have precise – and different – concepts does not help our understanding of the history of the present. In the same vein, I want to insist that over-generalizations, such as Jason Stanley's "the most telling symptom of fascist politics is division," do not help either. All politics, on one level, is about division; the question is how one divides, and with which consequences.[41]

Militant democracy was conceived as a response to fascism, but then quickly became caught up in the strategic use of analogies as part of a Cold War battle against communist parties and sympathizers. Many criticisms have been leveled against this approach: It is potentially elitist and technocratic; it might mirror extremists in its exclusionary tendencies;[42] it cannot be contained and will contaminate a political culture more broadly; it will have significant blind spots. All these views contain some valid points and constitute salutary warnings. But the basic idea, I believe, remains valid: Actors who exhibit a systematic tendency to undermine core aspects of democracy should have their rights restricted (after appropriate warnings). On one level, Natasha Lennard's observation that "fascism is un-bannable" is right; but it is also true that parties and movements that exhibit clear fascist characteristics *can* be legally banned.[43]

But – and this has been my other core claim in this chapter – fascism is in a sense the easy case today; by contrast, right-wing authoritarian populists in general have been careful not to be associated with violence, or with paramilitary movements that would conjure up memories of the twentieth century for both domestic and international audiences. I repeat the point that this does not mean that they are harmless; the claim to a monopoly of representing the "real people" points in an authoritarian direction; and the dismissal of some citizens as "not real" (and as positively threatening) is likely to have violent consequences on the ground. In some cases, the anti-pluralism will be so clear that the traditional machinery of militant democracy can be started; in many others, though, the evidence will simply be too limited (one learning effect among today's populist leaders has been plausible deniability under many circumstances). It is then that the argument – in the eyes of some, a banality – that democracy must ultimately be defended by democratic majorities really means something.

Notes

1 Larry Diamond, "Facing Up to Democratic Recession," *Journal of Democracy* 26 (2015), pp. 141–55; Anna Lührmann and Staffan I. Lindberg, "A Third Wave of Autocratization Is Here: What Is New About It?," *Democratization* 26 (2019), pp. 1095–113.

2 My own view is that close attention to individual national contexts remains crucial; this is not at the expense of, but rather a precondition for, understanding how practices (and toolkits) of autocratization are being shared across borders.

3 Steven Levitsky and Lucan Way, "The Myth of Democratic Recession," *Journal of Democracy* 26 (2015), pp. 45–58.

4 Natasha Lennard, *Being Numerous: Essays on Non-Fascist Life* (New York: Verso, 2019), p. 9.

5 Udi Greenberg, "What Was the Fascism Debate?," *Dissent* (Summer 2021) www.dissentmagazine.org/article/what-was-the-fascism-debate   (accessed 20 October 2021). The fact that the concept also mobilizes – and that there are overlaps between social scientific and political concepts – does not warrant the conclusion that fascism necessarily "expresses loathing more than it identifies a reality or a growing series of realities" or that fascism "does not so much isolate a thing as it does some stigmatizing." For this view, see Bruce Kuklick, *Fascism Comes to America: A Century of Obsession in Politics and Culture* (Chicago: University of Chicago Press, 2022), p. 3.

6 That such a leaning process has taken place is amply documented in Serguei Guriev and Daniel Treisman, *Spin Dictators: The Changing Face of Tyranny in the Twenty-First Century* (Princeton: Princeton University Press, 2022).

7 For a similar exercise with different assumptions, see Dylan Riley's "What Is Trump?," which uses "four comparative axes: geopolitical context, economic crisis, relations of class and nation, and, finally, the character of civil society and political parties." Dylan Riley, "What Is Trump?," *New Left Review* 114 (2018), pp. 5–31.

8 Roger Griffin, *Fascism* (Cambridge: Polity, 2018).

238   *Jan-Werner Müller*

9 Robert O. Paxton, *The Anatomy of Fascism* (London: Penguin, 2011), p. 23.
10 This is not to deny that, in the US, war veterans play an especially important role in far-right violence. See Kathleen Belew, *Bring the War Home: The White Power Movement and Paramilitary America* (Cambridge, MA: Harvard University Press, 2018).
11 Cas Mudde, *The Far Right Today* (Cambridge: Polity, 2019); Spencer Ackerman, *Reign of Terror* (New York: Penguin, 2021).
12 David Bell, "Fascism or Caesarism?," *Eurozine*, September 2020, www .eurozine.com/fascism-or-caesarism/ (accessed 21 October 2021).
13 Griffin, *Fascism*, p. 87.
14 Ibid.
15 I have tried to explain this notion of a formation of "new peoples" in *Contesting Democracy: Political Ideas in Twentieth-Century Europe* (London: Yale University Press, 2011).
16 Klaus Theweleit, *Männerphantasien*, 3rd ed. (Berlin: Matthes & Seitz, 2020).
17 I am grateful to Erika A. Kiss for drawing my attention to this aspect of Woolf's *A Room of One's Own*.
18 Sara R. Farris, *In the Name of Women's Rights: The Rise of Femonationalism* (Durham, NC: Duke University Press, 2017).
19 Juan Linz, *Totalitarian and Authoritarian Regimes* (London: Lynne Riener, 2000).
20 "Should We Even Go There? Historians on Comparing Fascism to Trumpism," *The Guardian*, 1 December 2016, www.theguardian.com/us-news/2016/dec/01/comparing-fascism-donald-trump-historians-trumpism (accessed 21 October 2021).
21 Kate Manne, "The Logic of Misogyny," *Boston Review*, 11 July 2016, http://bostonreview.net/forum/kate-manne-logic-misogyny (accessed 17 May 2020).
22 Larry M. Bartels, "Ethnic Antagonism Erodes Republicans' Commitment to Democracy," *Proceedings of the National Academy of Sciences*, 15 September 2020, www.pnas.org/content/pnas/early/2020/08/26/2007747117.full.pdf.
23 Ibid.
24 The original formulation of the idea of militant democracy can be found in Karl Loewenstein, "Militant Democracy and Fundamental Rights I," *American Political Science Review* 31 (1937), pp. 417–32; Karl Loewenstein, "Militant Democracy and Fundamental Rights II," *American Political Science Review* 31 (1937), pp. 638–58. For more on the history and theories of militant democracy, see Giovanni Capoccia, *Defending Democracy: Reactions to Extremism in Inter-war Europe* (Baltimore: Johns Hopkins University Press, 2004); for a more general, non-European comparison, see Gregor Paul Boventer, *Grenzen politischer Freiheit im demokratischen Staat: Das Konzept der streitbaren Demokratie in einem internationalen Vergleich* (Berlin: Duncker & Humblot, 1985); Gregory H. Fox and Georg Nolte, "Intolerant Democracies," *Harvard International Law Journal* 36, no. 1 (1995), pp. 1–70.
25 See Gereon Flümann, *Streitbare Demokratie in Deutschland und den Vereinigten Staaten: Der staatliche Umgang mit nicht gewalttätigem politischem Extremismus im Vergleich* (Wiesbaden: Springer, 2015), p. 94. In general, accounts of militant democracy too casually suggest that the masses are consciously

choosing "extremism" or even outright dictatorship at the ballot box; this tendency started in Loewenstein's original account that portrayed fascism as a form of emotionalism to which the masses had fallen victim.

26 I partly mention this because the defense of "European values" – such as democracy and human rights – was long said to have been hampered by a lack of "instruments" and appropriate "mechanisms." This diagnosis – whose technocratic language is not accidental – overlooks that means are in fact available; the problem is that the crucial actors do not want to use them.

27 See also Patrick Major, *The Death of the KPD: Communism and Anti-Communism, 1945–1956* (Oxford: Oxford University Press, 1998).

28 Many states eventually repealed the decree.

29 Peter Niesen, "Anti-Extremism, Negative Republicanism, Civic Society: Three Paradigms for Banning Political Parties" in Shlomo Avineri and Zeev Sternhell, eds., *Europe's Century of Discontent: The Legacies of Fascism, Nazism and Communism* (Jerusalem: Magnes Press, 2003), pp. 249–68; Peter Niesen, "Banning the Former Ruling Party," *Constellations* 19 (2012), pp. 540–61.

30 Venice Commission (European Commission for Democracy through Law), *Guidelines on Prohibition and Dissolution of Political Parties and Analogous Measures* (2000). Available at: www.venice.coe.int/webforms/documents/default .aspx?pdffile=CDL-INF%282000%29001-e (accessed 19 November 2019). On page 5, the guidelines add: "[L]egal measures directed to the prohibition or legally enforced dissolution of political parties shall be a consequence of a judicial finding of unconstitutionality and shall be deemed as of an exceptional nature and governed by the principle of proportionality."

31 Samuel Issacharoff, *Fragile Democracies: Contested Power in the Era of Constitutional Courts* (New York: Cambridge University Press, 2015).

32 Ronald Dworkin, "The Right to Ridicule," *New York Review of Books*, 23 March 2006, www.nybooks.com/articles/2006/03/23/the-right-to-ridicule/ (accessed 26 May 2020).

33 Jeremy Waldron, *The Harm in Hate Speech* (Cambridge, MA: Harvard University Press, 2014).

34 Jonathan Quong, "The Rights of Unreasonable Citizens," *Journal of Political Philosophy* 12 (2004), pp. 314–35.

35 That story is told in the 2015 documentary *Welcome to Leith*, directed by Michael Beach Nichols and Christopher K. Walker.

36 For an ingenuous set of possibilities along these lines, see Corey Brettschneider, *When the State Speaks, What Should It Say?* (Princeton: Princeton University Press, 2012).

37 Stephen Gardbaum, "Comparative Political Process Theory," *International Journal of Constitutional Law* 18 (2020), pp. 1429–57.

38 Larry Bartels, *Democracy Erodes from the Top* (Princeton: Princeton University Press, 2023).

39 It is certainly no longer plausible to read Putin as a de Gaulle-like figure, in the way Marlene Laruelle did in *Is Russia Fascist? Unraveling Propaganda East and West* (Ithaca: Cornell University Press, 2021). But other elements of Putinism post-2014 or so are more debatable. For instance, war mobilization

seems as much about escaping financial constraints and the miseries of contemporary Russia as about glorifying violence and heroism.

40 Geoff Eley, "What Is Fascism and Where Does It Come From?," *History Workshop Journal* 91 (2021), pp. 1–28, here p. 7.

41 Jason Stanley, *How Fascism Works* (New York: Random House, 2018), p. xvi.

42 Anthoula Malkopolou and Ludvig Norman, "Three Models of Democratic Self-Defense: Militant Democracy and Its Alternatives," *Political Studies* 66 (2018), pp. 442–58.

43 Lennard, *Being Numerous*, p. 17.

10 Weimar and Modernity

Richard Ned Lebow and Ludvig Norman

In this concluding chapter we revisit Weimar and its lessons. We offer some generalizations about these lessons, their evolution and appeal, and what they say about historical analogies and their role in politics. Our arguments build on those of the preceding chapters and make comparisons across them to say something more general about the motives, means, and consequences of analogical reasoning. We also consider the continuing hold of Weimar and its collapse on contemporary political and cultural imaginations.

We started our volume with the observation that Weimar has made a formidable comeback in public and political debate. The Western world has changed dramatically in the ninety years since Weimar, but the collapse of Germany's first republic remains a central trope of political thinking. In its contemporary incarnations, Weimar analogies are widely used to make sense of contemporary Western politics, especially the perceived fragility and decline of democracies. Weimar, however, represents more than a failure of democracy. It has long served as a synecdoche for modernity and its tensions. Modernity's cultural and political consequences are hotly contested, and Weimar, then as now, is regarded as the quintessential expression of its evils and promises. Building on our contributions, we highlight the multiple ways in which Weimar has served as a focal point for competing understandings of the conditions characterizing modern society and the implications for politics.

Our authors demonstrate how the breakdown of the Weimar Republic serves as the paradigmatic case for social and political collapse and as a seemingly inexhaustible well of lessons. Many of these lessons rest on competing understandings of the tensions built into modern society and how they are best addressed. Some of the most important tensions are those between markets and democracy, the masses and their representatives, the role of expertise versus popular rule, tradition and change, hierarchy and equality, order versus fluidity, and personal freedom versus social conventions. Scholars, commentators, novelists, filmmakers, and television producers use Weimar to foreground these

241

tensions. The historical analogies and political lessons they offer can be read as expressions of their hopes and fears. Weimar lessons are accordingly a kind of political and social barometer. They often tell us more about the people who make or invoke them than about the situations they purport to describe.

Historical analogies and lessons are used to make sense of the world and advance political projects. Drawing on our chapters, we offer some thoughts about these cognitive and instrumental purposes. We also consider how analogies, once embedded, become reference points for political thinking, and how that can shape the wider outlooks of politicians, the media, and ordinary people. We close with some general suggestions for improving the quality of historical analogies and their associated lessons.

Weimar Lessons

Historical analysis and lesson construction began in the immediate aftermath of the Weimar Republic's collapse. These lessons were propagated by historians, politicians, and jurists, many of them refugees, traumatized by the Nazis. Some of them would play important roles in the political and intellectual life of postwar Germany, where their understanding of Weimar and its collapse shaped their efforts to design a successor republic. In later decades, their lessons were used to assess the *Bundesrepublik*'s political health. Even when the Republic came to be regarded as robust, Weimar remained a preoccupation. Analogies were now deployed to show the many differences between it and its predecessor. Peter C. Caldwell demonstrates how contrasting analyses of Weimar were mobilized to support different interpretations of postwar German identity and how those identities could be understood in relation to the society that produced the Weimar Republic and that some held responsible for its collapse. With the re-emergence of a nationalist right in the aftermath of reunification, the focus for many has swung back toward similarities.

Analogies are closely connected to political orientation but not in deterministic ways. Douglas Webber describes how multiple and quite different analyses and lessons emerged within the same political party, the German Social Democratic Party (SPD). Some emphasized structural conditions and others gave more weight to the responsibility of particular agents for Weimar's demise. Future chancellor Willy Brandt castigated the SPD leadership for their lack of courage and failure to exploit the preparedness of their rank-and-file supporters to strike and fight to save Weimar. Webber notes that some SPD parliamentarians favored dramatic action but that many union leaders urged caution in response to what they judged as a lack of support among workers for a general strike. For instance, former finance minister Rudolf Hilferding, an influential figure in the SPD, had warned that a general strike would escalate into a civil war. Peter Breiner notes that Otto Kirchheimer insisted that the SPD merely sought to uphold the status quo of a failed constitutional arrangement, even to the point of tolerating a dictatorship when other parties defected.[1] Wilhelm Hoegner, postwar prime minister of Bavaria, emphasized the negative impact of the SPD's ideological orientation. Beliefs that socialist revolution was inevitable, with the party merely acting as its midwife, made members insensitive to the need to act.

Like Caldwell, Webber describes the Republic's coup de grace as an inside job. It was carried out "by political representatives of traditional elites who had become increasingly hostile towards democracy and sought to engage Hitler and the Nazis to provide them with the mass political base they lacked themselves and to crush the labour movement and the Left."[2] Weimar is for Webber an early example of the most common route to democratic breakdown: executive aggrandizement.[3] It was an incremental process; over the course of three years, the power of the Reichstag and of local authorities was progressively curtailed.[4] From this perspective, the Republic collapsed because the military, bureaucracy, clerics, scientists, businessmen, and landowners – and much of the middle class – were antidemocratic. Those further to the left considered social structure the ultimate cause of Weimar's demise. Stalinist economist Fred Oelssner insisted that "'a small group of powerful masters of firms and finance who control billions' had taken down the democracy; to avoid similar conditions and results in the future, a resolute people's democracy had to resist the reconstruction of capitalism."[5] For the SPD, competing understandings of Weimar's collapse became in part a way to make sense of German society and in part a self-reflection and scrutiny of the party's own ideological underpinnings.

Postwar, social democratic understandings of Weimar have emphasized the critical role played by the Great Depression. From this perspective, Weimar becomes the primary manifestation of what can happen to democracies when they are unable to balance the operation of open markets with the substantive material and democratic needs of the people. Abandoning the value of equality paves the way for antidemocratic political actors promising the restoration of greatness for the chosen people. The initial self-reflection within the SPD, pointing to the party's complacency when faced with the erosion of democratic institutions, has gradually become less prominent.

Recognition that mass unemployment and poverty radicalized many members of the working and middle classes made postwar Social Democrats extremely sensitive to the dangers of economic downturns. In the 1970s, then finance minister, and later chancellor, Helmut Schmidt repeatedly warned of the destabilizing consequences of significant unemployment. As chancellor, he would regularly refer to the political dangers of pursuing the kind of deflationary economic policy Germany pursued between 1930 and 1932. For Schmidt and his generation of Social Democrats, Douglas Webber writes, "a strong welfare state, labor codetermination, and good and close relations between business, labor, and the government were key ingredients of the Federal Republic's relative (democratic) political stability – ingredients that distinguished it from the failed Weimar Republic."[6] From this perspective, without the Great Depression the political system would not have suffered a prolonged crisis as the Nazis would not have been able to mobilize a large segment of the population. In the US, Webber notes – as does Lebow – that the Depression helped to bring about the election of the Democratic president Franklin Roosevelt and the New Deal. In Scandinavia and New Zealand, it was followed by the election of Labor or Social Democratic governments. In the most advanced industrial countries, the political fallout of the Depression thus diverged widely. Nevertheless, one of the most stable lessons drawn from Weimar by the left is that economic crisis fomented its demise. More recently, rising inequalities attributed to globalized neoliberal capitalism have been identified as the primary condition for the increasing support for far-right movements and parties.[7]

Early Weimar lessons were informed by attempts to make sense of German society. They were motivated by a desire to prevent a future catastrophe, but they were also self-serving. Peter Caldwell provides a detailed account of the debates that occurred during the 1948 Herrenchiemsee Convention, which brought together jurists and politicians to draft the Basic Law for the constitution of what would become the *Bundesrepublik*. It became clear that party representatives were using arguments by analogy to support their own approach to a voting law that was intended to strengthen their party. They sought to mobilize fears about another democratic collapse to advance party interests.

More generally, Weimar offered and continues to offer a multiplicity of lessons based on different understandings of the fundamental conditions of politics in modernity. Peter Breiner argues that Weimar is a unique case of political theorizing because participants "already knew in the midst of it that it would be a paradigmatic example from which to draw lessons for the future."[8] Like Webber, he argues that participants "differed markedly" in their judgment of just what it exemplified but that they were united in an agreement of its fundamental significance as a lens through which to understand core aspects of politics and law. For Walter Benjamin, it was a lesson "that the 'state of emergency' [*Ausnahmezustand*] in which we live is not exception but the rule."[9] For Carl Schmitt, it was a dissipation of politics in the party competition and hidden procedures of liberal democracy.[10] For Karl Mannheim, it was an opportunity for conflicting incommensurable political ideologies to gain insight from one another over the features of political reality they share in common and to which they are blind.[11] For jurist Otto Kirchheimer, the Weimar Republic suffered from "an unresolvable tension between, on the one hand, a liberal constitutional framework with no clearly defined principle of sovereignty, and, on the other, capitalism along with its attendant struggle of classes and the political parties through which that struggle took place."[12] Modernity as characterized by deep, perhaps unresolvable, tensions runs through these perspectives, and Weimar is identified as the principal site where they are most clearly manifested.

Caldwell follows Breiner in describing Weimar as a seemingly inexhaustible primary source for political theorizing. He too describes how German postwar analyses of Weimar and its collapse resulted in a range of overlapping and competing perspectives on the conditions for democratic politics. Werner Conze and Karl Dietrich Bracher advanced competing explanations for Weimar's collapse based on contrasting analyses of the general conditions for politics after World War I. Both, however, emphasized the role of mass politics. Pro-Nazi historian Conze maintained that the Republic self-destructed because of the irreconcilable tensions between mass democracy and parliamentary liberal democracy. Like Carl Schmitt, he maintained that these tensions could be controlled only by a strong leader with authoritarian powers supported by a robust administrative state. The dysfunctional connection among people, parties, and parliament, which, according to Conze, was inherent in democracy, meant that Weimar could never have survived. For the pro-democratic Bracher, Weimar was handicapped by the authoritarian culture of Germany, but destroyed by its last chancellors, who conspired to replace it with an authoritarian regime.[13] In his reading, the Republic's breakdown emerges as a story about a society that could not free itself from the authoritarianism deeply embedded in German culture.

Like Bracher, German economist Wilhelm Röpke and intellectual historian Friedrich Meinecke identified core tensions in modernity and the German state's inability to navigate them. Röpke argued that German worship of power led to more political parties, giant cartels recognized by the state, massive welfare systems, imperialism, and a monopoly capitalism that promoted a more centralized state control at the expense of individual freedom. He traced this evil to the nineteenth century, when monopoly capitalism and its macro-level concerns replaced liberal egalitarianism and its focus on individuals. He also connected Weimar's failure with the more general rise of the masses in the West. Theodor Heuss, who would become first president of the *Bundesrepublik*, was adamant that the Weimar Constitution was not fundamentally flawed, as many came to believe. The Republic was destroyed by those who rejected parties, pluralism, and democracy, and the German people were all too willing to be enslaved by the Nazis. This was an interesting argument from someone who voted in favor of the 1933 Enabling Act that cemented Hitler's power.[14]

Amel Ahmed offers another take by showing how Weimar was mobilized in support of a narrow Schumpeterian model of democracy, intended to reduce the power of the left by minimizing the possibility of mass mobilization and participation. This model of democracy found traction among postwar American intellectuals and officials because it offered justification for their Cold War strategy of support for anti-Soviet conservative and right-wing governments. Government was reframed as an institution to allow and moderate elite competition. In a more fundamental sense, it reflected a particular view of modernity, one in which capitalism was regarded as triumphant but still threatened by demagogues capable of mobilizing the discontented.

At the heart of these several analyses of the structural conditions of modernity lies the so-called problem of the masses, allegedly easy to manipulate by opportunistic politicians. For conservative democrats, this phenomenon necessitated efforts to reduce the potential for irresponsible and power-hungry politicians to exploit voters. Belief in the perils of mass democracy came to shape perceptions of the conditions of possibility for democratic politics in many national settings, and also informed the design of international cooperative arrangements put in place after the war.[15]

Peter Breiner demonstrates that the so-called problem of the masses was central to postwar American political science. Robert Dahl, perhaps the most admired student of American politics in the 1960s, explained the collapse of Weimar in terms of the rapid introduction of the masses in politics and warned of the perils of broad political participation. For Dahl, universal suffrage was granted so suddenly in Germany that there was insufficient time for "the arts of competitive politics [to be] mastered and accepted as legitimate among the elites."[16] Breiner observes that

Dahl and others focused primarily on elites and relegated citizens to the role of spectators and consumers, rather than active participants in politics. They regarded widespread and active political participation not as a sign of democratic strength, but as an indicator of instability and something that democratic systems should try to avoid.[17] The danger was greatest, as Dahl argued, in settings where the public had not been adequately socialized into a democratic culture. In his influential 1966 co-authored book *Comparative Politics*, Gabriel Almond extended this claim to postwar Germany. In his view, the legacy of Weimar and the Nazi dictatorship denuded postwar Germany of any strong political culture that would support democratic institutions. The *Bundesrepublik* appears stable only because citizens support it for the benefits it delivers. This is in sharp contrast to England, Almond insisted, where support for the political order had long since been internalized.[18] Almond and Verba assumed the superiority of Anglo-American culture and treated Weimar as the paradigmatic negative role model.[19]

Political scientists funded by the Social Science Research Council propagated the notion that ideology threatened democracy, whose primary purpose was to articulate and aggregate demands.[20] Democratic success depended on economic development and the middle class it created. The goal of creating or strengthening middle classes elsewhere was given perceived urgency by the Cold War.[21] American liberal social scientists sought to tame politics and create a liberal utopia.

Given this perspective, Peter Breiner notes, many comparative politics scholars misread Kirchheimer's attack on the non-ideological, catch-all political party whose leaders attempted to gain power by cobbling together programs likely to gain electoral support.[22] Kirchheimer was highly critical of de-ideologized party politics and their absence of contentious mass mobilization, something that had been typical of prewar democratic regimes. American political scientists transformed Kirchheimer's negative characterization into a positive one to support their claims that pluralist political systems could overcome the destructive polarization that characterized Weimar. Kirchheimer warned correctly – as recent developments demonstrate – that depoliticization and de-ideologization in liberal regimes were sources of political alienation and resentment.[23]

Amel Ahmed also addresses this theme. Her focus is on contemporary studies of Western democracy and the risk posed by populism and authoritarian politicians. In the US, the election of Donald Trump in 2016 rekindled interest in Weimar and led to a spate of studies that use it as a template for assessing the fragility and robustness of democracies. Much of this literature uses Hitler's rise to power as its starting-off point and concludes that it was made possible by democracy's openness, which allows aspiring autocrats to gain power by exploiting its very rules and institutions. Such an analysis promotes a largely tactical view of democracy's defense, stressing the way in which these rules and institutions can be manipulated to keep populism at bay. Ahmed argues, with good reason, that this approach is based on an historically impoverished understanding of Weimar history and treats the symptom rather than the cause of populism.

Modernity was also a source of lessons for those further on the right who opposed modernity in lieu of trying to tame it. Political theorist Leo Strauss and his acolytes are prominent examples. William Scheuerman describes Strauss's overall narrative as a dramatic *Verfallsgeschichte* (story of inevitable decline), set in motion by political thinkers such as Niccolò Machiavelli and Thomas Hobbes who rejected the ancient commitment to permanent natural right. Decline, for Strauss, is inevitable once natural right gives way to relativism, and Weimar is one, albeit dramatic, exemplar of this process.[24] Weimar showcased modern, relativistic values, undermining the ethical, social, and political commitments essential to any political order.[25] Its collapse was inevitable. Modernity, understood as the switch from natural right to relativism, was the problem, and Weimar was the paradigmatic case for its untenability.

Weimar also supported more forward-looking narratives. In Sweden, Ludvig Norman tell us, the Republic's collapse played a rather different and altogether less important role.[26] Swedes saw their country as the paragon of Scandinavian social and political organization, and did not look to Weimar for political lessons. Social democracy had consolidated its position in the 1930s and there was little sense in Sweden that democracy needed protection from internal enemies that would otherwise destroy it.[27] Norman engages with the works of two of the main intellectual architects of Swedish social democracy from the 1930s onward, Alva and Gunnar Myrdal. The Myrdals, and Alva Myrdal in particular, played a pivotal role in drawing up the contours of wide-ranging social programs in the 1930s, in significant parts centered on how to push back declining birth rates in Sweden, and engineering a democratic population policy.[28] Theirs was a distinct vision of how Swedish society was navigating the transition from traditional to modern society. For the Myrdals, Sweden was charting a unique course in dealing with the tensions arising from this transition. The perhaps most striking finding here is Weimar's *absence* as a source of lessons regarding democracy's fragility. Notable also is the sharp contrast between their views of people in general (and Swedes in particular) as fundamentally decent and reasonable and prevalent views in Germany and elsewhere of the perils of mass democracy.

From the perspective of the Myrdals, democracy's demise and the rise of totalitarianism Europe, specifically Nazism in Germany but also communism, were understood as occurring elsewhere, on a different branch of history. Swedish society, they argued, had developed a widespread commitment to equality and practical rationality, creating the conditions for a democratic mindset deeply embedded in Swedish culture. This was in contrast to the situation in many parts of Europe, and in Germany in particular, where, Alva Myrdal noted, society had been severely stunted by World War I. Rationality had been eclipsed by irrational nationalism and ideologies informed by delusions of grandeur had supplanted knowledge production based on the sober assessment of facts. For the Myrdals, this was in large part attributed to the fact that Germany and other European countries had lost the best of a whole generation during World War I. Many had died, and those who had survived emerged traumatized and psychologically stunted, with grave consequences for scientific and political thinking.[29]

Weimar's downfall did come to represent a cautionary tale even here, but primarily as a manifestation of what happens if irrationality is allowed to shape social engineering. As such, democratic collapse and chaos were treated as wholly external threats, serving as a counterexample, and not something that would emerge from tensions intrinsic to democracy itself – and, above all, not in Swedish society. For Swedish social democracy, if any lesson could be taken away from Weimar, it was to stay the course already embarked on, completing the transition to a fully modern society, and hope that the wildfire of war raging across Europe would not spread to Sweden.[30]

There are points of overlap between the Myrdals' perspectives on Germany and the strain of analysis that focused on Germany as an exception, rooted in the notion that Germany's development prior to Weimar and its collapse had been radically different from that of its neighbors. Known as the *Sonderweg* thesis, it was advanced by some German historians who considered their country's political development unique and a deviation from the pattern established by Britain, France, and the countries of northwest Europe.[31] Webber notes that, in contrast to the UK and France – and, he might add, the US – Germany did not develop a strong liberal bourgeoisie in the nineteenth and early twentieth centuries.[32] In the words of Ralf Dahrendorf, it became an "industrial feudal society," in which the landowning aristocracy transformed the bourgeoisie rather than the other way around.[33] These circumstances resulted in far less hospitable conditions for democracy than elsewhere. There are, nevertheless, many reasons for wariness about the *Sonderweg* thesis, chief among them the dubious assumption that there was a single pattern followed by Germany's neighbors. The thesis instead implies that Weimar's collapse and the subsequent takeover by the Nazis were specific to Germany, thus making lesson-drawing from this particular case less relevant for other settings.

Historical lessons, and Weimar's demise in particular, tend to be based on interpretations of events that are considered overdetermined. There is a strong incentive to frame lessons this way because they would not have much weight if based on events recognized as contingent. If the importance of agency is recognized, system-level explanations lose most of their luster. As Lebow has argued elsewhere, if World War I could have been averted in the absence of the assassination of Franz Ferdinand, or with recognition of the benefits of defensive military strategies, more deterministic explanations such as the balance of power and expected changes in this balance could not be described as definite causes and any lessons based on them would not be compelling. The most that could be said is that these factors made war more or less likely.[34] The same is true for Weimar. If the Republic could have survived in the absence of the Great Depression, Hitler's death on the Western front during World War I, or better management of party coalitions, than any lessons based on its collapse must be treated as provisional and highly context-dependent. They are not determinative, but at best suggestive.

There is a general tendency to see the past as overdetermined and the future as undetermined. Baruch Fischoff was the first to document what he calls "the certainty of hindsight bias." People upgrade the probability of events once they have occurred.[35] This bias is reinforced by the very nature of the scholarly enterprise. Historians and social scientists make reputations by proposing new explanations or theories to account for major events, such as the two World Wars, the fall of the Roman Empire, and the collapse of Weimar. Confronted by ever growing explanations for events of this kind, none of which can usually be dismissed out of hand, they appear massively overdetermined. The need for psychological closure also plays a role. Those who see the world to a great extent ordered and predictable display a need for psychological closure and are hostile to suggestions of contingency – unless it helps to explain away an outcome inconsistent with their worldviews or preferred theories.[36] Not surprisingly, social scientists, and certainly international relations scholars, cluster toward this end of the order and predictability continuum. Historians, by contrast, tend to see the world as more chaotic and less predictable.[37]

In line with such perspectives, historical scholarship on World War I has shifted noticeably in the last decade in its take on its origins. The hundredth anniversary of that event witnessed the publication of a score of serious studies, none of which accepted the conventional view of Europe in 1914 as dry kindling waiting for a match.[38] To varying degrees, these authors all stress the contingency rather than determinism of war in 1914, and those who offer any lessons do so with considerable caution. This, we argue, would also seem like a reasonable perspective on Weimar.

Amel Ahmed takes up the question of inevitability in the case of Weimar. Each of the works she examines goes to great lengths to convince readers that Hitler's rise to power could have been forestalled. Benjamin Hett faults the conservative elites, who, despite finding Hitler contemptible, supported him for their own political ends.[39] Peter Fritzsche similarly focuses on the failure of the political class to check extremism, arguing that, even after he became chancellor, Hitler's dictatorship was highly contingent.[40] This transformation occurred during his first one hundred days, when the Nazis succeeded in uniting a previously divided public. This turn to contingency is essential for arguments in favor of a tactical approach to democracy's defense. As with World War I, arguments for and against contingency are not so much based on a reading of history as they are on the needs of ideologically driven theories or explanations. Levitsky and Ziblatt also focus on political elites, and especially the role of parties as critical gatekeepers. They, too, argue that Hitler might have been prevented by a Grand Coalition. In cases where democracy has survived, they argue, it is because parties "make a concerted effort to isolate and defeat them." They maintain that, within the political class, "[u]nited democratic fronts can prevent extremists from winning power, which can mean saving democracy."[41]

Weimar might best be put in perspective by comparing it to the French Revolution. It also produced a similar set of diametrically opposed analyses and lessons that continue to resonate in the West. The opposing takes on Weimar can be regarded as an extension of the fundamental divide created by the French Revolution. On one side are those who welcome modernity and embrace equality and individual choice, and on the other those who are committed to the hierarchies and the order they generate. These opposing worldviews are deeply connected to our understandings of who we are or want to be.[42] When worldviews and their lessons become entangled with self-identifications and political identities and projects, they become reinforcing and more strongly held and resistant to change. This may help explain why these lessons endure even when they are discredited by empirical research.

Weimar as Cultural Symbol

Our contributors describe the Weimar Republic as an important reference point for political thinking, associated with manifold meanings and tied to competing visions of modernity. These meanings also extend outside politics and inform Weimar as a symbol and a source of interpretations of modern culture in broader society.

This symbolism began with the choice of the Thuringian city of Weimar as the venue for proclaiming the Republic in the aftermath of the Kaiser's abdication. Ever since, Weimar has become a synecdoche for this political order. It was chosen in part because of its role as a focal point of the German Enlightenment and home of the leading figures of the literary genre of Weimar Classicism. This genre included two of Germany's most distinguished writers: Johann Wolfgang von Goethe and Friedrich Schiller. In the nineteenth century, noted composers such as Franz Liszt made Weimar a music center. Artists and architects Henry van de Velde, Wassily Kandinsky, Paul Klee, Lyonel Feininger, and Walter Gropius among others worked in the city and founded the Bauhaus movement, the most important German design school of the interwar period. The socialists emphasized the connection between the Republic and the city, situating and defining the former as an outgrowth and continuation of the liberal democratic tradition and the very best of German culture. For the left, Weimar represented a taste of what modernity could offer.

As a symbol, Weimar took on a range of different meanings and became a battleground for competing perspectives. Even before the Republic fell, the Nazis did their best to make Weimar a counter-symbol. In 1926, the National Socialist German Workers' Party held its party convention in Weimar. Adolf Hitler visited Weimar more than forty times prior to 1933. In 1930, Wilhelm Frick became minister for internal affairs and education in Thuringia, the first Nazi minister in Germany.

Weimar as a symbol took on a different valence in the postwar era. The film *Cabaret*, produced in 1972, highlighted Berlin nightlife, but also the rise of fascism and its ever present threat to the culture industry, artistic life, and individual freedom. At the outset, we see a Nazi expelled from the Kit Kat Club, but in the final scene the cabaret's audience is dominated by uniformed Nazis. The more contemporary blockbuster German television series *Babylon Berlin*, which premiered in 2017, has been distributed to a global audience via diverse streaming platforms. Jill Smith tells us that it offers the Weimar Republic as a cautionary tale regarding the fragility of Western democracies. It portrays Weimar Berlin as a center for hedonistic nightlife, sexual experimentation, and social freedom.

Reviews of *Babylon Berlin* in the mainstream German and Anglo-American press perpetuate what Smith calls "the *Cabaret* syndrome." The series propagates the dubious claims that the so-called sexual decadence of Weimar played a key role in the Republic's decline and was responsible in part for the rise of the Nazis. *Babylon Berlin* nevertheless cleverly complicates and expands the cast of stock Weimar characters found in *Cabaret* and German and English novels about the period. It foregrounds the daily triumphs and trials of the Weimar-era "New Woman" and the prominent role of experiments with gender and sexuality.[43] It also dramatizes how erotic entertainment venues served as spaces for the negotiation of political, gendered, and sexual power.

Babylon Berlin offers a distorted portrayal of Weimar politics, with its unrelieved focus on communists and the nationalist right. There is only one scene in which identifiable Social Democrats appear, despite the fact that Berlin remained an SPD stronghold throughout the Republic.[44] *Babylon Berlin* is a land of extremes. Such decadence and radical politics certainly existed, but the space between them, where most people lived and functioned, is largely ignored. Also irritating, Smith argues, is the treatment of sexuality. In no other German city did such a robust pluralism thrive as it did in Weimar Berlin, where discourses on prostitution sometimes surpassed late twentieth-century debates on sex work and non-normative sexualities in their nuance and progressivism.[45] However, *Babylon Berlin* remains squeamish when it comes to sex work and ambivalent when it comes to gender parity. It has no interest in presenting sexuality as a form of liberation, especially not for women. Rather, sexuality is more often presented as a cause for shame and political vulnerability.

Weimar Today

The Weimar analogy and lessons have returned with a vengeance. But our contributors make clear that, especially in a German context, Weimar never went away. As the perceived vulnerability of democracies increases, analysts and other pundits invariably look back at Weimar for confirmation of their fears – or, more rarely, justifications for their optimism – and for policy guidance.

One of the lessons of Weimar that has found considerable traction in contemporary debates concerns political elites making light of far-right challenges to democratic institutions. Examples include the willingness of center-right parties in Europe to form governing coalitions with parties recently seen as political pariahs. In the US, the failure of Republicans to publicly denounce Trump's assault on the electoral system has triggered similar analyses. For liberals, this kind of behavior puts democracy at risk. Their opponents accuse them of fearmongering.

Fear for democracy, Jan-Werner Müller argues, has prompted a double identification with Weimar. Some European and American analysts frame the problems their political systems face as the same that confronted Weimar and advocate what they believe might have preserved it. They describe today's neo-authoritarian leaders and movements as fascist and propose militant democracy as a solution. Müller argues that contemporary antidemocratic forces are neither fascist nor neo-fascist. They are far-right wing but they do not glorify violence, make it central to their identity, or advocate confrontation and territorial expansion. He further contends that modern-day populism is not so much about anti-elitism as it is about anti-pluralism and the commitment to keep citizenship and privileges for "the real people."[46]

Müller warns against militant democracy. It seeks to constrain the rights of individuals, organizations, and parties committed to destroying the democratic order. It is based on the questionable counterfactual that intervention of this kind could have prevented the Nazis from coming to power. Müller denounces the illusion that fire can be fought with fire, that democracy can be limited against some opponents without limiting democracy for everyone. Protecting democracies through the courts and political parties, he maintains, is a more ethical and effective strategy. Advocacy of militant democracy ignores the degree to which liberal democracy is in part responsible for the threat it now faces. Liberal analysts also fail to recognize that those who want to overturn democracy have also learned from the past: specifically, how to avoid the restraints that military democracy might impose on them.

Fascists came to power only with the support of liberal democratic elites. This happened in large part because of liberal fears of communism. Today's far right invokes the threat of Islam as well as its own victimhood. It is a different kind of victimhood than that associated with Versailles but has similar psychological appeal. Democratic parties have lost confidence in themselves and have not hesitated to mimic the right when it comes to immigrants and Islam. Some have gone into coalition with right-wing parties, as in Austria, Italy, and Sweden. They have made right-wing authoritarianism a more visible and pronounced threat. Mainstreaming the far right seems currently to be the greatest threat to democracy.[47]

Scheuerman's chapter sheds light on the use of Weimar to bolster authoritarian politicians and parties. He notes that the Trump presidency, and especially his attempt to derail the electoral process, aroused profound concern among American intellectuals. The conservative political analysts and jurists connected to the Claremont Institute were a glaring exception. Drawing on Strauss's ideas of modernity as a story of moral relativism and decline and Weimar as its paradigmatic example, they were enthusiastic supporters of Trump. Despite their declared opposition to moral relativism and nihilism, they looked the other way when faced with Trump's transgressive behavior, rampant lying, and disregard for democracy and the rule of law. This was far less of a problem for them than the true enemy: the administrative state and decadent liberal egalitarianism, both of which they regarded as a fundamental perversion of the founding fathers' intentions.[48] The rules and laws that created obstacles for Trump, they argued, were products of this corruption of the constitution. The so-called Claremonsters are an extreme manifestation of a postwar American conservative tradition that has used Weimar to attack modernity and liberal democracy. As Scheuerman notes, Weimar was mobilized to condemn student movements and the civil rights movement as evidence of societal decline. It now provides a justification for autocratic executive power as the only means to forestall chaos.[49]

For decades, Weimar had overwhelmingly negative connotations in Germany and the US. The principal political reference was to the *Weimar Verhältnisse* (Weimar conditions) that helped bring about its collapse and boded ill for the *Bundesrepublik*. Nowadays, Germans have rediscovered the positive political side of Weimar, notably the progressive character of its constitution. This is evident in speeches by the president of Germany, Frank-Walter Steinmeier, and the president of the Bundestag, Wolfgang Schäuble.[50] One repeatedly hears the phrase "*Bonn ist nicht Weimar* (Bonn is not Weimar) and we Germans recognize positive features of the Weimar constitution from which Bonn profited."[51] The CDU/CSU/SPD parliamentary motion on the one-hundredth anniversary of the Republic's founding described it as "ever connected with the striving for democracy and freedom" and its constitution the embodiment of "Enlightenment principles" that "carry forward the liberal tradition."[52] It remains to be seen if references to Weimar will undergo such a transition outside Germany.

Why Weimar?

Why do people turn to some events and not others? And why do some lessons based on them gain widespread acceptance quite independently of their scientific status? Why not, for instance, Republican Spain, taken over by fascists after a long and costly civil war? One intuitive answer is of course that Weimar was followed by Hitler and the Nazis, who became emblematic of the human capacity for evil. If Weimar's collapse had merely led to a nasty authoritarian regime, like that of Franco's Falangists, it would not have garnered the same interest. Consider, too, that the scholars who began the debate about Weimar were German refugees to Britain and America, some of whom became extremely influential both in academia and in politics. What might have remained an internal debate became an international one.

The drama and tragedy of Weimar make it an attractive model for stories about politics. One depiction portrays its citizens as dancing on a volcano soon to erupt.[53] As we mention in our introduction, for much of the nineteenth century the French Revolution played a similar role; it served as a malleable focal point onto which social and political hopes and fears were projected. It, too, supplied warnings about the perils of upending established institutions, about how the Enlightenment quickly gave way to chaos, terror, and the subsequent restoration of the monarchy. Weimar, similarly, contains a story about both the promises of a democratic and progressive society and the subsequent fall into totalitarian terror.

Jill Smith's chapter explores a different dimension of Weimar's appeal. Cognitive scientists have shown how vividness enhances credibility, and films and television shows are vivid in a way that scholarly books or articles aimed at wider audiences are not.[54] Films and television influence people and policymakers alike not only because of their dramatic and memorable representations, but also because they are more straightforward and less intellectually demanding. Smith finds that these are both important underlying reasons for the appeal of the movie *Cabaret* and the television series *Babylon Berlin*.

The Breiner and Caldwell chapters demonstrate that analogy can serve as a tool for articulating positions and as a spur to more careful reasoning. Caldwell thinks that even vague political analogies make it possible to arouse or alleviate fears by transforming them into political fables. Our three Weimar narratives – decline and collapse, conscious self-destruction, and radical imagining of a better future – can all be understood in this light. For Breiner, Kirchheimer's analysis of Weimar is the source of a critique of liberal democratic institutions in Germany and elsewhere.

Ahmed adds to this perspective. The analogies made by Schumpeterians favoring a procedural model of democracy are a substitute for good history, or an excuse for not engaging with the complex story of Weimar. In this instance, the fable came before the history and was not so much designed to preserve democracy as to constrain it by keeping power in the hands of conservative elites.

Scheuerman's chapter offers further insights into these themes. He suggests that the selective and misleading manner in which right-wing Straussians recount Weimar's collapse highlights the flexible and open-ended contours of any turn to political analogies. Their efforts also dramatize the intellectual and political dangers of analogies. He notes the dangerous irony that Straussians associated with the Claremont Institute are so obsessed with Weimar's alleged relativism and nihilism that they have become oblivious to how their political agenda mirrors elements of its disturbing legacy. By vaunting executive power and authoritarian presidentialism as the necessary response to relativism, they mimic Carl Schmitt. Worse still, they embrace Donald Trump and a brand of Republicanism far more threatening to their values than liberal democracy.

Norman's chapter shows how analogies can become attractive not only as a source of substantive lessons but also as a way to articulate and strengthen a sense of self that is based on fundamental difference and uniqueness. The Myrdals' self-image as a science-based avant-garde in social reform, in contrast to the irrationalism of German society, allowed little room for critical self-reflection. They laid out an extremely progressive course for Swedish society, but they also embraced and developed the rationale for more troubling aspects of the welfare state regime, in particular a wide-ranging sterilization program aimed at parts of the population deemed undesirable and of "substandard quality."[55] Norman argues that the insistence that this program was science-based and driven by fundamentally democratic concerns seems to have closed the door to more critical perspectives that could have highlighted what in hindsight appear to be obvious parallels to ideas of racial hygiene.

Analogies can thus work to feed into an elevated sense of self, radically separated from what the analogy is thought to represent. In the Swedish example, Weimar's collapse emerges as a mirror image, an alternative universe where irrationality reigns supreme, and the subsequent Nazi regime similarly emerges in sharp contrast to the democratically informed program of social engineering that became prevalent in the early 1930s. As noted above, there are parallels here with the *Sonderweg* thesis in the sense that it allows observers to conclude that what happened in Germany could never have happened here and, by implication, that one's own society is entirely devoid of the fundamental flaws thought inherent to German prewar society.

We must also consider path dependency. Once embedded, analogies increase the likelihood that other analogies based on the same premises or assumptions will both be made and gain acceptance – and the opposite is true for those antagonistic to them. This is a well-known cognitive phenomenon. There is often also an institutional reinforcement. Analogies advance political projects and increase or help maintain the power of those who advance or benefit from them. Influential actors will use resources at their disposal to further propagate their favored analogies and associated lessons and sideline or discredit opposing ones. This is evident with Munich, where research critical of deterrence was more difficult to publish, as were opinion pieces critical of its heavy-handed application to the Soviet Union and China. Weimar analogies have been influential but have never quite had the same hold on the public mind or offered the same advantages to political authorities. Part of the reason for this may be that there are many Weimar lessons and analogies and no consensus about them in Germany or elsewhere. Of perhaps equal importance, the need to turn to them has not arisen because, until recently, Western democracies were perceived as robust. Germany was an exception, and, as our contributors document, Weimar was the template against which the fragility and robustness of the *Bundesrepublik* was assessed.

Conclusions

Our review of the Weimar lessons and the concept of analogy suggests that analogies are a means of making sense of the world, justifying one's projects to oneself and others, selling them to important constituencies, and, if successful, confirming the analogies and possibly oneself. These uses are closely related, as are self and other, the political and psychological.

There is ample evidence of analogies used for explanation and prediction. All the Weimar lessons discussed in this volume served this purpose. They were intended to account, at least in part, for the collapse of the Republic. They became analogies where they were invoked to assess contemporary fragility and support policy prescriptions to reduce it. They were employed as justifications for past and present actions.

For motivational in lieu of cognitive reasons, negative outcomes appear to predominate. There are many fewer analogies and lessons from successes in politics. However, in economics, the stability and growth of democratic, capitalistic economies have spawned all kinds of lessons on both the right and the left, although many of these lessons are now being questioned. There may be two reinforcing reasons for the greater "appeal" of political failures than successes. Some failures have catastrophic consequences, as did the Great Depression, the collapse of Weimar, appeasement, and the Holocaust. People suffered enormously, providing – as noted earlier – strong emotional and intellectual commitments to keep them from happening again. Success, by contrast, produces contentment, even euphoria on occasion, and with it less interest in revisiting the past. Following the principle of "If it works, don't fix it," people direct their intellectual energies elsewhere. Cognitive psychologists have documented the self-serving bias. It tells us that people tend to attribute their successes to their character and their failures to circumstances.[56] This, too, would produce a more thorough investigation of failures.

Repetitive use of even good historical lessons and analogies can degrade them. This is readily apparent in contemporary references to Hitler and the Nazis. In 1990, President George W. Bush claimed that Saddam Hussein was worse than Hitler and that the US had to go to war to remove him before he invaded another country.[57] It is unclear if Bush made this comparison out of ignorance or duplicitously. His son, George H. W. Bush, described Saddam "as a modern-day Hitler" in his speech to the American people announcing the invasion of Iraq.[58] The opposition also invoked Hitler. German Chancellor Gerhard Schröder was running for re-election on an anti-war platform at the time, and his justice minister, Herta Däubler-Gmelin, accused Bush of starting a war – just like Hitler – to divert the public from domestic problems.[59] In recent years, Hitler comparisons have routinely been used for almost every autocrat from Hungary to China, the EU, Israel, Donald Trump, Islamic fundamentalists, same-sex marriage, the "extermination" of the wealthy and the poor.[60]

The Holocaust has been equally abused. Pat Robertson brazenly claimed: "Just what Nazi Germany did to the Jews, so liberal America is now doing to evangelical Christians ... It's no different."[61] People for the Ethical Treatment of Animals (PETA) has consistently and shamelessly abused the memory of the Holocaust for its animal rights agenda. Needless to say, such comparisons have been vocally condemned by historians, the Jewish community, and Holocaust survivors. Elie Wiesel, among them, hastened to say: "I don't compare anything to the Holocaust."[62]

Weimar has given rise to only a minor version of this phenomenon. It has been deployed, by both right and left, as a frame of reference to analyze Germany, the US, the UK, Russia, and other countries. Under Stalin, Soviet foreign policy in the early postwar era was shaped in large part by a Weimar analogy. The Depression had destroyed the Weimar Republic and given rise to a fascist regime that was bent on world conquest. This was an inevitable product of capitalism. There would be another depression, and it would produce fascist dictatorships that would seek once again to destroy the Soviet Union.[63] Weimar was mobilized again following the demise of the Soviet Union.[64] The short-lived rise of Vladimir Volfovich Zhirinovsky and his right-wing nationalist party to a position of surprising political strength encouraged comparisons to Hitler. By describing himself as a tyrant and claiming that he would "act like Hitler in 1932," Zhirinovsky invited the comparison.[65] It was also raised by Yegor Timurovich Gaidar, head of the democratic Russia's Choice party and Yeltsin's deputy prime minister for economic reform. In January 1992, he pressed for a market economy to stave off political corruption and spoke of "a struggle against the Weimar syndrome in a stagnant market economy, in which the rich become richer and the poor become poorer."[66]

In the US, it was mobilized by Democrats in the aftermath of Donald Trump's election, and, in response, in their judgment to his trampling on the constitution. For almost every use of the analogy there was an article or post somewhere questioning its relevance or urging caution about the simplistic, even misleading, use of analogies.[67] The most serious abuse comes from the American right, where, for example, the National Rifle Association and its supporters falsely claimed that Weimar gun laws paved the way for Hitler and his consolidation of power.[68]

Analogies spawn lessons, but lessons also give rise to analogies. The process risks becoming self-referential. Richard Evans claims that "it's very dangerous simply to think in historical parallels."[69] But parallels are precisely what good historians and social scientists should be looking for. Analogy is at the core of most reasoning. Comparisons between things or situations are essential to understanding. We cannot do so in their absence. Analogies not only help us make the kinds of comparisons we address in this book; they also help formulate the concepts and worldviews that enable these analogies. Historians would be forced to close up shop if they could not make comparisons. The challenge is to make good comparisons. In his chapter, Peter Caldwell suggests that analogies can "pose hard questions ... and lead to discussions about the uncertain future of democracy." Analogy should be utilized, not as a single definite parallel or likeness, but as a kind of contingent, even literary device that focuses attention on lasting fears, hopes, and challenges; as a tool for articulating party-political positions; and as a spur to more careful reasoning.[70] Analogies are at best useful starting points for contemporary analysis, diagnosis, and policy prescriptions.

To be used effectively as analytical tools, analogies must be carefully specified. Those who invoke them must be very clear about how the original situation is relevant to the present one. Toward this end, they must tell us why whatever condition or event they are focusing on had the effect it did in the original case, and if there were enabling conditions that were critical. When applied to the contemporary situation, they must further show that these conditions are present – or, if not, why the same effect is to be expected.

Webber's cautious approach to what we can learn from Weimar today serves as a useful example. His discussions take as their entry point the considerable differences between the conditions that characterized social and political life in Weimar and those that characterize contemporary democratic societies. High levels of political violence, coupled with extreme ideological polarization, as well as the widespread suspicion toward democracy as a form of government in Weimar Germany supply stark contrasts to what we see today, even in countries where the far right has made a remarkable journey from the political margins into the mainstream. Webber highlights a more general lesson that we might take to heart: We should not be complacent about democracy, its durability, or imagined permanence, and we should take every opportunity to deepen its institutions. Careful historical analysis combined with open-ended recommendations that serve as reminders of what we care about in a political system, rather than deterministically tinged advice on how to achieve particular ends, seems a promising approach.

Crude analogies ignore agency and treat conditions as deterministic. Analogies of this kind are rife in the media and all too common in academia. Carefully constructed analogies consider causal as well as enabling background conditions, such as institutions, political culture, past events, path dependency, and agency. This limits their applicability, but at the same time has the potential to make analogies stronger and more relevant if parallels in context can be documented. Even when this is possible, analogies are at best starting points for narratives that make forecasts rather than point to predictions. These narratives are tentative probes that can and must be reshaped or redirected in response to new information. Ideally, they should also stipulate what would have to happen to increase or decrease our confidence in any of the storylines based on the analogy.[71] Used in this way, historical analogies can be fruitful starting points for serious historical research and contemporary analysis.

Notes

1 Peter Breiner, "The Paradigmatic Example of Weimar and Postwar Political Science: The Case of Otto Kirchheimer," this volume, citing Otto Kirchheimer, "Verfassungswirklichkeit und Politische Zukunft der Arbeiterklasse" in Wolfgang Luthardt, ed., *Otto Kirchheimer von der Weimarer Republik zum Faschismus: Die Auflösung der Demokratischen Rechtsordunung* (Frankfurt: Suhrkamp, 1972), p. 76.

2 Douglas Webber, "An Unheroic but Understandable Failure: German Social Democrats and the Collapse of the Weimar Republic," this volume, quoting Franz von Papen, as quoted in Wolfgang Michalka and Gottfried Niedhart, eds., *Die ungeliebte Republik: Dokumente zur Innen- und Aussenpolitik Weimars 1918–1933* (Munich: Deutscher Taschenbuch, 1980), p. 362.

3 On this point, see also M. Steven Fish and Jason Wittenberg, "Failed Democratization" in Christian Haerpfer, Patrick Bernhagen, Ronald F. Inglehart, and Christian Welzel, eds., *Democratization* (Oxford: Oxford University Press, 2009), pp. 249–64; Ethan B. Kapstein and Nathan Converse, *The Fate of Young Democracies* (Cambridge: Cambridge University Press, 2008); Steven Levitsky and Daniel Ziblatt, *How Democracies Die* (New York: Crown, 2018).

4 Webber, "An Unheroic but Understandable Failure."

5 Caldwell, "Bonn's Weimar."

6 Webber, "An Unheroic but Understandable Failure."

7 Hans-Georg Betz, *Radical-Right Wing Populism in Western Europe* (Houndmills: Macmillan, 1994); Hanspeter Kriesi, "The Populist Challenge," *West European Politics* 37, no. 2 (2014), pp. 361–78; Chantal Mouffe, *For a Left Populism* (London: Verso, 2018).

8 Breiner, "The Paradigmatic Example of Weimar and Postwar Political Science."

9 Walter Benjamin, "Geschichtsphilosophische Thesen" in Seigfried Unseld, ed., *Illuminationen: Ausgewählte Schriften* (Frankfurt: Suhrkamp, 1969), p. 272.

10 Carl Schmitt, *The Crisis of Parliamentary Democracy*, trans. Ellen Kennedy, Studies in Contemporary German Social Thought (Cambridge, MA: MIT Press, 1988), p. 20.

11 Karl Mannheim, *Ideology and Utopia: An Introduction to the Sociology of Knowledge*, trans. Louis Wirth and Edward Shils (New York: Harcourt, Brace, 1936), pp. 154, 163–4.

12 Breiner, "The Paradigmatic Example of Weimar and Postwar Political Science."

13 Caldwell, "Bonn's Weimar."

14 "Heuss' Pro-Hitler Vote Verified," *New York Times*, 21 September 1949, www.nytimes.com/1949/09/21/archives/heuss-prohitler-vote-verified.html? url=http%3A%2F%2Ftimesmachine.nytimes.com%2Ftimesmachine% 2F1949%2F09%2F21%2F92662608.html (accessed 21 November 2022).

15 Ludvig Norman, "Democracy's Fragility and the European Political Order: Functionalism, Militant Democracy and Crisis" in Richard Ned Lebow and Ludvig Norman, eds., *The Robustness and Fragility of Political Orders* (Cambridge: Cambridge University Press, 2023), pp. 176–202.

16 Robert A. Dahl, *Polyarchy: Participation and Opposition* (New Haven: Yale University Press, 2008), pp. 38–9.

17 Breiner, "The Paradigmatic Example of Weimar and Postwar Political Science."

18 Gabriel A. Almond and G. Bingham Powell, Jr., *Comparative Politics: A Developmental Approach* (Boston, MA: Little, Brown, 1966), p. 319.

19 Gabriel A. Almond and Sidney Verba, *The Civic Culture: Political Attitudes and Democracy in Five Nations* (Princeton: Princeton University Press, 1963).

20 Harold R. Lasswell, *Politics: Who Gets What, When, and How?* (Indianapolis: Bobbs-Merrill, 1952 [1936]).

21 Nils Gilman, *Mandarins of the Future: Modernization Theory in Cold War America* (Baltimore: Johns Hopkins University Press, 2003); Michael E. Latham, *Modernization as Ideology: American Social Science and 'Nation Building' in the Kennedy Era* (Chapel Hill: University of North Carolina Press, 2000); Begüm Adalet, "Transnational Constructions of Social Scientific Personae During the Cold War: The Case of Comparative Politics" in Mark Solovey and Christian Dayé, eds., *Cold War Social Science* (London: Palgrave Macmillan, 2021), pp. 315–43.

22 Breiner, "The Paradigmatic Example of Weimar and Postwar Political Science." See, for example, Joseph LaPalombara and Myron Weiner, eds., *Political Parties and Political Development* (Princeton: Princeton University Press, 1966).

23 Breiner, "The Paradigmatic Example of Weimar and Postwar Political Science."

24 William E. Scheuerman, "Weimar on the Potomac? Leo Strauss Goes to Washington," this volume.

25 Scheuerman, "Weimar on the Potomac?"

26 For an example, see the work of Danish constitutional lawyer Alf Ross, whose writings on democracy supplied a rather different perspective compared with the more protective "militant" conceptions of democracy emerging from German scholars. Alf Ross, *Why Democracy?* (Cambridge, MA: Harvard University Press, 1952).

27 Sofia Näsström, "Democratic Self-Defense: Bringing the Social Model Back in," *Distinktion: Journal of Social Theory* 22, no. 3 (2021), 376–96.

28 Alva Myrdal and Gunnar Myrdal, *Kris i Befolkningsfrågan* [*Crisis in the Population Question*] (Stockholm: Albert Bonniers Förlag, 1934); Alva Myrdal, *Nation and Family: The Swedish Experiment in Democratic Family and Population Policy* (New York: Harper and Brothers, 1941).

29 Alva Myrdal and Gunnar Myrdal, *Kontakt med Amerika* [*Contact with America*] (Stockholm: Albert Bonniers Förlag, 1941); Alva Myrdal, "Vår Plats bland Nationerna" [Our Place among the Nations] in Elsa Cedergren et al., eds., *Diskussion om Demokratin* (Stockholm: Albert Bonniers Förlag, 1941).

30 Myrdal, *Nation and Family*, p. v.

31 Geoff Eley, "The British Model and the German Road: Rethinking the Course of German History Before 1914" in David Blackbourn and Geoff Eley, *The Peculiarities of German History: Bourgeois Society and Politics in Nineteenth-Century Germany* (Oxford: Oxford University Press, 1984), pp. 1–158; Jürgen Kocka, "German History before Hitler: The Debate about the German *Sonderweg*," *Journal of Contemporary History* 23, no. 1 (1988), pp. 3–16.

32 Also on this point, see Friedrich Engels, *Revolution and Counter-Revolution* (London: George Allen and Unwin, 1891); Ralf Dahrendorf, *Society and*

Democracy in Germany (New York: W. W. Norton, 1979); Barrington Moore, Jr., *Social Origins of Dictatorship and Democracy: Lord and Peasant in the Making of the Modern World* (Boston, MA: Beacon Press, 1966); Karl-Dietrich Bracher, *Die Auflösung der Weimarer Republik: Eine Studie zum Problem des Machtverfalls in der Demokratie* (Dusseldorf: Droste, 1884), pp. 3–10.

33 Dahrendorf, *Society and Democracy in Germany.*

34 Richard Ned Lebow, *Forbidden Fruit: Counterfactuals and International Relations* (Princeton: Princeton University Press, 2010).

35 Baruch Fischoff, "Hindsight Is not Equal to Foresight: The Effect of Outcome Knowledge on Judgment under Uncertainty," *Journal of Experimental Psychology: Human Perception and Performance* 1, no. 2 (1975), pp. 288–99; S. A. Hawkins and Reid Hastie, "Hindsight: Biased Judgments of Past Events after the Outcomes are Known," *Psychological Bulletin* 107, no. 3 (1990), pp. 311–27.

36 Philip E. Tetlock and Richard Ned Lebow, "Poking Counterfactual Holes in Covering Laws: Cognitive Styles and Political Learning," *American Political Science Review* 95, no. 4 (2001), pp. 829–43.

37 Ibid.

38 John C. Röhl, *The Kaiser and his Court: Wilhelm II and the Government of Germany* (Cambridge: Cambridge University Press, 1994); Holger H. Herwig, *The First World War: Germany and Austria-Hungary, 1914–1918* (London: Arnold, 1998); Lawrence Sondhaus, *Franz Conrad von Hötzendorf: Architect of the Apocalypse* (Boston, MA: Humanities Press, 2000); Günther Kronenbitter, *Krieg im Frieden: die Führung der k.u.k. Armee und die Grossmachtpolitik Österreich-Ungarns 1906–1914* (Munich: Oldenbourg, 2003); Holger Afflerbach and David Stevenson, eds., *An Improbable War: The Outbreak of World War I and European Political Culture Before 1914* (New York: Berghahn Books, 2007); Christopher Clark, *Sleepwalkers: How Europe Went to War in 1914* (London: Allen Lane, 2012); Margaret Macmillan, *The War that Ended Peace* (London: Profile, 2013); Gerhard Hirschfeld and Gerd Krumeich, *Deutschland im Ersten Weltkrieg* (Frankfurt: Fischer, 2013); Gerd Krumeich, *Juli 1914: Eine Bilanz* (Paderborn: Ferdinand Schöningh, 2014); Manfred Rauchensteiner, *Der Erste Weltkrieg un das End der Habsburger-Monarchie* (Vienna: Böhlau, 2013); Thomas G. Otte, *July Crisis: The World's Descent into War, Summer 1914* (Cambridge: Cambridge University Press, 2014). For overviews and comparisons, see Richard Ned Lebow, "What Can International Relations Theory Learn from the Origins of World War I?," *International Relations* 28, no. 4 (2014), pp. 387–411; "World War I: Recent Historical Scholarship and IR Theory?," *International Relations* 28, no. 2 (2014), pp. 245–50.

39 Benjamin Hett, *Death of a Democracy* (New York: Henry Holt, 2018). Also, Levitsky and Ziblatt, How Democracies Die; Burt Neuborne, *When at Times the Mob Is Swayed: A Citizens Guide to Defending Our Republic* (New York: New Press, 2019); David Runcimann, *How Democracy Ends* (London: Basic Books, 2018); Timothy Snyder, *On Tyranny: Twenty Lessons from the Twentieth Century* (London: Bodley Head, 2017): Tim Duggan Books and

Jason Stanley, *How Fascism Works* (New York: Penguin, 2018); Tom Ginsburg and Aziz Huq, *How to Save a Constitutional Democracy* (Chicago: University of Chicago Press, 2018); Peter Fritzsche, *Hitler's First Hundred Days: When Germans Embraced the Third Reich* (New York: Basic Books, 2008).

40 Fritzsche, *Hitler's First Hundred Days*.

41 Levitsky and Ziblatt, *How Democracies Die*, p. 26.

42 On the questionable nature of identities but also their psychological, social, and political importance in the modern world, see Richard Ned Lebow, *The Politics and Ethics of Identity: In Search of Ourselves* (Cambridge: Cambridge University Press, 2012).

43 On gender and sexuality in the Weimar era, see Laurie Marhoefer, *Sex and the Weimar Republic: German Homosexual Emancipation and the Rise of the Nazis* (Toronto: University of Toronto Press, 2015); Richard W. McCormick, *Gender and Sexuality in Weimar Modernity: Film, Literature, and "New Objectivity"* (New York: Palgrave, 2001); Jill Suzanne Smith, *Berlin Coquette: Prostitution and the New German Woman, 1890–1933* (Ithaca, NY: Cornell University Press, 2013); Katie Sutton, *Sex between Body and Mind: Psychoanalysis and Sexology in the German-Speaking World, 1890s–1930s* (Ann Arbor: University of Michigan Press, 2019); and the chapter on "Bodies and Sex" in Eric D. Weitz, *Weimar Germany: Promise and Tragedy* (Princeton: Princeton University Press, 2007), pp. 297–330.

44 See Veronika Fuechtner and Paul Lerner, eds., "Forum: *Babylon Berlin*: Media, Spectacle, and History," *Central European History* 53 (2020), pp. 835–54, here pp. 841–2; Jill Suzanne Smith's conversation with Julia Roos, Bloomington, 1 October 2021.

45 Smith, *Berlin Coquette*, p. 189.

46 Jan-Werner Müller, "Militant Democracy: A (Supposed) Weimar Lesson Revisited," this volume.

47 Ibid. For a similar argument, see Peter Breiner, "End of Democracy or Recurrent Conflict: Minimalist Democracy, Legitimacy Crisis, and Political Equality" in Lebow and Norman, The Robustness and Fragility of Political Orders, pp. 54–91.

48 Scheuerman, "Weimar on the Potomac?"

49 Ibid.

50 "Herbst 1918: Vom Kaiserreich zur Republik," Deutscher Bundestag, 9 November 2018, www.bundestag.de/parlament/geschichte/revolutionskalender#url= L2Rva3VtZW50ZS90ZXh0YXJjaGl2L1zIwMTgva3c0NS1nZWRlbmtzdHVuZGU tOW5vdmVtYmVyLTU3NTU3OA==&mod=mod570028 (accessed 3 November 2021).

51 Michael F. Feldkamp, "Die Lehren aus Weimar," *Das Parlament*, 23 July 2018, www.das-parlament.de/2018/30_31/themenausgaben/564752-564752; "Rede von Bundestagspräsident Dr. Wolfgang Schäuble im Rahmen der Vorlesungsreihe, 100 Jahre Weimarer Republik an der Universität Freiburg: Berlin ist nicht Weimar. Über die Gefährdung der Demokratie," Deutscher Bundestag, 7 February 2019, www.bundestag.de/parlament/prae sidium/reden/2019/008-592858 (both accessed 3 November 2021).

52 Resolution of the CDU/CSU and SPD in "Orte der Freiheit und Demokratie: 100 Jahre Weimar Reichsverfassung – Demokratiker Aufbruch und Scheitern der ersten deutschen parlamentarischen Republik," Deutscher Bundestag, 25 February 2019, https://dip.bundestag.de/vorgang/orte-der-freiheit-und-demokratie-100-jahre-weimarer-reichsverfassung/250203?f. deskriptor=Weimar&rows=25&pos=3 (accessed 04 November 2021).

53 Thomas W. Knieshe and Stephen Brockman, eds., *Dancing on the Volcano: Essay on the Culture of the Weimar Republic* (Rochester: Camden House, 1994).

54 Hawkins and Hastie, "Hindsight"; Philip E. Tetlock and Richard Ned Lebow, "Poking Counterfactual Holes in Covering Laws: Cognitive Styles and Historical Reasoning," *American Political Science Review* 95, no. 4 (2001), pp. 829–43.

55 Ludvig Norman, "Swedish Social Democracy and Weimar: Engineering the Democratic Population with the Myrdals," this volume.

56 Fritz Heider, *The Psychology of Interpersonal Relations* (New York: Wiley, 1958); James Larson, "Evidence for a Self-Serving Bias in the Attribution of Causality," *Journal of Personality* 45, no. 3 (1977), pp. 430–41; Jari-Erik Nurmi, "Cross-Cultural Differences in Self-Serving Bias: Responses to the Attributional Style Questionnaire by American and Finnish Students," *Journal of Social Psychology* 132, no. 1 (1992), pp. 69–76; Steven J. Heine, Darrin R Lehman, Hazel Rose Markus, and Shinobu Kitayama, "Is There a Universal Need for Positive Self-Regard?," *Psychological Review* 106, no. 4 (1999), pp. 766–94.

57 Tom Raum, "Bush Says Saddam Even Worse Than Hitler," *AP News*, 1 November 1990, https://apnews.com/article/c456d72625fba6c742d17f1699b18a16 (accessed 3 November 2021).

58 David E. Sanger, "Bush's Doctrine for War," *New York Times*, 18 March 2003, www.nytimes.com/2003/03/18/international/middleeast/bushs-doctrine-for-war.html (accessed 3 November 2003).

59 "Angeblicher Bush–Hitler–Vergleich: Däubler-Gmelin fühlt sich völlig falsch verstanden," *Der Spiegel*, Politik, 20 September 2002, www.spiegel.de/politik/deutschland/angeblicher-bush-hitler-vergleich-daeubler-gmelin-fuehlt-sich-voellig-falsch-verstanden-a-215061.html (accessed 3 November 2021); Peter Connolly-Smith, "'Connecting the Dots': Munich, Iraq, and the Lessons of History," *History Teacher* 43, no. 1 (2009), pp. 31–51.

60 "Nazi Analogies," Wikipedia, 11 September 2021, https://en.wikipedia.org/wiki/Nazi_analogies; Zachary Karabell, "The Trouble with Hitler Analogies," *Wall Street Journal*, 30 November 2018, www.wsj.com/articles/the-trouble-with-hitler-analogies-1543506780 (both accessed 4 November 2021); Gavriel D. Rosenfeld, "An American Führer? Nazi Analogies and the Struggle to Explain Donald Trump," *Central European History* 52 (2019), pp. 554–87.

61 See the video at Elias Isquith, "Pat Robertson: Liberalism Turns People into Nazis," *Salon*, 21 October 2013, www.salon.com/2013/10/21/pat_robertson_liberalism_turns_people_into_nazis/; (accessed 3 November 2021).

62 For a justification of Hitler–Trump comparisons, see Waitman Wade Beorn, "It's Not Wrong to Compare Trump's America to the Holocaust. Here's Why," *Washington Post*, 16 July 2018, www.washingtonpost.com/news/post

everything/wp/2018/07/16/its-not-wrong-to-compare-trumps-america-to-the-holocaust-heres-why/ (accessed 3 November 2021).

63 Joseph Hansen, "Stalin's Speech Reflects Fear of World War III; Shifts Line on Character of Imperialist Conflicts," *Militant* 10, no. 9 (1946), p. 6; Robert C. Tucker, "The Emergence of Stalin's Foreign Policy," *Slavic Review* 36, no. 4 (1977), pp. 563–89.

64 Robert C. Williams, "Virtuous Republics and Eternal Empires: Goose Steps, Weimar on the Volga and Other Specious Analogies," *German Politics & Society* 14, no. 1 (1995), pp. 1–16; Gary P. Russell, "Exploring the 'Weimar Russia' Analogy," *Defense Technical Information Center*, 1 December 1999, https://apps.dtic.mil/sti/citations/ADA376027 (accessed 4 November 2021).

65 Williams, "Virtuous Republics and Eternal Empires."

66 Ibid.

67 Robert Gerwarth, "Weimar's Lessons for Biden's America," *Foreign Policy*, 26 February 2021, https://foreignpolicy.com/2021/02/06/weimars-lessons-for-bidens-america/; Rosenfeld, "An American Führer?"; Mike Cormack, "Are There Any Parallels between US and Weimar Republic?," CGTN, 6 September 2020, https://news.cgtn.com/news/2020-09-06/Is-America-the-new-Weimar-Republic-Tz3RRmt3Uc/index.html (all accessed 4 November 2021).

68 Dave Kopel and Richard Griffiths, "Hitler's Control: The Lessons of Nazi History," Independence Institute, 22 May 2003, https://davekopel.org/NRO/2003/Hitler's-Control.htm (accessed 4 November 2021); Stephen P. Halbrook, "Nazi Firearm Laws and the Disarming of the German Jews," *Arizona Journal of International and Comparative Law* 17, no 3 (2000), pp. 483–537. For a critique, see Bernard E. Harcourt, "On Gun Registration, the NRA, Adolf Hitler, and Nazi Gun Laws: Exploding the Gun Culture Wars (A Call to Historians)," *Fordham Law Review* 73, no. 2 (2004), pp. 653–80.

69 Richard Evans, "Too Close for Comfort," *Slate*, 10 February 2017, https://slate.com/news-and-politics/2017/02/historian-richard-evans-says-trumps-america-isnt-exactly-like-the-third-reich-but-its-too-close-for-comfort.html (accessed 4 November 2021).

70 The reference is to Richard Rorty's approach to contingency and situatedness in discussions of self and society and the need for literary analogies as ways to think through life problems: Richard Rorty, *Contingency, Irony, and Solidarity* (New York: Cambridge University Press, 1989).

71 On forecasting, see Steven Bernstein, Richard Ned Lebow, Janice Stein and Steven Weber, "Social Science as Case-Based Diagnostics" in Richard Ned Lebow and Mark L. Lichbach, eds., *Theory and Evidence in Comparative Politics and International Relations* (New York: Palgrave-Macmillan, 2007), pp. 229–60.

Index

Milton Keynes UK
Ingram Content Group UK Ltd.
UKHW021925220924
448664UK00013B/106

9 781009 484305